# DARE Primer on Global Queer Theologies

# DARE Primer on Global Queer Theologies

Edited by

Lisa Isherwood

and

Hugo Córdova Quero

Series Editor: Graham McGeoch

Published in 2025 by SCM Press

Editorial office
3rd Floor, Invicta House,
110 Golden Lane,
London EC1Y 0TG, UK
www.scmpress.co.uk

SCM Press is an imprint of Hymns Ancient & Modern Ltd
(a registered charity)

Hymns Ancient & Modern® is a registered trademark of
Hymns Ancient & Modern Ltd
13A Hellesdon Park Road, Norwich,
Norfolk NR6 5DR, UK



British Library Cataloguing in Publication data

A catalogue record for this book is available
from the British Library

ISBN: 978-0-334-06682-8

EU GPSR Authorized Representative
LOGOS EUROPE, 9 rue Nicolas Poussin, 17000, LA ROCHELLE, France
E-mail: Contact@logoseurope.eu



Typeset by Regent Typesetting

# Contents

*About the Authors* ix
*Foreword* xv
*Introduction – Lisa Isherwood and Hugo Córdova Quero* xvii

**Part 1 Hermeneutics and Interpretation**

1 Queer Hermeneutics: Liberation Techniques 3
*Mercy Aguilar Contreras*

2 Stabanized African Biblical Hermeneutics: Exploring the Contours of an African Izitabane Biblical Hermeneutics 23
*Charlene van der Walt*

3 Theological Faggotting (*Via[da]gem*) *or* Cruising with Frida Kahlo 36
*André S. Musskopf*

**Part 2 Ecclesiology and Communities**

4 Decolonizing Human Sexuality in Ecumenical Conversations 55
*Masiiwa Ragies Gunda*

5 Being-Blessed: The Primacy of Sophianic Love through the Gifts of Sex-Gender Diversity 78
*Ángel F. Méndez Montoya*

6 *Trans-Struere*: Transing Theological Deconstruction 89
*Alex Clare-Young*

**Part 3 Poimenics and Activism**

7 Gay Bodies and God: Envisioning the Fundamental Principles of an LGBTIQ+-Affirming Theopastoral Competence 107
*Joseph N. Goh*

8 Faith, Sexuality and Human Rights: Reconciliation and Theological Reflections for LGBTIQ+ People in Africa 122
*Jide Macaulay*

9 Towards a Healthy Pastoral Work 136
*Adelard Kananira*

**Part 4 Christology and Embodied Theology**

10 Grace: Times of *Cuir* Alchemy 153
*Marilú Rojas Salazar*

11 Embodied Theology of Liberation: Intersecting Violence on Dalit and Queer Bodies 172
*Samuel Mall*

12 *Izitabane Zingabantu* Ubuntu Theology: Amplifying Voices of South African *Izitabane* 185
*Tracey Maswazi Gumede*

**Part 5 Soteriology and Eschatology**

13 (W)hol(e)y Saved: Queering Constructs of Salvation from a Naga Perspective 203
*Inatoli Aye*

14 A Queer Trinitarian Reading of Communion and Otherness 219
*Miguel H. Díaz*

15 In Search of Queer *O/utopia*: A Haunting (Impossibility of) Queer Archive 236
*Mayuko Yasuda*

## Part 6 Mariology and Hagiography

16 Manifesting the Mediatrix: Queering Ecclesiology through Spiritual Activism 255
*Molly Greening*

17 Queer Mary: A Reflection on Gender, Sexuality, Violence and Resistance in the Symbol of the Virgin in Latin America 272
*Giovanna Sarto*

18 Into Queer Silence: Resisting the Theological Voice 285
*Zaccary Haney*

## Part 7 Apologetics and Prophetic Witness

19 Visions of Hope from a Transgender Perspective 301
*Andrés Herrera Gré*

20 Caledonian Antisyzygy: Defiantly Dissonant Theology for a Quantum Generation 316
*Judith Tatton-Schiff*

21 Folding, (Un)Folding and (Re)Folding the World: An Approach to the Intellectual Itinerary of Darío García Garzón 331
*Anderson Fabián Santos Meza*

*Glossary* 355
*Acknowledgements* 358
*Index* 359

# About the Authors

**Mercy Aguilar Contreras** is a feminist, queer and decolonial theologian who studies Latin American Liberation Theology and queer theologies. She is currently a minister at the Pilgrim Lutheran Church in El Salvador. Her research focuses on issues of the Bible, theology and gender training. She coordinates the Ecumenical Research Center in El Salvador (CIE). She is a junior researcher at Institute Sophia in St. Louis, Missouri, pursuing a Master in Divinity.

**Inatoli Aye** is a doctoral candidate at the University of Wales Trinity St David. She holds an MA in Intercultural Theology (2019) from Protestant Theological University in Groningen, the Netherlands, a ThM in Systematic Theology (2018) from Princeton Theological Seminary in New Jersey, and a Bachelor of Divinity (2016) from Bishop's College in Kolkata, India.

**Alex Clare-Young** is a theologian and minister in the United Reformed Church, UK. Alex (they/he) writes and speaks on queer, disabled and trauma theologies, with a special interest in trans theologies. Alex's lived experiences of being queer, trans, disabled, neurodiverse and of church-related trauma, inform their work. Alex currently ministers to Solidarity Hub, a group in Cambridge exploring social justice and deconstruction, and tutors at the Cambridge Theological Federation. Alex expresses themselves through words, music and textile craft, and they live in rural fens with their wife Jo and their dog Digger.

**Hugo Córdova Quero** is Associate Professor of Critical Theories and Queer Theologies and Director of Digital Learning at Starr King School for the Ministry (SKSM) in Oakland, California. Upon his appointment he became the first academic globally to hold a position with the title 'Queer Theologies'. He also serves as the Director of Institute Sophia in St. Louis, Missouri, where he holds the Marcella Althaus-Reid Chair in Queer Theologies and Critical Theories. He earned a PhD in Interdisciplinary Studies in Religion, Migration, and Ethnic Studies (2009) and an MA in Systematic Theology and Critical Theories (2003), both from the Graduate Theological Union (GTU) in Berkeley, California, as well as an MDiv. (1998) from ISEDET University in Buenos Aires, Argentina. Córdova Quero is a member of the research groups Emerging Queer Asian & Pacific Islander Religion Scholars (EQARS) and the Queer Migrations Research Network.

**Miguel H. Díaz** is John Courtney Murray, SJ, University Chair in Public Service at Loyola University Chicago. Dr Díaz served under President Obama as the ninth US Ambassador to the Holy See. He co-edited the series Disruptive Cartographers: Doing Theology Latinamente (Fordham University Press). He is the editor of the multi-authored Volume One, *The Word Became Culture* (2024), and the author of the third volume, *Queer God de Amor* (2022). Díaz is a member of the Atlantic Council, a member of the Ambassadors Circle at the National Democratic Institute (NDI), and a member of the Board and Senior Fellow for Religion and Peacebuilding for the Alliance for Peacebuilding (AfP).

**Joseph N. Goh** is Senior Lecturer in Gender Studies at the School of Arts and Social Sciences, Monash University Malaysia. Goh (he/they/any) holds a PhD in gender, sexuality and theology, with research interests in queer and LGBTIQ+ studies, human rights and sexual health issues, diverse theological, spiritual and religious studies, and qualitative research. Goh is the author of numerous publications, including *Doing Church at the Amplify Open and Affirming Conferences* (2021), *Becoming a Malaysian Trans Man* (2020) and *Living Out Sexuality and Faith* (2018). He owns a personal website at https://www.josephgoh.org/.

**Molly Greening** is full-time instructor in the Theology Department and a faculty affiliate of the Institute for Racial Justice at Loyola University Chicago. They also received their PhD in Integrative Studies in Ethics and Theology (2023) and their dual MA/MA in Theology and Women's Studies/Gender Studies (2016) from Loyola University Chicago. Their research focuses on taking responsibility for colonial legacies of violence by narrating histories of interconnectivity at the intersection of religion, race, gender and nation-building.

**Tracey Maswazi Gumede** is a queer theologian and activist from South Africa. She has a background in psychology and communications from the University of South Africa (2013) and has a Master's of Theology in Gender and Religion from the University of KwaZulu-Natal (2021). Tracey is pursuing her PhD in Theology within the Gender and Religion programme at the University of KwaZulu-Natal. Her research focuses on homophobic hate crimes and developing inclusive theological resources. As a resource person for the All Africa Theological Education by Extension Association, she plays a crucial role in addressing issues of human sexuality in this faith context.

**Masiiwa Ragies Gunda** is Programme Executive for Overcoming Racism, Xenophobia, and Related Discrimination at the World Council of Churches (WCC) and an adjunct professor at the Ecumenical Institute at Bossey. He holds a Bachelor of Arts (Honours) in Religious Studies (2001) and a Master of Arts in Religious Studies (2003) from the University of Zimbabwe. He earned his PhD in Intercultural Applied Biblical Studies from the University of Bayreuth, Germany, in 2010. With over a decade of experience in teaching at universities and theological institutions, Gunda has authored over 50 publications, including three books. His research focuses on the intersection of religion, human sexuality and social justice.

**Zaccary Haney** is a doctoral candidate in Systematic Theology at Loyola University Chicago. As an instructor of record, he teaches Introduction to Theology and Christianity through Time. Zaccary completed his MA in the Study of Religion at the University of Chicago Divinity School (2015). His research considers methods in queer and trans historiography, the relationship between the past and the present, and intersections between medieval mysticism and contemporary queer theory. Zaccary's dissertation, 'Perverse Convergences', places contemporary values in conversation with those of Aelred of Rievaulx as it constructs an apophatic arc that refocuses theological attention on lived material realities.

**Andrés Herrera Gré** is Communications Assistant at Otros Cruces. He holds a BA in Journalism from Universidad Central de Venezuela (2010) and a BA in Pastoral Theology from Seminario Semisud (2014). Andrés is also a certified spiritual director from Still Harbor (2022) who works with trans and queer people in Latin America specifically.

**Lisa Isherwood** is Professor Emerita of Feminist Liberation Theologies at the University of Winchester. Her work explores the nature of incarnation within a contemporary context and includes areas such as the body, gender, sexuality and eco-theology. She has written, co-authored or edited 32 books, including *The Power of Erotic Celibacy* (2006), *The Fat Jesus: Feminist Explorations in Boundaries and Transgressions* (2007), *Introducing Feminist Christologies* (2001), *Liberating Christ* (1999), *Patriarchs, Prophets and Other Villains* (2007) and *The Poverty of Radical Orthodoxy* (2012).

**Adelard Kananira** is a journalist and screenwriter from Burundi, now living in Italy. He holds a Bachelor's degree in Mass Communication from St. Lawrence University in Kampala, Uganda, a Master's in Political Science from Sophia University Institute in Florence, and another Master's in Philosophy and Ethics of Relations from the University of Perugia. He is also a Netflix scholarship recipient for a Screenwriting and Production Specialisation Master's from Sacred Heart Catholic University in Milan. As the founder and coordinator of the Gay Christian Africa initiative, he advocates for intercultural pathways to foster inclusion, leadership, global citizenship and the common good.

**Jide Macaulay** is Founding Pastor and CEO of House of Rainbow CIC, a Black LGBTIQ+ organization. Born in London to Nigerian parents, Jide is an openly gay British-Nigerian Christian minister who has been a dynamic and inspirational voice in faith communities since 1998. He holds a degree in Law, a Master's in Theology and a Post-graduate certificate in Pastoral Theology. Jide is a passionate HIV-positive activist, author, poet and preacher. He has received several awards, including the 2003 and 2007 Black LGBT Community Award for 'Man of the Year' in recognition of his work helping people of faith reconcile their sexuality and spirituality. He was also shortlisted for the National Diversity Awards 2014 for 'Positive Role Model'. A dedicated global leader, Jide served from 2007 to 2013 as Executive Board member and Co-Chair of the Pan Africa International Lesbians and Gay Association (PIA), and he is the current Africa Regional Representative at the Global Interfaith Network. He serves on the Board of Trustees at Kaleidoscope Trust UK, is the Chairperson of INERELA+ Europe and has been awarded the nOSCAR'S Award in 2014, 2017 and 2018. Jide is also a Trained Volunteer Champion at Africa Children's Charity, continuing to advocate for marginalized communities with passion and dedication.

**Samuel Mall** is ordained presbyter of the Diocese of Chandigarh, Church of North India (CNI), since 2008. He earned his Bachelor of Divinity (BD) and Master of Theology (MTh) degrees, focusing on constructing Dalit Christology in conversation with Historical Jesus Studies. Currently he is pursuing a Doctor of Theology (DTh). After completing his MTh in 2010 he served as the Programme Coordinator for Training Development and Empowerment at the CNI Synod Programme Office in Nagpur, facilitating clergy and laity training across CNI dioceses. Presently he is an Assistant Professor of Christian Theology at Bishop's College, Kolkata, teaching courses to Bachelor of Divinity and Bachelor of Christian Studies students. His research interests include Christology, Dalit Theology, Religious Pluralism, Religious Nationalism and Contextual Theologies in India.

**Ángel F. Méndez Montoya** is full-time Professor and researcher at Universidad Iberoamericana in Mexico City. He holds a PhD in Philosophical Theology (University of Virginia), an MA in Philosophy (St Louis University), an MA in Theology and MDiv in Divinities (Aquinas Institute of Theology) and a BA in Dance (University of Texas-Austin). He is the author of *The Theology of Food: Eating and the Eucharist* (2009), *Festín del deseo: hacia una teología alimentaria* (Aliosventos, México), and *Teopoéticas del cuerpo: la danza, la teología filosófica y las intermediaciones de los cuerpos* (2023).

**André S. Musskopf** is Professor in the Religious Studies Department of the Universidade Federal de Juiz de Fora and coordinates the recently created research group 'indecencies – religion, gender, and sexuality'. He holds a Bachelor's (2001), Master's (2004) and PhD in Systematic Theology from Escola Superior de Teologia/Faculdades EST. His areas and themes of research interest are Feminist Studies, Gender Studies, Queer Studies, Masculinities, Homosexuality and Sexual Diversity, in their relation to Theology and Religion. He is a lecturer in his areas of expertise in academic, religious, grassroots and social movements in Brazil and internationally.

**Marilú Rojas Salazar** was born in 1969 in Orizaba, Veracruz, Mexico. She has a PhD in Systematic Theology from the Roman Catholic University of Leuven. She is Feminist Theologian and Subject Professor in the PhD of Critical Gender Studies at the Ibero-American University of Mexico City; founder of TEIFEM (Feminist Theologians and Researchers of Mexico); director of the magazine *Sophias* (journal of interdisciplinary reflection on feminist theology in Mexico); and founding member of the UPM Academy of Theology in Mexico. She is guest professor at Lasalle University and feminist researcher in favour of reforms of the Roman Catholic Church.

**Anderson Fabián Santos Meza** is a doctoral candidate at Pontifical Xavierian University (PUJ), where he also obtained a Philosophy degree (2021). He serves as Editor and Proofreader at PUJ's Faculty of Theology. Concurrently he is a Junior Researcher at Institute Sophia in St. Louis, Missouri, where he is also a member of the research group Intercultural, Interdisciplinary, and Interreligious Group on Decoloniality, Migrations, and Sexuality (GIDMS). Additionally he is Assistant Editor for the journal *Conexión Queer*, showcasing expertise in Queer Theologies. His academic interests encompass Medieval Philosophy, Contemporary Mysticism, Queer Theory and Latin American Theology.

**Giovanna Sarto** is a doctoral candidate in Religious Studies at the Federal University of Juiz de Fora in Minas Gerais, Brazil. She holds an MA in Religious Studies (2022) and a specialization in Religion, Society and Culture (2020) by the same institution. In 2024 she was a visiting scholar at IMRI of the University of Dayton, Ohio. She is a member of the Research Groups Indecências – Religion, Gender and Sexuality (ReGeSex). She is currently the main editor of the academic journal *Sacrilegens*, which since 2022 has been rated A3 (the third highest Brazilian rating out of nine possible) by the National Commission for Religious Studies and Theology. Currently Giovanna is conducting her research with funding from CAPES as part of the scholarship programme supporting higher education research in Brazil.

**Judith Tatton-Schiff** is an ordained United Reformed Church (URC) Minister. She has a PhD in Practical Theology from the University of Wales Trinity St David (2024), an MTh from the University of Glasgow (Practical and Pastoral Theology, 2014) and a BD from the University of Edinburgh (Divinity, 2006). Particular areas of academic focus are sexuality and relationality, identity, theological ethics and moral injury. As a URC minister, Judith has served in Glasgow and Derby and previously as a Metropolitan Community Church (MCC) minister in Edinburgh and across Scotland.

**Charlene van der Walt** is Global Coordinator for Theological Education for Act Church of Sweden and an Honorary Associate Professor in Gender and Religion at the School of Religion, Philosophy and Classics at the University of KwaZulu-Natal in South Africa. Prof. Van der Walt also remains associated with the change-making work of the Ujamaa Center for Biblical and Theological Community Development and Research. Charlene's primary research interests include Queer Theory/Theology, Queer Biblical Hermeneutics, LGBTIQ+ activism and change-making, Contextual Bible Study, and emerging experimental pedagogies in the study of Religion and Theology.

**Mayuko Yasuda** is NT scholar and a Coordinator for Gender Justice for the Asia Pacific region in the Evangelical Lutheran Church in America. She received her PhD from the Lutheran School of Theology in Chicago, and her interests lie in feminist, queer and postcolonial interpretations of the Bible. Being a queer feminist herself, Dr Yasuda advocates for gender and queer justice in classrooms, churches and academia through teaching and publications. Her recent publication in English includes 'Rethinking Eschatologies with Postcolonial and Queer Perspectives', *Annual of the Japanese Biblical Institute* 47 (2022), pp. 70–92.

# Foreword

This book is the fruit of the work of the Council for World Mission (CWM). From its very beginning, the mission of CWM has extended beyond the confines of worship and faith communities into public arenas where services relating to education, health, welfare and ecology are provided, assessed and re-envisioned. Since the 1970s, CWM has wrestled with how to decolonize mission globally and locally – its praxis, pedagogy and theory – and how to proclaim fullness of life at a time when all of life is threatened.

CWM is committed to radical discipleship and prophetic spirituality. Through the Discernment and Radical Engagement (DARE) Programme, CWM conveys its prophetic role in the present sociopolitical, economic, ecological and global landscapes. DARE is inspired by liberation theologies that have emerged from the diverse context of struggles, its praxis, pedagogies and theories; and it explores, shares, transforms and tries to make sense of divinities, scriptures, traditions, responsibilities, destinies, practices, experiences and biases. DARE is open to the signs of the times and committed to the mission from the margins. Engagement with the margins is the first step for mission, theology and the ecumenical movement to manifest their radical, liberating, decolonizing spirits.

DARE and liberation theologies are radically interdisciplinary, interreligious and intersectional in their approach. This accompanies the shifts in academic trends but transcends those trends to root DARE in praxis, pedagogies and theories of struggles for liberation, decolonization and counter-imperial testimonies. As DARE is one of the key priorities of CWM's missiological discernment, I hope this series of publications out of Global DARE Conferences will inspire, encourage and empower mission, theology and movements towards liberation and reconciliation!

*Revd Dr Jooseop Keum*
*CWM General Secretary*

This book was supported by the Council for World Mission (CWM) through its DARE Programme (Discernment and Radical Engagement)

# Introduction

LISA ISHERWOOD AND
HUGO CÓRDOVA QUERO

The *DARE Primer on Global Queer Theologies* seeks to amplify the voices of queer Christian theologians from across the globe, integrating their perspectives into academic discussions and spiritual practices. The CWM Discernment and Radical Engagement (DARE) forum is a radical interdisciplinary, interreligious and affective platform that not only keeps abreast of shifts in academic trends but also transcends those trends to root the spirit of DARE in praxes, pedagogies and theories of struggles for liberation, decolonization and counter-imperial testimonies. In light of that spirit, this book highlights the engagement of queer Christian theologians with multiple theological disciplines, including systematic theology, pastoral care, missiology, ritual and liturgical experiences and broader spiritual traditions. By centring these perspectives, the primer showcases how queer theologies do not only critique but also reimagine traditional theological frameworks, challenging inherited doctrines and practices.

These theologians bring fresh insights into the lived realities of queer communities, offering interpretations that expand theological horizons while addressing issues of inclusion, justice and authenticity. They critique oppressive structures within religious institutions, advocate for transformative pastoral practices, and enrich liturgical experiences by incorporating queer narratives and symbols. In doing so they construct deeply contextual theologies, embodying a dynamic interplay between faith and identity.

This collection of chapters underscores the transformative potential of queer theologies to reshape theological understandings, religious practices and missional approaches. It invites readers to reflect on how these theologies foster more inclusive and life-affirming spiritual pathways, thus contributing to a richer and more diverse theological landscape.

A recurring theme in these reflections is the nuanced exploration of the intricate relationship between faith and sexuality. These theologians deeply engage with the complexities of how belief systems intersect with the lived experiences of queer individuals, weaving together a rich tapestry of insights that highlight the spiritual journeys of those often marginalized within religious contexts. Their work sheds light on the struggles, resilience and creativity of queer believers, revealing how faith can be both a source of challenge and empowerment. They offer profound and transformative perspectives on spirituality and identity by grounding their analyses in specific cultural and personal contexts.

Moreover, these theologians courageously confront the formidable challenges rooted in religious institutions' political and hierarchical structures. Their narratives expose the struggles and tensions that queer individuals face as they navigate faith communities often shaped by exclusionary practices and doctrines. They critically analyse how institutional power dynamics intersect with sexuality and faith, revealing how traditional religious systems perpetuate marginalization.

By bringing these realities to light, they critique oppressive structures and envision transformative pathways towards greater inclusion and justice. Their work underscores the importance of dismantling harmful ideologies and practices within these institutions, advocating for reforms that honour the dignity and spiritual agency of queer believers. Through their theological reflections they challenge the status quo and invite institutions and individuals to reimagine faith communities as spaces of radical hospitality, equity and mutual flourishing.

The primary objective of this scholarly project is to cultivate liberative and contextual theologies that honour the richness of local diversity while integrating the embodied practice of the Christian faith. These theologies emerge from lived experiences, cultural particularities and the dynamic interplay between tradition and innovation, offering profound insights into faith as practised in diverse contexts.

The theories and schools of thought that inform and shape these theological reflections are central to this endeavour. They are indispensable tools, enabling theologians to navigate complex intersections of culture, identity and spirituality. These frameworks help articulate a theology that addresses marginalized communities' unique challenges and enriches the broader Christian tradition with fresh perspectives. This project seeks to contribute a distinctive voice to global theological discourse – one that emphasizes liberation, celebrates diversity and embodies the transformative power of faith in action.

This collection endeavours to bridge the gap between academic discourse and the lived realities of queer individuals, contributing to theological scholarship while serving as a practical guide for fostering inclusivity and empathy in faith communities. Such a dual focus reflects the profound interconnectedness of thought and action, where theological reflection is not merely theoretical but deeply rooted in the lived experiences of those it seeks to affirm and uplift.

At the heart of this work lies an acknowledgment of the dynamic intersectionality that shapes global queer experiences. Intersectionality recognizes that identity is multifaceted, encompassing gender, sexuality, race, culture and socio-economic status. These diverse factors create unique contexts for faith and spirituality, where traditional theological narratives often fail to address the complexities of marginalization and resistance. Queer theologians thus engage with these realities, offering liberative praxis as a foundation for an embodied and life-affirming faith. This praxis involves reimagining doctrines, rituals and community structures to reflect God's inclusive love. It challenges exclusionary practices and seeks to create spaces where queer identities are celebrated as integral to the divine image. This collection amplifies these efforts, offering insights into how theology can transform not only academic perspectives but also the lived experiences of believers.

The *DARE Primer on Global Queer Theologies* invites readers – scholars, clergy and laypersons alike – to participate in this transformative theologizing. It calls for a re-examination of faith traditions in light of queer experiences, emphasizing the importance of justice, empathy and liberation. Through this work, theology becomes a tool for healing and hope, bridging divides and fostering communities where every individual is affirmed in their full humanity and spiritual identity.

A hope we nurture is that queer theologies will no longer be seen as simply contextual theologies and thereby have little or no impact on what is considered mainstream theology. As truly inspirational and Spirit-inspired theologies, they have much to offer for the continued development of theology. That is not to say they are not from contexts, namely the lived realities of believers, but rather to suggest that this is the beating heart of how theology was once understood, not as it has become in seminaries and the academy. It is time to release theology from the shadow of the Enlightenment and place it once more in the flesh and blood realities of the lives of believers. As we know too well, the label 'contextual' allows many university courses to ignore the wealth of knowledge within them and place them, if we are lucky, as a side issue that students can follow in their own time. What passes as normative theology has been inattentive to the problems of marginalization and has largely refused to engage with human difference and diversity, which has led to the oppression of the outsider. Our point is that if these concerns are called 'contextual theology', they can be dismissed as lesser, as not the real work of serious theologians. Perhaps the problem in Christian theology stems from the belief in one sole all-powerful God, making it difficult for theologians to embrace the different ways people of diverse backgrounds and embodied living understand and relate to this God. However, we suggest that any theology that ignores these realities cannot be understood as a valid representation of the divine.

As editors, engaging with such a diverse range of scholars has been a privilege, and we thank you for your contributions, which have come from your hearts. Your words will impact the readers and, by extension, the communities they are part of. Thank you everyone! We are also immensely grateful to CMW and, particularly, Graham McGeoch for enabling this project through setting in place a committee and funding a symposium. For queer scholars from around the globe, it is genuinely affirming that your organization would stand alongside and enable dialogue.

*Thank you all!*
*Lisa and Hugo*
*September 2025*

# PART I

# Hermeneutics and Interpretation

1

# Queer Hermeneutics: Liberation Techniques

MERCY AGUILAR CONTRERAS

*(translated by Hugo Córdova Quero)*

## Introduction

More than 500 years after the colonization of Latin America the traces of coloniality remain deeply ingrained in reality, particularly in racialized, stigmatized and feminized bodies. These bodies bear the imprint of a bleached history imposed upon them – a history that sought to erase all traces of the mud from which they were formed. Coloniality (Quijano, 2000, 2014) and patriarchy, as central techniques of colonial domination, have persistently targeted women and the most vulnerable groups. This dynamic operates by layering criteria that position some individuals below the threshold of the human, thereby perpetuating racist and sexist prejudices.

Racialized and stigmatized bodies, therefore, bear the enduring marks of an imposed, whitewashed history – one that sought to obliterate the essence of their origins. Yet the emergence and growing influence of feminist, queer and decolonial movements have ushered in powerful transformative forces. These movements actively reclaim and reinterpret original techniques of liberation, peeling away the figurative makeup that had whitened bodies, emotions, desires and sexualities. Like a snake shedding its skin, these schools of thought have initiated a profound bodily and subjective transformation process. Through the reimagining of liberation techniques, they have cultivated a renewed and original experience of theological and spiritual (re)incarnation:

> For Sloterdijk, the human being is an animal that has always been at an evolutionary disadvantage compared to other animals since its physical capabilities do not reach in any way what fur, claws, night vision, and different abilities allow other inhabitants of nature. However, in

> the face of this disadvantage, it developed technology, culture, and other tools that enable it to make everything around it have a degree of artificiality. (Castro-Gómez, 2012, p. 65)

Recreating original liberation techniques begins with human realities, interpretations and lived experiences. Its purpose is to construct emancipatory, plural and diverse hermeneutics – techniques designed to disrupt the hegemonic languages of domination and control tied to race, gender and sexuality. This approach challenges the notion that every human being emerges from a fixed natural reality, proposing that humanity is a continuous construction and reconstruction process. According to Michel Foucault, technique is the only will imposed in this process.

Coloniality, as a technique of domination, becomes inscribed on to white bodies, framing them as reproducers of a binary, dichotomous, cis-heterocentred construct of male and female. That construct, however, originates in a history built upon the same dichotomy: dominant men and subordinated women. These women were whitened and conditioned to nurture the offspring of the Western New World – a world constructed through the intersecting technologies of gender, race and class. Within this framework, the patriarchal world established itself through absolutist rule and the systematic imposition of women's roles.

The binary now evolves into a monogender paradigm, as Aura Estela Cumes (2009) posits. She argues that colonization configures the world as the realm of 'the One' – a single truth, a singular god, one man, one language, one culture, one epistemology and one dominant history. The dominant subject is embodied in the figure of 'man', with Europe representing the archetype of 'the One' (Cumes, 2012). It is essential to highlight that Cumes' perspective vindicates critical thinking as both an ethical-political principle and a methodology. Her work exposes how the project of coloniality continues to shape and define reality in Latin America.

Regardless of the denomination or methodology adopted by the current system of things, it invariably leads to the questioning and acknowledgement of patriarchy as the most pervasive colonial technique of domination and the inferiorization of women. Patriarchy positions men or the masculine at the centre of existence, framing them as the creators of the 'new world' while excluding women and diverse bodies from this role. This hierarchical framework constructs a reality where women are deemed inferior, systematically nullifying all forms of life that deviate from masculinity.

The colonial technique introduced gender, race and sexuality as fixed biological determinisms, subjecting women to a dual form of dispossession. As Cumes (2012) argues, every devaluing category of colonialism constructs a specific form of dispossession against the peoples of Abya Yala. Moreover, this dispossession operates through the imposition of a biopolitical system (Foucault, 2007) that organizes human lives while expropriating and annihilating cultural worlds.

According to Foucault (2008), knowledge is the primary intervention technique in the body, where the human being transforms. This concept is pivotal for understanding the different systems of colonization imposed in Latin America. It is essential to grasp the dynamics of colonialism – including its use of language and categories of dispossession, which enforce power relations that dehumanize bodies.

Beginning in the 1960s, Foucault employed the concept of the *dispositif* to challenge the notion that the modern subject is individual, autonomous and rational. This perspective suggests that personal identity is in a state of perpetual reconstruction, shaped by a variety of social, historical and discursive forces that evolve and transform over time (Foucault, 2008, p. 63). Foucault examines how the modern subject has been constructed and how social conditions influence the structure of human existence and its historical evolution.

Central to Foucault's analysis are the technologies of the self, which he explored by studying the classical era. He investigates the interplay between subjectivity and truth and the technologies of power that shape individual behaviour and discipline. These frameworks reveal the mechanisms through which individuals are governed and transformed within the broader power structures.

The technologies of the self (Foucault, 2008, p. 48) enable individuals to perform a range of operations on their own body, soul, thoughts, behaviour or any other aspect of their being, resulting in a transformation of themselves. These operations constitute a comprehensive process through which the subject actively reshapes their existence. Within this framework the *dispositif* emerges as a form of knowledge that acts upon the body, ensuring the subjugation of life, as it is intrinsically linked, according to Foucault, to specific forms of domination.

In his 1966 lecture *The Order of Things*, Foucault (1970) inaugurated a reconstruction of hermeneutics – an archaeological and genealogical archive aimed at interpreting reality, particularly the modern subject, while challenging any fixed notion of truth through the lens of technique. This reinterpretation of the contemporary subject through technique lays the foundation for new hermeneutics that disrupt the universalizing interpretations of the West, especially regarding techniques used in classical theologies. Foucault's work reveals that the categories crafted by coloniality to define and dominate bodies result from anthropotechnical processes of colonization, processes that utilize the techniques of language and knowledge to perpetuate power. These methods are used to control bodies, desires and sexualities while simultaneously transforming individuals through their internalization of these techniques.

This is why the metaphor of the snake shedding its skin as a technique of liberation resonates deeply with the transformations led by feminist and queer pilgrims in Latin America. The process of 'becoming' has undergone profound shifts: becoming a woman now entails becoming black, Latina, Mestiza, indigenous and queer. Recovering the 'mud skin' symbolizes a deliberate dismantling of the whiteness imposed on brown bodies. It is a transformation that has been both painful and revealing. The shedding of skin has exposed subtle and profound wounds from the past, as well as the complicity embedded in daily practices that sustain the colonial project.

Being confined within a bleached body and the embodied techniques of coloniality has necessitated a profound reckoning with our complicity in the establishment and perpetuation of ongoing colonial processes. Such self-examination exposes the depth of these wounds and highlights the urgent need for continuous transformation to escape the colonial frameworks that continue to shape identities and lives. The construct of whiteness – as a technique of intervention on the body – operates as a network that binds bodies through various technologies of subjectivation and the regulation of behaviour. Thus, the body becomes the quintessential domination device, reproducing and materializing the modern colonial and capitalist world system. Consequently the representations of the body form a cartography imposed by the colonial world as a boundary and frontier that has proved nearly impossible to transcend. The body, therefore, becomes an organic archive upon which the colonial system is inscribed (Preciado, 2002).

This embodied cartography has made the body a critical site of reflection in decolonization processes, given that it remains a primary territory of colonial intervention. The body is subjected to and controlled by a mechanism labelled the 'soul', a comprehensive technology for producing Eurocentric subjectivity (Wynter, 2024). That system constructs an army of cis-heterocentred bodies that, through a Western lens, marginalize the hermeneutic knowledge of the body. Within this framework, thought is divorced from the body, as the body has historically been interpreted as the prison of the soul, stripping it of its original function as a site of transformation. Reclaiming the body as a locus of resistance and transformation challenges this historical narrative. It seeks to disrupt the technologies of domination that continue to regulate and confine human potential within colonial structures.

This invites us to reflect on the various components of the colonization project and how they are intricately woven into networks that bind bodies through diverse techniques of control over life. According to Jacques Derrida (1986), Western concepts and categories are grounded in two absent imaginaries: the myth of creation or creationist theory on the one hand, and the notion of the end of time on the other. Throughout history these imaginaries, masquerading as presences, have shaped theological, political, cultural and religious knowledge in the West, perpetuating a persistent metaphysical problem. In contrast, indigenous myths often diverge from these Western imaginaries by emphasizing cyclical time and interconnectedness rather than linear creation or apocalyptic endings. Such myths position humanity within a relational web of life, rejecting the hierarchical binaries central to Western metaphysics. For example, many indigenous cosmologies perceive creation as an ongoing process rooted in reciprocal relationships with nature. Unlike the static framework of 'beginning and end', indigenous world views embrace continuity and regeneration, challenging the metaphysical constructs that sustain colonial domination and Eurocentric epistemologies.

For Foucault (2007), Western language is a self-referential system representing thought. Consequently, the challenge of alternative hermeneutics lies in redefining the technique of representation – developing languages and knowledge that emerge from bodily, sexual and gender representations. The objective is to craft a language that arises from life itself, one that does not merely represent itself but instead gives voice to the bodily, sexual and spiritual experiences of diverse lives. In this context, María Lugones (2014) asserts:

> The task of the decolonial feminist begins by seeing the colonial difference, emphatically resisting her epistemological habit of erasing it by seeing it. She sees the world with new eyes, and then she must abandon her 'woman's enchantment' with the universal and learn about others who resist colonial differences. (p. 115)

The recreation of the original techniques of the peoples of Abya Yala has enabled the proliferation of knowledge and practices as techniques that challenge and displace the anthropocentric hegemony over the management of life. This implies that the peoples of Abya Yala bring forth an epistemological matrix – a self-intervention technique – that destabilizes the ontological and epistemological foundations of Western thought. This matrix unveils a historical framework, accompanied by textual corpora, that restores the past and the liberation techniques taken away by colonization. That epistemological matrix inscribes itself on to cosmo-sentient bodies, bodies that convey an alternative message with different senses of life, challenging the origin and order of the world and interrogating the hermeneutic principle of a universal idea of one god, one man and one culture. These cosmopolitan bodies reveal the existence of other ways of life that cannot be comprehended through the binary, patriarchal-colonial paradigm.

Such representations of bodies emerge as a community of spectres, returning from a history of death to reappear in life. They are accompanied by an epistemological matrix and liberation techniques that give rise to other cultural worlds. These worlds are deeply connected to the spirits of a denied past, to bodies that have drawn sustenance from alternative sources of meaning. The spectral community symbolizes a reawakening of the voices and knowledge silenced by colonization, offering a profound critique of the imposed universality of colonial systems:

> The phantasmal moment comes upon him (*le moment fantomal lui survient*) and adds a supplementary dimension, a simulacrum, an alienation or an additional expropriation. Namely, a Body! a Flesh (*Leib*)! For there is no phantasm, there is never becoming a spectre of the spirit without, at least, an appearance of flesh in a space of invisible visibility, as a disappearance of an apparition. For there to be a ghost, a return to the body is necessary, but to a body more abstract than ever. (Derrida, 1998, p. 144)

The people of Abya Yala reemerge as a community of bodies and spectral worlds yet to come, challenging the trajectory of colonial history. They bring forth the denied past and the bodies discarded by coloniality, affirming the life and identity of their communities. By reconnecting the past with the present, they move within a temporality where the past continuously becomes. Through this circularity they return to an original time – a primordial moment where they perpetually reconstitute themselves as a people and a community.

This resurgence of peoples and marginalized bodies has enabled the construction of categorical frameworks in which diverse bodies can navigate and interpret themselves, breaking away from colonial and Eurocentric universals. The peoples of Abya Yala transcend colonial theorization, situating us in a primordial space where life flows, transforms and mutates. In this space the body is stripped bare, transcending the contradictions imposed by gender, class and race as fixed biological determinisms. Returning to their origins, they reclaim the political significance of difference and diversity.

Thus, no biological order of gender, class or race determines the future or history of 'women'. Instead women are woven into the historical and counter-hegemonic fabric of these people's traits and narratives. Consequently the becoming of women as diverse bodies is not a peripheral concept but a counter-hegemonic one – diverse, plural and integral to the lived realities of Abya Yala.

## Queer Hermeneutics as Techniques for Liberation

Hermeneutics has been essential for the subject's understanding of themselves, as it has been committed to providing answers to the existential challenges that human beings face. This hermeneutic task has historically been rooted in some of humanity's most archaic religious and theological beliefs. Yet these beliefs continue to operate technically in the psyche of the human being today. The fundamental function of hermeneutics has been transforming human beings and establishing judgments, rules, norms, beliefs, laws and imaginaries that guide individuals towards understanding themselves.

Therefore, hermeneutics serves pedagogical and anthropological functions as it is constructed and consolidated in bodies through the subjectivation of its discourse. In this sense, hermeneutics takes on a technical role in the production and organization of life. Historically it has been one of the primary disciplines within various religious traditions. It has been used to transmit concepts, imaginaries and beliefs about the world's origin and human beings. Despite its metaphorical origins, particularly in biblical hermeneutics, it has acquired an anthropological dimension of governance over bodies.

In this context biblical hermeneutics is one of history's primary domination devices. As Giorgio Agamben (2014) asserts:

> The term *dispositif* refers to the process through which a pure government activity is carried out without any foundation in being. For this reason, devices must always imply a process of subjectivation; that is, they must produce their subject. (p. 16)

Hermeneutics has historically produced a subject subordinate to the various institutions that govern the discourse of classical theologies and hegemonic Christianity. Hermeneutics mobilizes discourses, beliefs, concepts and imaginaries that capture the human being and subject them to the device's will. As Agamben (2014) further states: 'The device, then, is above all a machine that produces subjectivities, and only as such is it also a machine of government' (p. 23).

From a Western world view, hermeneutics is grounded in the various techniques of domination embedded in knowledge, particularly in its conceptualizations. Theology – as a discipline concerned with the knowledge of God – has undergone multiple transformations, each attempting to create the best concept and metaphor for God that responds to reality. Since modernity and the anthropological turn, religious knowledge and its foundations, imaginaries and languages have been scrutinized, primarily through biblical-theological interpretation methods. These methods have affirmed that religion, in its historical form, has often served political interests. Religion – by instrumentalizing spirituality and the concept of God as a technique of domination – has perpetuated itself as one of the significant systems of colonization and oppression in Latin America.

During colonization, Christianity, through its Western interpretation, became the hegemonic religion in Latin America. It functioned as a technology of upbringing, shaping and transforming the subject of the new Western world. With the hermeneutic turn of the twentieth century, new methodologies and approaches to interpreting biblical texts emerged, strengthening the discourses and practices of different groups that resisted literalist interpretations of the Bible.

For this reason theological work in Latin America was deeply influenced by the various movements that emerged in the twentieth century – including Feminist, Queer, Indigenous and Ecological Movements – and the reception of critical theories of modernity that appeared in the West. This has created a fertile ground for the proliferation of knowledge that challenged the ongoing processes of colonization in Latin America. We can assert that theologies have also undergone their pilgrimage. Just as feminist and diversity movements began their path of liberation grounded in various sexual, feminist and queer theories, theologies have become bodily, sexual and gendered knowledge – allowing themselves to be transformed and incarnated in these realities.

Theological knowledge begins to reimagine itself by engaging deeply with these realities, dismantling the constructs of body, sexuality and gender imposed by colonial and Western paradigms. In this process, theology metaphorically 'recovers its skin', stripping away layers of imposed ideology to reveal its authentic, vulnerable body. This act of undressing theology marks a hermeneutic shift, a reinterpretation that exposes its inherent fragility. Similar to the journey of feminism, this shedding of skin is both painful and transformative. It requires disembodying and rejecting the Western theological framework, a construct disguised as a 'natural order' yet designed to oppress and control bodies. By confronting and aborting the colonial god embedded within its theological body, theology embraces its nakedness, a state that allows for the possibility of rebirth. This vulnerable and embodied rebirth becomes the foundation for redefining the theological task from these emancipatory and decolonial perspectives.

The theological nakedness – of diverse bodies – represents one of the founding experiences we encounter in the testimonies of faith from various diverse communities. It is a word that emerges from anguish, from the theological orphanhood created by the patriarchal god who does not recognize his paternity in these bodies. Consequently this experience of nakedness undoubtedly leads to the creation of a different theology, as it symbolizes revelation, discovery and knowing through self-exposure.

Nevertheless, queer hermeneutics must seek the rescue of human experience in its concrete reality, striving to overcome the metaphysical problem of the West through a language of presence. This entails moving beyond the transcendental principles of the West, where an entire imagery of the origin of the human being operates. This does not imply a rejection of science or a dismissal of technological logic but rather an awareness that humans are responsible for their creation and are the sole agents capable of altering their programming. Hence human beings have an original technique of continuous construction and reconstruction. Santiago Castro-Gómez (2012) articulates this perspective as follows:

> Technique, in this case, is not the tools that man manufactures but the set of coordinated, strategic, regulated actions oriented to achieving a precise purpose. We could say that technique is the product of man's *practical intelligence*, which allows him to 'dispose' of the environment and submit it to his vital needs. It is not that man makes 'use' of technique, but that man is, in himself, a *technical animal*. The technique is not something aggregative but *constitutive* of the human animal. Or, to put it another way, as a consequence of his organic infradotation, man is compelled to think and act *technically*. And it is this compensatory ability that allowed him to become Homo sapiens. (p. 65; emphasis in the original)

This technical action enables individuals to construct queer hermeneutics as techniques of self-intervention that assist in developing strategies for creating alternative spaces of liberation. These spaces allow individuals to live their diversity freely and disconnect from the methods of domination and intervention that affect the body, gender and sexuality. Thus, hermeneutics emerges from its technical capacity to liberate itself, meaning that within its organic and genetic constitution, the anthropotechnical framework of its theological creation is organized.

For Castro-Gómez (2012), anthropotechnique operates in two ways: one is applied to dominate others, and the other is used to liberate oneself. Consequently the anthropotechnique concept highlights how one human's intervention over another remains an enduring historical force. Therefore the task of queer hermeneutics is to reappropriate the body's technical capacity and the various technologies that shape subjectivity. It involves producing a new subject by creating critical discourses that work on our bodies to dismantle Western knowledge. Such knowledge functions as a domestication technique, consistently placing us in vulnerable positions and subject to domination.

As Peter Sloterdijk (2012, p. 17) suggests, thinking about human self-formation requires more than seeing people as workers or as devoted believers; it must consider how life itself is exercised. Humans are not only makers or ritual practitioners – they are beings whose actions and habits shape and enhance themselves. Just as past centuries were defined by production or reflection, Sloterdijk proposes that the future is marked by deliberate exercise, highlighting the ongoing work we do on ourselves to shape our capacities and subjectivities. This understanding of self-formation resonates with reclaiming interpretative and bodily practices in theology.

The goal, therefore, is not to construct hegemonic hermeneutics but to reclaim the technical skills necessary for crafting our interpretations. This approach seeks to challenge the foundations of classical hermeneutics by employing liberation techniques and emphasizing the language of bodily presence – particularly in areas often neglected by traditional theologies: the body, sexuality and liberation methodologies. In the Gospel of John the *Logos* was made flesh and dwelt within a body. The Hebrew Bible depicts the *Ruâh* as a liberating force that once hovered over the waters. Christian tradition interprets this passage in Genesis as the *Logos*, destined to transform the world. The *Logos* did not remain confined to the metaphysical realm of absence. Still, it took on a tangible, historical presence by incarnating in Jesus' body, moving theology beyond abstraction and into the lived reality of embodied existence.

The *Logos* begins by transforming itself to transform the world. Thus, each person who embodies this *Logos* as a divine intervention technique recreates the original human intervention technique (Contreras Forero, 2021). As a result, human beings become their saviour, turning the theological endeavour into a technical knowledge of liberation by embracing this *Logos*. Consequently, it distances itself from the theological upbringing imposed by scholars, philosophers, religious figures, pastors and politicians who use technologies of domination over their bodies. According to Castro-Gómez (2012):

> To show the functioning of this anthropotechnique is humanism since it implies the explicit commitment of some men to rescue others from barbarism by means of their systematic training (Sloterdijk, 2009). Humanism is an instrument for the domestication and taming of man by man in order to save him from his animalistic tendencies. Insofar as it aims to make beasts civilized men, humanism functions as a set of anthropogenic techniques operated by a select elite of breeders (literate and expert). (p. 68)

Hence, as I have noted, this first type of anthropotechniques is an operation carried out by some individuals on others who have become breeders of various systems of domination. They reproduce individuals who embody different techniques of domination through breeding. Consequently the need for an original technique – a primordial process of teaching and liberation – brings us back to the image of the incarnated *Logos* as the first technique of divine intervention upon humanity. In this sense, theology becomes part of an anthropotechnique that shapes the human being, either for domination or liberation.

Historically this process has been used to dominate others. However, when theology is understood as a technique of self-intervention aimed at freeing us from the techniques of domination, it enables us to construct stories, narratives and hermeneutics that focus on the care of the self. Such a shift implies new modes of subjectivation, where knowledge is tied to the subject's ethical transformation rather than subjection. The transformation of subjectivity and corporeality through liberation techniques allows the individual to take charge of their being, abandoning the narratives of upbringing that once formed and subjected them. Therefore, upon becoming aware of their historical programming, human beings as technical animals emerge as being emancipated from the techniques of domination constructed by the various upbringing systems: religious, cultural and political (Contreras Forero, 2021).

## The Body as a Technique of Liberation

Historically the body has been one of the most significant absentees in theological thought, often regarded as holding less theological value or significance. Classical theologies – rooted in dominant imaginaries – perpetuate a view of the body that excludes it from the sacred and divine realms. Such exclusion has diminished the body's role in theological discourse and led to a profound absence of language to address the body and its lived experience. As a result the body has been marginalized, and its complexities and significance are largely ignored in theological discussions that emphasize the spiritual and metaphysical over the material and embodied. For Hugo Córdova Quero (2023):

> Religious discourses are intrinsically related to social and cultural contexts and shape perceptions about gender, sexuality, bodies, the heterosexual division of labor, and gender role expectations. Navigating the complex construct of each of these elements requires an exercise in conceptual calibration. That is, the ways in which these elements have been loaded with meaning refer to negotiations of power and contextualities that are not always common to each interlocutor and that are anchored in the context of each culture. (p. 42)

It is for this reason that queer theologies initiate a reconstruction of the language and experience of the body and sexuality and mainly express the sacred union between theology and the body. Specifically, the theological reappropriation of the body is a hermeneutic place and a place of nurturing diverse bodies. Such an incarnated God has the uterotechnical ability (Sloterdijk, 2009) to create bodies that have the capacity to produce and transform themselves. That is to say, those bodies can be born again, as the Gospel of John 3.4–8 describes:

> Nicodemus said to him, 'How can anyone be born after having grown old? Can one enter a second time into the mother's womb and be born?' Jesus answered, 'Very truly, I tell you, no one can enter the kingdom of God without being born of water and Spirit. What is born of the flesh is flesh, and what is born of the Spirit is spirit. Do not be astonished that I said to you, "You must be born from above." The wind blows where it chooses, and you hear the sound of it, but you do not know where it comes from or where it goes. So it is with everyone who is born of the Spirit.' (NRSV)

Juan Mateos and Juan Barreto (1982) – in their commentary on the Gospel of John – analyse:

> Jesus' answer is categorical (*I tell you the truth*) and enunciates a condition that admits no exceptions.
>
> The expression that is translated: *again*, means in Greek at the same time *again* and *from above*. Jesus does not admit the presuppositions of Nicodemus: the Law cannot bring man to the level required by the kingdom of God; the Law is 'from below' (3:31); it is not the source of life (1:4b); life comes 'from above,' from a new birth. Such is the con-

> dition for perceiving the reign of God; whoever is not born again, receiving a different life that originates from above, cannot even imagine what it is. The Law does not give an idea of it, nor is it a means to attain it. (p. 191; emphasis in the original)

In the context of Jesus' teachings, the concept of the Kingdom of God diverges significantly from traditional Jewish expectations. While many believed that the Kingdom would come through strict adherence to the Law and the arrival of a Messiah who would enforce its observance, Jesus emphasized a more profound, personal transformation. According to Jesus, the Kingdom was not merely a social or political ideal but a reality that required a spiritual rebirth. This rebirth was not about continuing in the past practices of the Law but about embracing a new way of living that transcended previous conceptions of righteousness and sin. The process of becoming 'born again' involves a fundamental shift, creating space for the actual realization of God's reign in human life:

> The reign of God was Israel's goal, its ideal. In the Pharisee mentality, the Messiah, who was to inaugurate it, would be the first teacher and observant of the Law. The kingdom would be realized because every Israelite would be 'just' according to that standard, and the ungodliness of the 'sinners' or unbelievers would be banished.
>
> For Jesus, the kingdom of God, being a social reality, is linked, however, to personal change *if one is not born again*. To be born again means becoming independent of a past and beginning an experience and a life. Each one is the result of a personal and communitarian history, but this is neither a basis nor a preparation for the kingdom of God. Continuity with a past of patient assimilation of the principles and practice of the Law does not bring us closer to it. The hope of forming man for the kingdom of God by relying on the Law is illusory; a new beginning is required. To reach the goal that God offers to humankind, his kingdom, and the finished and perfect human society, Nicodemus must renounce his programme. (Mateos and Barreto, 1982, p. 19; emphasis in the original)

Breaking free from the world's programming – its norms, codes and traditions – is crucial to understanding true rebirth. It involves shedding the cultural garments that confine bodies within cis-heteropatriarchal closets. Breaking with the past and transforming one's programming as a subject of this world is a key characteristic found in queer theologies, according to Córdova Quero (2023):

> As Marcella Althaus-Reid stated … we find ourselves in a terrain where it is not possible to have precise definitions of each theology presented here. The 'queer' – because of its permanent state of fluidity and de/(re)construction – resists being pigeonholed in the closets of the essentialist definitions of modern theories. Therefore, queer theologies are in constant change, evolution, and testing by their very postmodern imprint. In the background, they are the fruit of a long journey that has taken Christian thinkers and scholars almost two thousand years to (un)walk. (p. 16)

Therefore the change manifested by queer theologians, who refuse to remain confined by traditional norms, embodies the word as articulated in the Gospel of John. This Gospel expresses the inseparable unity between theology and the body. That unity undoubtedly challenges the theological foundations of classical theologies as the body acquires an ethical and theological commitment to liberate itself from traditional norms. It does so by transforming and altering the cis-heteropatriarchal programming embedded in classical hermeneutics, which has historically dominated the body and sexuality. The human being also has the potential to transform their world through the various techniques of liberation that arise from reclaiming the body as a theological space.

Consequently an individual's self-understanding is grounded in their bodily structure and sexual and gender experiences. That technical union of embodiment reveals the shared qualities and intimate unity between the *Logos* and the body in its transformative capacity. Thus, the technical or uterotechnic ability of queer bodies to produce and transform themselves enables them to reclaim desire and sexuality as a language through which to speak about God. This is particularly significant, as hegemonic theologies have historically co-opted the transformative power of desire and sexuality. As Marcella Althaus-Reid (2022) states:

> The sexually hegemonic theological project, extremely idealistic and strongly dependent on a colonial model, has systematically marginalized and silenced the revelation that occurs in intimate acts in what is perceived as the chaotic unfolding of intimate human relationships throughout history. (p. 70)

Queer theological work aims to dissolve the tension between theology and the body by constructing metaphors, imaginaries and hermeneutics that merge into a unified thought and experience. Doing so creates an intimate unity between God, the human body, its desires and its sexuality, all serving as a language for speaking about God. Such a union leads us to a concept of new birth – an evolved self-understanding of the body, its desires and its sexuality. Therefore, the theology of new birth suggests no immutable nature or fixed human essence. Instead human beings shape themselves according to their environment and experience. That is the genesis of their new existence, a rebirth that is not biological but technical. Castro Gómez (2012) describes this process in the following way:

> In this context, immunological practices that Sloterdijk calls 'anthropotechnical' appear. By this name, he refers to the set of techniques through which men of different cultures have tried to systematically protect themselves from the blows of fate and the risk of death. (p. 67)

Therefore, human beings are often born into a world that is not their own. They must take on the ethical and theological responsibility to transform both themselves and their world into a liveable space – one where the body, desire and sexuality can express themselves freely. This process represents the construction of what the Gospels term *Basileia tou Theou* [the Kingdom of God], which the biblical scholar Elisabeth Schüssler Fiorenza (1989) contests. Through liberation techniques, Schüssler Fiorenza reimagines the *Kingdom of God* through a feminist lens, suggesting that the term *Basileia tou Theou* should be understood not as a hierarchical, patriarchal vision but as a concept that challenges and dismantles *kyriarchal* structures. *Kyriarchy* refers to intersecting systems of domination and power – such as patriarchy, racism and classism – that perpetuate inequality and oppression. Schüssler Fiorenza offers an alternative vision through *Ekklesia*, the church or community of believers, redefined as a space of justice, equality and liberation. In this reimagined *Ekklesia*, traditional hierarchical systems of domination are replaced with mutual respect, empowerment and inclusive solidarity. It becomes a space where the community collectively works to transform the world, beginning with changing the self. Thus, The *Ekklesia* represents a technical reality where human beings actively create a just society through their actions, commitment and ongoing personal and collective change.

Building on the previous vision of *Ekklesia* as a space for transformation and liberation, queer theologians also embody this ethical and theological commitment through the reimagining and reshaping of their bodies, sexuality and gender. By embracing a radical reconfiguration of identity and rejecting the cis-heteropatriarchal systems of domination, queer theologians bring forth new principles of life grounded in justice, inclusivity and mutual respect. In their lived experiences they engage with the body not as a site of oppression but as a space for liberation and redefinition. Such a transformative process, which echoes the feminist and decolonial commitments discussed earlier, disrupts systems that marginalize diverse bodies and offers a powerful challenge to traditional theological and societal norms. Through their actions and theological reflection, queer theologians actively contribute to the creation of a world that honours all forms of being, challenging and transcending the constraints of past frameworks and the cis-heteronormative dicta that have shaped Christianity and theology. For instance, Córdova Quero (2023) comments on this in the Introduction to his book *Teologías Queer Globales* [Global Queer Theologies]:

> By making visible the rich and complex differences of people and communities doing and thinking about different queer theologies, we seek to contribute to the liberation of Christianity from the closet in which it has been trapped. Each queer theologian and each queer community of the faithful contributes to and constitutes itself as the subject of that liberation. Therefore, the intention behind this book is neither apologetic nor contestatory – although its dissent can be understood as such – but somewhat proactive. That is, while the contexts and issues to which each queer theology responds critique both aspects, to some extent, they are also continuations of non-hegemonic Christian thought in those settings. Thus, the readers of these pages have before them no longer a 'weapon' to be used against the 'enemies' but a tool to de/(re)construct the stifling sex-gender realities in which they live and develop their faith. This book is a contribution to the conscientization and formation of queer faithful and communities seeking to embody the Christian faith beyond the confines of cis-heteropatriarchal dictates. (pp. 17–18)

In other words – as Córdova Quero (2023) affirms – queer theologies serve as a tool to de/(re)construct the realities and programming of this suffocating world in which many queer bodies find themselves. Therefore, the revelation of Jesus to Nicodemus is crucial for understanding that this revelation reveals an existential problem within the world of Nicodemus. It is important to remember that Nicodemus belonged to the sect of the Pharisees, who grounded their faith in the law, which was often overshadowed by their cultural and political traditions that took precedence over the will of God. Nicodemus's ontological and programming issues regarding his self-understanding and perception of the world are resolved by being born again in the Spirit. This rebirth empowers humans with a new self-comprehension based on the Kingdom's values.

Similarly, the Mexican theologian Ángel F. Méndez Montoya (2019) states:

> Cuir theology is inexhaustible, for there are always new frontiers yet to be deconstructed, to be discovered and explored. It not only longs for another possible world beyond the dichotomous, antagonistic and hierarchical fixations that justify the exclusion of 'other' bodies considered inferior and defective by the dominance of heteropatriarchal technologies but also for their perpetual inscription in an intermediate space between human and divine agency. (p. 742)

Such a liberatory exercise by queer theologians undoubtedly provides essential tools for reclaiming our bodies, desires and sexuality. This process, rooted in queer theologies, offers a profound means of transforming these realities into technical practices of ongoing liberation. Queer theologians, such as Hugo Córdova Quero and Marcella Althaus-Reid, emphasize the importance of reclaiming the body as a site of divine presence, not one of sin or shame. Córdova Quero (2023), for instance, highlights the need for a queer liberation that reimagines theology by embracing the fullness of human experience, including sexuality and gender, as sacred and integral to our relationship with God. Similarly, Althaus-Reid's (2005) concept of 'indecency' challenges traditional Christian morality, suggesting that God's love and presence are not confined to cis-heteronormative or patriarchal structures. For her, the liberation of the body from such constraints is an essential aspect of spiritual freedom.

In both of their works, the enjoyment of our bodies and the freedom to love and be loved by God are acts of personal liberation and radical theological practices. These theologians call for a transformative vision where queer bodies and desires are affirmed as holy and deserving of the same respect and care as any other form of being. Through their contributions, queer theologies empower individuals to live freely, breaking from the oppression of cis-heteronormative structures and embracing a theology that celebrates diverse bodies, identities and expressions of love as reflections of divine beauty.

## Conclusion

Historically hermeneutics has been an endeavour predominantly by theological thinkers, scholars, philosophers, religious leaders and pastors. With this technical skill, they have traditionally constructed theology as an anthropotechnical endeavour, a method of shaping humanity and the world, primarily for purposes of domination. It has been achieved through narratives, norms, imaginaries, languages and other mechanisms. As a result, theology has become associated with techniques of control and domination, losing its transformative and liberating potential in addressing the realities of oppression.

In contrast, queer hermeneutics recovers the technical abilities inherent in human beings, constructing a subject capable of both self-transformation and the transformation of reality. It does so by recreating the various liberation techniques derived from our peoples and the bodies that theologies of domination have historically marginalized. By restoring the nature of the human being as a technical animal, queer hermeneutics initiates its liberation processes. This involves an epistemic rupture with the Western world view and an emancipation from the metaphysics of absence. The metaphysics of presence, by contrast, is more closely related to nature and the corporeal than to transcendence or the supernatural.

Technique is an intrinsic ability of humanity, tied to the material world as a product of consciousness and human nature. It is part of humankind's creative function, allowing for the rejection and alteration of existing programming when it no longer serves survival. Therefore, technique emerges as a fundamental capacity for human transformation, representing one of the most primitive capabilities of human beings.

The work of various thinkers has been instrumental in exposing and denaturalizing the techniques of domination historically imposed on bodies. Theories of sexuality and gender challenge socially constructed norms and power structures that regulate bodily autonomy and identity, revealing how such systems exert control over expressions of desire, gender identity and embodiment. By interrogating these dynamics they shed light on how bodies have been disciplined and marginalized, offering critical tools for liberation and resistance. Historically these mechanisms have perpetuated the idea of a universal human being, shaped and constrained by cis-heteropatriarchal values and norms. Through the transformative power of these techniques, such values have embedded themselves as universal anthropotechnical systems, reinforcing the binary construction of man and woman as fundamental to human nature. This binary framework has not only obscured the diversity of human experiences but also obstructed the natural and fuller realization of what it means to be human.

It is within this context that queer theologies, drawing on the technical construction of liberation hermeneutics, manage to free themselves from the petrification of humanity imposed by cis-heteropatriarchal systems. By reimagining the relationship between the body, identity and divinity, queer theologies initiate a process of human, bodily and sexual realization that affirms the sacredness of diverse experiences and identities. This transformative journey begins with the self, challenging the rigid binaries of nature and technique that have historically restricted expressions of humanity. Queer theologies emphasize that the body is not merely a site of control but a space for liberation, where the divine is encountered through embodied experiences. By deconstructing universal anthropotechnical systems with their oppressive norms and embracing fluidity, they disrupt the dichotomous relationship between the natural and the constructed, offering a vision of humanity that celebrates diversity and affirms the sacred in all forms of being.

## References

Agamben, Georgio (2014), *Que es un dispositivo? Seguido de El amigo y de La iglesia y el reino*, translated by Mercedes Ruvitoso, Ciudad Autónoma de Buenos Aires: Adriana Hidalgo Editora.

Althaus-Reid, Marcella (2005), *La teología indecente: Perversiones teológicas en sexo, género y política*, Barcelona: Edicions Bellaterra.

Althaus Reid, Marcela (2022), *Dios cuir*, translated by Leslie Pascoe Chalke, Ciudad de México: Universidad Iberoamericana.

Castro-Gómez, Santiago (2012), 'Sobre el concepto de antropotécnica en Peter Sloterdijk' ('On Peter Sloterdijk's Concept of Anthropotechnics'), *Revista de Estudios Sociales* 43, pp. 63–73.

Contreras Forero, Sergio Nicolás (2021), 'El humano: Un animal técnico, la educación como técnica constructora del hombre', doctoral dissertation, Chía: Facultad de Filosofía y Ciencias Humanas, Universidad de la Sabana.

Córdova Quero, Hugo (2023), *Teologías Queer Globales*, Saint Louis, MO: Institute Sophia Press.

Cumes, Aura Estela (2009), 'Multiculturalismo, género y feminismos: mujeres diversas, luchas complejas', in *Participación y políticas de mujeres indígenas en contextos latinoamericanos recientes*, edited by Andrea Pequeño, Quito: FLACSO, Sede Ecuador, pp. 29–52.

Cumes, Aura Estela (2012), 'Mujeres indígenas, patriarcado y colonialismo: Un desafío a la segregación comprensiva de las formas de dominio', *Anuario Hojas de Warmi* 17, pp. 1–16, at https://revistas.um.es/hojasdewarmi/article/view/180291, accessed 01.12.2024.

Derrida, Jacques (1986), *De la gramatología*, Madrid: Siglo XXI editores.

Derrida, Jaques (1998), *Espectros de Marx: El estado de la deuda, el trabajo del duelo y la Nueva Internacional*, Madrid: Editorial Trotta.

Foucault, Michel (1970), *The Order of Things: An Archaeology of the Human Sciences*, translated by Alan Sheridan, New York: Vintage Books.

Foucault, Michel (2007), *Nacimiento de la biopolítica*, Ciudad Autónoma de Buenos Aires: Fondo de Cultura Económica.

Foucault, Michel (2008), *Tecnologías del yo: Y otros textos afines*, Ciudad Autónoma de Buenos Aires: Editorial Paidos.

Lugones, María (2014), 'Colonialidad y género', in *Tejiendo de otro modo: Feminismo, epistemología y apuestas descoloniales en Abya Yala*, edited by Yuderkys Espinosa Miñoso, Diana Gómez Correal and Karina Ochoa Muñoz, Popayán: Editorial Universidad del Cauca.

Mateos, Juan and Juan Barreto (1982), *El Evangelio de Juan: Análisis lingüístico y comentario exegético*, Madrid: Ediciones Cristiandad.

Méndez Montoya, Ángel F. (2019), 'El amor en los últimos tiempos: La inscripción escatológica en cuerpos afines a un deseo infinitamente cuir', in *Teologías* queer*: Devenir el cuerpo* queer *de Cristo*, edited by Stefanie Knauss and Carlos Mendoza-Álvarez (*Concilium* no. 383), Estella: Editorial Verbo Divino, pp. 737–46.

Preciado, Paul B. (2002), *Manifiesto contra-sexual*, Madrid: Editorial Opera Prima.

Quijano, Aníbal (2000), 'Colonialidad del poder y clasificación social', *Journal of World-Systems Research* 6, no. 2, pp. 342–86.

Quijano, Aníbal (2014), 'Colonialidad del poder, eurocentrismo y América Latina', in *Cuestiones y horizontes: De la dependencia histórico-estructural a la colonialidad/descolonialidad del poder*, edited by Edgardo Lander, Ciudad Autónoma de Buenos Aires: CLACSO, pp. 777–832.

Schüssler Fiorenza, Elisabeth (1989), *En memoria de ella: Una reconstrucción teológico- feminista de los orígenes del cristianismo*, translated by María Tabuyo, Bilbao: Editorial Desclée de Brouwer.

Sloterdijk, Peter (2009), *Esferas I*, Burbujas, Madrid: Siruela.

Sloterdijk, Peter (2012), *Haz de cambiar tu vida*, Valencia: Pre-Textos.

Wynter, Sylvia (2024), *Desestabilizar la colonialidad de Ser/Poder/Verdad/Libertad: Hacia lo humano, después del hombre, susobrerepresentación – un argumento*, Ciudad de México: Cráter Invertido/Taller XD.

2

# Stabanized African Biblical Hermeneutics: Exploring the Contours of an African Izitabane Biblical Hermeneutics

CHARLENE VAN DER WALT

## Remaining at the Threshold

In another book chapter entitled '"Better is never better for everyone; it always means worse for some": Could there be space in an African women's theology for those known as Izitabane?' (Van der Walt, 2021a), I reflected on the apparent lack of African women's theological engagement with the embodied lived realities navigated by African *Izitabane*.[1] I started this initial reflection by focusing on my homecoming within the Circle of Concerned African Women Theologians (the Circle) and how I found within this collective a creative and productive space to reflect on contextual issues navigated by African women. I found the orientation towards justice propagated by the Circle compelling. In this vein, Isabel Phiri and Sarojini Nadar argue that one of the key characteristics of African women's theology is a particular ideological investment as it is aimed at community transformation and labours fundamentally to enable and enhance communities that aid the collective well-being and flourishing of all its members (Phiri and Nadar, 2006). In light of this focus and commitment, I found the lack of engagement and invested reflection on the lived reality faced by African *Izitabane* – like myself – concerning and problematic. Although dimensions of my life and embodied experience found a homecoming within the contours and commitments expressed by the Circle, there were dimensions of my personhood that seemed best left out of the equation.

The same applies if we shift our critical focus to African women's biblical hermeneutics. Although there have been some who have taken up the task of engaging the biblical text in the African context by drawing on the insights of queer scholarship and by engaging the lived realities faced by African *Izitabane*, it is still an approach and a focus that is sorely absent from the body of scholarship that constitutes African women's biblical hermeneutics (Maier et al., 2016; Dube, 2017; Van der Walt, 2015, 2016a, 2016b, 2021b, 2022a, 2022b; Claassens et al., 2021; Van der Walt and Davids, 2022). That is particularly problematic if we consider the reality that the biblical text is often used in contemporary African faith communities to condemn LGBTIQ+ people as an abomination before God and to label same-sex love as unnatural, un-Christian and un-African.

During the last General Assembly of the World Council of Churches that took place in Karlsruhe, Germany – between 31 August and 8 September 2022 – a working group consisting of queer people and clergy, gender and sexuality experts, and faith leaders who have been journeying together since 2012 launched a document entitled *Conversations on the Pilgrim Way: Invitation to Journey Together on Matters of Human Sexuality* (WCC, 2022). The document set out to highlight issues of gender and sexuality as an important area for collective reflection and engagement for the diversity of member churches and organizations that convene under the banner of the World Council of Churches. Considering the diversity of members and the ideological and confessional disparities represented by members, this was indeed no small task. The document set out to place church and faith conversations about human sexuality in a contextual and time framework to highlight again the importance of embodied representation in conversations relating to human sexuality, and highlight some of the violence and vulnerabilities faced by LGBTIQ+ people in hostile contexts. The resource again offers theoretical, theological and vocabulary resources to enable faith communities to have difficult conversations concerning sexuality and spirituality. It is a crucial resource; through some fancy terminology, groundwork signifies a good starting point for critical engagement by diverse faith communities.

A second accompanying publication developed by the Rainbow Pilgrims of Faith is entitled *Reconciliation from the Margins: Personal Stories of Queer Persons of Faith* (Söderblom et al., 2022). The resource created by the Rainbow Pilgrims of Faith for the World Council of Churches is one of many contemporary initiatives designed to raise awareness among people of faith and faith communities about human sexuality and sexual diversity. These resources are fundamentally designed with the church and faith communities in mind. Numerous resources and processes developed by the Ujamaa Centre and Inclusive and Affirming ministries have also aimed to create spaces for life-affirming conversations about sexuality in faith communities. Although this is work that I remain committed to, I am also grappling with questions about who this work is for and how our efforts benefit those most vulnerable in African faith settings because of their sexual diversity or non-normative gender expression. In this current contribution I therefore aim to highlight work being developed with, for and among queer people as we critically, contextually and in a counter-normative way engage the biblical text.

The title *Reconciliation from the Margins* queerly asks the question of who determines the agenda for change. Are the journey and outcome of liberation for the poor and marginalized determined by the centre, or can we trust those on the margin to choose their destiny? The title hints at its orientation, and it is a vital resource drawing on feminist and queer insights as the value of storytelling foundationally underpins it as a method to allow context to speak and to showcase the deep intersectional complexity of situated narratives as a starting point for our theological engagement. *Reconciliation from the Margins* offers stories from around the globe and a diversity of faith contexts speaking to the integration of sexuality and spirituality, the reading of the Bible and ethics, and the navigation of calling and 'coming out' in hostile landscapes. The rich and complex stories speak to diverse experiences and contexts, yet many striking similarities and themes emerge.

The narrative offered by Felicia (2022) from Ghana speaks, as so many others, to an early awareness of sexuality diversity and the intersection with spirituality. Where some find the integration less troublesome and have a deep and innate sense of God's love and care, Felicia finds the integration process challenging. She shares the story of a Sunday school teacher whose teaching and interpretations of scripture impacted her entire life and how she navigated her sexuality and her journey of spirituality. She states: 'My Sunday school teacher had always made me believe that homosexuality is the greatest sin on earth, and it comes with the greatest punishment among other condemnations' (Felicia, 2022, p. 8).

These foundational teachings caused Felicia to experience a lack of personal integration as she found it hard to accept herself and struggled with the marginalization that she experienced in her faith community and the exclusion from her family and kinship relationships. She continues: 'Things became hard. I saw myself as a sinner and a black sheep of the family. I was always isolating myself, keeping distance between myself and the other members of the family as they started to suspect my sexuality' (p. 8).

She concludes her story by sharing the extreme isolation and humiliation that she experienced from those closest to her:

> I never found peace in the house as my grandmother would pour insults on me anytime she sets her eyes on me; all sorts of humiliations. All those living in my area heard about my sexuality, as my grandmother took the chance of shouting every morning at me in an ever-louder voice. No one in the family wanted to associate with me. (p. 8)

Felicia's story so painfully expresses something of the vulnerability of LGBTIQ+ people navigating sexual and gender diversity in African faith spaces. When reading Felicia's story and those of others from around the globe who offered their narratives as witnesses to the presence, experiences and struggles of LGBTIQ+ people in faith communities, it was significant to note how central were the reading of the Bible and the teaching developed from Bible reading in the exclusion and marginalization experienced by LGBTIQ+ people. From these stories it is clear that rather than functioning as a conversation starter, the Bible or sacred scriptures and the teaching developed from these foundational scriptures often function as a proverbial dead end to creative and imaginative explorations of what the contours of diverse life together constitute.

## Engaging the Systemic

LGBTIQ+ people in the Southern African context are often referred to as *Izitabane*, a derogatory indigenous term aimed to strip LGBTIQ+ people of their humanity and to objectify sexually diverse people as the other. As Amanda Swarr (2009) highlights, *Izitabane* originated from the question *Usistela bani?*, which translates as 'What kind of a sister are you?', Such a question arose in local communities when an LGBTIQ+ person was noticed.

Although it might seem strange or counterintuitive, especially for those who have borne the brunt of violent exclusion and othering on their bodies, I deliberately and queerly choose to use the term *Izitabane* when referring to African LGBTIQ+ people. Drawing on the counter-normative imperative of Queer Theory, I decided to reappropriate a derogatory term to create space through discomfort for more authentic conversations about the embodied presence. I lived the realities of LGBTIQ+ people in the African context. By employing this term I intentionally aim to trouble or destabilize the derogatory and to reflect on the presence and agency of LGBTIQ+ people in the African context. Although African *Izitabane* is often engaged in the context of violence and dehumanization, through the reappropriation of this term, I also want to celebrate the agency, creativity and possibility for connection and community that African LGBTIQ+ people embody.[2] This indigenous term, although derogatory, speaks to the presence of LGBTIQ+ people in the African context and refutes notions of queerness as being impossible, un-African or a Western import. African *Izitabane* are human beings among other human beings and in community with other humans who make life and meaning in a diversity of contextual settings.

Underlying constructions, ideas and practices that either negate the existence of *Izitabane* or that aim to annihilate African LGBTIQ+ people are the ideology of econo-heteropatriarchy (West, 2020; Van der Walt, 2021b). The term articulates the systematic and institutionalized implications when dominant ideologies such as patriarchy, cis-heteronormativity and capitalism align to inform dominant constructions and lived realities concerning gender and sexuality. Foundational to the systemic ideology of econo-heteropatriarchy is a biological essentialist understating of sex that finds expression in the pervasive binary classification of sex in a binary male/female. From this flows an insistence on the alignment of biological sex, understood in a binary, with gender identity and sexual orientation. Men are not only constructed as the polar opposite of women but also as of superior status and higher value. What it means to be a man in a cis-heteropatriarchal system finds expressions in hegemonic constructions of masculinity that frame men primarily as powerful providers, protectors and penetrators (Ngcobo, 2022). Decision-making power regarding issues of sexuality and reproduction is reserved for men in a cis-heteropatriarchal system. Within this frame, reproduction is understood as a moral imperative, which leads to stable notions of what constitutes a 'natural family'.

Circle theologians have done much to critically engage patriarchy in the African context as a life-denying system that enables the oppression of women. The founding mother of the Circle, Mercy Amba Oduyoye (1986), skilfully describes feminism as a hermeneutical tool when stating:

> Feminism has become the shorthand for the proclamation that women's experiences should become an integral part of what goes into the definition of being a human. It highlights the woman's world and her worldview as she struggles side by side with the man to realize her full potential as a human being … Feminism then emphasizes the wholeness of the community as made up of male and female beings. It seeks to express what is not so obvious, that is that male-humanity is a part with female-humanity, and that both expressions of humanity are needed to shape a balanced community within which each will experience a fullness of being. Feminism calls for the incorporation of

> the woman into the community of interpretation of what it means to be human. (p. 21)

The lived realities faced by African *Izitabane* point to the fact that beyond patriarchy, the systemic ideology of cis-heteronormativity warrants critical engagement. Cis-heteronormativity is the result of a systematic normalization of cis-heterosexuality. It is often informed by a particular way of reading the Bible and infused by patriarchy and static understandings of culture. Gust Yep (2014) describes this process as follows:

> The process of normalizing heterosexuality in our social system actively and methodically subordinates, disempowers, denies, and rejects individuals who do not conform to the heterosexual mandate by criminalizing them, denying them protection against discrimination, and refusing them basic rights and recognition, or all of the above. (p. 24)

Cis-heteronormative discourse describes reality primarily and exclusively from the position of the cis-heterosexual. According to Andrew Martin et al. (2009):

> [T]his is the idea, dominant in most societies, that heterosexuality is the only 'normal' sexual orientation, only sexual or marital relations between women and men are acceptable, and each sex has certain natural roles in life, so-called gender roles. (p. 6)

The ideologies of patriarchy and cis-heteronormativity are profoundly informed and bolstered by dominant cultural realities and foundational values and religious teachings, practices and interpretations of foundational scriptures. The systemic reality underpinned by econo-cis-heteropatriarchy is not a mere conceptual construction or an idea. Still, it has very real consequences for bodies and finds expression in the complex lived realities situated at the intersection of socio-economic realities, class, race, gender and sexuality. Those who do not fit the cis-heteropatriarchal ideal are often policed, shamed or violated in an attempt to keep the norm intact. Consequently, LGBTIQ+ people in the South African context navigate daily life and existence at the heart of this intersection and often experience abuse, dehumanization and violence as a result of counter-heteronormative expressions of sexuality and gender identity. In this sense, to Stabanize it to turn *Izitabane* – a noun used to name those who do not fit the econo-heteropatriarchal ideal – into a verb. Stabanize is to *Izitabane* what queering it to queer. It is a word aiming to centre the experience and realities of *Izitabane*.

## African *Izitabane* Reclaiming the Bible as a Source for Liberation and Life

Considering the way that African faith leaders and faith communities have appropriated the Bible to exclude and objectify African *Izitabane*, it should not come as a surprise that African LGBTIQ+ people often consider the Bible as something that belongs to the church or the academy (West and Van der Walt, 2019). Biblical narratives are drawn on anecdotally within ethical debates and discussions in African faith communities as a clear textual example of God's adverse judgement of LGBTIQ+ people and of those who navigate gender, desire and love outside of the cis-heteropatriarchal binary directive (Van der Walt and Davids, 2022; Van der Walt, 2023). These practices and the understanding of the positionality and ownership of the Bible lead us again to ask critical questions about power. Who gets to interpret and proclaim the results of that interpretation? Who gets to determine the dominant narrative?

That is, of course, not the first time that these questions have been asked by the poor, marginalized or disenfranchised when it comes to the position of the Bible concerning dominant ideologies, cultural construction and foundational narratives. Jeremy Punt (2002) argues in this regard:

> The history of the interpretation of the Bible is a history of power and control ... Attempts to say what the Bible 'really means', to get to *the* meaning, always stood in service of purposes determined by ecclesial, socio-political, ethnic, nationalistic or other such concerns. Attempts to subvert existing claims to the Bible and its meaning often served similar, if opposing, interests. Although the very notion of the meaning of the biblical texts are denied by some today, it has to be acknowledged that many people continue to find the Bible a valuable guide for their lives. The Bible as site of struggle involves, however, more than difference of interpretive opinion. The Bible is involved in the discourse of power and is drawn into a struggle for interpretive control as well as, eventually, ownership thereof. (p. 425; emphasis original)

In light of the constant and pervasive power dynamics present in all Bible interpretation processes, Elisabeth Schüssler Fiorenza (1985) articulates the task of feminist biblical interpretation as a political one because the Bible and its interpretation have constantly been used as weapons against the liberation of women.

In the same way, a Stabanized African biblical hermeneutics implies a creative balance between, first, the critique of current life-denying interpretative practice that exposes and destabilizes dominant and pervasive power dynamics that are aimed at keeping the norm intact. Second, the dynamic work of imagining a different way to engage the Biblical text allows for more outstanding agency and diversity regarding the interpretative process. Rather than thinking about Bible reading as an objective activity that belongs in churches and universities, to be overseen by faith leaders and scholars, the call is for an imaginative 'taking back of the word' by *Izitabane* and those often marginalized because of fundamentalist engagement with scripture (Shore-Goss and West, 2000). Rather than letting churches or academia decide what the Bible means, *Izitabane* are called to read the Bible for themselves with others and to draw on their own embodied stories as an entry point into the creative process of reading the Bible in the community. A Stabanized biblical hermeneutics thus sees African *Izitabane* reading the text by drawing on their interpretative recourses and centring their own experience. In line with the impulse of queer scholarship, it transforms *Izitabane* from a derogatory insult to an active attempt to centre the African LGBTIQ+ experience in the hermeneutical process.

In the final part of this chapter I aim to explore some of the foundational contours of a Stabanized African biblical hermeneutics that draws on insights from African biblical hermeneutics, African feminist biblical hermeneutics and contextual and intercultural biblical hermeneutics. The contribution draws on ongoing work to develop an *Izitabane Zingabantu* Ubuntu theology. *Izitabane Zingabantu* Ubuntu theology broadly calls for an embodied reclaiming of all that is life-affirming within faith landscapes, reimagining community, engagement with the sources of faith and remembering our communal sacramental identity (Davids et al., 2019).

Although this is not a comprehensive or final articulation of what constitutes a Stabanized African biblical hermeneutic as the work remains ongoing, developing and emerging, I aim to explore four foundational contours in the remainder of the chapter: a commitment to the embodied contextual, the collective, the counter-normative and the continuous. I offer these contour lines as part of a more significant and developing project aiming to establish a Stabanized African biblical hermeneutics.

First, I turn my attention to the embodied contextual. This dimension implies an acknowledgment that all Bible reading is done in an embodied and contextual way. We read the Bible in our context and from our position through our embodied experience filter. Although some might claim objectivity in Bible interpretation, our bodies and lived experiences remain the first membrane through which we engage our interpretative process. Rather than an obstacle, this reality allows us to bring the embodied stories of our own lives into conversation with the stories of the Bible. Truly engaging the contextual implies a thick, intersectional, embodied analysis of what constitutes the contextual when we critically engage with life-denying systems and situations. A Stabanized biblical hermeneutic has an epistemological commitment to the embodied lived reality of those affected, being the starting point for reflection.

That implies that LGBTIQ+ people should be present to read the text for themselves and to share their own embodied experiences in communal faith settings. Rather than talking about LGBTIQ+ people and prescribing what bodies should be doing, this dimension would imply an openness and welcoming orientation by African faith communities to speak with LGBTIQ+ people and to collectively reflect on the reality of what bodies are doing in intimate settings and how this links to notions of hospitality, faith, salvation and flourishing that are so central to the Christian gospel. As with African women's theology, telling personal and contextual stories is a unique tool for gaining insight, making sense of reality and informing identity formation and the interpretative process (Phiri and Nadar, 2006). When insisting on the importance of authentic LGBTIQ+ stories to serve as an entry point for more profound and intersectional engagements with a contextual, I do not mean by this that LGBTIQ+ people should 'perform their pain' for African faith communities to be conscientious, but rather a collective invitation to greater vulnerability and sharing from an embodied more profound contextual place (Terblanche and Van der Walt, 2022).

These spaces could be safer and more welcoming when arguing for these collective faith settings. Therefore, a pertinent issue that warrants our critical engagement is reflections on how we work towards creating safety, mutuality, accompaniment and care in the spaces where we engage each other in an embodied and contextual manner.

Second, closely related to the first contour examined above, Stabanized biblical hermeneutics calls for collective engagement. Similarly, Adriaan van Klinken (2020) considers the importance of participatory work when he reflects on the study of religion from a decolonial perspective. The polarized nature of the conversation about sexual diversity is well known and particularly poignant in faith settings. To a certain extent, the echo chambers of homogenous physical and virtual communities contribute to this as ethical and social reflection is conducted among those who think and argue within the same paradigm. As discussed elsewhere, it is crucial to read the Bible not only with those who look like us or who think like us but to meet together with others (and their Bible reading, which is so different from our own), creating space for more bodies to matter in our collective communities (Van der Walt, 2016a, 2016b). Reading the Bible with others as we engage in issues of human sexuality and gender expression will imply a collective willingness to take a risk, an imperative to suspend judgement and a commitment to creating co-constructed spaces for knowledge production. Instead of allowing faith leaders or academic practitioners to claim final authority when it comes to the reading of the biblical text, this approach calls for alternative interpretative spaces where the interpretative resources of a diversity of interpreters are not only tolerated or acknowledged but celebrated and considered the starting point for collective knowledge production.

Third, and foundational to a Stabanized biblical hermeneutic is the commitment to practices and processes that allow for the troubling and destabilization of the norm or what is considered normative in service of liberation and justice. Although sexual orientation and gender expressions are central to the queering process, they are not singularly confined to gender and sexuality issues. Rather they represent an intersectional ideological commitment to the interrogation and destabilization of any social construct and the privilege that insider states hold to any dominant construction, be it race, class, age, gender, sexuality or ability. To Stabanize is a verb, and the process of disruption is achieved by destabilizing the processes, spaces and role-players involved in the process of reading the Bible (Van der Walt, 2022b).

Fourth, and in conclusion to this chapter, a Stabanized biblical hermeneutic invites a continuous and collective process of critical engagement, reflection and interpretation. In opposition to the knowledge economy propagated by econo-heteropatriarchy, where individual ownership and exclusive knowledge are valued and celebrated, this approach insists on the incomplete, the partial and the value of failure. In line with the argument made by Jack Halberstam in *The Queer Art of Failure* (2011), this approach insists on failure. It calls for a realization that we are not enough on our own, do not know it all and do not have the final answers when it comes to the interpretation of the Bible. It calls for an awareness of the partiality of our understanding and orientation of curiosity.

## Notes

1 In the second segment of this chapter I offer a reflection on the choice and contours of choosing for the term *Izitabane* to refer to African LGBTIQ+ people and the theoretical and contextual implications of this choice.

2 The ongoing complexity in navigating the representation of LGBTIQ+ people in public discourse is well illustrated in the top 2022 queer articles featured on MambaOnline.com. We see the pervasive trends of violence and discrimination that are being countered by stories of liberation and queer agency (Igual, 2022).

## References

Claassens, L. Juliana, Christl M. Maier and Funlola O. Olojede, eds (2021), *Transgression and Transformation: Feminist, Postcolonial and Queer Biblical Interpretation as Creative Interventions*, London: Bloomsbury Publishing.

Davids, Hanzline, Abongile Matyila, Sizwe Sithole and Charlene van der Walt (2019), *Stabanisation: A Discussion Paper About Disrupting Backlash by Reclaiming LGBTIQ+ Voices in the African Church Landscape*, Johannesburg: The Other Foundation, at http://theotherfoundation.org/faith-and-religion/, accessed 01.12.2024.

Dube, Musa W. (2017), 'Dinah (Genesis 34) at the Contact Zone: Shall Our Sister Become a Whore?', in *Feminist Frameworks and the Bible: Power, Ambiguity, and Intersectionality*, edited by L. Juliana Claassens and Carolyn J. Sharp (Library of Hebrew Bible/Old Testament Studies #630), Leiden: Brill, pp. 39–57.

Felicia (2022), 'I never found peace in the house of my grandmother', in *Reconciliation from the Margins: Personal Stories of Queer Persons of Faith*, edited by Kerstin Söderblom, Martin Franke-Coulbeaut, Misza Czerniak and Pearl Wong, Oslo: Rainbow Pilgrims of Faith, pp. 8–9.

Halberstam, Jack (2011), *The Queer Art of Failure*, Durham, NC: Duke University Press.

Igual, Roberto (2022), 'Mamba's 21 Most-Read Queer Stories of 2022', *Mamba Online*, at https://www.mambaonline.com/2022/12/30/mambas-21-most-read-queer-stories-of-2022/, accessed 0.12.2024.

Maier, Christl M., Madipoane Masenya, Jacqueline E. Lapsley, Charlene van der Walt, Mercedes García Bachmann and L. Juliana Claassens (2016), 'Assessing the Use of Gender in Current Biblical Scholarship: A Panel Discussion at the IOSOT Congress in South Africa', *Lectio Difficilior* 2, pp. 1–32.

Martin, Andrew, Annie Kelly, Laura Turquet and Stephanie Ross (2009), 'Hate Crimes: The Rise of "Corrective" Rape in South Africa', *ActionAid* 15, pp. 1–20.

Ngcobo, Siwakhile (2022), 'Powerful, Penetrator, Provider: A Religio-Cultural Analysis of Masculinity Production in Men's Conference Promotional Media in the African Pentecostal Context', Master's thesis, Durban: University of KwaZulu-Natal.

Oduyoye, Mercy Amba (1986), *Hearing and Knowing: Theological Reflections on Christianity in Africa*, Maryknoll, NY: Orbis Books.

Phiri, Isabel and Sarojini Nadar (2006), 'Treading Softly but Firmly: African

Women, Religion and Health', in *African Women, Religion and Health: Essays in Honor of Mercy Amba Ewudizwa Oduyoye*, edited by Isabel Phiri and Sarojini Nadar, Pietermaritzburg: Cluster Publications, pp. 1–16.

Punt, Jeremy (2002), 'From Re-writing to Rereading the Bible in Postcolonial Africa: Considering the Options and Implications', *Missionalia: Southern African Journal of Mission Studies* 30, no. 3, pp. 410–42, 425.

Schüssler Fiorenza, Elisabeth (1985), 'The Will to Choose or to Reject: Continuing Our Critical Work', in *Feminist Interpretation of the Bible*, edited by Letty M. Russell, Philadelphia, PA: Westminster Press, pp. 125–36.

Shore-Goss, Robert E. and Mona West, eds (2000), *Take Back the Word: A Queer Reading of the Bible*, Cleveland, OH: Pilgrim Press.

Söderblom, Kerstin, Martin Franke-Coulbeaut, Misza Czerniak and Pearl Wong, eds (2022), *Reconciliation from the Margins: Personal Stories of Queer Persons of Faith*, Oslo: Rainbow Pilgrims of Faith.

Swarr, Amanda Lock (2009), '"Stabane," Intersexuality, and Same-Sex Relationships in South Africa", *Feminist Studies* 35, no. 3, pp. 524–48.

Terblanche, Judith and Charlene van der Walt (2022), 'Towards Global Citizenship Education in South Africa: Cultivating Deliberative Encounters in the Context of Gender-Based Violence', in *Global Citizenship Education in the Global South: Educators' Perceptions and Practices*, edited by Emiliano Bosio and Yusef Waghid, Leiden: Brill, pp. 198–220.

Van der Walt, Charlene (2015), '"It's the Price I Guess for the Lies I've Told That the Truth It No Longer Thrills Me ...' Reading Queer Lies to Reveal Straight Truth in Genesis 38', in *Restorative Readings: The Old Testament, Ethics, and Human Dignity*, edited by L. Juliana Claassens and Bruch C. Birch, Eugene, OR: Wipf & Stock Publishers, pp. 57–74.

Van der Walt, Charlene (2016a), 'Is "Being Right" More Important Than "Being Together"? Intercultural Bible Reading and Life-Giving Dialogue on Homosexuality in the Dutch Reformed Church, South Africa', in *Christianity and Controversies over Homosexuality in Contemporary Africa*, edited by Ezra Chitando and Adriaan van Klinken, London: Routledge, pp. 125–40.

Van der Walt, Charlene (2016b), 'Danger! Ingozi! Gevaar! Why Reading Along Can Be Bad for You', *Scriptura: Journal for Contextual Hermeneutics in Southern Africa* 115, no. 1, pp. 1–12.

Van der Walt, Charlene (2021a) '"Better is never better for everyone, it always means worse for some." Could there be space in an African Woman's Theology for those known as Izitabane?', in *Religion, Patriarchy and Empire: Festschrift in Honour of Mercy Amba Oduyoye*, edited by Lillian Siwila and Fundiswa Kobo, Pietermaritzburg: Cluster Publications, pp. 389–414.

Van der Walt, Charlene (2021b), 'Come On, Come Out, Come Here, Come Here... Queer Expressions of Desire in Genesis 28–31', in *Transgression and Transformation: Feminist, Postcolonial and Queer Biblical Interpretation as Creative Interventions*, edited by L. Juliana Claassens, Christl M. Maier and Funlola O. Olojede, London: Bloomsbury Publishing, pp. 145–60.

Van der Walt, Charlene (2022a), '"The Bra Is Wearing a Skirt!" Queering Joseph in the Quest to Enhance Contextual Ethical Gender and Sexuality Engagements', in *Sexual Reformation? Theological and Ethical Reflections on Human Sexuality*, edited by Manitza Kotze, Naida Marais and Nina M. Van Velden, Eugene, OR: Wipf & Stock Publishers, pp. 94–109.

Van der Walt, Charlene (2022b), '"I Won't Behave Myself. I Won't Hate Myself": Harnessing the Multi-Colored Butterfly in Genesis 37 as an *Izitabane* Icon', in *Building Bridges Towards a More Humane Society: Explorations in Contextual Biblical Interpretation*, edited by Kirsten van der Ham, Geke van Vliet, Peter-Ben Smit and Klaas Spronk, Geneva: Globethics.net, pp. 31–50.

Van der Walt, Charlene (2023), 'Moving Beyond the Text as Slogan: Reading Genesis 19 in the Context of LGBTIQ+ Lived Realities in African Faith Contexts', in *Context Matters: Old Testament Essays from Africa and Beyond Honoring Knut Holter*, edited by Madipoane Masenya (Ngwan'a Mphahlele), Marta Høyland Lavik, Ntozakhe Simon Cezula and Tina Dykesteen Nilsen, Atlanta, GA: SBL Press.

Van der Walt, Charlene and Hanzline R. Davids (2022), 'Heteropatriarchy's Blame Game: Reading Genesis 37 with Izitabane During COVID-19', *Old Testament Essays* 35, no. 1, pp. 32–50.

Van Klinken, Adriaan (2020), 'Studying Religion in the Pluriversity: Decolonial Perspectives', *Religion* 50, no. 1, pp. 148–55.

West, Gerald O. (2020), 'A Trans-Textual and Trans-Sectoral Gender-Economic Reading of the Rape of Tamar (2 Sam 13) and the Expropriation of Naboth's Land (1Kgs 21)', in *Faith, Class, and Labor: Intersectional Approaches in a Global Context*, edited by Jin Young Choi and Joerg Rieger, Eugene, OR: Wipf & Stock Publishers, pp. 105–21.

West, Gerald O. and Charlene van der Walt (2019), 'A Queer (Beginning to the) Bible', in *Queer Theologies: Becoming the Queer Body of Christ*, edited by Stefanie Knauss and Carlos Mendoza-Álvarez (Concilium #383), London: SCM Press, pp. 109–18.

World Council of Churches (WCC) (2022), *Conversations on the Pilgrim Way: Invitation to Journey Together on Matters of Human Sexuality*, Geneva: WCC Publications.

Yep, Gust A. (2014), 'The Violence of Heteronormativity in Communication Studies: Notes on Injury, Healing, and Queer World-Making', in *Queer Theory and Communication: From Disciplining Queers to Queering the Discipline(s)*, edited by Gust A. Yep, New York: Routledge, pp. 11–60.

# 3

# Theological Faggotting (*Via[da]gem*) or Cruising with Frida Kahlo

ANDRÉ S. MUSSKOPF

## Introduction

The first version of 'Veadagens teológicas' ('Theological Faggotting') (Musskopf, 2008a) was published as part of a collection to celebrate Frida Kahlo's 100th anniversary (Eggert, 2008b). Frida herself would not have considered that her anniversary since she chose 7 July 1910 to be her birthdate – instead of 6 July 1907 – as a homage to the Mexican Revolution (Dexter and Barson, 2005, p. 215; also referenced in her diary: Kahlo, 1995, p. 127). Still, a group of Latin American scholars joined in a project in which each was invited to write an article dialoguing with one of her paintings. I immediately chose *La Venadita* – known in English as *The Little Deer* or *The Wounded Deer*. That is how the epistemological proposal of 'theological faggotting' started to develop in my work and has accompanied me now for some time.

In this first exploration (Musskopf, 2008a),[1] I used the Portuguese word *veadagens* in reference to the name of the animal *veado* (deer). Only later I used the spelling *viadagens* when referring to the more commonly used Brazilian slang word *viado* for 'faggot', a perspective that was also present in the Spanish version, where it appears as *mariconajes* – in reference to *marica* (sissy) (Musskopf, 2017a). Such a change happened when I incorporated the article in my PhD dissertation (Musskopf, 2008b; subsequently published as a book in Musskopf, 2012), bringing together other elements in the construction of 'itineraries for a queer theology in Brazil'.

Although I presented different versions of this work in English at the American Academy of Religion in 2008 and the DARE Conference in Mexico in 2018, it has never been published in this language. Therefore, this text is an exercise in translation, both languages and contexts. I am dealing with at least three languages (mainly Portuguese, Spanish and

English) and more diverse contexts (generally speaking Brazil, Mexico and English-speaking countries). Much as descriptions of words and realities can cross those boundaries, they cannot fully express all the dimensions of what is at stake. Those limitations, however, should not prevent the possibility of establishing connections and dialogue in the encounter between readers and text.

In what follows I relive different steps taken in the dialogue with Frida and her painting *La Venadita*, exploring several aspects of this encounter and how they present themselves from the first connection established between the central figure of the 'deer' and the Brazilian notion of *veado-viado*. The reflection, then, unfolds as an experience of *cruising* in which different aspects of the painting and the painter and connections with other experiences lead to a theological elaboration that is representative of a Brazilian and Latin American queer theological epistemology. In conclusion I briefly relate this exercise to my latter work that expanded and consolidated the perspective of theological faggotting.

## Coincidences and Method: *Veadagem* and a Word on *Cruising*

> To write about this theme, I had to go to my garden and plant flowers, cook, wash the dishes, finish sewing a curtain for the front window of my house, dress my three-year-old son, hug him, cuddle him, tell my ten-year-old daughter, for the fifth time, to finish getting dressed or she would be late for the movies. Not in that order because it all took place almost simultaneously. And I did many of those things purposefully (especially the sewing, gardening, and cooking) simply as a way of making myself think more about the theme. (Eggert, 2005, p. 92)[2]

A similar process took place with me when confronted with the idea of writing about Frida and *La Venadita*. Aside from my admiration of the painter and fascination with the painting, it was not before several 'coincidences' that I could start writing. One of them was reading the most recent edition of a popular gay magazine in Brazil. In one of the articles, Jean Wyllys (2007) speaks of the admiration of gay men over thirty years old for the singer Maria Bethânia. According to him, 'Her way of singing love fits the stains in our sheets, even the tears. Her celebration of life, the drumming, and the laughter are in the temperature of our beer. Her religious syncretism welcomes our beliefs' (p. 13).

In another article, João Silvério Trevisan (2007) – discussing the *guei* [gay] way of speaking – states:

> The homosexual subculture developed itself with more subtle mechanisms: it usually uses ambiguity or *escracho*. Thanks to its ambiguity, the history of homosexuality requires a magnifier lens to find its signs and interpret them. See, for example, the image of Saint Sebastian arrowed. From Medieval European painters to the Japanese writer Yukio Mishima, in the 20th century, it has been taken as an iconic representation of the homosexual desire.

Those references and their coincidences with my subject of reflection prompted me to write and, from the start, think about it as *veadagem* [faggotting] as present it this way. I soon realized that my computer's grammar corrector did not acknowledge such a procedure. In the *Aurélio* dictionary of the Portuguese language, I found a short and not very enlightening definition for *veadagem*: 'Act, saying or ways proper to deer [*veados*]; *bichice*' (Ferreira, 1986, p. 1757). The first definition refers to the mammal – of the order of the artiodactyls, of the family of the cervids – and an effeminate man. *Bichice* – presented as a synonym – is derived from a slang word to refer to *bicha* [homosexuals] and refers to the ways of the effeminate (Ferreira, 1986, p. 254). Therefore, according to this definition, in Brazilian popular culture, 'deering' [faggotting] refers to that which is considered proper to 'deer' [faggots] and can be used to classify the actions or attitudes that are outside the socially accepted norms of masculinity. It also refers to unnecessary, futile, inadequate, a *frescura*, so to speak.

This other word – *frescura* – [freshness], according to Aurélio, is: 'Daring, cynical or impudent procedure or expression; pimp, grotesque. Effeminatement. Excessive sentimentalism. Fussiness. Attachment to conventions, to prejudices; conventionalism, coldness ...' (Ferreira, 1986, p. 812). According to James Green (2000):

> In Brazil, at the turn of the [nineteenth] century, the word fresh, with a double meaning of 'puto' and also expressing freshness, joviality or amenity in the climate, became an ambiguous term commonly used to mock effeminate men or those who supposedly had 'passive' anal relations with other men. [...] The multiple uses of the term appear in the *Dicionário moderno*, a small satirical compilation of the erotic and pornographic slang published in 1903: '*Fresh* – Airy adjective of depraved modernization. Almost cold, bland, soft, that which doesn't have heat nor heating. The one who does fresh things [*frescuras*], who has the blow of the breeze [...]' evokes a relation between social degeneration and modernization, such as if the process of urbanization and

> transformation of traditional costumes were guilty of the homoerotic behaviour. (p. 64)

The reference to popular gay magazines and other ordinary things and experiences can, thus, be labelled as *bichice*, *frescura* or *veadagem* [faggotting] by more strict academic standards. The idea of dealing with art, especially with such a unique artist as Frida, may be seen differently. But a theological reflection that ventures into faggotting has no other choice. Using the words of Trevisan (2007), it uses the mechanisms of 'ambiguity and *escracho*' to articulate the experience of the sacred in people's reality. This ambiguity and *escracho*, as Trevisan (2000, pp. 231–331) argues, is also part of Brazilian culture in general, sanctioned and experienced nationally every year during carnival, for example.

When the original text was introduced in my PhD dissertation, I framed the methodological procedures described above. Further, I used them in the analysis/dialogue with Frida's painting *La Venadita* and other elements introduced later with Timothy Koch's (2001) reflection on *cruising* as a hermeneutical approach to biblical interpretation. Although this notion – and the practice – was already present from the beginning, Koch's proposal gave it a name and a more precise framework.[3] Koch explores the lived experience of gay men and connects it to Audre Lorde's (2007 [1984]) reflection on the 'power of the erotic', defining *cruising* as:

> using our own ways of knowing, our own desire for connecting, our own understanding and instinct, our own response to what attracts us and compels us ... as in our social lives, choosing to *cruise* here means to take on our own authority and responsibility in following whatever it is that comes in our way, since that is what speaks to our own desires. (as cited in Koch, 2001, p. 16)

This perspective points to the embodiment dimension, highlighting that all knowledge is produced in, with and through the body. Theology, in its hermeneutical task of articulating the manifestation of the sacred in daily life, is an embodied enterprise resulting from that which awakens the senses and arouses desire. In my encounter with Frida and *La Venadita*, the hermeneutical perspective of *cruising* was set in motion. It enables the production of knowledge that occurs in rubbing bodies.

## Starting with the Deer/Faggot: Establishing the Connection and Stating the Presence

At the centre of the painting *La Venadita* stands the unmistakable figure of a deer. Its prominence indeed gets the attention of any Brazilian not versed in art history in the twentieth century and/or Frida's work. To Brazilians, the image of a *veado* [deer] is associated with homosexual men and, thus, causes discomfort (or excitement). The association of the animal with homosexuality is a mystery in Brazilian – queer – historiography. But it became an insult and, more recently, has been resignified by segments of the LGBTIQ+ movement as a sign of pride and/or provocation.

There are at least three more popular hypotheses about the identification between the deer and homosexuals in Brazil. The first one refers to an event in the gay community in the 1920s, which later took on mythical meanings. According to James Green (2000): '[a] chief policeman ordered the prison of all homosexual men that were found in a certain park ... As the policemen tried to arrest the young men, they ran like a deer' (p. 143).[4] Another hypothesis, also suggested by many homosexuals, is that the identification comes from Walt Disney's character Bambi for its sweetness and tenderness, indicating effeminacy (Parker, 1991, p. 77; Green, 2000, p. 180). The direct identification with the character and not with the animal itself would also come from the fact that the (male) animal with its antlers, in European countries, is a symbol of virility, which goes against the popular image of homosexual men as effeminate (Leonel, 2007; Coutinho, 2013).

A third hypothesis points to the connection with the word *transviado*, which became popular in the 1960s when talking about rebellious youth in Brazil. That would also explain the change in the spelling, considering that when it refers to homosexual men, it is usually spelled *viado* instead of *veado* – for the animal (Leonel, 2007). According to Green (2000), it is not the word *veado* that comes from *transviado*. Still, the opposite, since – according to his research – the former became popular before Bambi was created. He argues that the word *veado* appears in a text published in 1938, where it is used to refer to homosexuals. So for Green, the association of *transviado* with homosexuals is a later development, playing 'phonetically with the two main pejorative words used to express homosexuality: *viado* [faggot] and *travesti* [transvestite]' (p. 365).

Tracing this genealogy, even if inconclusive, allows us to present the social subjects identified with the terminology and imagery the painting may evoke in this particular context. Connecting the central figure in Frida's painting *La Venadita* (a deer) with Brazilian homosexuals (*viados*) triggers the process of cruising as a methodology and prompts *veadagem* or faggotting as an epistemology that implies acknowledging the presence of the deer/faggots. Their recognition and visibility have become a fact in the most diverse social interaction spaces. That is why, as in religion and theology, they have dared to come out of the closets and say their word. Frida's deer – or the deer-Frida – may become, then, a means and a way of positioning and saying oneself as a deer-faggot.

## The Deer-Frida: Expressing Oneself Through Mixtures and Ambiguities

The being that occupies the centre of the painting *La Venadita* is Frida's creation. Even if her face gives it its particularity, the body, the ears and the antlers leave no doubt: its animal body carries the marks of what is perceived and named as male. Its face has makeup, and its head has ornaments – earrings and a crown of horns – which are constructions of the female. Its name – *La Venadita* – also points to the feminine grammatical form.

Crossing gender norms and expressions is part of Frida's work and life. Some examples are the well-known family pictures in which she appears in male attire, and the painting *Self-Portrait with Cropped Hair*.[5] In *La Venadita* the mixture between or the erasure of male and female is tied to the hybridism between the male animal (deer) and the female painter (Frida), resulting in an ambiguous or non-conforming gender figure.

The same kind of mixture is present in her diary, where she draws a hybrid figure formed with the head of a bull and the body of a woman, which might represent the Roman god Janus as well as the Minotaur of Picasso and the surrealists' Greek mythology (Kahlo, 1995). According to Lowe (1995):

> Kahlo's reference to Janus is not accidental. Janus, god of the New Year, is usually portrayed looking back and forward. What it sees in the past, in the page on the left [of the diary], is the imponent profile of a woman with pride, strong – Kahlo as insignia of a Roman coin. But when Janus (and Kahlo) contemplate the right side, to the future, they foresee disaster: Kahlo's image, looking like a marionette with the limbs disjointed, oscillating on the top of a classical column. Parts of her fall – an eye and a hand – both used to produce art. Above the

figure precariously equilibrated Kahlo writes: 'I am disintegration'. (p. 224)[6]

One of the hypotheses for Frida's use of the deer is that it was 'an attempt to change the date of her birthday (marked in the Aztec calendar by the sign of death) to the sign of the "deer", and this way alter her fate' (Ankori, 2005, p. 42), as mentioned in the introduction to this chapter. In the same way, it can also be – one more – expression of her alter ego, a mirror or duplication of herself, an idea rooted in the Aztec belief system (Barson, 2005, p. 64). Other interpretations suggest that the deer may be Granizo, Frida's pet who was her partner and wandered through the courtyard of the *Casa Azul* and appears in some pictures and paintings with her (Lowe, 1995, p. 265) – thus the male body.

Besides all those possibilities – or somehow articulating all of them – the deer in the painting represents Frida's right foot, one of the sources of her constant physical pain and a reflection of her 'disintegration'. In her accident, while travelling on a bus, 'she suffered 11 fractures in her right leg – which had already been deformed by childhood polio – her right foot was displaced and smashed' (Sitwell, 2005). Those wounds marked her walk for the rest of her life and ended up causing the amputation of her foot in 1953. 'Feet' appear singly drawn all over her diary, often accompanied by the phrase: *Pies para qué los quiero si tengo alas para volar* [Feet why do I want them if I have wings to fly], which is the most vivid expression (Kahlo, 1995, p. 134).

It is impossible to dissect and separate all the possible meanings and intentions represented by the deer-Frida. That is part of their 'pedagogy' (Berté, 2018) and their way of expressing their unfinished and ongoing knowledge about themselves and their reality. Mixture and ambiguity are intrinsic elements of this cruising that is just beginning.

## The Frida-Deer: Multiple Connections and Identifications

Frida underwent several surgeries from July 1945 to January 1947 and painted 'three of her most vivid paintings that deal openly with her illnesses, surgeries, and recoveries' (Lowe, 1995, p. 232). *La Venadita* was one of them. In the first painting – entitled *Without Hope* (1945) – Frida depicts the diet imposed on her by doctors to help her gain weight (Alcántara and Egnolff, 2001, p. 81). In *Tree of Hope – Keep Strong* (the second painting), the Aztec duality of the sun and moon is reflected in the two Fridas: one lying on a stretcher, face down, with bleeding wounds, and the other dressed in a *Tehuana* – a Zapotec dress – holding the corset that supports her spine and a flag bearing the painting's title. In the third painting – *La Venadita* – Frida's body becomes the body of the 'wounded deer'.

Although natural elements – animals and plants – appear in many other of her paintings, according to Gannit Ankori (2005):

> Whereas in the 1930s she depicted herself *with* plants and animals, later, as her involvement with Oriental philosophy deepened, she showed herself *as* a plant or animal ... in *Roots* the plant actually becomes an integral part of Kahlo's Self. Similarly, beginning in 1937 she painted herself with various animals around her; by 1946 she imagined herself as an inseparable hybrid 'bird-being' or 'deer-being'. (p. 42; emphasis original)

The pages of Frida's diary from this period express the multiple connections she experiences and expresses in her paintings. She mixes a significant quantity of Egyptian, Aztec, Eastern and Roman symbols. The 'wounded deer' creates its symbolic potential to include other identifications in its hybridity.

In Frida's memories, the deer comes back in a tribute to her friend Isabela Villaseñor, who died in 1953 and is identified in the pages of her diary as 'deer, painter, poet' [*venada, pintora, poeta*], amid symbols of the revolution (Kahlo, 1995, pp. 264–6). An illustration that reminds me of Franz Marc presents a slender deer, and the red of the blood is no longer a symbol of pain but empowers the animal itself in a utopic vision of harmony expressed through the red orbit with the inscription *TAO*, a symbol of life strength in Buddhism (Lowe, 1995, p. 265). The memory of 'Chabela' Villaseñor and the dream of another society lives in the red of the flag without forgetting the pain: '*Colorado, colorado, colorado, colorado*, like the blood shed when they kill a deer [*venado*]' says the poem that ends this passage in her diary (Kahlo, 1995, p. 13).

The Frida-deer offers itself as a possibility for a theologizing that crosses the rigid borders of social, political, cosmological and identity conventions. As stated by Oriana Baddeley (2005):

> It is likely that we will all keep looking for some special person hidden within the wider phenomenon that is Frida. It might be a person whom we want to be, or a person whom we know we will never be, but the desire for connection remains. What is wished for is probably the simplest yet most impossible of things: to have our own knowledge of this distant woman's painful secrets acknowledged through her reciprocal friendship or love, to release our own stories in an outpouring

of empathy. Perhaps the marvel of Kahlo is that she can be constantly reinvented by different audiences, who find in her work what it is they are looking for. (p. 52)

That is why *La Venadita* may not *be* a Brazilian homosexual, but we may call her our own. She is a being full of mixtures and ambiguities with whom we can connect and identify, and who gives voice to our own stories. Frida Kahlo is the one who, in making herself *veado/viado* [deer/faggot], calls us into, and guides us through, the process of faggotting. She is our Saint Sebastian in his most symbolic homoerotic representation and his most painful torture.

## Disturbing Arrows: The History of Wounds and the Affirmation of Beliefs

Frida's painting *A Few Small Nips* was inspired by a story from a newspaper in which the assaulter of a woman stated precisely that the stabs were only 'a few small nips' (Dexter and Barson, 2005, p. 2).[7] In the same way, the reports of violence against LGBTIQ+ people do not seem to move or demote homophobic perpetrators who see them as innocent and incidental inconsequential acts, or they actually characterize them as deliberately conscious and justified. 'A good faggot is a dead faggot' (Mott and Cerqueira, 2003, p. 114). The arrows spiked in *La Venadita* may be seen as the arrows spiked in the bodies of LGBTIQ+ people; faggot body and faggot blood.

The suffering and the pain represented in Frida's paintings are usually interpreted as a response to mistreatment and betrayals by her husband, Diego, or an expression of her crises and illnesses. *The Wounded Deer* – painted in a period in which she was exposed to several surgical interventions – undoubtedly contains this concrete physical pain in its representation. A drawing in the last pages of her diary suggests some identification with the arrows of the wounded deer as she appears completely naked, with eleven arrows pointing to where she had had surgery (Kahlo, 1995, p. 161).

But maybe the more disturbing effect of the arrows of the wounded deer is the suggestion of their identification with the martyrdom of Saint Sebastian and his portrayal in Christian (and homoerotic) sacred art (Alcántara and Egnolff, 2001, p. 82; Ankori, 2005, p. 42; Mucci, 2006; Adriano, 2008); the appropriation of Saint Sebastian as a (homo)erotic icon has a long history. According to Adriano (2008):

> The complex calvary of holy heresies encapsulated by Saint Sebastian must have started with the image created by Fra Bartolomeo (1473–1517), an Italian painter of the Florence school, 'specialized' in religious themes. His painting in fresco about the martyr was taken off the walls of the church by the monks, under the 'accusation' that it was the source of sinful thoughts during the confessions of women and induced the faithful to erotic daydreams.

Since then, painting, literature, and cinema have created innumerable representations of this Christian martyr and accentuated his homoerotic identification to the point of him being known as the 'patron of homosexuals'. According to Adriano (2008), it was a:

> mix of vamp and Narcissus, intrepid guy and ready to die, the 'patron of soldiers, homosexuals and people who suffer plagues' serves as emblem for a rebellious, censorship and faith battle underlined by a myth that reached the twentieth century demarcating a curve 'between the secularization of the sacred and the elevation of the profane to sacred'.

In 2006, the Grupo Gay da Bahia (2003), in Brazil, proclaimed:

> WE, GAYS, LESBIANS, TRANSVESTITES AND TRANSEXUALS present here, in the Church of Saint Sebastian of the Benedictine Monastery of Salvador, proclaim today, January 20th, 2000, this Church as a Homosexual Sanctuary of Brazil, and Saint Sebastian the patron of gays, lesbians, transvestites and transsexuals of Brazil.
>
> Following a tradition of gay people that lasts since the first millennium of the Christian Era, and which made of Saint Sebastian the main icon and model of homosexuality, we solemnly proclaim, in this first anniversary of Saint Sebastian in the third millennium, our faith that our patron saint will give us strength to win the enemies and the evil that still threatens our life and our happiness, and that from this new millennium on, Brazil's homosexual community will be respected with the same rights of other citizens.

Frida's deer has a guaranteed space in Saint Sebastian's homoerotic genealogy. Besides the visual identification from the arrows that spear its robust and slender body, Frida's face, which gives an identity to the animal, lends the queer and sexually ambiguous components incarnated by the painter in the intensity of her life. The already mentioned non-conforming gender, her intimate relationships with men and women, and the incorporation of cultural symbols marked precisely by free, transgressive and rebellious sexuality such as *La Llorona* and *La Malinche/*

*La Chingada* (Ankori, 2005, pp. 34–6, 40–1; Barson, 2005, pp. 69–70) are also part of that construction. According to Ankori (2005):

> in several paintings, she assumed the identities of 'evil women' who personified forces undermining the 'proper' social order, such as *La Llorona* and *La Malinche*. In her art, she also expressed her sexual ambiguities, androgynous traits, and homosexual tendencies. (p. 31)

Such deconstruction-construction-reconstruction occurs not only in her work but also in her body. Frida incorporates several constituting elements of her identity in a precise way in her clothes, accessories and in the way she wears her hair. One of the most famous images incorporated by Frida is the *Tehuana*. According to Christina Burrus (2005): 'Ritually, nearly every morning until the end of her life, Kahlo decked herself out like an idol, constructing her image, establishing a style of dress whose interaction with her pictorial style rapidly became apparent' (p. 202). This ritual very much resembles the process of 'mounting' by drag queens, who construct through make-up, clothes, wigs, accessories, gestures, a persona, subverting gender and sexuality norms.

The arrows denounce our – Frida's and the faggots' – transgressive sexuality that breaks the patterns and limits of cis-heteropatriarchy, defined by culture, economy, politics and religion. They do not represent only the pain and suffering of policing violent mechanisms but point to our sexual histories, the source, the material and the methodology of our theological doing. *La Venadita* not only uses religious symbols to express Frida's reality – and her understanding of it – but she becomes the personification of a religiosity that breaks away from ecclesiastical dogmas and doctrines and which, because of that, announces the religiosity of those who transit at their margins. Therefore, from the history of our wounds, old beliefs can be resignified and appropriated, and new ones can emerge in unpredicted constellations.

## Syncretizing Words and Landscapes: Building New Webs of Meanings

According to Emma Dexter (2005):

> not only is *The Little Deer* 1946 an extraordinary exploration of psychic alienation and gender confusion, but its symbolism is strongly indebted to pre-Columbian rites and rituals of rebirth and renewal, as well as to popular Mexican love songs of the 1930s and Hindu Karmic beliefs of reincarnation. (p. 21)

Religiosity and religious symbolism are all over Frida's work as part of the popular culture she liked so much. One way this manifests is through the use of ex-votos or *retablos* 'style':

> paintings made as a gesture of gratitude for salvation, a granted prayer, or a disaster averted and left as offerings in churches or at saint's shrines. They are generally painted on small-scale metal panels and depict [through the drawing and the inscription] both the incident ... and the Virgin or saint to which they are offered. (Barson, 2005, p. 65)

The relationship with *La Venadita* is self-evident, although she subverts its meaning and uses it to express her experience. She becomes herself the portrait of disaster, the saint, the offering and the prayer at the same time.

Sentences taken from popular songs – *corridos* – appear in some of Frida's paintings. One of these *corridos* also seems to have inspired *La Venadita*, although its text does not appear in the painting (Barson, 2005, p. 62). The only inscription in *La Venadita*, besides the name and the date, is the word *carma*. This reference to the Oriental concept is substantiated in the landscape that portrays it – in the background – visible among trees, water and lightning. According to Ankori (2005, p. 42), water represents the divine essence, and lightning symbolizes the possibility of illumination (Nirvana). By expanding her belief system, Frida visualizes – and paints – the possibility of another cosmovision, not based on the separation of the other but on the fusion with the 'fabric of life'.

Besides mixing and fusing herself with the animal of which her head is an extension – as aforementioned – Frida fuses herself with the whole of nature. According to Emma Dexter (2005), the 'still life genre [is] meaningless, as Frida creates a unifying vision of the wholeness of creation'. Accordingly:

> Her still life output also reflects the development of her personal philosophy, moving from early paintings that dramatize the formation and consolidation of national and cultural identity, to works that express regenerative and sexual forces within nature, to canvases in which the human, the natural and the divine are melded into one. (Dexter, 2005, p. 25)[8]

The creation depicted in *La Venadita* is hurt: the deer is wounded and the branch is broken. It has been a while since feminist, gay and queer theologies, in their eco-theological perspectives, have pointed to the relation between the destruction of nature and the exclusion and violence against women and LGBTIQ+ people. J. Michael Clark (1993), for example, stated: 'I can see how our experiences of homophobia, exclusion, and expandability in our society are also reflected in the ways our society disvalues and disposes of the earth itself' (p. xi; see also Spencer, 1996). The principle that guides this expendability is the despising and the elimination of diversity any time it does not fit the projects of profit and economic development.

The themes, concepts and realities get mixed up, confused and entangled in Frida's work and *La Venadita* specifically, just as they do in life. Thus, she offers an embodied image of what Brazilian and Latin American theology could be if it left aside its systems, orthodoxies and moralism. In its theological work, it expresses the sensuality and eroticism that arise from the concrete bodies and their indecencies.

## From *Veadagem* to *Via(da)gem*: Concluding Remarks and Later Developments

Revisiting 'Veadagens teológicas' and presenting some of the elements of the original reflection here, besides making it available in English, is an attempt to accomplish an exercise in *doing* – rather than describing conceptually – theological faggotting, using cruising as a methodology. As mentioned in the introduction, in my reflections there was a change in the spelling to *via(da)gens teológicas* as new elements were incorporated. Such a change in the spelling and its use to articulate and express the argument of my PhD research and dissertation made explicit the importance of my first encounter and dialogue with Frida and *La Venadita* and its potential to articulate those new elements.

The change from *veado* (the name of the animal, deer) to *viado* (explicitly used concerning homosexuals or queer people in Brazil) allowed for a more explicit expression of its connection to queer politics and studies as developed in the early 1990s. Besides, it allowed for a play with two different words in Portuguese: *viagem* [travelling] and *viadagem* [faggotting]; thus *via(da)gem*. *Viagem* implies that the production of theological knowledge is accomplished as 'travelling', in which the itineraries are always open and multiple. It is also a direct reference to liberation theology and its call for a 'theology on the way' or a 'pilgrim theology' proposing to discover and signal other routes, walking where many theologies refuse to go. Nonetheless, *viagem* proposes that theology needs to walk (travel) in places even liberation theology has mostly not dared to go yet – *lugares mais 'frescos'* ['fresher' places] (Musskopf, 2012, p. 459).

In this perspective, *viadagem* then proposed a concrete way of doing this 'travelling' as it is situated in the field of reference that questions the system that is responsible for the oppression, discrimination and marginalization of any identity or practice constructed outside of cis-heteropatriarchal patterns as understood by queer studies from a Brazilian – and Latin American, as *mariconaje* – context. In this 'transition', I laid down my itineraries (in the sex/gender system, in church and religion, in the academy, in activism and politics) as a 'personal phenomenology' (Gebara, 2000, p. 85), as a 'biographical theology' (Althaus-Reid, 2003, p. 8) made of 'formative experiences' (Josso, 2004; Musskopf, 2012, pp. 26–8).

Therefore, while sewing together my itineraries, I felt it essential to establish a broader dialogue about Brazilian religiosity and sexuality. Such a process led me to explore its history, uncover and inhabit unexpected landscapes of homosexual, gay and queer theologies, and engage deeply with the concept of ambiguity. This engagement involved a conceptual discussion and the sexual narratives of three trans individuals: Maria Florzinha, Júlia Guerra and Lolita Boom-Boom.

Drawing on the Brazilian context of religiosity and sexuality – as well as the tools provided by homosexual, gay and queer theologies – I developed a theological epistemology that fosters queer theological thinking in Brazil. The aim was to bring together diverse voices and experiences around the notion of ambiguity and to present a theological reflection that thoughtfully considers the Brazilian context while addressing its pressing issues:

> In the concept of *via(da)gem*, ambiguity is not an error or mistake, but a way of thinking that, in the stories of Maria Florzinha, Júlia Guerra, and Lolita Boom-Boom and in the figure of Frida Kahlo's 'Venadita,' finds its narrative and plastic expression producing a knowledge and a theology where the borders are always moving and unstable. On those grounds the search for meaning in the fugacity of the daily experience of struggle for survival allows for producing a theology that is itself moving and transient since it is not concerned with eternal values and future salvations, but with the meaning of the lives that construct and reconstruct themselves, invent and reinvent themselves in each movement, since they are overflowing of meaning. There, the subjects of theology can be what they want and produce their knowledge with sharp tongues that subvert not only the norms of the correct writing, but, by reinventing language, create other spaces for this production. In those spaces, theology is done as *via(da)gem* [faggotting], always plural, adjective and written in lowercase [or tiny] since it does not

> intend to express the experience of all but point, through ambiguity as an epistemological principle, for the liberation of theology and enunciate, once more, libertarian theological reflections. (Musskopf, 2012, pp. 463–4)

This is how the *veadagem* elaborated in dialogue and cruising with Frida and *La Venadita* became *via(da)gem*. Ultimately, Frida's work reflects what it means to be human, the world and the sacred, and the connections between those dimensions of reality. Exposing her intimacy reveals the world with its pains and pleasures and constructs her faith without seeking purity, objectivity or ultimacy. According to Althaus-Reid (2003): 'it is in scenes of intimacy and the epistemology offered by those excluded from the heterosexual political Project in Theology that unveilings may occur' (p. 14). She adds: 'The surprising conclusion is that in the present time revelation needs to be Queer, because it needs to come from a Queer God, manifest in the people whose lifestyle and values cannot be easily assimilated by capitalist spirituality' (p. 158).

Frida's faggotting in *La Venadita* allows for a theological faggotting that continues as we travel through contemporary landscapes, speaking with tongues of fire and having conversations that may offer ways out of the crisis, violence and injustices that pierce our bodies and wound the body of the world, all the while kidnapping and disappearing the body(ies) of god(s) in closets and pits.

## Notes

1 Recently a revised version of the original text has been published as part of a book series called *Ensaios teológicos indecentes* [indecent theological essays] in a "Pocket Theology" format (Musskopf, 2023).

2 All quotations from references in other languages were translated by the author.

3 I have used *cruising* as a methodology in other works and in relation to other subjects/bodies as, for example, in 'Cruising (with) Marcella' [Althaus-Reid] (Musskopf, 2010), and 'Cruising (with) [Martin] Luther' (Musskopf, 2017b).

4 The author collected this story from members of the LGBTIQ+ community but never found a written or documented confirmation of it.

5 For discussions on androgyny and gender in Frida's work, see Ankori (2005, p. 41) and Barson (2005, pp. 56, 66). For a theological reflection on the painting, see Ströher (2008).

6 For a theological reflection on this passage of her diary, see Althaus-Reid (2008).

7 See Eggert (2008a) for a theological reflection on this painting.

8 See Cardoso Pereira (2008) for a theological reflection on Frida's still-life paintings of fruit and flowers.

## References


Adriano, Carlos (2008), 'Os mil martírios de São Sebastião', *UOL Online* (13 January), at https://memorialdeipaumirim.wordpress.com/2008/01/13/sao-sebastiao-no-imaginario-da-arte, accessed 01.12.2024.

Alcántara, Isabel and Sandra Egnolff (2001), *Frida Kahlo and Diego Rivera*, New York: Prestel.

Althaus-Reid, Marcella (2003), *The Queer God*, London: Routledge.

Althaus-Reid, Marcella (2008), 'Yo soy la desintegración...', in *[Re]leituras de Frida Kahlo*, edited by Edla Eggert, Santa Cruz do Sul, RS: EDUNISC, pp. 94–100.

Ankori, Gannit (2005), 'Frida Kahlo: The Fabric of her Art', in *Frida Kahlo*, edited by Emma Dexter and Tanya Barson, London: Tate, pp. 31–45.

Baddeley, Oriana (2005), 'Reflecting on Kahlo: Mirrors, Masquerade and the Politics of Identification', in *Frida Kahlo*, edited by Emma Dexter and Tanya Barson, London: Tate, pp. 47–53.

Barson, Tanya (2005), '"All art is at once surface and symbol": A Frida Kahlo Glossary', in *Frida Kahlo*, edited by Emma Dexter and Tanya Barson, London: Tate, pp. 55–79.

Berté, Odailso (2018), *O movimento criativo e pedagógico de Frida Kahlo*, Santa Maria, RS: Editora UFSM.

Burrus, Christina (2005), 'The Life of Frida Kahlo', in *Frida Kahlo*, edited by Emma Dexter and Tanya Barson, London: Tate, pp. 199–207.

Cardoso Pereira, Nancy (2008), 'Para comer com os olhos e contemplar com a boca', in *[Re]leituras de Frida Kahlo*, edited by Edla Eggert, Santa Cruz do Sul, RS: EDUNISC, pp. 146–56.

Clark, J. Michael (1993), *Beyond Our Ghettos: Gay Theology in Ecological Perspective*, Cleveland, OH: Pilgrim Press.

Coutinho, Genilson (2013), 'Luiz Mott fala sobre a origem do termo veado', *Doisterços* (18 September), at https://www.doistercos.com.br/luiz-mott-fala-sobre-a-origem-do-termo-veado/, accessed 01.12. 2024.

Dexter, Emma (2005), 'The Universal Dialectics of Frida Kahlo', in *Frida Kahlo*, edited by Emma Dexter and Tanya Barson, London: Tate Publishing, pp. 11–29.

Dexter, Emma and Tanya Barson, eds (2005), *Frida Kahlo*, London: Tate Publishing.

Eggert, Edla (2005), 'Grace and the world below the Equator', in *The Grace of the World Transforms God*, edited by Nancy Cardoso, Edla Eggert and André S. Musskopf, Porto Alegre, RS: Editora Universitária Metodista, pp. 92–103.

Eggert, Edla (2008a), 'A apatia de quem olha: A violência naturalizada', in *[Re]leituras de Frida Kahlo*, edited by Edla Eggert, Santa Cruz do Sul, RS: EDUNISC, pp. 75–83.

Eggert, Edla, ed. (2008b), *[Re]leituras de Frida Kahlo*, Santa Cruz do Sul, RS: EDUNISC.

Ferreira, Aurélio B. H. (1986), *Novo Dicionário da Língua Portuguesa*, Rio de Janeiro, RJ: Editora Nova Fronteira.

Gebara, Ivone (2000), *Rompendo o silêncio – Uma fenomenologia feminista do mal*, Petrópolis, RJ: Editora Vozes.

Green, James (2000), *Além do carnival*, São Paulo, SP: UNESP.

Grupo Gay da Bahia (2003), 'São Sebastião patrono dos homossexuais', at http://www.midiaindependente.org/pt/blue/2003/01/45957.shtml, accessed 01.12.2024.

Josso, Marie-Christine (2004), *Experiências de vida e formação*, São Paulo, SP: Cortez Editora.

Kahlo, Frida (1995), *The Diary of Frida Kahlo: An Intimate Self-portrait*, New York: H. N. Abrams.

Koch, Timothy (2001), 'A Homoerotic Approach to Scripture', *Theology & Sexuality* 7, no. 14, pp. 10–22.

Leonel, Vange (2007), 'A natureza transviada', *G-Magazine* 9, no. 113 (February), p. 106.

Lorde, Audre (2007 [1984]), *Sister Outsider*, Berkeley, CA: Crossing Press.

Lowe, Sarah M. (1995), 'Translation of the Diary and Commentaries', in *The Diary of Frida Kahlo: An Intimate Self-portrait*, New York: H. N. Abrams, pp. 201–92.

Mott, Luiz (n.d.), 'A origem do termo "viado"', *Revista Lado A*, at http://www.revistaladoa.com.br/website/artigo.asp?cod=1592&idi=1&id=2192, accessed 01.12.2024.

Mucci, Latuf Isaias (2006), 'Figuração cinematográfica de São Sebastião, mito gay', *Fazendo Gênero* 7, at http://www.fazendogenero7.ufsc.br/st_35.html, accessed 01.12.2024.

Musskopf, André S. (2008a), 'Veadagens teológicas', in *[Re]leituras de Frida Kahlo – Por uma ética estética da diversidade machucada*, edited by Edla Eggert, Santa Cruz do Sul, RS: EDUNISC, pp. 101–20.

Musskopf, André S. (2008b), *Via(da)gens teológicas – itinerários para uma teologia queer no Brasil*, doctoral dissertation, São Leopoldo, RS: EST.

Musskopf, André S. (2010), 'Cruising (with) Marcella', in *Dancing Theology in Fetish Boots: Essays in Honour of Marcella Althaus-Reid*, edited by Lisa Isherwood and Mark D. Jordan, London: SCM Press, pp. 228–39.

Musskopf, André S. (2012), *Via(da)gens teológicas*, São Paulo, SP: Fonte Editorial.

Musskopf, André S. (2017a), 'Mariconajes teológicas', in *Frida Kahlo, relecturas – Hacia una ética estética de la diversidad lastimada*, edited by Edla Eggert, Ciudad de México: Casa Unida de Publicaciones, pp. 137–60.

Musskopf, André S. (2017b), 'Cruising (with) Luther – Indecent Lutheran Theologies from the South, or What makes a Lutheran Theology Lutheran', *Consensus: A Canadian Journal of Public Theology* 38, no. 2, at https://scholars.wlu.ca/consensus/vol38/iss2/3, accessed 01.12.2024.

Musskopf, André S. (2023), *Veadagens teológicas*, Rio de Janeiro, RJ: Metanoia.

Parker, Richard G. (1991), *Corpos, prazeres e paixões*, São Paulo, SP: Best Seller.

Sitwell, Ros (2005), 'Humor and Anguish', *Morning Star Online* (14 June), at http://www.morningstaronline.co.uk/index2.php/free/culture/arts/humour_and_anguish, accessed 01.12. 2024.

Spencer, Dan (1996), *Gay and Gaya*, Cleveland, OH: Pilgrim.

Ströher, Marga J. (2008), 'Autorretrato con el pelo cortado – A fabricação de um corpo estético de rupturas', in *[Re]leituras de Frida Kahlo*, edited by Edla Eggert, Santa Cruz do Sul, EDUNISC, pp. 121–38.

Trevisan, João Silvério (2000), *Devassos no paraíso*, Rio de Janeiro, RJ: Record.

Trevisan, João Silvério (2007), 'O linguajar do gueto guei', *G-Magazine* 9, no. 113 (February), p. 14.

Wyllys, Jean (2007), 'O favo de seu mel', *G-Magazine* 9, no. 113 (February), p. 13.

# PART 2

# Ecclesiology and Communities

# 4

# Decolonizing Human Sexuality in Ecumenical Conversations

MASIIWA RAGIES GUNDA

## Introduction

The World Council of Churches (WCC) and several other global ecumenical bodies were established to serve as conduits of unity, and they continue to act as examples of it. However, there have been times when fragmentation has threatened the very essence of these bodies. A variety of factors has triggered this fragmentation. Issues such as the circumcision of gentiles, the nature of Jesus Christ, racial segregation, the ordination of women and gender equality, sexual orientation and practice, as well as sexual and reproductive health and rights, are among the themes around which ecumenism has faced challenges. These challenges have persisted in the past and continue to impact ecumenism today.

The greatest threat to Christian unity and ecumenical fellowship today has been the acceptability of sexual diversity in the faith community. The history of Christianity has seen an evolution of the almost universal primacy of cis-heteronormativity – man–woman sexual relations – to multiple sexualities being acceptable in some areas while vehemently opposed in other areas. Europe and North America have, in the past two decades but especially in the past few years, significantly moved towards diversity and inclusion. Sexual minoritized groups have been welcomed into the Christian church, welcomed into the various ministries, and lately welcomed into holy matrimony. In Africa and Asia, sexual minoritized groups have faced rejection, exclusion, remedial responses, stigmatization and criminalization.

The case of the Uganda Anti-Homosexuality Act 2023 sanctioned by the Parliament of Uganda has further strained relations between and among Christian communities. The divide is sometimes simplistically expressed in terms of the global North versus the global South, but the reality is more complicated than this. To begin with, neither the global

North nor the global South has a single reaction or position when it comes to human sexuality, especially the place of sexual minoritized groups. In this chapter, I seek to pose two questions: How did we get to where we are now? Can ecumenical partnership be reduced to whether we agree or disagree on human sexuality?

## Defining Human Sexuality

I will briefly define human sexuality, as conversations on this topic often stem from varying interpretations of its meaning. According to the World Health Organization:

> Sexuality is a central aspect of being human throughout life and encompasses sex, gender identities and roles, sexual orientation, eroticism, pleasure, intimacy and reproduction. Sexuality is experienced and expressed in thoughts, fantasies, desires, beliefs, attitudes, values, behaviours, practices, roles and relationships. While sexuality can include all of these dimensions, not all of them are always experienced or expressed. Sexuality is influenced by the interaction of biological, psychological, social, economic, political, cultural, ethical, legal, historical, religious and spiritual factors. (WHO, 2024)

I want to highlight some key aspects of this definition. First, WHO (2024) describes sexuality as an integral part of human life, encompassing the entire lifespan 'from birth to death'. Second, sexuality is not one thing but an intersection of many things. Third, sexuality is influenced by various factors, external and intrinsic. Fourth, sexuality has spiritual and religious dimensions to it. In short, sexuality has elements that could be regarded as learned but also inert. A human rights approach informs the WHO definition; hence it emphasizes the individuality of sexuality.

In its multiple processes of engaging around human sexuality, the WCC Central Committee received the document *Conversations on the Pilgrim Way*.[1] In this document the approach to human sexuality is faith-based, and it says the following about human sexuality:

> Human sexuality is much more than sexual feelings or sexual intercourse. It is an important part of who every person is. It includes the complexity of feelings, thoughts, and behaviours, of being female, male, or transgender, being attracted and attractive to others, and being in love, as well as being in relationships that may include var-

ious forms of sexual intimacy. Hence human sexuality and how it is perceived and addressed in society have profound implications for a person's identity and quality of life. Sexuality concerns relationships and potential vulnerability to be marginalized or taken advantage of, as well as risks pertaining to sexual and reproductive health. (WCC, 2022, p. 11)

As we did with the WHO definition, some elements of this definition are worth highlighting. First, sexuality is a reality for all individuals. Second, sexuality encompasses many dimensions. Third, sexuality has social dimensions that sometimes pit individuals against communities and vice versa. On assessing human sexuality, Manoj Kurian (2017) invokes ideas of creation, gift, goodness and divine intention to suggest there is nothing intrinsically wrong with human sexuality. His contention drifts towards sexual ethics which he contends ought to be guided by the values of faithfulness, consent, loving and the giving of life.

Allow me to proffer yet another definition in which sexuality is that part of being human that further cements an individual's relational nature and social obligation, bringing the individual into communion with the living, the dead and the spirit world expressed through relationships and practices within the purview of the community. Henry Chukwudi Ezebuilo (2023) states that 'Sexuality is the way people experience and express themselves sexually. Sexuality, in other words, encompasses all the ways people experience and express themselves as sexual beings. This may include biological, physical, emotional, or social feelings and behaviors' (p. 58). According to Okechi Samuel Okafor (2018), 'the African continent ... is one of the continents where many nations still place value on human sexuality and sexual union as a group order than individual matter' (p. 1). The African philosophical maxim, 'I am because you are', was applied across a whole range of life, including in understanding human sexuality. The group mores and interests took precedence over individual interests.

Based on the three definitions above, it is essential to note the complexity of human sexuality as a dimension of being human, which interfaces with several other dimensions of being human, expressed in and through feelings, thoughts, relationships and practices. Let me also highlight that in two definitions, the individual has a pronounced presence and stake in how sexuality is expressed. In contrast, in the third, the individual represents and lives sexuality under the guidance of the community. In short, I am arguing that there seems to be a communal-centred and an individual-centred approach to human sexuality in communities, past and present. It is also apparent in these definitions that sexuality elicits very diverse reactions in communities, exposing some cultural diversities. The examples below demonstrate the importance of context in moral discernment:

> In the case of human sexuality, for example, the various contexts of Christians affect how they respond to sexual ethics and norms. For instance, it is normal in Africa for a mother to breastfeed in public, but it is considered less acceptable in the global North. Similarly, an African man may marry more than two wives, but still oppose same-sex marriages. A Western Christian may accept same-sex marriage but oppose polygamy. The way moral discernment is contextual explains some of the disagreements associated with human sexuality in global Christianity. Morality is contextual in most cases. (WCC, 2022, p. 24)

When it comes to sexual intimacy there are societies where the demonstration of sexual intimacy through hugging and kissing in public is celebrated, mainly in European and North American contexts. In contrast, in most African communities such acts are frowned upon as indications of loose morals, especially for women. Yet even in such African communities, sexuality is celebrated in art, music and theatre. However, this celebration of sexuality does not, as erroneously assumed by early missionaries and explorers, translate into reckless and indiscriminate sexual practices (Okafor, 2018).

The story of Africa and African nations, states and communities' understanding of human sexuality is now a composite story affected by its pre-colonial traditions, colonial and Christianization interventions, and postcolonial hybridization of human sexuality. In the following section I will briefly define colonial ideology, coloniality, decolonization and decoloniality and show how colonial ideology and coloniality have impacted the understanding of human sexuality.

## Definitions of Key Terms and Concepts

My main contribution to this chapter is that European powers' colonization of Africa impacted African communities' conceptions of human sexuality. I also posit that the challenges we face today regarding human sexuality stem from the imposition of colonial mores and the creation of a hybrid conception of human sexuality in African Christian communities. Decolonizing human sexuality and fostering decoloniality in our activities and conversations provide a pathway to deepening and strengthening ecumenical partnerships.

The *colonial ideology* denotes a system of ideas and beliefs that legitimized the European move to conquer, subdue, dominate and rule the world. The ideas of 'natural selection', 'survival of the fittest', 'white supremacism' and 'hierarchy of human races' were central in legitimizing colonization, and the belief in the 'white man's burden' to civilize, evangelize and industrialize the 'heathens' made colonization sound and look like an honourable service to the peoples of the world. We now know it was far from being honourable! The association of white and good in Christian scriptures, liturgies and traditions, coupled with encounters with diverse peoples in the age of explorers, led to the rise of the racialization of humanity into 'white' and 'black' and some in-between, resulting in the institutionalization of white supremacism and whiteness (Harris, 2018). The service provision offered by missionaries under the influence of white supremacism and whiteness had a place in the sustenance of the domination of Africans by Europeans. White supremacism and whiteness 'reflect the Eurocentricity behind the Christianization of Africans, with angels represented according to European codes equating Whiteness with perfection, beauty, and purity. When positive values are only represented through White characters, it is impossible to develop a positive image of Blackness' (Mokoko Gampiot, 2017). Colonization was, therefore, the total domination of conquered peoples expressed through governance, epistemologies, theologies, economies and social and legal systems. Nothing, including human sexuality, could have escaped the colonial gaze!

We are aware that as Europe was rising from the ashes of the Second World War, many colonized nations, states and peoples took advantage to demand the end of colonization and their independence. This period is known as decolonization, beginning in the 1950s. *Decolonization* refers to resisting colonization, unlearning the epistemologies of colonialism, undoing the outcomes of colonization and, finally, unbeing or unbecoming what the colonial ideology has made us into. While in its early manifestations, decolonization was thought 'to refer to the formal processes of political change' (Horrell, 2023, p. 39). Political domination was the most visible manifestation of colonization, and the early processes of decolonization focused on 'governance power' in politics, society, church, education and industry. I think the most potent power of colonization was the least visible, the 'back office' of the colonial project – the systems, epistemologies, theologies, social norms and values. *Decolonization* involves challenging the particular systems – legal, policy, economic and ecclesial, modes of knowing, social norms and values – that have been superimposed through colonization. It is a process to remember, reclaim and reimagine; it is about recreating a community worthy of the label 'Body of Christ' by affirming and re-affirming the marginalized and suppressed voices (Ramantswana, 2017, pp. 74–5). What is it about human sexuality in Africa that has been colonially marginalized? What is it about human sexuality that needs decolonization?

*Coloniality* refers to the continuity of the colonial form of domination, exploitation and racialization by the dominant racial groups in the post-colonial era (Ramantswana, 2016, p. 181). The end of direct political control and domination sometimes clouds the view, making coloniality operate in the spaces as an invisible force that maintains the privileges that flow to the elites. It refers to the ongoing influence and authority of colonial systems, epistemologies, theologies and moral frameworks, even in contexts where the colonizers are no longer physically present. Bode Igboin (2023) writes: 'The history and experience of colonialism and its constant recalibration in postcolonial Africa have adversely affected African Indigenous cosmologies, epistemologies, cultures and experiences' (p. 7). While direct colonization ended, coloniality allowed colonial ideology, systems and practices to persist. In what ways is coloniality manifesting in our human sexuality conversations?

*Decoloniality* is understood and defined concerning coloniality and decolonization, by which it refers to the commitment to perpetual resistance to manifestations of coloniality in society and a commitment to decolonize continually. Decoloniality concerns itself with resisting not simply Eurocentric perspectives but colonial ideologies of superiority, privileges, domination and exploitation (Idamarhare, 2014, p. 53). The beneficiaries of coloniality are not permanently fixed, hence the focus on ideology, systems and epistemologies. As we gather here, 'epistemic decolonization' is critical (Horrell, 2023, p. 39) because human sexuality conversations are directly impacted by the centuries of 'colonial epistemicide'. What will decoloniality in human sexuality look like?

## Human Sexuality in Pre-Colonial African Communities

To begin with, the idea of African sexuality is itself a colonial concept that we need to use with caution. That concept emerged in Europe, and its purpose was to enable the state to control human bodies and exploit them for capitalist productive endeavours. If human sexuality is a foreign concept, what can we say about sexuality in African communities before their encounters with European empires and kingdoms? In this section, I briefly articulate what is known about life in some pre-colonial African communities that might shed light on what we are calling human sexuality. Before these encounters, African communities were organized into extended families, clans and tribes associated with geographical locations. These communities' social, political and economic lives were organized into villages, chiefdoms and kingdoms. A group of families formed a village, several villages came together to create a chiefdom and chiefdoms united to establish a kingdom. Other than the hunter-gatherer communities across Africa (Lee and Hitchcock, 2001), most communities that now form the majority of African states were agriculturalists – crop and animal husbandry – with some mining also taking place. Life in these communities revolved around group interests and was regulated by 'group norms and values', which were systematically inculcated and enforced 'through a well-organized and consistent socialization process' (Okafor, 2018).

A sedentary way of life among African communities naturally came with specific demands, especially around labour production, to increase productivity and food security and create an environment conducive to raising children and caring for older people (Gunda, 2010, p. 163). This is the context within which what we now call sexuality can be best understood. In this context, sexuality became a matter for the community because it was an instrument for growing the community, for sealing friendships and political and economic alliances. Individuals had a responsibility and duty to use their sexuality within the guidelines provided by the family or community (Gunda, 2010, pp. 163–5). With sexuality occupying such a strategic position in these communities, it naturally followed that sexuality education needed to be introduced from an early age. This education was conveyed through various means, including folktales, children's games such as *Mahumbwe* (where children recreate and reimagine family setups and life), initiation rites, *chiramu* (sex games between in-laws), sex education, music and dance, and ritual ceremonies (Okafor, 2018). In most of these communities, sexuality was celebrated publicly, with the use of metaphors and euphemisms allowing deep sexuality conversations to occur with children unaware of what was being discussed until they came of age. This public presence of sexuality, however, did not result in 'indiscriminate sexual activity especially premarital sexual union, there were stringent unwritten rules, which guided and enforced discipline among the members of the society' (Okafor, 2018).

The ideas and concepts of multiple sexual orientations that are mutually exclusive and independent of each other – heterosexuality, homosexuality and bisexuality – are also a European invention. They were imposed upon African communities through colonization and evangelization. Many in Africa have argued that there were no persons in Africa who were heterosexual, homosexual, bisexual, intersex or transgender. Now that these labels exist, some people exhibit the traits to be regarded as such (Tamale, 2013). In some pre-colonial African communities there is no doubt that sexual unions between men and women were the dominant manifestation and expression of sexuality. Producing children was a responsibility for all individuals and was essential to the well-being of their families and communities. Yet there were exceptions – some women and men could not bear children for whatever reason. In some communities there were strategies for covering up this deficiency. Among the Shona, a woman's family could provide a second wife to the husband. In contrast, a man's family could arrange for a brother to bear children for his brother by engaging in sexual intercourse with the impotent brother's wife, in most cases with her consent (Gunda, 2010, pp. 169–70). We can speculate that not only was impotence the reason for men having no children; maybe some men could bring themselves to have sex with a woman, but they were not attracted to women. There were cases when a woman reported that their husbands 'did not touch them in the bedroom' as part of the reason why they were not pregnant.

Many Ugandans have spoken loudly about their support of the Anti-Homosexuality Act 2023, presumably because homosexuality is un-Ugandan. However:

> among the Langi in northern Uganda, there is an alternative gender known as *mudoko dako*. These 'effeminate males' are allowed to marry men. The fact that the usual 'common sense' sex markers would fail to classify *mudoko dako* clearly points to the limitations within the colonial knowledge system to understand humanity outside the constructed binaries of male/female. Similarly, the Imbangala of Angola shocked English traveller Andrew Battell in the 1590s when he discovered that 'they have men in women's apparel, whom they keep among their wives'. In other words, the appearance of humans like *mudoko dako* marks 'the limit of Being, that is, the point at which Being distorts meaning'. (Tamale, 2022, pp. 58–9)

From West Africa, Ifi Amadiume (1987) spoke of 'male daughters and female husbands', demonstrating how a wealthy female could acquire wives to bear children for her, while in some families, daughters were conceptualized as sons for them to inherit the position of head of the family from their fathers. While sex might have been fixed, gender was fluid. In a story that is widely known among Christians in Africa, on 3 June the Anglican Communion commemorates the Ugandan Martyrs Day, whose background is vital for conversations on human sexuality:

> In the pre-colonial kingdom of Buganda in East Africa, intimate relations between the king and his male pages represented an important mode of asserting political obedience. As missionaries reconfigured these intimacies under the generic category of the 'sexual' and associated them with the Christian notion of 'sin', some pages began to refuse yielding to what seemed now to be their king's 'unnatural desires'. Consequently, in 1886, the king burnt 30 pages alive on a pyre. (Meiu, 2015, pp. 1–2)

Another dimension of human sexuality that has invited the attention of many people has to do with circumcision, especially among women, in a practice that is now internationally known as Female Genital Mutilation (FGM). I cannot claim to speak authoritatively on this practice, but while it involves cutting off some parts of female genitalia, there is another practice or other practices that are the opposite of FMG. As part of the sexuality education of girls and young women, Amadiume (2006) observes that:

> some traditional African societies such as some ethnic groups in northern Mozambique, Zambia, and southern Tanzania practice what is variously called labia stretching or labia elongation or enlargement in their female puberty and initiation rituals, which is the opposite of cutting. We do not hear much about this practice or the experiences of sex in these African cultures. Sex as pleasure is counter to fundamentalist or purist thinking that insists on sex as sin, sex as duty, sex as marital right and sex as male domination. When solely viewed from the reasons stated above or from the perspective of the ramifications of FGC, sex would incorrectly seem mechanical and only for male gratification and female procreation for which a woman is simply a depository. This simply restates and reinforces the perspective and practice of male power over female sexuality and this is not the whole story of sexuality in Africa. (p. 3)

Labia elongation is practised in communities and is seen as increasing a woman's desirability for the pleasures she will be able to give to herself and her husband. There are also some communities in which young women ready for marriage were given 'sex education' to prepare them for marriage. Sex education was not the only education; it was part of sex education that individuals were exposed to from early on in their lives.

The missionaries or Western colonial settlers were not responsible for introducing these same-sex practices in the kingdom of Buganda or any other pre-colonial community. They introduced a new way of looking at these practices (Blevins, 2011). In most pre-colonial African communities, sexual practices and relationships were not simply right or wrong in themselves; they depended on their consequences on relationships in the family and community (Jeater, 1993; Gunda, 2010, pp. 171–2). This has led some scholars to argue that most taboos around sexuality in Africa should be 'attributed to European Christian missionaries who measured the degree of repentance [or authenticity of conversion] with the extent of rejection of one's traditional custom and value' (Okafor, 2018, p. 3). While sex-talk was shrouded in euphemisms and metaphors, 'sex and human sexuality were freely discussed and children properly educated on sexual matters, before the coming of the Europeans' (Okafor, 2018). Amadiume (2006) states that: 'Many traditional cultures seem to have traditional ways of talking about and teaching about sexual pleasure, while at the same time practicing customs that regulate women's sexuality' (p. 6).

To conclude this section it is essential to highlight that discussing sexuality through song, dance, rituals, euphemisms and metaphors is inherently African. Similarly, sexual education conveyed through folktales, children's games, initiation rituals and practices is deeply rooted in African traditions. The presence of a fluid environment for gender, sex and sexuality – where one could freely identify as heterosexual, homosexual, bisexual or transgender without the expectation of adhering to a single expression of sexuality – is also a hallmark of African authenticity. If these diversities are intrinsically African, why are misunderstandings, outright disagreements and even the breakdown of relationships arising over aspects present in Africa and Europe long before Christianity? This question naturally leads to exploring the impact of colonization, evangelization and human rights on the conceptions of human sexuality in Africa.

## Colonial Ideology, European Evangelization and Human Sexuality in Africa

European exploration unveiled an entirely unfamiliar world to the European gaze, introducing encounters with peoples who looked and lived differently. Those encountered on these journeys had skin that was not as pale, hair and eyes that differed in texture and shape, and cultures and ways of life that stood apart from European norms. Among the many thoughts that emerged in European minds, the idea of European supremacism proved pivotal to what would follow.

European explorers interpreted these differences in physical appearance, culture, language and general ways of life as evidence of a qualitative hierarchy among humans. In this imagined hierarchy, Europeans were seen as the most developed, with Africans with the darkest skin and highest melanin levels at the lowest rung and others positioned somewhere in between. While past empires and kingdoms had alternated in their dominance, Europeans of the exploration age perceived this hierarchy as permanent. They believed it was their duty to 'parent, civilize, evangelize, and teach commerce' to these so-called 'primitive beings'.

This self-imposed 'burden of the white man' became the foundational rationale for colonization, following centuries of 'chattel enslavement' during which Europeans orchestrated the hunting, capture, trafficking and enslavement of productive Africans. These are stories for another day. What is critical for us is that:

> Colonialism is not satisfied merely with holding a people in its grip and emptying the native's brain of all form and content. By a kind of perverted logic, it turns to the past of the oppressed people, and distorts, disfigures and destroys it. This work of devaluing pre-colonial history takes on a dialectical significance today. (Fanon, 2005, pp. 210–11)

What enslavement and colonization did in the context of human sexuality in Africa was to create a dualism in which African communities' ideas and practices were compared or, better still, judged against European ideas and practices. European settlers and missionaries created 'images of African sexuality as pathological, perverse and primitive ... the sexuality of the European in opposition as healthy, normal and civilized (Ezebuilo, 2023, p. 57). Armed with the colonial logic that they knew everything better than everyone else, they clearly misunderstood African communities' public displays and celebration of sexuality (Kungu and Chacha, 2022, p. 19). This misunderstanding and detesting of African sexuality led to colonial narratives that continue to be alive across Africa today.

Most of the colonial settlers and missionaries were 'white males' from a context where women were primarily confined to keeping house and bearing children, always assuming they were regarded as 'chaste women'. According to Paul Schrader (2020):

> Reitzenstein postulated a theory that human development from 'natural' to 'civilized' peoples is accompanied by a growing differentiation of the gender order. While 'civilized nations', as he argued, are marked

> by a clear-cut separation between male gainful employment and female domestic work, 'natural peoples', at the other end of the scale, could be described by their levelling social orders where both genders work on comparable positions. A similar scheme could be observed, as he added, in the case of sexuality. Whereas in 'civilized' societies women live their sexual lives as a 'passive devotion' to male 'active' sexuality, within 'natural' societies, in contrast, the sexual conduct of both genders could be described as 'active', 'lustful', or 'rude'. The problematized sexuality of African women was, in this perspective, not a result of bodily pathologies but rather the end result of social structures that made women 'almost like men'. The sexualization of African women and their de-feminization went, in this account, hand in hand. (p. 137)

Against this background, African women were a scary proposition for European white males, and they were neither simply domesticated nor did they hide their bodies. That led to a growing obsession by these white males with the sexuality of African women, to whom they attributed 'hyperfecundity and sexual profligacy', while Africa was thought to be 'a wild space of pornographic pleasures in need of sexual policing' (Kungu and Chacha, 2022, p. 20). Stuart Cloete (1958) bluntly says of the women of Africa:

> One is suddenly aware of the immense fecundity and sexuality of Africa. Many of the women were beautiful once you become used to African beauty. One could see why they were all women. They were in a sense without souls. They were bold and without innocence. They said with their dark eyes; we are women. You are a man. We know what you want. (p. 51)

Coming from a background that had thoroughly constrained sexuality, Africa was the opposite, yet in its celebration of sexuality, African communities were still regulating sexuality, especially its reproductive dimension. This was not always visible to the outsider, hence the 'myriad stereotypical myths regarding the sexualities of "black" peoples ... constructing this phenomenon as either "exotic, mysterious, [and] uncivilized" or as hypersexual' (Kungu and Chacha, 2022, pp. 20–1), sometimes even regarded as 'natural' as opposed to the advanced and developed sexual mores of Europe since Africans were considered primitive (Schrader, 2020, p. 128). African sexuality was constructed and presented as dominated by 'the unbridled black female sexuality, excessive, threatening and contagious, carrying a deadly disease' (Kungu and Chacha, 2022, p. 21; Arnfred, 2004). According to Sylvia Tamale (2011):

> Texts from 19th century reports authored by white explorers and missionaries, reveal a clear pattern of the ethnocentric and racist construction of African sexualities. Western imperialist caricatures of African sexualities were part of a wider design to colonize and exploit the black race. Narratives equated black sexuality with primitiveness. Not only were African sexualities depicted as primitive, exotic and bordering on nymphomania, but it was also perceived as immoral, bestial and lascivious. Africans were caricatured as having lustful dispositions. Their sexualities were read directly into their physical attributes; these attributes were believed to reflect the (im)morality of Africans. The imperialists executed this mission through force, brutality, paternalism, arrogance, insensitivity and humiliation. (pp. 14–15)

The colonial logic accompanied by European Christian moralization painted an Africa that was struggling with sexual licentiousness bordering on libertinism as opposed to their civilized, rigidly controlled cis-heteronormativity. In their observations of sexuality in Africa, and significant for this conversation, where Europe had persecuted and killed persons whose sexuality deviated from the cis-heteronormative hegemony, the explorers and missionaries were shocked by what they saw:

> University Anthropology Professor Evans-Pritchard was also puzzled by the phenomenon. In 1951 he wrote about the Nuer of South Sudan: 'What seems to us, but not at all to Nuer, a somewhat strange union is that in which a woman marries another woman and counts as the pater [father] of the children born of the wife. Such marriages are by no means uncommon in Nuerland, and they must be regarded as a form of simple legal marriage, for the woman-husband marries her wife in exactly the same way as a man marries a woman. (Tamale, 2022, p. 62)

In the sixteenth century, an English explorer, Andrew Batell:

> who had been imprisoned in the 1590s by the Portuguese in the territory of modern Angola, wrote about the practices among the Imbaanga: 'They have men in women's apparel, whom they keep among their wives.' Later, Sir Richard Burton, researching the Portuguese sources from the sixteenth century, found observations of the instances of male homosexuality among the Kongo tribes. (Ananyev and Poyker, 2020, p. 5)

In recent decades, studies have attested to the existence of multiple fluid sexual practices in pre-colonial African communities with varying degrees of attitudes towards the 'non-reproductive' expressions of sexuality. Rose Jaji (2017) writes:

> Anthropological sources document the practice of homosexuality in traditional African societies where it had varying meanings. Contrary to the orthodoxy that portrays African cultures as discriminatory, most of these cultures tolerated diversity and treated gender, sexuality, and sexual orientation as continuums rather than binaries in which one was either a man or a woman and heterosexual or homosexual. Flexibility in gender, sexuality, and sexual orientation as sociocultural constructions enabled people to move back and forth between masculinity and femininity depending on the requirements of specific situations or circumstances. (pp. 2–3)

Friedrich Julius Bieber's work reveals how Western perspectives projected interpretations of sexuality on to African contexts. By describing Ethiopian practices and attitudes towards sexuality, Bieber explored assumed cultural contrasts, portraying Ethiopia as a space of sexual openness in comparison to European norms, as evidenced by his observation on Abyssinian frankness:

> Austrian ethnographer and traveller Friedrich Julius Bieber, a practitioner of a supposedly innovative 'sexual ethnology'. In the first decade of the 20th century, he participated in several private and state-funded research expeditions to Ethiopia, subsequently publishing a large number of research articles with a particular focus on sexual questions in German and Austrian ethnological and sexological journals. He wrote about allegedly favoured sex positions among Ethiopians, marriage customs, and the spread of homosexuality and sex work. In these pieces, Bieber portrayed sub-Saharan Africa as a space of free sexual development and libertinage. 'Any form of hypocrisy concerning sexual acts, is an alien concept to the Abyssinians. They deal with natural acts in a natural way, and they talk about them frankly and without any shyness.' (Schrader, 2020, p. 128)

Even some of the most vocal proponents of homophobia in Africa today have moved beyond the denial or rejection of the presence of some dimensions of sexuality that could be regarded as falling under the concept of homosexuality:

> Theresa Okafor, a Nigerian recipient of the anti-gay and anti-abortion advocacy group World Congress of Families 2015 Woman of the Year Award also claims: 'In the 19th Century, we had homosexuality. It has always existed in the pagan society in Africa. In Uganda for instance, the king was homosexual and was making ... sexual advances towards his young pagers in his courts. And it is precisely the missionaries from the West, who stepped in and made those pagers convert to Christianity and told them the righteousness of sexuality and why it is wrong to yield to the advances of the king ... If homosexuality was in our pagan society, what is progressive? what is new about it? It was there! And it was the missionaries who came and changed all of that ... There is nothing new, it has always been there. And right now, we are fighting it – it is like retrogressive – it is [going back to] where we started ... [traditional life].' (Kerry Eleveld, 2015, as cited in Kaoma, 2016, p. 65)

While same-sex practices and relationships were observed, this reality led to two contradictory conclusions from European explorers and missionaries, with one view suggesting that if such practices were found among the most primitive peoples, it meant that homosexuality was a natural human instinct, while others, using the European classification of sexual practices and relationships into natural and unnatural acts, accused the Arabs, Portuguese and Italians of introducing this unnatural sexuality (Gunda, 2010, p. 122; Schrader, 2020, p. 128). With the colonial establishments and Christian missions sharing their misunderstanding of African sexuality, a legal and evangelization attack on it emerged. Monogamy was institutionalized and legalized, and by implication, polygyny or polygamy became criminalized. Similarly, Christianity pronounced traditional sexuality in its fluidity and polygamy sinful and uncivilized. Male same-sex practices, especially anal sex, were criminalized by the enactment of the Sodomy Laws, beginning with the passing of the Buggery Act 1533, which criminalized anal sex and bestiality, which were both capital offences (Kirby, 2013). Tamale (2011) affirms:

> Religion, especially Christianity and Islam, stressed the impurity and inherent sin associated with women's bodies. Through religion and its proselytising activities, Africans were encouraged to reject their previous beliefs and values and to adopt the 'civilised ways' of the whites. With these new developments came the emphasis on covering and hiding body parts. Indeed, one of the most effective methods of controlling African women's sexuality has been through the regulation of their dress codes. Perhaps the most notorious post-colonial cases on the continent in this regard were the draconian laws on women's dressing

> sanctioned by dictators Kamuzu Banda of Malawi and Idi Amin of Uganda. A new script, steeped in the Victorian moralistic, antisexual and body-shame edicts, was inscribed on the bodies of African women and with it an elaborate system of control. (p. 16)

Through colonial laws and Christian injunctions, sex-talk, sexuality education and public celebration of sexuality were placed under a veil of secrecy and shame, 'marriage [monogamous] is, in this context, the only legitimate arena for sexual expression. Any sexual expression outside of this boundary is condemned as sin' (Ahlberg et al., 2009, pp. 106–7; Okafor, 2018). With these developments, African sexuality was being extinguished and, in its place, Western, Victorian conceptions of sexuality were being implanted:

> As Christian missionaries tried to implement monogamous marriage practices and the small family norm onto colonized subjects and societies, colonial administrations intended to regulate sexual behaviour in order to prevent the spread of venereal diseases, or settler populations attempted to uphold the racialized barrier between colonizing and colonized subjects by regulating sexual contacts between both groups, sexuality, in any case, occupied a prominent place within colonialist discourses, strategies, and governance plans ... As a result, a significant number of travelogues, ethnographic studies, missionary reports, and administrative statistics from the colonies, all dealing in one way or another with the issue of sexuality, circulated in Germany at the turn of the century. (Schrader, 2020, p. 131)

Presently, in conversations around human sexuality – focusing on LGBTIQ+ individuals as well as comprehensive sexuality education – Africa takes a firm stance in its objections, rejection and resistance. It criticizes what it perceives as the embrace of decadent Western culture and mores while steadfastly clinging to what it refers to as 'its moral culture'. However, as evidenced in this chapter, this so-called 'moral culture' is the 'colonial culture and mores' forcibly and coercively implanted in Africa (Meiu, 2015) by colonial and European Christian institutions, epistemologies and theologies. Coloniality continues to determine our conceptions and perceptions because colonial ideology unsettled, altered and delegitimized existing indigenous knowledge and knowledge systems through the processes of colonialism and imperialism (Tamale, 2022, p. 58). Sadly most homophobic Africans are arguing while steeped firmly in the realm of colonial thinking, their antagonists from Europe and North America are similarly steeped in the realm of colonial thinking and coloniality, in which white European ideas, practices and conceptions are considered superior, reasonable, scientific, objective, theologically sound and therefore not to be questioned or challenged but are rather to be adopted and embraced unquestionably. This is the same approach that took African communities where they are currently. The toxicity of the current impasse continues to dehumanize and indignify the real lives of individuals whose sexuality has been magnified to deny the totality of their personhood.

'For centuries Christianity and colonialism squeezed Africans on every side, trying to make them subjects of God and empire. Both empires – the empire of the spirit and the empire of the European powers – attempted to claim Africans for themselves' (Wariboko, 2019, p. 60). Unfortunately, coloniality and a resurgent Christian Right accompanied by the supposed progressive white European Christian Left continue to squeeze Africans into an identity crisis or crises.

What is clear from earliest observations by Europeans and current studies by Africans is that some women and men had relations of an intimate nature with other women or men, respectively, and that these relations were never understood as exclusive of such individuals' responsibilities towards the interests of their families and communities. There were no rigid, mutually exclusive sexual identities in these communities. The current debates around same-sex relationships are manifestations of the continuing impact of colonial thinking and/or coloniality across the divide. On the one side are those who embrace the colonial positions that made European-Victorian sexual mores and conception of sexuality a superior form of sexuality to which progress and civilization would lead. On the other side are those who are also holding on to the superiority of European ideas and concepts and insisting that all others adopt such ideas and concepts, exceptionally as such ideas are now packaged as part of the Human Rights discourse, which is supposed to be universal and to which progress and civilization leads. Can Africans embrace human rights without embracing their full import? Can white European Christian leftists engage in a dialogue from a position of equality and not of superiority? Can an intentional decolonial approach create a firmer basis for ecumenical cooperation?

## Decolonization of Human Sexuality

Based on how entrenched antagonists are on human sexuality – especially LGBTIQ+ persons – there is little hope for finding common ground. Sadly this polarization is costing lives, directly or indirectly. This happens, on the one hand, through vicious, violent attacks and murders.

Eudy Simelane – a South African women's national football team player – was violently sexually assaulted and then murdered in 2008. In Uganda, gay rights activists have been murdered: David Kato in 2011 and Brian Wassa in 2019. In Kenya, Edwin Chiloba – a gay model and activist – was found murdered in Kapsaret in 2023.

On the other hand, mental health complications lead to increased cases of suicides among sexual minorities (Moagi et al., 2021). While we argue, real lives are being lost, and none of us is doing these vulnerable persons, created in the Image of God, any favours because we are more worried about winning the argument than actually saving and serving lives. We remain entrenched, dig in deeper or seek out each other. From the beginning, the faith we follow has thrived on motion. My call is for an intentional decolonial motion from both sides because we are all in desperate need of decolonization:

> Decoloniality is a path to heal the wounds of coloniality. And since colonial wounds are not physical but mental (which Ngũgĩ wa Thiong'o clearly understood in the expression 'decolonizing the mind,' ... and mental wounds are inflicted by words and assumptions that sustain the words, colonial wounds are perpetrated by epistemic weapons. (Mignolo, 2016, pp. vii-viii)

In the past there have been aspersions that decolonization is for those negatively impacted by colonization. That is only a recipe for sustaining coloniality. Colonization and its systems under the almost invisible coloniality continue to exert influence and authority on all of us. To decolonize is to un-learn, un-do and un-be what colonization made us into, irrespective of which side of colonization we stand on. We both need to reach a point of conviction in our hearts and minds that white supremacism is sinful and that whiteness is not divinely ordained. As declared by the WCC Fifth Assembly held in Nairobi in 1975 (Pillay and Gunda, 2024), racism is also a sin. We must affirm that there is only one human family, whose diversities are shaped by environmental factors rather than essential differences, and commit to standing against all instances and systems that perpetuate inequalities, discriminations, dominations and deprivations inflicted upon sisters and brothers based on their appearance or supposed origins. Decolonization and decoloniality are revolutionary commitments that will disrupt the world as we know it and allow for a new creation. We can embrace our agency for this latest creation or defend our privileges and the status quo.

Decolonization challenges us to ask ourselves: How colonial have we been in our conversations around human sexuality, especially when it comes to LGBTIQ+ persons? By raising this question we should recall that colonial logic assumes there is one superior and correct position. It is the duty of the one who knows, the colonizer, to indoctrinate those who do not understand this proper knowledge, and it is the duty of the one who supposedly does not know to accept the teaching without questioning. Have we exhibited colonial tendencies in our engagements around human sexuality? What are the ways in which our partners' colonial tendencies become apparent in our efforts to build a strong ecumenical partnership, sometimes making it feel more like ecumenical colonization than like true partnership?

As a starting point, it is essential to create safe spaces where it is possible to encourage a 'discourse on responsible sexuality without guilt, fear or ill-health' (Amadiume, 2006, p. 1). Safe spaces are not spaces of agreement but rather respectful spaces where everyone is welcome, has a voice, is listened to and listens in return. Disagreements should be seen as opportunities for deeper dialogue and conversation, not justifications for breaking relationships. I wonder how much listening we have genuinely done and whose voices have been privileged in that process. If we have taken the time to listen to LGBTIQ+ persons in our communities across Africa, what are their aspirations?

They are pleading for recognition of their humanity, for acknowledgment of the Image of God within them and for assurances of a life free from violence, one that allows them to walk the streets like any other individual. They seek recognition of the fullness of their lives – they are professionals, friends, sons, daughters, uncles and aunties; they are not defined solely by their sexuality.

Decolonization calls us to challenge the 'colonizing narratives' that claim 'they are paedophiles', 'they are indecent' or 'they deny God'. We know these narratives are untrue, just as we now know the colonial depictions of Africa as a hotbed of pornographic sexual escapades were equally false.

The power of the colonial project lies in the colonial meta-narratives and narratives entrenched through education, Bible study, church teachings, laws, theologies and ecclesiastical structures. To decolonize is to develop counter-narratives that will undo the colonial narratives. To develop decolonial counter-narratives, we need to listen to the lived experiences of those who stand on the margins of the house of God. That allows decolonization to challenge, reject and disrupt the epistemological privileging of European ideas and practices. It is critical not to lose sight of the fact that it also challenges all epistemologies with a colonizing tendency or agenda. According to Amadiume (2006): 'African educated elites are mistaken to assume to know more about sexuality than the illiterate masses or traditional villagers' (pp. 4–5). Decolonization seeks to create a platform on which all epistemologies have a place on the table, including the epistemologies that colonization tried to exterminate. They, however, have been resilient, and their legacies and residues are still alive in our different communities if we dare to investigate and learn. Unfortunately, 'contemporary conceptualizations of "African sexuality" continue to be informed by earlier colonial and Western, Victorian-era imaginations' (Kungu and Chacha, 2022, p. 21).

## Closing Remarks

European kingdoms and empires colonized Africa thoroughly, allowing European control of education, governance, economy and social life. European missionaries' evangelization of sub-Saharan Africa was equally thorough, allowing missionaries to control their converts' spirituality, morality, theology, education and social life. While it is true that colonization and evangelization were two separate movements, it is essential to acknowledge that these were intersecting, reinforcing each other by providing each other with material and moral support.

Human sexuality was heavily regulated in Europe both legally (by the state) and morally (by the Christian church); a rigid gender binary had become the only way of understanding human beings, with white males being the standard and epitome of being human and white women reduced to the next best thing, good enough for home care and making babies. Women were expected to hide inside dresses with a passive and submissive demeanour. When European explorers, colonizers and missionaries – all of them primarily white males – encountered communities on the African continent, they were shocked and excited by the degree of openness with which these communities handled their sexuality. Women's bodies were not hidden away! Talking about sex – with clearly age-appropriate strategies, although most Europeans missed this element – was not a problem! These communities did not even fear sex. On the contrary, they celebrated their sexuality through song, dance and rituals. The gender binary from Europe could not explain what they were seeing. A mission to erase this was started; out went the African celebration of sexuality, and in came the European secrecy, regulation and rigidity of sexuality. Today we are confronted by a supposedly African argument upholding colonial sexuality in a battle of supremacy against European sexuality that seems to be getting closer to pre-colonial African sexuality, with its indifference towards diversities and public celebration of sexuality. African women's bodies are being counselled to be hidden away, and other sexualities face the risk of capital punishment. These entrenched positions demonstrate colonial tendencies, which we must challenge, undo and unlearn. Decolonizing is revolutionary, disruptive and discomforting, but a new edifice emerges from the ruins it creates!

## *Note*

1 The document *Conversations on the Pilgrim Way* (WCC, 2022) was prepared by the Reference Group on Human Sexuality and was set up as part of the recommendations by the WCC Tenth Assembly, Busan 2013. While the Central Committee received it, there were strong objections by several WCC members.

## References

Ahlberg, Betty M., Anne Kamau, Francis Maina and Amina Kulane (2009), 'Multiple Discourses on Sexuality: Implications for Translating Sexual Wellness Concept into Action Strategies in a Kenyan Context', *African Sociological Review* 13, no. 1, pp. 105–23.

Amadiume, Ifi (1987), *Male Daughters and Female Husbands: Gender and Sex in an African Society*, London: ZED Books.

Amadiume, Ifi (2006), 'Sexuality, African Religio-Cultural Traditions and Modernity: Expanding the Lens', Africa Regional Sexuality Resource Centre, at http://www.arsrc.org/downloads/features/amadiume.pdf, accessed 01.12.2024.

Ananyev, Maxim and Mikhail Poyker (2020), 'Christian Missions and Anti-gay Attitudes in Africa', *NICEP Working Paper* #4, Nottingham: Nottingham Interdisciplinary Centre for Economic and Political Research, at https://nicep.nottingham.ac.uk, accessed 01.12.2024.

Arnfred, Signe, ed. (2004), *Re-Thinking Sexualities in Africa*, Uppsala: Nordic Africa Institute.

Blevins, John (2011), 'When Sodomy Leads to Martyrdom: Sex, Religion, and Politics in Historical and Contemporary Contexts in Uganda and East Africa', *Theology and Sexuality* 17, no. 1, pp. 51–74.

Cloete, Stuart (1958), *Congo Song*, New York: Monarch.

Eleveld, Kerry, 'World Congress of Families Attendee explains how U.S.-based Groups spread Homophobia in Africa', at http://www.dailykos.com/story/2015/ll/03/1444045/-World-Congress-of-Families-attendee-explains-how-U-S-based-groups-spread-homophobia-in-Africa, accessed 27.7.2025.

Ezebuilo, Henry Chukwudi (2023), 'Sexuality and Human Nature: An African Perspective', *Ochedo: An African Journal of Innovative Studies* 4, no. 1, pp. 56–73.

Fanon, Frantz (2005), *The Wretched of the Earth*, translated by Richard Philcox, New York: Grove Press.

Gunda, Masiiwa Ragies (2010), *The Bible and Homosexuality in Zimbabwe: A Socio-historical Analysis of the Political, Cultural and Christian Arguments in the Homosexual Public Debate with Special Reference to the Use of the Bible* (BiAS Series #3), Bamberg: University of Bamberg Press.

Harris, Max (2018), 'Racism and White Defensiveness in Aotearoa: A Pākehā Perspective', *E-Tangata* (10 June), at https://e-tangata.co.nz/comment-and-analysis/racism-and-white-defensiveness-in-aotearoa-a-pakeha-perspective/, accessed 01.12.2024.

Horrell, David G. (2023), 'The Ethical Challenge of Decolonisation and the Future of New Testament Studies', *Studies in Christian Ethics* 36, no. 1, pp. 36–57.

Idamarhare, Andrew O. (2014), 'Africentric Hermeneutics: Methodology towards Decolonizing Biblical Studies in Africa', *Journal of Sociology, Psychology and Anthropology in Practice* 6, no. 1, pp. 44–54.

Igboin, Bode O. (2023), 'Contextuality, Interculturality and Decolonisation as Schemes of Power Relations', *HTS Teologiese Studies/Theological Studies* 79, no. 4, pp. 1–11.

Jaji, Rose (2017), 'Homosexuality: UnAfricanness and Vulnerability', *The Zambakari Advisory* (March), at https://ssrn.com/abstract=3148335, accessed 01.12.2024.

Jeater, Diana (1993), *Marriage, Perversion and Power: The Construction of Moral Discourse in Southern Rhodesia 1894–1930*, Oxford: Clarendon Press.

Kaoma, Kapya (2016), 'Unmasking the Colonial Silence: Sexuality in Africa in the Post Colonial Context', *Journal of Theology for Southern Africa* 155 (July), pp. 49–69.

Kirby, Michael (2013), 'The Sodomy Offence: England's Least Lovely Criminal Law Export?', in *Human Rights, Sexual Orientation and Gender Identity in the Commonwealth*, edited by Corinne Lennox and Matthew Waites, London: University of London Press, pp. 61–82.

Kungu, Joseph N. and Beatrice K. Chacha (2022), 'Decolonizing African Sexualities: Between Continuities and Change', *International Journal of Social Sciences and Management Review* 5, no. 2, pp. 14–30.

Kurian, Manoj (2017), 'Critical Analysis of Churches' Stand on Human Sexuality and a Way Forward', in *A Theological Reader on Human Sexuality and Gender Diversities: Envisioning Inclusivities*, edited by Roger Gaikward and Thomas Ninan, Delhi: ISPCK, pp. 152–68.

Lee, Richard B. and Robert K. Hitchcock (2001), 'African Hunter-Gatherers: Survival, History, and the Politics of Identity', *African Study Monographs* 26 (March), pp. 257–80.

Meiu, George Paul (2015), 'Colonialism and Sexuality', in *The International Encyclopedia of Human Sexuality*, edited by Patricia Whelehan and Anne Bolin, Chichester: Wiley, pp. 239–42.

Mignolo, Walter D. (2016), 'Foreword: Decolonial Body-Geo-Politics at Large', in *Decolonizing Sexualities: Transnational Perspectives-Critical Interventions*, edited by Sandeep Bakshi, Suhraiya Jivraj and Silvia Posocco, Oxford: Counterpress, pp. vii-xviii.

Moagi, Miriam Mpho, Anna E. Van Der Wath, Priscilla M. Jiyane and Richard S. Rikhotso (2021), 'Mental Health Challenges of Lesbian, Gay, Bisexual and Transgender People: An Integrated Literature Review', *Health SA Gesondheid* 26, pp. 1–12.

Mokoko Gampiot, Aurélien (2017), *Kimbanguism: An African Understanding of the Bible*, translated by Cécile Coquet-Mokoko (Signifying (on) Scriptures Series), University Park, PA: Pennsylvania State University Press.

Okafor, Okechi Samuel (2018), 'The Indigenous Concept of Sexuality in African Tradition and Globalization', *Global Journal of Reproductive Medicine* 6, no. 1, pp. 1–5.

Parliament of Uganda (2023), 'The Anti-Homosexuality Act, 2023' (26 September), Kampala: Parliament of Uganda, at https://www.parliament.go.ug/sites/default/files/The%20Anti-Homosexuality%20Act%2C%202023.pdf, accessed 01.12.2024.

Pillay, Jerry and Masiiwa Ragies Gunda (2024), 'Anti-Racism and the Fight against Discrimination Today', *Ecumenical Review* 76, no. 3 (July), pp. 182–91.

Ramantswana, Hulisani (2016), 'Decolonising Biblical Hermeneutics in the (South) African Context', *Acta Theologica Supplement* 24, pp. 178–203.

Ramantswana, Hulisani (2017), 'Decolonial Reflection on the Landlessness of the Levites', *Journal of Theology for Southern Africa* 158, pp. 72–91.

Schrader, Paul (2020), 'Fears and Fantasies: German Sexual Science and its Research on African Sexualities, 1890–1930', *Sexualities* 23, no. 1–2, pp. 127–45.

Tamale, Sylvia (2011), 'Researching and Theorizing Sexualities in Africa', in *African Sexualities: A Reader*, edited by Sylvia Tamale, Oxford: Pambazuka Press, pp. 11–36.

Tamale, Sylvia (2013), 'Exploring the Contours of African Sexualities: Statutory, Customary and Religious Laws', paper presented at the Conference on Law and Religion in Africa: Comparative Practices, Experiences and Prospects, University of Ghana, Accra.

Tamale, Sylvia (2022), 'Challenging the Coloniality of Sex, Gender and Sexuality', *Intellectus: The African Journal of Philosophy* 1, no. 1, pp. 57–79.

Wariboko, Nimi (2019), 'Colonialism, Christianity, and Personhood', in *A Companion to African History*, edited by William H. Worger, Charles Ambler and Nwando Achebe, Hoboken, NJ: John Wiley & Sons, pp. 59–75.

World Council of Churches (WCC) (2022), *Conversations on the Pilgrim Way: Invitation to Journey Together on Matters of Human Sexuality*, Geneva: WCC Publications.

World Health Organization (WHO) (2024), 'Sexual Health: Definitions', at https://www.who.int/health-topics/sexual-health#tab=tab_2, accessed 01.12.2024.

5

# Being-Blessed: The Primacy of Sophianic Love through the Gifts of Sex-Gender Diversity

ÁNGEL F. MÉNDEZ MONTOYA

*(translated by Hugo Córdova Quero)*

For you love all things that exist,
and detest none of the things that you have made,
for you would not have made anything if you had hated it.
(Wisdom 11.24, NRSV)

## Ecumenical and Interreligious Blessing in a Roman Catholic Church: Prelude to the Sacramentality of Diverse Love

As a prelude, I would like to share my experience of having received the blessing of our marriage union with my husband, with whom I contracted a civil marriage months before this ecumenical and interreligious liturgical celebration. In Mexico, in 2015, the Supreme Court of Justice approved the law of equal marriage that guarantees that all people – regardless of their sex-gender experience – can legally marry, granting the same rights for cis-heterosexual marriages. Taking advantage of this civil initiative, my husband and I contracted this civil and political right, but at the same time we wanted a religious blessing to celebrate with family and friends of diverse faiths.

The ceremony occurred in December 2019 in a Roman Catholic church in Mexico City's *Centro Histórico* (historic town centre). The ecumenical and interfaith liturgy was created by a fellow feminist theologian in conjunction with my husband and me. My husband is of indigenous descent, which goes back to Montezuma, so we insisted on integrating sacred elements of the Meso-American world view. In the centre of a sixteenth-century church we placed a Mayan altar with apples, bean seeds and corn cobs. A professional pre-Hispanic music group provided music. There were readings of a passage from the Song of Songs and a poem by Netzahualcoyotl.

We were joined at the ceremony by family members, friends, theologians from Roman Catholicism and various Christian churches, as well as people from religions other than Christianity and people who do not follow any religious creed or have a belief in God. A Roman Catholic priest presided over the liturgy, and another Roman Catholic priest shared the homily. The blessing was led by an Afro-Caribbean lesbian feminist theologian representing the Metropolitan Community Churches. She invited everyone in attendance to raise their hands with their palms towards us to send a communal blessing. This was one of the most endearing liturgical gestures that has left a beautiful memory in our hearts. Although the ceremony was by no means a replica of the Roman Catholic sacrament of marriage, I felt that it provided a space of human-divine 'sacramentality' from a blessing emanating from a spirit of ecumenical and interreligious love, recognizing and celebrating publicly and in the name of God our dissenting love.

For the Roman Catholic Church, the theology of sacramentality allows us to recognize God's presence in the world and history. This broadens a notion of the sacrament limited to liturgical and canonical spaces and ceremonies. At the same time, sacramentality sheds light on the meaning of being blessed by the presence of God in daily life, thus recognizing the world and history as sacraments of God and, therefore, sharers in divine love. For this very reason the ecumenical and interreligious blessing we received in the Roman Catholic church was an experience of human sacramentality as a sacrament of God and divine sacramentality coming from love without boundaries, the sacrament of eccentric love.

## *Fiducia Supplicans*: Supplicants Trust the Divine Blessing

Two months after our marriage blessing, several official communiqués were issued from the Dicastery for the Doctrine of the Faith – previously known as the Congregation for the Doctrine of the Faith – prohibiting all liturgies from blessing same-sex unions. That brought about a series of statements from the Vatican that culminated in December 2023 with the Declaration *Fiducia Supplicans: On the Pastoral Meaning of Blessings* (Dicastery for the Doctrine of the Faith, 2023).

In the Roman Catholic Church, Pope Francis showed an ambiguous position regarding the recognition and welcoming of LGBTIQ+ people.

In some ways this attitude also reflects the feelings of many people within the Roman Catholic Church, where a large number of members reject the inclusion of people of sexual diversity, while communities that desire inclusion and even celebrate Sunday Masses of diversity and inclusion are growing and becoming more visible. On multiple occasions Pope Francis promoted non-discrimination, non-violence and non-criminalization towards people in LGBTIQ+ populations. The Pope had gay friends and met with sexually diverse people to listen and address their concerns. For example, Pope Francis met with LGBTIQ+ human rights activists and human rights defenders representing several countries. Of particular note is his interview with Nava Mau – a Mexican transgender actress – who reports that she will never forget the blessing she received from the Pope and his words of hope when he told them not to stop fighting for their rights (Beltrán, 2024). In addition, Francis publicly acknowledged his approval of equal civil marriages for societies and nations in the contemporary world. However, whether out of personal conviction or pressure from more conservative sectors of the church, the Pope did not take official and doctrinal steps.

The *Fiducia Supplicans* Declaration makes explicit and reiterates that the sacrament of marriage is exclusively for cis-heterosexual couples. In this sense, this Declaration offers no change in the doctrine and theology of the sacrament of marriage, upholding and reiterating the position of a hegemonic cis-heteropatriarchal church:

> In any case, precisely to avoid any form of confusion or scandal, when the prayer of blessing is requested by a couple in an irregular situation, even though it is expressed outside the rites prescribed by the liturgical books, this blessing should never be imparted in concurrence with the ceremonies of a civil union, and not even in connection with them. Nor can it be performed with any clothing, gestures, or words that are proper to a wedding. The same applies when the blessing is requested by a same-sex couple. (§ 39)

The Declaration prohibits any liturgy or sacrament that might suggest or imply that marriage may recognize 'irregular status' couples and same-sex unions. However, the document specifies that this does not preclude blessing all persons and creation. In this sense, *Fiducia Supplicans* affirms the foundation of the practice and theology of blessings as 'sacramentals' in a constant process of evolution:

> Indeed, they lead us to grasp God's presence in all the events of life and remind us that, even in the use of created things, human beings are

> invited to seek God, to love him, and to serve him faithfully. For this reason, blessings have as their recipients: people; objects of worship and devotion; sacred images; places of life, of work, and suffering; the fruits of the earth and human toil; and all created realities that refer back to the Creator, praising and blessing him by their beauty. (§ 8)

In this sense, blessing persons in same-sex unions, while not expressing a sacramental relationship with the status of 'marriage', does confirm the ecclesial rationale for blessing sex-diverse unions rather than being cursed. There is no ambiguity here. The effect of the blessing is confirmed as an ascending value insofar as we bless God for his infinite love, but the descending value is also confirmed, coming from the generous gesture and the radical divine love:

> from God upon those who – recognizing themselves to be destitute and in need of his help – do not claim a legitimation of their own status, but who beg that all that is true, good, and humanly valid in their lives and their relationships be enriched, healed, and elevated by the presence of the Holy Spirit. These forms of blessing express a supplication that God may grant those aids that come from the impulses of his Spirit – what classical theology calls 'actual grace' – so that human relationships may mature and grow in fidelity to the Gospel, that they may be freed from their imperfections and frailties, and that they may express themselves in the ever-increasing dimension of the divine love. (§ 31)

Blessing is an openness to divine transcendence that shows that God is not indifferent to the whole of creation but instead makes us participants in his radical love. This is very important because, in my own experience of being part of the LGBTIQ+ collective in the Roman Catholic Church, I recognize that the message to us has been one of a curse rather than a blessing, and we have been told that the final destination for us is hell. The curse comes from an imagined God who hates us and not from a God who loves us without restraint. *Fiducia Supplicans* rejects this position of fundamentalism of hatred and reiterates and makes explicit that we are all blessed. Ontologically, our very being has as its source an unrestricted love: 'For you love all things that exist, and detest none of the things that you have made, for you would not have made anything if you had hated it' (Wisdom 11.24, NRSV).

Again, this Declaration does not advance its cis-heteropatriarchal canonical stance that excludes LGBTIQ+ persons from the sacrament of marriage. It does, however, reiterate a theology that breaks down the institutional boundaries of diverse religious affiliations, even secular ones, to affirm the interreligious ecumenism of divine love that blesses us all and the importance of celebrating in the world being blessed perpetually by God's love:

> 'the root of Christian meekness' is 'the ability to feel blessed and the ability to bless ... This world needs blessings, and we can give blessings and receive blessings. The Father loves us, and the only thing that remains for us is the joy of blessing him, and the joy of thanking him, and of learning from him ... to bless.' (§ 45)

The Declaration insists that we are always loved and blessed: 'In this way, every brother and every sister will be able to feel that, in the Church, they are always pilgrims, always beggars, always loved, and, despite everything, always blessed' (§ 45).

*Fiducia Supplicans* may be a starting point for future 'fissures' and 'twists' in Roman Catholic theology. Thus, it celebrates the sacramentality of same-sex union blessings in churches worldwide. This in turn could further twist the celebration of the sacrament of egalitarian marriage and thus confirm the sacramentally queer/*cuir* character of God's love.

## Being Blessed: The *Cuirization* of Diverse Love

In the English language the term *queer* means weird, strange, strange, out of the normal/normative, eccentric, twisted. Nevertheless it is also a term that, in English-speaking contexts, expresses a discourse of hatred and violence towards sexually diverse people. *Queer* is an offensive homolesbobitransphobic term that marginalizes non-heteronormative people. However, it is exciting how this term has been twisted by LGBTIQ+ activist movements in political marches in public spaces, to mean pride, dignity and defence of the human rights of sexually diverse people.

In this chapter, I use the hybrid term queer/*cuir* to express ourselves from Latin American contexts and other epistemologies of the global South. We use phonetic Spanish to integrate the English root and reiterate the dimension of political activism and resignification of dignity and pride that these struggles of LGBTIQ+ collectives maintain. At the same time, queer/*cuir* is a term that we use here to include all bodies that are abject or subordinated not only because they belong to dissident sexuality collectives but also because they are racialized bodies, bodies of undocumented migrants, indigenous bodies, poor, disabled, old; in short, bodies that do not matter for cis-heteropatriarchal and colonial systems as supremacist, extractivist and hegemonic. We use the verb *cuirizar* [to *cuirize*] to signify the act of twisting these cis-heteropatriarchal and colonial attitudes to provoke imagining and generating a more liveable life, as in the case of this particular reflection. In this life, we all experience the blessings of an overabundant and overflowing divine love.

We propose, then, to *cuirizar* and twist the theology of blessings to same-sex unions within the Roman Catholic Church. In reality these twists are also inspired by movements and Christian churches that initiated and have continued with religious celebrations to bless and communally confirm the commitment of love between sexually diverse persons. In contemporary theology these kinks require an ecumenical and interreligious spirit to overcome institutional boundaries and find alliances and collective struggles among pluralistic communities of faith at the global level – as is the intention of this collective book on global queer theologies.

While I speak in the first person from my biographical horizon, as a *cuir* theologian, I also include communal voices that resonate with plural, diverse and dissident religious experiences. In particular I consider myself a Roman Catholic in the diaspora precisely because of this dissident and queer/*cuir* location of thinking and doing theology. I think theological reflection is an exercise of constant signification and resignification of our experiences of God and the importance of doing it from the concrete contexts in which we are situated, from what we indeed are, not from fear, lies or dishonesty. My theological reflection is in the first person. Still, it also integrates intersectionality, those who, within and beyond Christian churches, have been condemned to live precariously as a result of the counter-blessings generated by hateful, fundamentalist, racist and cis-heteropatriarchal discourses and actions. My purpose is to glimpse the primacy of divine love that blesses all creation and invites us to bring about a more liveable life, a blessed life for every person on the face of the Earth and all the planet's ecosystems. With this I invite us to embrace, radically and courageously, the joy of the superabundant blessings of God, who loves us first, especially those who live most precariously.

Therefore, to *cuirize* the theology of blessings in the Roman Catholic Church I propose that we first venture to bring God out of the closet and let ourselves be moved and stirred by queer/*cuir* God, who opens cracks in the walls of masculinization of a cis-heteropatriarchal, whitewashed and colonial god (Althaus-Reid, 2022). God must be freed from the closets of hatred and necrophilia, a god who punishes, crushes and annihilates God's creation to set them free. God radically loves all creation. God is queer/*cuir* as non-binary, not belonging to a single gender or perhaps embracing all gender, and as polyamorous because of his overabundant love for the diversity and complexity of the cosmos created and blessed with his love. For a Christian glimpse, the divine nature is queer/*cuir* by lovingly sharing itself amid a communal loving presence, which loves diversity within the very relational and self-giving unity of divine love. It is an eccentric love, outside of itself, moving towards the other and sharing itself in a Trinitarian dynamic of divine love. God is eros and agape, at the same time desire and fullness, both giver and receiver and the very action of this eternal and infinite erotic-agapeic love. Amid this polyamorous act, God creates and continues to develop and bless the whole of creation. Because God is queer/*cuir*, we are all blessed. Wherever there is love we find the blessing of this extravagant and eccentric love initiated by God, who radically loves and blesses us first. If the Church blesses people, animals, houses and other objects created by human beings, as well as elements in nature such as trees, water and crops, why not bless genuine love unions between people, including same-sex unions?

Second, to *cuirize* the theology of the blessings of same-sex unions it is necessary to revisit a sophianic theology, where God is Sophia, 'she who is' (Johnson, 1993). God-Sophia is a mother who delights in God's creative act and counsels with her wisdom, with which she blesses all creation (Prov. 8.22–31). That is a theology of the feminine figure of Sophia as a gift and source of divine wisdom. She is divine discernment and action, full of creativity and blessings. She is the divine breath (Prov. 7.25) that invites us to taste/know – in the Latin root, *sapere* – the gifts and blessings of a radical, *cuir*, extravagant love given unconditionally to all creation. With the invocation of the sophianic blessings of divine love, same-sex unions become a sign of God's love communion but also a sacrament of this same love. Here, we are invited not only to discern in favour of the practice of communally blessing same-sex unions but also to twist it even further to the point of celebrating them communally as a sacrament of marriage.

Third, I propose to *cuirizar* not only the blessings but the sacrament of marriage predominantly cis-heterosexual in the Roman Catholic Church, taking as a foundation the theopolitical dimension of same-sex marriages. The acceptance of the civil law of same-sex marriage expresses the political struggle of activist movements, public marches and demands for the recognition of the human rights of LGBTIQ+ persons and collectives. At the same time, these marriages can be seen theologically as expressions and sacraments of the divine love embodied in the love promised between the couple and amid the celebrating community. Thus, the blessings and sacrament of same-sex marriage could become an event that is both political and theological, or theopolitical:

a communal celebration to celebrate the diversity of gifts, blessings and transformations that queer/*cuir* loves to bring about. We invite all the churches of the world, including all religious communities globally, to celebrate without fear that we are blessed by a love that transcends all boundaries, an eccentric and overflowing love that breaks with the necropolitics of lesbohomobitransphobic hatred and violence.

Finally, I propose to *cuirize* the theologies of blessings and marriage in the Roman Catholic Church, reiterating the importance of living, without fear and hatred, a more liveable life through honesty with oneself, society and God. As the openly gay theologian and priest James Alison has pointed out, we need to heal the wounds left by doctrinal practices and discourses within the Roman Catholic Church and other fundamentalist Christian churches, which declare that being gay is a defect, a flawed version of cis-heterosexuality (sdmani, 2021).

Love is love, but for these cis-heteropatriarchal positions it is only possible for cis-heterosexual unions. Otherwise non-heteronormative love is 'sin' and to bless it is 'blasphemy', repeating with these condemnations a sacrificial mechanism that follows the logic of a masculinized and resentful God in search of scapegoats to heal the 'deviation of conscience' of those non-cis-heteronormative creatures. This counter-blessing or curse generates fear, anxiety and trauma and very often leaves irreparable damage to LGBTIQ+ people. Alison (2001) has warned us about the reality of a homophobic Roman Catholic Church where there are many, many priests, religious and church leaders who, even though they are queer themselves, condemn, with their double talk, non-heteronormative love, living locked in rigid closets of dishonesty and self-hatred, which then translates into hatred towards the 'others'. That creates fundamentalist positions regarding human sexuality, which promote living in dishonesty and fear. These attitudes make us sick with hatred, which also boycotts the overabundance of the blessings of divine love that has no end and knows no boundaries.

## Conclusion: The Sacramentality of the Blessings of Queer/*Cuir* Marriages

Contrary to this cis-heteronormative fundamentalist stance, Wisdom 11.24 expresses the foundation and importance of God's sophianic love that comes out of the cis-heteropatriarchal closet to be shared and given to all of creation, particularly the most vulnerable people. For LGBTIQ+ people and all the myriad abject bodies, this has great importance because here God *cuirizes* the hegemonic-fundamentalist logic of hatred and resignifies the sacrament of marriage with his immeasurable sophianic love. The blessing expresses the donation of divine love so radical that it transfigures and resignifies all hatred and abhorrence towards abject bodies, sharing divine love and blessings without reserve. At the beginning of creation we find this superabundant and joyful love that gives itself without reserve. In the end times, in the resurrected life, the consummation of this radical love, infinitely *cuir*, will take place (Méndez Montoya, 2019). The flow of time in the here and now is overflowing with this protology and eschatology that re-signify the 'present'. Past and future constitute the crevices of the here and now, impregnating them with the ineffable divine desire that blesses every human relationship, precisely where there is love. Suppose the vital desire consists in being recognized. In that case, God desires us first and foremost, and his recognition and blessing dignify the 'indecent' (Althaus-Reid, 2005), re-signifying those bodies that live precariously.

God's sophianic desire for loving self-giving is shared within God's Trinitarian community, participating in a perichoretic dance of infinite love for the Other, being perpetually energized by a desire for common-union in diversity (Isherwood and Jordan, 2010). The divine community is loving affinity without subordination. It is unity in plurality, a co-eternal dance of donation and reception, overflowing loving recognition of the other, and intensely intimate coexistence with the Other, in the Other and for the Other. All creation's plurality and immeasurable diversity are akin to this dance of radical love. Such perichoretic love crosses all our bodies and makes us participants in the dance of divine wisdom, letting us know that love is love, and wherever there is love, there is God (Córdova Quero, 2011).

On several occasions I have heard the fundamentalist argument that 'You love the sinner, but not the sin'. Such a declaration assumes non-heteronormative love to be sinful and thereby justifies hatred, exclusion, criminalization and violence – even murder – of LGBTIQ+ individuals, couples and communities. However, love is love and God is love, so divine love has the potential to be embodied in loving relationships. Therefore, sex-divergent loving relationships are not a sign of sin but of overflowing blessing. This does not imply denying the reality of sin. Hatred is a sin. Violence, denial and subordination of the other is sin. Blessings and diverse marriage can generate sacramental practices of resistance and healing to those manifestations of sin that curse the loving relationships of people with non-heteronormative sexogenic experiences.

The *Fiducia Supplicans* Declaration still follows cis-heteropatriarchal canonical and doctrinal models, recognizing only the sacramentality of marriages between man and woman and with procreative intentions.

However, its theology of blessings to couples in irregular status and same-sex unions reiterates a theology based on the importance of divine love that subverts and twists the neoconservative fundamentalisms that preach hatred and curse. This Declaration has elicited a positive response in many churches worldwide, where more and more are daring to celebrate Roman Catholic and ecumenical liturgies to bless and celebrate diverse loves. In an ecumenical and interreligious spirit, the sacrament of matrimony is being celebrated, even without the official approval of the hierarchical and clerical church.

With this *cuirization* I do not intend to idealize egalitarian marriages, nor am I proposing that they become a replica of cis-heterosexual couples. That would produce supremacist discourses, minimizing the sex-affective life of all those people and queer/*cuir* relationships who, for example, have no intention or desire to marry or live a marital relationship. Nor am I suggesting that sex-diverse couples must necessarily replicate cis-heteronormative patterns for their married life. I am not recommending a single form of psycho-affective life for sexual diversity. Still, I invite everyone to open up about how to make marriage more open to procure experiences of diverse, complete, dignified and blessed love. With good humour, festivity, celebration, honesty and courage, let us continue to resist hegemonic theologies and cis-heteropatriarchies that arouse so much hatred and violence, to open ourselves to the surprises of the queer/*cuir* love of God who loves radically. And, thus, incarnate the blessings of a love that knows no limits in diverse and plural forms.

I recall the experience of my civil marriage and the ecumenical and interfaith blessing we received in a Roman Catholic church. I still delight in the many blessings we received in our ecumenical, interfaith, decolonial and queer/*cuir* liturgical celebration. All the people in the Roman Catholic Church – priests, religious men and women, bishops and lay people, representatives of spiritualities of native peoples, family members and friends, believers and atheists – gave us their blessing. There we felt the manifestation of God's overflowing and sophianic love that made us know and taste that we are all blessed, that another church and another world is possible here and now.

This autobiographical and first-person experience is intended only as a prelude to possible transformations in the sacrament of marriage within the Roman Catholic Church. In supplicant trust we pray for the transformation of our religious communities so that we let God be God and do not impede his superabundant blessings. I understand there is still much to be *cuirized* for divine blessings to pass through our bodies and communities of faith in Christian churches, other religions and spiritual traditions beyond Christianity.

## References

Alison, James (2001), *Faith Beyond Resentment: Fragments Catholic and Gay*, Spring Valley, NY: Crossroad.

Althaus-Reid, Marcella (2005), *La teología indecente: perversiones teológicas en sexo, género y política*, Barcelona: Bellaterra.

Althaus-Reid, Marcella (2022), *Dios cuir*, Mexico City: Universidad Iberoamericana.

Beltrán, José (2024), 'El papa Francisco, a la actriz trans Nava Mau: "Seguid luchando"', *Nueva Vida Digital*, 24 November, at https://www.vidanuevadigital.com/2024/11/24/el-papa-francisco-a-la-actriz-trans-nava-mau-seguid-luchando/amp/, accessed 01.12.2024.

Córdova Quero, Hugo (2011), 'Sexualizando la Trinidad: aportes desde una teología de la liberación queer a la compresión del misterio divino', *Cuadernos de Teología* 30, pp. 53–70.

Dicastery for the Doctrine of the Faith (2023), 'Declaration *Fiducia Supplicans*: On the Pastoral Meaning of Blessings', 18 December, Vatican City: Libreria Editrice Vaticana, at https://www.vatican.va/roman_curia/congregations/cfaith/documents/rc_ddf_doc_20231218_fiducia-supplicans_en.html, accessed 01.12.2024.

Johnson, Elizabeth (1993), *She Who Is: The Mystery of God in Feminist Theological Discourse*, Spring Valley, NY: Crossroad.

Isherwood, Lisa and Mark D. Jordan, eds (2010), *Dancing Theology in Fetish Boots: Essays in Honour of Marcella Althaus-Reid*, London: SCM Press.

Méndez Montoya, Ángel F. (2019), 'Love in the Last Days: The Eschatological Marking of Bodies Resembling an Infinitely Queer Desire', in *Queer Theologies: Becoming the Queer Body of Christ*, edited by Stefanie Knauss and Carlos Mendoza-Álvarez (*Concilium* No. 383), Estella: Editorial Verbo Divino, pp. 91–99.

sdmani (2021), 'Gay Catholic Priest [Testimony]', 8 June, at https://www.youtube.com/watch?v=Cs84mGfDReU, accessed 01.12.2024.

# 6

# *Trans-Struere*: Transing Theological Deconstruction

ALEX CLARE-YOUNG

## Introduction

My name is Alex Clare-Young and my pronouns are they/he. I start by introducing myself because my research and writing practice as a queer theologian centres standpoint theory: the idea that there is no view from nowhere (Harding, 2001). I cannot research and write theology from any standpoint than my own. Thus, where do I stand? Well, actually, I do not. Part of my standpoint is that of a full-time wheelchair user. I am also neurodivergent – AuDHD to be specific – and am trans. I transitioned towards male around fifteen years ago and live with little attention to – or understanding of – the binary categories of male and female. I am an ordained minister and theologian in the United Reformed Church. I live in a rural part of the UK. My socio-economic reality is complex and always has been. My lived experiences include power and oppression; aspects of my identity are normative and others are subaltern. In particular I acknowledge the power of being the researcher and writer who tells people's stories.

This chapter emerges out of my growing interest in deconstruction. This interest began during my doctoral studies, where participants identified as trans, non-binary and Christian and shared their life and faith experiences. Each of them are deconstructing in various ways, though many would not use that term. My interest in deconstruction has deepened as I minister with a new faith community, Solidarity Hub. The fifteen members of the Hub are each exploring faith from a unique standpoint, and most are questioning or deconstructing in one way or another. In contrast, many of the church members that host Solidarity Hub would struggle with the word 'deconstructing', wondering if it seeks to undermine the faith that is so important to them.

## Introducing *Trans Formations* Participants

My doctoral research, published in the book *Trans Formations* (Clare-Young, 2024), concerned trans theologies. I interviewed ten trans and non-binary people about their identities, experiences and theological understandings. I also engaged in autoethnography – exploring my identity, experiences and theological understandings in dialogue with participants. Participants have diverse identities on every axis – gender, age, religious belonging, socio-economic background, education, ethnicity and heritage, and more. Nevertheless participants all experienced deconstruction in a multitude of ways. I write:

> Throughout our conversations, we reflected on the limited nature and scope of our human understandings of God. Every person I spoke with questioned how much we can really know about God, considered how limited language affects the way that we talk about God, and explored how understandings of God's gender are sometimes overly impacted by these limitations. (Clare-Young, 2024, p. 144)

In *Trans Formations* I do not explore the topic in any greater depth; however, this chapter considers participants' views on deconstruction.

## Introducing Solidarity Hub

Solidarity Hub is the community among whom I currently minister. I am serving as a Special Category Minister in Cambridge. In this case, that means I minister among people at the margins of or outside established churches rather than those inside them. My ministry began with a project of attending to the voices of people in bars, clubs, shops and community spaces in the city. It developed into a new faith community called Solidarity Hub. The Hub describes itself as follows:

> Cambridge Solidarity Hub aims to reduce loneliness, increase social cohesion, work for social and eco justice, and develop authentic spirituality by creating expansive spaces that are relevant, safe, accessible and have the potential to influence change. At the heart of the Hub is a collective of dreamers and doers who gather to create new spaces for social and eco justice. (Solidarity Hub, 2024)

Members of Solidarity Hub are diverse in terms of age, gender and socio-economic background. They share a concern for social justice and an interest in theological exploration and/or deconstruction. Most members are disabled, neurodivergent and/or LGBTIQ+. These experiences of subaltern identity are woven into their theological questioning. In 2024 we had a round-table conversation about deconstruction, which is considered further in this chapter.

## Introducing *Trans-Struere*

The title of this chapter, *Trans-Struere*, is the name I have given to an idea that overlaps my doctoral research and ministry. The word 'construction' has its roots in the Latin word *construere*, which itself has roots in *con-*, meaning 'together', and *struere*, meaning 'to pile up' (Etymology Online, 2001–24). Building up knowledge and systems together is not necessarily harmful until the weight of tradition becomes constrictive rather than constructive; that is where the 'de' of deconstruction comes in. Deconstruction attempts to break down or untangle theological constructions that have become constrictive (Ward, 2003). However, in my experience, deconstruction can become a regulated and restrictive system. I wonder, then, whether *trans-struere* – a combination of the roots *trans* (meaning across, beyond, to change) and *struere* (to pile up, to build, to create) – may facilitate a more transformative ethic of theological exploration. Whereas systematic approaches prioritize logic, *trans-struere* prioritizes affect (Koivunen, 2013).

## Introducing this Chapter

I begin the main section of this chapter by exploring the trajectory – in trans-related theologies – from apologetics to theological material. This is, in effect a review of theological literature about trans identities, some of which is written by trans people. I also explain why I believe that trajectory is essential and how this chapter is a part of it. I explore *trans-struere*, drawing on conversations with research participants and Solidarity Hub members. I conclude by considering the impact and ongoing work related to *trans-struere*.

## Trajectory: From Apologetics Towards Theologies

In the literature review of my doctoral research I explored the trajectory of theologies related to trans identities. This literature review did not go on to form part of the subsequent book. Trans-related theological research is on a trajectory from apologetics towards theologies. This trajectory has four steps: (1) apologetics, (2) pastoral writing, (3) theologies about trans people, (4) theologies by trans people. Each of these steps is essential, valuable and ongoing. Nevertheless there is a need to grow this relatively new field to include more of each step rather than over-focus on apologetics.

The first step is trans-apologetic literature, which explains or defends trans identities. It is a phrase that I use to highlight the similarities between Christian apologetics and trans-apologetics – both of which seek to defend something rather than explore it more freely. While trans-apologetic writing sometimes contains theological aspects its scope is usually limited to the defence of trans identities; usually including attempts to teach about what it means to be trans and to then argue against anti-trans interpretations of scripture. Trans-apologetic literature is an essential component of the foundations of grounded and/or constructive theologies written by trans people. I do not argue that it should not exist, though I suggest that we now must move beyond it (Beardsley and O'Brien, 2016; Chalke, 2018; Savage, 2006).

The second step is pastoral writing. The experiences of trans people have been explored in the fields of clinical and pastoral care, as well as practical theology. These texts, which focus on providing clinical and pastoral care for trans people, are not explicitly theological. They do, however, highlight the connections or, more often, disconnections between religious belonging and trans well-being and, as such, show the need for more work to be done in the area of trans-related theology. In the fields of clinical and pastoral care, practitioners and scholars have explored the experiences of trans people intending to improve care (Conroy, 2010; Levy and Lo, 2013; Yarhouse, 2015; Rubano, 2016; Dowd, Beardsley and Tanis, 2018; Cornwall, 2019).

The third step is theologies about trans people. Susannah Cornwall's work has also been key in the move from understandings of trans experiences towards trans-written grounded and/or constructive theologies. In 'Recognizing the Full Spectrum of Gender', Cornwall (2012) argues effectively that there is a need for theology that recognizes trans identities, experiences and understandings.

Six years later the *Journal of Feminist Studies in Religion* issued a volume of papers initiated by a round-table conversation on Max Strassfeld's 'Transing Religious Studies'. Strassfeld (2018, p. 53) argues that rather than assuming that theology is 'cis-gendered', religious studies scholars must 'trans religious studies to engage the depths of trans religiosity'.

While many papers that respond to Strassfeld focus on religious studies rather than theology, five responses move the discussion towards trans-written theologies. Ellen T. Armour (2018, pp. 58–63) makes a persuasive argument for increased attention to trans identities and experiences. Building on ontological theory, Armour (pp. 62–3) suggests that trans-lived experiences have the potential to 'trouble' the lines between religion and non-religion and theory and praxis. By doing so, she shows the potential of trans-written theologies. Her paper is, however, an examination of trans identity rather than a conversation with trans people. As such, any arising theology would be a theology of trans phenomenology rather than a trans-written theology. What I mean is that Armour studies the phenomenon of being trans rather than listening explicitly to trans voices. This phenomenological character is typical of texts written about trans people by cis people.

A notable exception is the work of Cornwall (2022) in *Constructive Theology and Gender Variance*. In her significant monograph Cornwall takes the voices of trans people seriously while persuasively arguing for the relevance of her voice in trans theology. Drawing on themes around creatureliness, Cornwall successfully integrates the voices of trans people into an intersectional consideration of what it means to be human. In so doing, she points to the relevance of trans theology both in and beyond the lives of trans people. The global relevance of trans voices is an essential part of the argument for an increase in trans theology.

The fourth step is theologies by trans people. These are still sparse. Notably, Marcella Althaus-Reid and Lisa Isherwood's *Trans/Formations* (2009) is an early and significant contribution that weaves rich theological insights with narrative explorations of trans lives, as shared by trans and cis individuals. That hints at the importance of liberation and body theologies in the trajectory towards trans theologies. Rachel Mann's (2020) *Dazzling Darkness* and my book *Transgender. Christian. Human* (Clare-Young, 2019) are two examples of trans-written theologies that are grounded in both autobiography and apologetics. While both Mann and I point towards theological concepts, we still feel the need to defend our identities and our place in Christian theology and the church. *Trans Formations* (Clare-Young, 2024) represents my effort to move beyond autobiography into autoethnography and participatory research. This approach deepens my understanding of my identity, experiences and insights while expanding this work in trans theology to include the identities, experiences and insights of ten other trans-Christians. In the present chapter, I further broaden trans theology to bring a trans lens to a wide range of people, some of whom are not trans. In doing so, I point further to the relevance of trans voices in dialogue with cis voices in the creation of a queer, trans-theological method that has the potential for widespread impact.

## Rationale

I believe that this trajectory and, within it, the concept of *trans-struere* is vital in three contexts: (1) theological institutions, (2) churches and (3) the public square. Before moving to consider *trans-struere* directly, I briefly consider these contexts.

In theological institutions, the move towards trans-written theologies can answer misunderstandings of being trans that are rooted in the idea of a cartesian split between body and mind (Chalke, 2018). Trans apologetic theologies sometimes cite the idea that trans people are 'born in the wrong body', but this is not borne out in research on trans people. This, and other reductive understandings of transness, can only be countered by the trans people who know our bodies and minds better than anyone else. In countering limited narratives we can explicate understandings of gender more broadly and deeply. In churches the move towards trans-written theologies has the capacity to facilitate a move beyond inclusion to affirmation and leadership.

Finally, in the public square, trans-written theologies can move beyond the logic of culture war towards the effect of psychological safety. This is where *trans-struere* comes in. This concept is not so much a theology as a methodology, lens or hermeneutic. Transing deconstruction enables us to destabilise the binaries of faith/doubt, church/secular, systematic/deconstructive. Instead, authentic emotional responses of questioning, liminality and uncertainty are encouraged. The celebration of doubt and queering counters the damage of confidence-breaking self-apologetic stances and debate-stirring false objectivity.

## *Trans-Struere* in *Trans Formations*

We now turn to deconstruction, which leads to *trans-struere*, beginning with my theological research involving trans Christians. While I did not ask any specific questions about deconstruction in my research with trans Christians, the concept of theological uncertainty repeatedly arose. It was striking that this topic was explicitly linked with transition.

One participant – a non-binary genderqueer minister – wrote about their deconstruction being a natural part of the transition, explaining that:

> Things are a lot less black and white – I'm much more comfortable sitting in grey areas and much more comfortable in not knowing, in not being sure – I think that's really important. So much of my early

> faith was all about 'Well this is this and this is that and there's no in between', whereas now it's so much more the case that there are things I don't know and I'm probably not ever going to know, and that's OK, and that actually my faith is made richer because of that.

Prior to their transition this participant experienced religion as a context within which there was no room for doubt. They came to realize that doubt was a key part of faith. This trajectory towards doubt moved from doubt as being impossible, through the possibility of doubt, to doubt as good, as a core component of faith. They further argued that 'Where you begin the journey is significant. Being non-binary reshapes my understanding of God, as it influences how I interpret God's actions, God's church and God's people.' This is a clear description of standpoint theory. This participant came to understand their location – their viewpoint – as a non-binary person as central to their understanding. As such, being non-binary informs their theology, anthropology and practices. Their ability to understand God from that location of being a non-binary person includes a non-binary questioning of God. This non-binary queering lens repeats through their understandings of God's essence, character, actions, church and people.

The same person wondered if one day they would need to rescue queer kin from the constriction of the church, saying:

> On the days when I really despair for the church that I'm working for, and everything, I remember that there are so many LGBTI people who just need a way out, and if nothing else, I'm in a burning building making sure that people get out before the roof collapses.

This raises the question of a second type of location – or viewpoint – in the conduct of deconstructive theology. Can deconstruction occur from within the church or is the church a burning building? Can we fix the roof or do we need to go outside? Is this effort predominantly about bringing people into the church – or a particular view of faith (or getting them out of it) or a specific view? I do not have answers to these questions or think I should. Instead they are key questions to hold in mind as we continue to consider deconstruction.

Another non-binary person felt that a differing hermeneutic perspective was inherent to all subaltern – or marginalized – people, not only queer people. They explained that:

> I think it's in a way ... being queer, but also just the experience of being part of any kind of marginalized group. I am more and more moving

> away from a mainstream hermeneutics to hermeneutics of social justice in all its aspects, becoming more and more aware of intersectional elements of theology, which I think is really growing on the edge, and for me, queer theology.

For this person, intersectionality was vital to theological hermeneutics (Crenshaw, 1991). They felt that queer theology was not only about considering queer perspectives but, more widely, considering all experiences of oppression and how they overlap or combine. For them, social justice was not only about action but also about hermeneutics. Theological research and questioning should be done with a lens of social justice.

It was not only non-binary participants who had things to say on deconstruction. Three trans people had striking perspectives on how their theological interpretations have changed in transition. An older woman – who describes herself as having a trans history – said that:

> Transition was what prodded me into asking the questions ... I think before I still had a bit of this picture of God as a man with a long white beard sitting on a cloud. It wasn't that I exactly thought that but I never unthought it from being a child ... We can only understand God in fragments ... I would say that God is to be mischievous.

Another trans woman explained that she wrote a play about God wearing a dress to rescue God from the constriction that they experienced in the gender-conforming laws and practices of the Hebrews. In both cases, the use of play in deconstruction is apparent. I love describing God as a verb, 'to be mischievous'. This mischievous nature of God is further reflected by the idea of God dressing up to escape cis-hetero-patriarchal normativity.

A young trans man also implied that deconstruction was essential for them and was an ongoing process:

> My relationship with faith feels quite ambiguous at the moment because it's certainly shifted over the last four years since I first came out as a queer person ... I've started to have broader theological questions, partly through queerness, but I think also partly through being black as well. I have questions around interpretations of the Bible, and lots of reflections on where things have been abused or misused or in harmful ways. I guess I'm trying to decide whether there is anything still good, whether there is still something valuable here or whether it all needs to go. I currently feel like there is something good.

This reflection clearly indicates the harm that constrictive theology can do. The young man is considering journeying away from church, from God, from scripture altogether due to the narrow interpretations of scripture that he has been exposed to as a young, trans, queer, black man. However, he continues to wrestle with scripture:

> Passages that talk about like sexual morality, I don't really know how you could or would redeem those, because first of all, I don't think there's a coherent sex ethic in the Bible anyway, but I think secondly, like from the bits that we do get in parts of the new Testament, I don't really agree and I don't think it's healthy, which feels like a very scary thing to say as someone who grew up evangelical and it's like, God's word, and there's not really room to question those things. I guess I mentioned the sexual and morality passages in particular because I think that has been significant to me and my journey of coming out has been moving away from that sense of regret, like repressing things and desires, that part of me, and realizing that actually there's a lot of life and fullness in being authentic to those things, obviously within respectful and consensual boundaries.

For him, deconstruction is a journey from regret, repression and limitations to a theology informed by travelling towards the fullness of life. He argued that for the Christian church to have any significance, it needed to deeply explore structural injustice and question why it is so apparent in scripture, the contemporary church and the wider world.

In light of these contributions, deconstruction is not primarily about breaking things down but, instead, about what effect is stirred up to trouble the gaps formed by constricted logic. The influence of grey and rainbow hues disrupts the binary logic of black and white. The journey's transformative nature unsettles the academic logic of objectivity. The presence of the firefighting non-binary priest challenges the ecclesial logic of control. The force of social justice activism shakes the mainstream hermeneutical logic. The act of questioning destabilizes the logic of certainty. The symbolism of her dress subverts the concept of a male God. The power of authenticity and fullness confronts the principle of biblical inerrancy.

## *Trans-Struere* in Solidarity Hub

While completing my PhD, I became a minister in the United Reformed Church in a Special Category ministry role. Out of this role a group called Solidarity Hub emerged. Several people in the group have expressed that they are deconstructing or deconstructed. Solidarity Hub currently consists of around fifteen people, many of whom are neurodivergent and/or LGBTIQ+. Recently we discussed what we mean when we talk about deconstruction. Members did not feel that deconstruction was destructive. Instead, one person affirmed:

> It's the dismantling of concepts including beliefs, values and communities, sort of picking apart and looking for what's worth keeping and what's worth recycling. It's not just like tear it down, although it can be that as well, and that's also OK. But that would be different, that would be just walking away from pain. I think there's something about the fact that you're naming it that that implies you're still engaging. If you're deconstructing something, you haven't turned your back on it.

This intervention is central to my reconfiguration of deconstruction as a *trans-struere*. This person destabilizes the binary logic of faith vs deconstruction that I often encounter in established churches. Instead, they suggest that deconstruction is a deeper engagement of faith. By wrestling with faith, similarly to Israel wrestling with a stranger or angel (Gen. 32), deconstructs refuse to shy away from conflict, instead fighting through it to seek new names for the concepts that seem alien to them.

Many of our group enjoy knitting or crocheting, so naturally a term related to wool entered the conversation. Someone said: 'I went to a talk a few years ago where they talked about unravelling, and I liked that because they talked about unravelling, but then at some point in the future, there'll be a re-ravelling.' This multi-sensory image enables a theology and practice driven by affect – rather than logic. Can you imagine the sensation of slowly unravelling a tangle of wool? There are knots when the thread must be woven under, over, through and between. Once unravelled, you must begin rewinding the wool into a ball so you can use it. This labour of love involves more knots, some bits that need to be unravelled and rewound repeatedly. It is a lifelong process.

Another person used the analogy of refurbishment, explaining that:

> as soon as you think you've got all the answers it's long past time to start breaking this all down. I don't normally like analogies but the best that I do like is to say that this is like refurbishing a house and you

> check the parts of the house, you see bits you can reuse in the rebuilding and you even make sure that the extension is in keeping, or in the same character as the house. It's on the same foundation, but then you kick in some of the other bits because they aren't right. There's a need for lots of change.

Similarly to ravelling, this is an emotive image. Imagine taking a sledgehammer or wrecking ball to the bits of theology that do not work for you. Then rebuilding brick by brick ensures that your new theology is in keeping with your core personal values. Smooth plaster carefully into the gaps, making sure you place an air brick to allow ideas to circulate.

Another used a nature-based image:

> Change is a constant thing. We go through autumn and winter. Bulbs don't flower all year round. There is a season to everything and you don't get rebirth without death either, so it's a cycle of belief. The continual death of the gods is essential. As soon as you feel you've got a certain god, you've got full knowledge of it, perhaps it's time to kill it and see what happens. And you know, if the Christ is real, then killing him is necessary. Human conceptions of God prior to that point are not good enough and need to be broken by and within humanity. As soon as you get to a static conception of God, break it because that's not God.

This brings Christology into our considerations of deconstruction. This person is queering the question: 'Why did Jesus have to die?' For them, divinity continuously shifts, whereas theological constructions risk becoming static or binary. They locate this transformation in nature, referring to seasons and the growth and death of plants. In doing so they inherently relate deconstructive theology to ancient Celtic and pagan religious practices of engaging with nature hands-on. What would it be like to do theology while jumping in a pile of autumn leaves or planting a spring bulb in the damp soil?

The idea of deconstruction is biblical. Someone said:

> When I read the Bible, I increasingly see a God that changes. In the garden, there's a God that walks around. When deciding whether or not to trash Sodom, there's a God that's open to argument. You have a God that wins wars and a God that's a pacifist. A God in the ether and a God that is man. There's this shift of character throughout the story. It's like searching for a shape-shifter. So it's perfectly OK to completely change your mind about God. The Bible does it every few years so it's sure OK for you to do it every few months.

This person raises a key theological debate: whether God can change (O'Hanlon, 1987). They point to the idea that human conceptions of God – be they in the Bible or our own lives – are continuously changing, which is OK. This recognition of ongoing theological transformation weaves threads of understanding between and around a God who contains multitudes, simultaneously being many things in many times and places. In other words, while God – existing beyond our human timeline – may not be subject to change, God can encompass multiple possibilities, even inconsistencies, within Godself, including those that are temporal and those that are atemporal.

As we began to get bogged down in metaphysics, someone helpfully suggested:

> The thing about ideas is that they are precarious. Church is precarious. It is always very close to falling apart. Churches want to be so certain, but I think they are very precarious actually. They are just one moment away from falling apart.

I reflected that:

> I'm seeing this image of a church made of glass and there are people inside and there are people outside and the people inside have rocks and the people outside have rocks. And the people outside are trying to like make beautiful patterns with the rocks to make sense of something and the people inside are throwing the rocks at each other, and at the people outside, and the glass church is going to fall apart. It's precarious because of how it causes people to act.

Near the end of our time together, someone suggested that 'Maybe hope is a process.'

Therefore, as a group, Solidarity Hub queried the logic of solid concepts, unchanging buildings, static time, an unchanging God, a strong church and a confident hope. Instead we explored the effect of unravelling and re-ravelling, of seasons, of a changing mind, of precarity and of the process of hope.

## Conclusion

Therefore, what might a praxis of *trans-struere* – which queers the space between certainty and deconstruction – be like?

Perhaps it might feel like knitting, crocheting or sewing a multi-hued, tactile understanding of God and what it means to be human, tenderly unravelling that understanding once in a while so that the raw materials can be reused. That might mean tentatively and carefully phrasing our understandings of God, being clear that they are open to question and change, and actively accompanying people in asking those questions without asserting definitive answers.

Perhaps it might feel like going on a journey with a pocket full of seeds, planting them in the ground in the places we pass through, acknowledging that some will die and some will grow, and not being too worried about whether or not we, personally, will ever see the flowers in full bloom. That might mean trying out new spiritual practices in our local contexts but not getting too worried about the outcomes of numbers. Instead, practising for the process of practising, not for a predetermined result. It might also mean practising seasonality – recognizing that there is a time for rest, backing off and solitude, just as there is a time for action, moving forward and dialogue.

Perhaps it might feel like spending time in and around a precarious, transparent, glass house of faith, carefully putting down our stones so that we might honour something of God in the space, the people in it and the people outside it. That might mean making the boundaries of faith spaces more porous, prioritizing dialogue over monologue and discussion over teaching. It might mean spending more time asking questions and less time asserting truths. It might mean that worship is upbeat and honouring rather than negative and shame-inducing.

It may feel like engaging in the process of hope by putting out the fires surrounding subaltern, marginalized kin by living out authenticity and fullness, by engaging in activism. In practice that might mean actively speaking out about social justice issues and speaking up for people who are subjected to culture wars, such as trans people. It might mean being more honest about our views, particularly when they diverge from the group-think of our churches. It might mean protesting or participating in movements, working actively for change.

These practices are not practices of *struere*. They are not piling up new traditions on top of old ones. Neither are they practices of deconstruction – tearing the building down. Instead these practices are *trans-struere*. Practices of change, of movement, of growth. Practices that bring good news.

This practice of *trans-struere* is not theology or practice in and of itself. Instead it is a theological method. It is about how we think theologically and how that theological thinking affects our actions. Thus, by unravelling and reravelling, for example, we might discover that some of our understandings of God were limited, and we might be able to reform new understandings to broaden our theology and enliven our practice.

By planting seeds we might discover limited ecclesiology, and we might be able to reform new churches to expand our ecclesiology and enliven our practice. By recognizing the precarity of our spaces, systems, and structure and worship, we might discover things about the limited ways we worship. We could reform new faith spaces to broaden our worship and enliven our practice. By engaging in the process of hope, we might discover things about our soteriology – our ideas around what salvation means – that are limited, and we might be able to reform our theories to broaden our grace and enliven our practice.

In other words, trans-theology extends beyond the experiences of trans people. It centres on amplifying marginalized voices, encouraging everyone to engage in a deeper, more expansive understanding of God. This approach invites all to embrace a transformative journey of hope, fostering inclusivity and mutual growth within spiritual and theological spaces.

## References

Althaus-Reid, Marcella and Lisa Isherwood (2009), *Trans/Formations*, London: SCM Press.

Armour, Ellen T. (2018), 'Transing the Study of Religion: A (Christian) Theological Response', *Journal of Feminist Studies in Religion* 34, no. 1, pp. 58–63.

Beardsley, Christina and Michelle O'Brien, eds (2016), *This is My Body: Hearing the Theology of Transgender Christians*, London: Darton, Longman & Todd.

Chalke, Steve (2018), *The Gender Agenda: Towards a Biblical Theology on Gender Identity, Reassignment and Confirmation*, London: Oasis Books.

Clare-Young, Alex (2019), *Transgender. Christian. Human*, Glasgow: Wild Goose Publications.

Clare-Young, Alex (2024), *Trans Formations: Grounding Theology in Trans and Non-Binary Lives*, London: SCM Press.

Conroy, Melissa (2010), 'Treating Transgendered Children: Clinical Methods and Religious Mythology', *Zygon* 45, no. 2, pp. 301–16.

Cornwall, Susannah (2012), 'Recognizing the Full Spectrum of Gender: Transgender, Intersex and the Futures of Feminist Theology', *Feminist Theology* 20, no. 3, pp. 236–41.

Cornwall, Susannah (2019), 'Healthcare Chaplaincy and Spiritual Care for Trans People: Envisaging the Future', *Health and Social Care Chaplaincy* 7, no. 1, pp. 8–27.

Cornwall, Susannah (2022), *Constructive Theology and Gender Variance: Transformative Creatures*, Cambridge: Cambridge University Press.

Crenshaw, Kimberle (1991), 'Mapping the Margins: Intersectionality, Identity Politics, and Violence against Women of Color', *Stanford Law Review* 43, no. 6, pp. 1241–99.

Dowd, Chris, Christina Beardsley and Justin Tanis, eds (2018), *Transfaith: A Transgender Pastoral Resource*, London: Darton, Longman & Todd.

Etymology Online (2001–24), 'Construct', at https://www.etymonline.com/word/construct, accessed 01.12.2024.

Harding, Sandra (2001), 'Introduction: Theory as a Site of Political, Philosophic and Scientific Debate', in *The Feminist Standpoint Theory Reader: Intellectual and Political Controversies*, edited by Sandra Harding, New York: Routledge, pp. 1–15.

Koivunen, Anu (2013), 'Yes We Can? The Promises of Affect for Queer Scholarship', *Kvinder, Køn og Forskning* [Women, Gender and Research] 3–4, pp. 19–30.

Levy, Denise L. and Jessica R. Lo (2013), 'Transgender, Transsexual, and Gender Queer Individuals with a Christian Upbringing: The Process of Resolving Conflict Between Gender Identity and Faith', *Journal of Religion & Spirituality in Social Work: Social Thought* 32, no. 1, pp. 60–83.

Mann, Rachel (2020), *Dazzling Darkness*, Glasgow: Wild Goose Publications.

O'Hanlon, Gerry (1987), 'Does God Change? – H. U. von Balthasar on the Immutability of God', *Irish Theological Quarterly* 53, no. 3, pp. 161–83.

Rubano, Craig (2016), 'Where do the Mermaids Stand? Toward a "Gender-Creative" Pastoral Sensitivity', *Pastoral Psychology* 65, no. 6, pp. 821–34.

Savage, Helen (2006), 'Changing Sex?: Transsexuality and Christian Theology', doctoral dissertation, Theology and Religion Department, Faculty of Arts and Humanities, Durham University, at http://etheses.dur.ac.uk/3364, accessed 01.12.2024.

Solidarity Hub (2024), 'Who Are We', at https://www.solidarityhub.co.uk, accessed 01.12.2024.

Strassfeld, Max (2018), 'Transing Religious Studies', *Journal of Feminist Studies in Religion* 34, no. 1, pp. 37–53.

Ward, Graham (2003), 'Deconstructive Theology', in *The Cambridge Companion to Postmodern Theology*, edited by Kevin J. Vanhoozer, Cambridge: Cambridge University Press, pp. 76–91.

Yarhouse, Mark A. (2015), *Understanding Gender Dysphoria: Navigating Transgender Issues in a Changing Culture*, Downers Grove, IL: IVP Academic.

# PART 3

# Poimenics and Activism

# 7

# Gay Bodies and God: Envisioning the Fundamental Principles of an LGBTIQ+-Affirming Theopastoral Competence

JOSEPH N. GOH

## Introduction

Informed and guided by the embodied Christian spiritualities of Malaysian Christian gay men, this chapter envisions several fundamental principles of an LGBTIQ+-affirming theopastoral competence. Embodied Christian spiritualities focus on the pivotal role of God in human lives, incorporate and integrate bodily experiences and are dialogical, outward-looking and other-centred (Blée, 2022). In the various ways in which they are lived out by men who are unapologetically gay and Christian, these spiritualities divulge how these men experience an affirming God with whom they have an intimate relationship through their corporeal existence. I am convinced that human experiences can be crucial sources and resources for an understanding of the person of God and God's operations in human lives (Kwok, 2000, pp. 38–50; Cheng, 2011, pp. 11–20), mindful that 'God chose to fully experience the reality of living in a human body, completely enfleshed' (Voelkel, 2017, p. 20).

I acknowledge that I draw solely on gay men's experiences and insights in this chapter and that there are critical differences in LGBTIQ+ experiences. I am hoping, however, that what I offer will also resonate with and benefit others of diverse genders, sexes and sexualities who do not identify as gay. Additionally, this chapter does not proffer a 'gay essence' or 'gay universal truth' or a specific 'gay spirituality'. The three men introduced below – indeed all gay men – do not share identical performances of gender, sexuality and faith. Instead, what appears is a snapshot from a spectrum of individuals for whom identities of gender, sexuality and faith are permitted to coalesce and inform each other. I am also cognizant that 'the gay self is not an incontestable truth' (Stuart, 2003, p. 28). A theopastoral project that leans on gay men's experiences and insights may be fitting and fruitful. Still, it must also continue to open itself up to ongoing discernment and critique.

I use 'theopastoral' and 'theopastoralities' to refer to the mutually informing synergy or integration between the theological and the pastoral in Christianity, whereby theological thought is informed by pastoral care and pastoral outreach is grounded in theological notions. My belief is that theopastoralities hold immense potential to support the life journeys of LGBTIQ+ Christians, but only if they are (re)shaped according to a trajectory of radical and courageous equity, respect and openness. An LGBTIQ+-affirming theology creates LGBTIQ+-affirming pastoral care and action, and vice versa. My coinage of the term 'theopastoral competence' borrows from the notion of cross-cultural competence, which Rehman Abdulrehman (2024) defines as:

> the ability to identify barriers to the ability to relate and empathize with people we perceive to be different, so we can help them like a fellow human, and a member of our community. In our understanding of our biases and the legitimacy of other worldviews, we can engage with others in a more equitable and democratic way that does not place ourselves above others, or vice versa. When we remove the barriers that come with bias and false and stereotypical interpretations, we are better able to relate and work with those we perceive to be different, from the common platform of a human experience. (p. 5)

Moreover, '*cultural competence* is an active, developmental, and ongoing process and is aspirational rather than achieved' (Sue and Sue, 2015, p. 46; original emphasis). Therefore, I interpret theopastoral competence as an ongoing aspiration towards fostering more significant equity and empathy in human society, building the capability, capacity and potential of Christian theological and pastoral systems to value all manner of human diversity, abolishing religious arrogance and manipulation, eliminating destructive notions and assumptions pertaining to human lives, and generating conditions that foster authentic and effective human growth and relationships.

I provide a brief outline of Malaysian LGBTIQ+ communities before explaining 'rebellion' as the theological rationale and trajectory behind the writing of this chapter. Thereafter, I analyse and interpret selected narratives of Christian gay men 'Henri', 'Artisan' and 'Aadesh' on their embodied spiritualities.[1] I end by presenting some thoughts on how such spiritualities can inform an LGBTIQ+-affirming theopastoral competence, which can then be instructional for any Christian community that is committed to the non-judgemental and affirming spirit of Christ even as it struggles to make sense of diverse genders, sexes and sexualities.

## Malaysia: Religious Conservatism and LGBTIQ+ Communities

Gender and sexual identities in the Malaysian context, as is the case in many other Southeast Asian countries, are often blurred and/or conflated (Jackson, 2003). Similarly, demeaning Malaysian terms such as *pondan*, *bapok*, *ah qua* and *pottaipayeh* are used indiscriminately for both people with same-sex attraction and people who are gender diverse. Bearing meanings that are similar to 'sissy', 'faggot' or 'poof', these terms relegate LGBTIQ+ people to realms of abnormality and iniquity. In response, Malaysians who are unwilling or unable to align themselves with the obligatory matrix of cis-heteronormative embodiment readily choose appropriate identity markers from a suite of categories under 'LGBTIQ+'. They do so not as passive clones of global North LGBTIQ+ embodiments but as Malaysians of Malay, Chinese, Indian, native, indigenous, 'mixed' and 'Other' ancestry who are mired in the particularities of a disabling environment.

As a profoundly conservative multi-ethnic and multi-religious country of 34 million people with a 64% Muslim majority (Countrymeters, 2024), Malaysia imposes both secular and religious laws on the gendered and sexual lives of its citizens. The Malaysian Penal Code (Commissioner of Law Revision, Malaysia, 1997) proscribes oral and anal sex for people of various gender and sexual identities and expressions, but this prohibition holds particular salience for gay men. *Syariah* (Islamic) laws bear specific stipulations for the criminalization of Muslim gay men, lesbian women and transgender people, often with horrific consequences such as flagellation (Commissioner of Law Revision, Malaysia, 2006). Christianity is a minority religion at 9% of the population (Countrymeters, 2024) and has no direct political impact on the country's governance. Nonetheless, its disapproval of both same-sex sexual activity and gender-affirming transformations mirrors and supports homonegative and trans-negative Muslim dictates.

Over the years, I have become acquainted with LGBTIQ+ Christians who have completely relinquished their faith, chiefly due to the homonegative and trans-negative behaviours of churches. Some eschew any form of institutional affiliation but customize life-giving spiritualities for themselves. There are others for whom regular church attendance is a non-negotiable aspect of their faith despite having to 'pass' as cisgender and heterosexual or avoid any conversation concerning non-normative genders, anatomies and sexualities. This chapter is devoted to those whose spiritual sensibilities fall under the latter two categories.

## Rebellion: A Way to Theologize

The Christian opprobrium of LGBTIQ+ expressions – and identities in some cases – is largely based on a seeming impasse of biblical prohibition, namely the infamous 'texts of terror' (Trible, 1984), which are read and weaponized through the country's various languages. In this regard, Malaysian biblical exegesis refuses to 'recognize that theology from the Biblical times is always time-bound, historically based[,] culturally conditioned and socially constructed' (Yap, 2020, p. 32). Malaysian churches also react strongly to an imagined onslaught of same-sex marriages in the country (NECF Malaysia, 2007).

A certain degree of dismissiveness towards LGBTIQ+ experiences exists in many Asian theologies,[2] of which Malaysian theologies are a part, which paradoxically claims to accord privilege to, draw on and respond to the everyday experiences of the people of Asia. In their varied forms, Asian theologies champion the idea that 'the totality of life is the raw material of theology' (Song, 1979, p. 15), and are 'carried out in conversation with the broader vision of the community and more subaltern versions of theologies of the people' (Clarke, 2012, p. 5). Indispensable theological resources include 'the cultures of peoples, the history of their struggles ... economic and political realities ... stories of oppressed people crying for justice, freedom, dignity, life, and solidarity' (Office of Theological Concerns, 2000, p. 29). Hence, 'any theology the church develops cannot be pure theory, but must be a deep conviction which has grown from experience and has been clarified by the needs and challenges of the church and society' (Athyal, 1995, p. 84). Moreover, as the Malaysian theologian Albert Sundaraj Walters (2002) acknowledges, 'theology is a living experience [which] must speak to the actual questions people are asking in the midst of their dilemmas; their hopes, aspirations and achievements; their doubts, despair and suffering' (p. 242). A significant defining feature of Asian theologies is their deep rootedness in all forms of embodied experience.

I argue, however, that these rather grandiose claims fall short of their aspirations. A general theological disregard of LGBTIQ+ issues, circumstances, experiences and knowledges is evident: not all embodiments and experiences qualify for, or meet the expectations of, the theological enterprise. Admittedly, LGBTIQ+ perspectives in Christianity are growing around the globe, as can be attested to in the works of numerous contemporary theologians, as well as religionists, psychologists, sociologists and social workers (Althaus-Reid, 2000; Cheng, 2011; Levy and Reeves, 2011; Boppana and Gross, 2019; Shore-Goss and Goh, 2020; Isherwood and Quero, 2021; Cornelio and Dagle, 2022; Rubano, 2022). There has also been a modest rise in LGBTIQ+-affirming theologies in Asia in recent years (Gaikwad and Ninan, 2017; Goh, 2021; Kuruvilla, 2017; Suleeman and Udampoh, 2019), including the occasional non-affirming theological piece that peddles celibacy and sexless friendships for people of same-sex attraction (Yeo, 2021), and subtly reinscribes sexual self-denial as the noblest response to sexual 'deviations'. Still, gender and sexual diversities are not common topics in Asian theological efforts. Indeed, as Patrick S. Cheng (2011) notes, 'LGBT lives and experiences have been excluded from traditional theological discourse' (p. 18).

Nonetheless, it is not only in Asian theologies that LGBTIQ+ experiences are regarded with such triviality. What emerges as somewhat peculiar is that most, if not all, local churches outwardly adopt a welcoming stance towards both closeted and out LGBTIQ+ people and include them in various faith-based activities – an ostensible display of 'inclusion'. Nevertheless, these churches also preach against the 'sins' of homosexuality and 'transgenderism', offer church-based reparative therapy under the guise of 'counselling' the 'sexually broken', promote a 'love the sinner, hate the sin' mentality and idealize celibacy among its LGBTIQ+ fold (Goh, 2016; 2018). Many Malaysian churches welcome LGBTIQ+ people into their spaces in the same breath that they denounce expressions of gender and sexual diversity.

This double-speak of acceptance and rejection exposes the ambiguity of 'inclusion', 'support' and 'welcome' in any theopastoral approach that has yet to attain a critical self-reflexive understanding of this inherent contradiction. The actual lived experiences of LGBTIQ+ Christians are dismissed in favour of an insistence on cis-heteronormative Christian ideals. 'Inclusion', 'support' and 'welcome' as articulated by these churches lack any semblance of genuine affirmation, which gestures towards 'an attitude of total and unconditional acceptance' (Goh, 2019, p. 189). It is a superficial embrace of LGBTIQ+ congregants that seeks to edit their subjectivities and an inability and a disinclination to battle for their full recognition in sacred communal spaces.

If the pastoral ministry shapes theological thought while pastoral outreach is rooted in theological principles, yet either/both theological and pastoral dimensions of Christianity remain antagonistic, dismissive, or indifferent towards LGBTIQ+ people, their knowledges, experiences and needs will inevitably be excluded from or inadequately addressed in theopastoral initiatives. These theopastoral patterns of disregard prompt the writing of this chapter, which aims to address them: 'Turning toward the body hermeneutically is ... an act of epistemological and redemptive rebellion', particularly the LGBTIQ body, as 'it exposes the veiled oppressive agenda of centuries of knowledge production made captive to the tyranny of the unitive center' (Sprinkle, 2009, p. 65). By focusing on the embodied epistemologies of gay men, I participate in such a rebellion.

## The Gay Body and God

Marcella Althaus-Reid (2000) aptly describes the synergy between sexuality and faith when she postulates that 'It is from human sexuality that theology starts to search and understand the sacred, and not vice versa' (p. 146). Henri, Artisan and Aadesh draw on their sexualities as a sort of starting point to know, understand and speak of God *as gay men.* In their conversations with me, each man brings to sharp relief an intimate relationship with God that flows into distinctive visualizations of God and the lavish presence of God in his life, a God who is lauded through his gay body.

For Henri, a 30-year-old self-described 'liberal Anglican' Tamil-Indian Malaysian and frequent church attendee, the idea of an absolutely affirming God forms the basis of his meaningful relationship with God:

> Me being gay is part of my relationship with God ... I realize that as a human being, yes, I have free will, I have the ability to make my choices and to live my life, but without God ... who sustains me, or without God who's there to guide me ... Without that in my life, I would be completely lost, and I wouldn't be able to, I mean there wouldn't be a purpose in my life.

Being gay is a conduit that connects Henri with God, allowing him to collaborate with God, who 'sustains' and 'guides' him in navigating and making sense of life's vicissitudes and 'purpose'. Hence the gay body is 'not a sensual obstacle to the moral and religious life; it [is] a vehicle to connect with God' (Shore-Goss, 2002, p. 12). That Henri's gay identity establishes only '*part* of [his] relationship with God' (emphasis added) suggests that his sexuality is a significant but not an all-encompassing element of his faith, and that his relationship with God probably comprises elements aside from his sexuality.

Henri realizes that the 'free will' that God has bestowed on him 'as a human being' is inextricably linked to a plethora of 'choices' with which he is tasked to chart his course in life, including options of repressing and/or cultivating his sexuality and faith. In order 'to live [his] life' to an optimal degree, he knows that he must remain steadfast as a gay and Christian man, a resolution that coheres with his relationship with God. Henri's embodied spirituality reveals him as 'someone who dares to embrace the totality of life in its relational form and its vulnerability, that is, its openness to being touched and changed by what is experienced' (Wu, 2000, p. 85). In other words, his is a transformative spirituality. Being open to God gives meaning to his being gay, and being open to his sexuality provides meaning to his relationship with God.

At a particular juncture during our conversation Henri recounted to me an experience of listening to a homonegative sermon in his church. Despite this pernicious episode, God remains crucial to his life journey:

> God is everywhere ... God is love, God is omnipotent, omnipresent ... God is this being, who, well, 'being' not being the best word to use to describe, but God is this being who ordains everything in life and especially my life, and I cannot run away from this presence of God, no matter how I try.

Henri discovers that God's love, omnipotence and omnipresence inspire him to continue being who he is. The articulation of these divine traits bespeaks his belief in a God who 'ordains everything in [his] life', including the mapping of his life as a gay man. This is an embodied spirituality that lies at odds with the more common pseudo-theological rhetoric that same-sex attraction is a distortion of God's plan; that conversion to cis-heterosexuality is attainable when a gay man collaborates tenaciously with an all-loving, all-powerful and all-present God. His enduring bond with God as a gay man disrupts the persistent inclination of churches 'to legislate which bodies are fit to "God's grace" and which ones are not' (Córdova Quero, 2020, p. 155).

I propose that the tentativeness with which he describes God as a 'being' could be significant. In his mind, 'being' could possibly allude to human beings who adhere unyieldingly to the belief that being gay and Christian are incompatible. In contrast, God exceeds the limitations and prejudices of '*human* beings' as a *Divine* '[B]eing' who is unconditionally accepting and affirming of human diversity. For Henri, to 'run away' from being a gay man is to flee the 'presence of God'. It is to turn his back on 'the *indelibility of divine imprint*' (Goh, Meneses and Messer, 2019, p. 178; original emphasis) on his life as a gay man.

Artisan, a Cantonese Chinese Malaysian and Pentecostal Christian in his late forties who frequents church services, expresses his faith in a God who is unreservedly accepting of him as a gay man:

> I believe he accepted, for who am I. Totally accept ... to a lot of people, Christianity is a religion, but to me, it's a personal relationship between me and God ... there are many things that happen in my life, then I draw my strength through prayers, through reading the Bible, and sometime interaction between fellow Christians, and this does actually help me and ... I feel he's everywhere. I know that he's with me, when the time that I'm down, when I'm fearful, or when I'm in danger, I always believe that he's nearby, he's around me.

In expressing the practical performances of Christianity in his life – such as prayer, scripture reading and community fellowship – Artisan explains the material elements of Christianity that sustain his relationship with God. He does not sense God in an abstract or impersonal manner but through concrete, embodied personal and communal human experiences, chiefly in periods of low mood, fear and 'danger'. That God is 'everywhere' is sensed and discerned through the gay body. As such, 'the body is not seen as an inconvenience that battles with the spirit, it is rather the flesh and blood in which God acts in the world' (Isherwood, 2024, p. 125).

Artisan supplies additional depictions of God that frame his relationship with God:

> He's like a father to me, you know, because as a father, his love for me is never-ending, and no doubt, I can't see him with my physical eye, but I can really know deep in me that he is there for me all the time ... He could be a friend at one time, he could be the father at one time, he could be the strength at times, or the power ... He's awesome, yeah, he is ... powerful ... he's divine. He's worthy, he's powerful, he's mighty, he's omnipresence.

Akin to Henri, Artisan sees God as the personification of unremitting love, a love that he parallels with fatherhood and friendship. Such a personification is essential for gay men like him, who are often assailed by theopastoral pronouncements that a proper and valid relationship with God is contingent on a cis-heteronormative identity (Kolysh, 2017; Campos et al., 2022). This unmitigated love of God that Artisan experiences translates further into images of God as 'strength' and 'power', which I suggest are vital for anchoring him in self-empowerment, self-confidence and resilience as a Christian gay man amid the disapproving stance of many Malaysian churches towards people of diverse genders, sexes and sexualities.

That Artisan is able to 'really know deep inside himself' the abiding presence of God through personal experience is vital. Instead of attempting to perceive God in corporeal form, he relies on 'deep' human experiences that index the presence of God in his life – including his life as a gay man – in which 'God expands, is not limited by the control of hegemonic tradition, and is not regulated by sanitized experiences' (Pádua Freire, 2021, p. 19). These experiences enable Artisan to ascribe further attributes such as 'awesome', 'divine', 'worthy', 'mighty' and 'omnipresen[t]' to God which, although ubiquitous in Malaysian Pentecostal traditions and therefore familiar to Artisan, reflect his heartfelt connection with God.

Aadesh is a 41-year-old Malayalee-Indian-Malaysian who identifies as spiritual and non-practising Roman Catholic. He informs me during our conversation that he no longer participates in church services. This decision is due mainly to 'the rejection of [the] church' of his sexuality and based on a profound reflection on the nexus between his sexuality and faith:

> I think gay people, because of the rejection of church, are more willing to find a truer sense of God and ... because of rejection of religion, God in relationship to their lives. I think all the structures start falling apart around them in religion, and then they start asking themselves, what am I left with? How do I create meaning with God or with spirituality in myself without these structures?

In asking a series of questions that pertain to the collapsing 'structures' of 'religion' in the lives of 'gay people', Aadesh is actually interrogating the failure of religious teachings and institutions in guiding and supporting him personally as a Christian gay man. His experience of Christian rejection due to his sexuality is, I submit, also one of abandonment, and he is left to fend for himself in matters of spirituality. Rather than relinquishing Christianity altogether, Aadesh creates spiritual meaning from this rejection and abandonment. He acknowledges that 'the rejection of church [and] religion' can be a fortuitous incident for him as it propels him towards the meaning-making and crafting of a personalized spirituality that prompts his search for 'a truer sense of God' and which nourishes and sustains him as a gay man. His experience demonstrates a 're-negotiation [that] has allowed the invisible presence of the True God to reveal herself more clearly – and queerly' (Buechel, 2015, p. 153) in the gay body.

Aadesh's description of God's omnipresence is very similar to that of Henri's and Artisan's, but he also includes other interesting perspectives:

> God is … this force, this field that is present in all of us … glimpses of which I see when I see people's goodness … God is the God that exists inside all of us, and when I understand that, I understand the world in a very different way … God has become far more personal … I find God existing inside of me.

Aadesh does not provide any explicit explanation for his use of 'force' and 'field' to describe his experience of God. Still, the notion of 'force-field' – in a segregated form in his narrative – suggests that God is, for him, a barrier of power and protection against manifestations of homonegativity, to which Aadesh is no stranger, as he made clear to me at various points during our conversation. What is notable here is his idea of a multiply incarnated God, one who 'exists inside all of us', a God who manifests godself in a proliferation of ways.

That he is able to perceive God in the 'express[ions]' of 'people's goodness' affirms that 'bodies are theologically revelatory' (Sprinkle, 2009, p. 80) – or perhaps as I see it, that bodies *can be* theologically revelatory. A homonegative God in theopastoral structures has given way to a 'far more personal' God who is encountered in human goodness in Aadesh's everyday life. It is possible that in this regard Aadesh has supportive and affirming acquaintances in mind. I suggest that his theological insight prompts him towards a renewed vision of 'the world' from an ethical perspective, in which he realizes that as someone who 'find[s] God existing inside of [him]', he is capable of both showing and hiding the presence of God through his actions.

## Fundamental Principles of an LGBTIQ+-Affirming Theopastoral Competence

Henri, Artisan and Aadesh understand that their 'deviant' and 'iniquitous' embodiments can actually form a powerful nexus between them and God, thereby signalling the reality that 'the first-hand experiences of sexually marginalized people should be respected and that they are the *subjects*, not the *objects*, of theology' (Wu, 2015, p. 35; emphasis added). By inviting God in God's various manifestations into the intimate spaces of their lives, their gay bodies generate embodied spiritualities that make meaning of sexuality through faith and faith through sexuality. These spiritualities, I submit, can inform the principles that undergird an LGBTIQ+-affirming theopastoral competence.

The three Malaysian Christian gay men indicate that being gay is integral to their relationships with God. They look to God for guidance, wisdom, inspiration and protection to live their lives productively as gay men rather than for miraculous 'healings' from same-sex 'distortions', 'afflictions' or 'diabolical oppression'. Gay men are cognisant of pastoral and doctrinal denunciations and dismissals of their sexual expressions on numerous fronts and interpret these rejections as institutional desertions. They recast these desertions as opportunities to encounter, understand and forge relationships with God while turning their attention to other spiritual strategies to nourish their faith. Gay men realize that the presence of God can be revealed and concealed through the actions and decisions of human beings and even through Christian teachings and institutions.

Embodied Christian spiritualities are practices that allow gay men to – borrowing the words of Pearl Wong (2015) – 'recognize not only the meaning of claiming their identity in relation to God, but also who God is in sexuality' (pp. 18–19). They can direct and illuminate the principles of an LGBTIQ+-affirming theopastoral competence on several levels, the most significant of which is arguably the role they play in restoring, including and foregrounding the wisdom of those who have been traditionally excluded and hidden from mainstream theopastoral discourses. An LGBTIQ+-affirming theopastoral competence upholds the idea that theopastoral pursuits must listen to, respect, learn from and empathize with the knowledges of God among people of diverse genders, sexes and sexualities. Such a stance is predicated on a deep comprehension, support and celebration of human diversity and fluidity.

An LGBTIQ+-affirming theopastoral competence understands that the ways in which LGBTIQ+ people understand and relate to God may and may not align with mainstream Christian expectations and, in that sense, adopts a liberative praxis. While some seek acceptance for their gender and sexual identities within churches, others do not feel the need for any shape or form of ecclesiastical approval to live as Christians. These individuals prefer to remain at the peripheries or outside official Christianity, often with stylized spiritualities. An LGBTIQ+-affirming theopastoral competence thus champions equity within multiplicity for all Christians. It acknowledges that LGBTIQ+ people are experts in their own lived experiences, including their experiences of God, but it also gently reminds LGBTIQ+ people that this expertise is not beyond scrutiny. As such, it confesses that its role is to guide and augment – rather than dictate and diminish – the personal and spiritual realities of LGBTIQ+ people.

An LGBTIQ+-affirming theopastoral competence humbles itself before the fact that cis-heteronormative ideals continue to shape Christianity. Still, it is also aware that these ideals must not be allowed to maintain their hegemonic status in theopastoral formulations. It continues to inform itself of Christian presuppositions surrounding LGBTIQ+ people as it boldly confronts and interrogates salient and subtle exclusionary doctrinal norms. It adamantly insists that 'God is revealed in and among the bodies of strangers, persons, and communities at odds with ideologies of the center' (Sprinkle, 2009, p. 80). It understands that 'inclusion', 'support' and 'welcome' must avoid any insidious agendas that attenuate the capacity of LGBTIQ+ people to flourish as LGBTIQ+ people. An LGBTIQ+-affirming theopastoral competence is firmly convinced of the role it plays in helping LGBTIQ+ people thrive in all aspects of life – particularly in human relationships and interactions – and in their lives in God.

## *Notes*

1 These are pseudonyms selected by the three men themselves, whom I interviewed for a larger qualitative project that examined the meaning-making of the sexual identities, sexual practices and belief systems among 30 Malaysian gay and bisexual men. The analysis and theorizing of their narratives in this chapter are guided by a Constructivist Grounded Theory Methodology. See Charmaz, Thornberg and Keane (2017).

2 I use 'Asian theologies' here to refer to theological productions by Asian scholars that address the interplay between Christianity and lived realities in South, Southeast and East Asia.

## References

Abdulrehman, Rehman (2024), *Developing Anti-Racist Cultural Competence*, Göttingen: Hogrefe Publishing.

Althaus-Reid, Marcella (2000), *Indecent Theology: Theological Perversions in Sex, Gender and Politics*, New York: Routledge.

Athyal, Saphir P. (1995), 'Towards an Asian Christian Theology', in *Biblical Theology in Asia*, edited by Ken Gnanakan, Bangalore: Asia Theological Association, pp. 77–89.

Blée, Fabrice (2022), 'What Can Postural Yoga Contribute to an Embodied Christian Spirituality? An Analysis of the Strengths and Weaknesses of Postural Yoga in the Light of Kashmir Đivaism', *Religions* 13, no. 2, p. 120.

Boppana, Shilpa and Alan M. Gross (2019), 'The Impact of Religiosity on the Psychological Well-Being of LGBT Christians', *Journal of Gay & Lesbian Mental Health* 23, no. 4, pp. 412–26.

Buechel, Andy (2015), *That We Might Become God: The Queerness of Creedal Christianity*, Eugene, OR: Cascade Books.

Campos, Michael Sepidoza, Clarence Darro del Castillo, Gregory Ching and Fides del Castillo (2022), 'Emotions towards God of Select LGBTQs in the Philippines and the Experience of Shame', *Intersections: Gender and Sexuality in Asia and the Pacific*, 48 (November), at http://intersections.anu.edu.au/issue48/campos.html, accessed 01.12.2024.

Charmaz, Kathy, Robert Thornberg and Elaine Keane (2017), 'Evolving Grounded Theory and Social Justice Inquiry', in *The SAGE Handbook of Qualitative Research*, edited by Norman K. Denzin and Yvonna S. Lincoln, Thousand Oaks, CA: SAGE Publications, pp. 411–43.

Cheng, Patrick S. (2011), *Radical Love: An Introduction to Queer Theology*, New York: Seabury Books.

Clarke, Sathianathan (2012), 'The Task, Method and Content of Asian Theologies', in *Asian Theology on the Way: Christianity, Culture and Context*, edited by Peniel Jesudason Rufus Rajkumar, London: SPCK, pp. 3–13.

Commissioner of Law Revision, Malaysia (1997), 'Malaysian Penal Code', at http://www.agc.gov.my/agcportal/index.php?r=portal2/lom2&id=1687, accessed 01.12.2024.

Commissioner of Law Revision, Malaysia (2006), 'Syariah Criminal Offences (Federal Territories) Act 1997', at http://www.agc.gov.my/agcportal/index.php?r=portal2/lom2&id=1431, accessed 01.12.2024.

Córdova Quero, Hugo (2020), 'Unfaithful Noxious Sexuality: Body, Incarnation, and Ecclesiology in Dispute', in *Unlocking Orthodoxies for Inclusive Theologies: Queer Alternatives*, edited by Robert E. Shore-Goss and Joseph N. Goh, New York: Routledge, pp. 154–73.

Cornelio, Jayeel and Robbin Dagle (2022), 'Contesting Unfreedom: To Be Queer and Christian in the Philippines', *Review of Faith & International Affairs* 20, no. 2, pp. 27–39.

Countrymeters (2024), 'Malaysia Population', at https://countrymeters.info/en/Malaysia, accessed 01.12.2024.

Gaikwad, Roger and Thomas Ninan, eds (2017), *A Theological Reader on Human Sexuality and Gender Diversities: Envisioning Inclusivity*, Delhi: ISPCK/NCCI.

Goh, Joseph N. (2016), 'Survivalist Sexuality-Faith Strategies in Biblical Meaning-Makings: Non-Heteronormative Malaysian Christian Men and Negotiations of Sexual Self-Affirmation', *QUEST: Studies on Religion & Culture in Asia* 1, pp. 38–53, at https://www.theology.cuhk.edu.hk/quest/index.php/quest/article/view/19, accessed 01.12.2024].

Goh, Joseph N. (2018), *Living Out Sexuality and Faith: Body Admissions of Malaysian Gay and Bisexual Men*, London: Routledge.

Goh, Joseph N. (2019), 'Practical Guidelines for SOGIESC Theologising in Southeast Asia: Foregrounding Gender Nonconformity, Sexual Diversity and Non-Dyadic Embodiment', in *Siapakah Sesamaku? Pergumulan Teologi Dengan Isu-Isu Keadilan Gender*, edited by Stephen Suleeman and Amadeo D. Udampoh, Jakarta, Indonesia: Sekolah Tinggi Filsafat Theologi Jakarta, pp. 186–211.

Goh, Joseph N. (2021), *Doing Church at the Amplify Open and Affirming Conferences: Queer Ecclesiologies in Asia*, Asian Christianity in the Diaspora, Cham: Palgrave Macmillan.

Goh, Joseph N., Kristine C. Meneses and Donald E. Messer (2019), 'An Ecclesiological Praxis of Inclusivity toward Sexual Diversity and HIV: Learning from Singapore and the Philippines', *International Journal of Public Theology* 13, no. 2, pp. 163–84.

Isherwood, Lisa (2024), '"This Is My Body"', *Feminist Theology* 32, no. 2, pp. 119–31.

Isherwood, Lisa and Hugo Córdova Quero, eds (2021), *The Indecent Theologies of Marcella Althaus-Reid: Voices from Asia and Latin America*, New York: Routledge.

Jackson, Peter A. (2003), 'Performative Genders, Perverse Desires: A Bio-History of Thailand's Same-Sex and Transgender Cultures', *Intersections: Gender, History and Culture in the Asian Context*, 9, at http://intersections.anu.edu.au/issue9/jackson.html, accessed 01.12.2024.

Kolysh, Simone (2017), 'Straight Gods, White Devils: Exploring Paths to Non-Religion in the Lives of Black LGBTQ People', *Secularism and Nonreligion* 6, no. 2, pp. 1–13.

Kuruvilla, Philip, ed. (2017), *Christian Responses to Issues of Human Sexuality and Gender Diversity: A Guide to the Churches in India*, New Delhi: ISPCK/NCCI.

Kwok, Pui-lan (2000), *Introducing Asian Feminist Theology*, Cleveland, OH: Pilgrim Press.

Levy, Denise L. and Patricia Reeves (2011), 'Resolving Identity Conflict: Gay, Lesbian, and Queer Individuals with a Christian Upbringing', *Journal of Gay & Lesbian Social Services* 23, no. 1, pp. 53–68.

NECF Malaysia (2007), 'Gay Church: A Response', at http://www.necf.org.my/newsmaster.cfm?&menuid=2&action=view&retrieveid=930, accessed 01.12.2024.

Office of Theological Concerns (2000), 'Methodology: Asian Christian Theology', in *For All Peoples of Asia: Documents from 1997 to 2001*, edited by Franz-Josef Eilers, Quezon City: Claretian Publications, pp. 329–419.

Pádua Freire, Ana Ester (2021), 'Dirty Martini: Toasting with Marcella Althaus-Reid', in *The Indecent Theologies of Marcella Althaus-Reid: Voices from Asia and Latin America*, edited by Lisa Isherwood and Hugo Córdova Quero, New York: Routledge, pp. 7–22.

Rubano, Craig A. (2022), 'Opening Doors to Resilience and a Gender-Diverse Pastoral Theology', *Pastoral Psychology* 71, no. 6, pp. 769–87.

Shore-Goss, Robert E. (2002), *Queering Christ: Beyond Jesus Acted Up*, New York: Pilgrim Press.

Shore-Goss, Robert E. and Joseph N. Goh, eds (2020), *Unlocking Orthodoxies for Inclusive Theologies: Queer Alternatives*, New York: Routledge.

Song, C. S. (1979), 'New Frontiers of Theology in Asia: Ten Theological Theses', *Southeast Asia Journal of Theology* 20, no. 1, pp. 13–33.

Sprinkle, Stephen V. (2009), 'A God at the Margins?: Marcella Althaus-Reid and the Marginality of LGBT People', *Journal of Religious Leadership* 8, no. 2, pp. 57–83.

Stuart, Elizabeth (2003), *Gay and Lesbian Theologies: Repetitions with Critical Difference*, Aldershot: Ashgate.

Sue, Derald Wing and David Sue (2015), *Counseling the Culturally Diverse: Theory and Practice*, Hoboken, NJ: Wiley.

Suleeman, Stephen and Amadeo D. Udampoh, eds (2019), *Siapakah Sesamaku? Pergumulan Teologi Dengan Isu-Isu Keadilan Gender* [Who Is My Neighbour?

Theological Reflections on Issues of Gender Justice], Jakarta: Sekolah Tinggi Filsafat Theologi Jakarta.

Trible, Phyllis (1984), *Texts of Terror: Literary-Feminist Readings of Biblical Narratives*, Philadelphia, PA: Fortress Press.

Voelkel, Rebecca M. M. (2017), *Carnal Knowledge of God: Embodied Love and the Movement for Justice*, Minneapolis, MN: Fortress Press.

Walters, Albert Sundararaj (2002), *We Believe in One God? Reflections on the Trinity in the Malaysian Context*, New Delhi: ISPCK.

Wong, Pearl (2015), 'Queering Binary Notions of Sexuality: Proclamation of a Bisexual Feminist', *in G♀d's image* 34, no. 2, pp. 14–24.

Wu, Rose (2000), *Liberating the Church from Fear: The Story of Hong Kong's Sexual Minorities*, Kowloon: Hong Kong Women Christian Council.

Wu, Rose (2015), 'A Pedagogy to Empower Queer Voices in Hong Kong', *in G♀d's image* 34, no. 2, pp. 29–35.

Yap, Kim Hao (2020), 'Toward Radical Inclusion', in *Unlocking Orthodoxies for Inclusive Theologies: Queer Alternatives*, edited by Robert E. Shore-Goss and Joseph N. Goh, New York: Routledge, pp. 27–33.

Yeo, Adriel (2021), 'Aelred and Sworn Brotherhood', *Asia Journal of Theology* 35, no. 1, pp. 100–120.

# 8

# Faith, Sexuality and Human Rights: Reconciliation and Theological Reflections for LGBTIQ+ People in Africa

JIDE MACAULAY

## Introduction

The discourse on reconciling sexuality with Christianity for LGBTIQ+ people is critical and demands urgent theological and practical attention. The entrenched imbalances within religious interpretations and rhetoric have placed LGBTIQ+ lives at significant risk. Homophobia, biphobia and transphobia are not merely societal attitudes but are often bolstered by conservative religious ideologies. Such attitudes counter the core tenets of Christian faith – love, mercy and compassion.

This chapter examines the oppressive forces of religious discrimination and abuse faced by LGBTIQ+ individuals, particularly within Christian communities in Africa. Drawing on personal experience and the work of House of Rainbow, I reflect on the challenges and opportunities for reconciling sexuality with faith by uncovering the often invisible theological barriers that impede inclusion. The chapter critically explores the intersection of faith, sexuality and human rights, delving into the theological obstacles that hinder acceptance and the complex dynamics between faith, culture and colonialism. It demonstrates how historical, theological and sociopolitical forces have perpetuated exclusion, primarily through the lens of colonial legacies and Western conservative ideologies, which have shaped and entrenched anti-LGBTIQ+ sentiments in African contexts. Engaging with these dynamics, the chapter advocates for a transformative path rooted in reconciliation and liberation. It emphasizes the necessity of inclusive theological interpretations that uphold justice and mercy alongside promoting human rights education and faith-based activism as essential means to foster healing and acceptance.

Ultimately this chapter envisions a future where faith communities embrace the radical inclusivity of God's love, offering a vision of dignity, decolonization and liberation for all people, regardless of their sexual identity. Such a transformative journey requires both a reimagining of theological narratives and a collective commitment to dismantling systems of oppression to cultivate a world where all individuals can thrive in the fullness of their identity.

## Theological Barriers to Inclusion

Religious communities, particularly within Christianity, have increasingly shifted towards conservatism, adopting exclusionary ideologies that undermine the dignity of LGBTIQ+ individuals. The historical and ongoing abuse of LGBTIQ+ people, amplified by rigid interpretations of scripture, has eroded any sense of hope or safety for many within the faith. At the heart of this oppression is the demand for LGBTIQ+ people to suppress their identity and deny their humanity to conform to cis-heteronormative ideals.

Such demands are antithetical to the biblical mandate for justice and mercy. As the prophet Micah declares, 'He has shown you, O mortal, what is good. And what does the LORD require of you? To act justly and to love mercy and to walk humbly with your God' (Micah 6.8). This verse underscores the divine call to justice and kindness, which should extend to all, regardless of sexual orientation or gender identity.

Cis-heteronormativity – the presumption that cis-heterosexuality is the default or preferred norm – has deeply infiltrated Christian theology and practice. This framework marginalizes LGBTIQ+ individuals, perpetuating the idea that they are 'other' or 'less than' in the eyes of God. Yet a close reading of scripture reveals a consistent theme of God's radical inclusion. The Ethiopian eunuch's story in Acts 8.26–40 exemplifies this inclusivity. Despite being a sexual and gender minority in his context, the eunuch is welcomed into the community of faith without condition, demonstrating that God's love transcends human-imposed barriers.

Theologians such as James Alison (2001) and Marcella Althaus-Reid (2000, 2003) have challenged cis-heteronormative theology, urging a re-reading of scripture through the lens of love and liberation. Alison argues that the resurrection reveals God's ultimate embrace of all humanity, dismantling systems of exclusion and oppression. This theological perspective invites faith communities to question the harmful norms that perpetuate injustice against LGBTIQ+ people.

For LGBTIQ+ Africans, the intersection of faith and sexuality is fraught with complexities. In many African contexts Christianity has been co-opted by colonial legacies to enforce cis-heteronormativity and suppress indigenous understandings of gender and sexuality. The result is a heightened level of stigma and violence against LGBTIQ+ individuals, both in Africa and within the diaspora.

In contemporary society the intersection of politics and religion often creates a toxic environment of hostility towards LGBTIQ+ people. This hostility is harmful and diabolical, undermining the principles of love and justice central to the gospel. The fight for the rights and dignity of LGBTIQ+ individuals – particularly those enduring profound challenges to their bodies, minds and souls – can no longer be ignored. To remain silent in the face of such oppression is to betray the command to love one's neighbour as oneself (Matt. 22.39).

The Bible consistently calls us to resist oppression. In Isaiah 1.17 the prophet encourages: 'Learn to do right; seek justice. Defend the oppressed. Take up the cause of the fatherless; plead the case of the widow.' This passage reminds us that advocating for marginalized groups, including LGBTIQ+ people, is an integral part of Christian discipleship.

Despite the strides made in education and human rights, the grip of patriarchy, religious dogma and traditional views on homosexuality continues to bind many LGBTIQ+ Africans and their families. These forces create a form of captivity, alienating individuals from both their faith and the modern world. Theologies rooted in patriarchy have historically upheld hierarchies that exclude women, LGBTIQ+ individuals and other marginalized groups. Yet scripture offers a counter-narrative. In Galatians 3.28 Paul proclaims: 'There is neither Jew nor Gentile, neither slave nor free, nor is there male and female, for you are all one in Christ Jesus.' That radical statement of equality challenges the structures perpetuating exclusion, urging believers to embrace the fullness of God's creation.

The works of liberation theologians such as Gustavo Gutiérrez (1973) and queer theologians like Patrick S. Cheng (2011, 2012, 2013) underscore the necessity of dismantling oppressive systems. Cheng emphasizes that queer theology is a theology of radical love – a love that breaks down barriers and affirms the dignity of all people.

The struggle to be both a devout person of faith and authentically express one's sexual orientation or gender identity remains one of the most profound challenges of our time. This tension is especially pronounced in contexts where cultural and religious norms are rigidly cis-heteronormative. For LGBTIQ+ individuals, reconciling their faith with their identity often feels impossible, as they face condemnation both from their spiritual communities and from society at large.

A more nuanced understanding of scripture is the theological foundation for reconciling faith and sexuality. The Bible emphasizes the intrinsic worth of every individual as a creation of God. Psalm 139.13–14 celebrates this truth: 'For you created my inmost being; you knit me together in my mother's womb. I praise you because I am fearfully and wonderfully made.' This passage affirms that LGBTIQ+ individuals are as fearfully and wonderfully made as anyone else, reflecting the divine image in all its diversity.

The work of theologians like James Alison, a Roman Catholic theologian and openly gay priest, has been instrumental in reframing the conversation about sexuality within faith communities. Alison's concept of 'the joy of being wrong' invites the church to rethink traditional teachings on homosexuality, embracing humility and openness to the Spirit's guidance.

## Intersections of Faith, Culture and Colonialism

For decades LGBTIQ+ individuals in Africa have faced relentless stigma and persecution. Hostile rhetoric from political and religious leaders exacerbates this hostility, making reconciliation with faith communities an uphill battle. Former Zimbabwean President Robert Mugabe's infamous statements, in which he likened LGBTIQ+ people to animals and threatened violence against them, epitomize the toxic environment faced by many. Such rhetoric not only dehumanizes LGBTIQ+ individuals but also emboldens acts of violence and discrimination.

The complicity of religious leaders in this oppression is a profound moral failure. The gospel of Jesus Christ offers a clear mandate to stand against such injustice. In Matthew 25.40 Jesus declares: 'Truly I tell you, whatever you did for one of the least of these brothers and sisters of mine, you did for me.' By failing to protect and affirm LGBTIQ+ individuals the church neglects its duty to care for the 'least of these'.

President Jacob Zuma's statements to the news highlight tension in leadership regarding LGBTIQ+ rights in Africa (Macupe, 2024). On the one hand, he emphasizes respect for South Africa's progressive constitution, which guarantees equal rights to all citizens, including LGBTIQ+ individuals. On the other, this neutrality often contrasts with the lived realities of LGBTIQ+ people, who face systemic oppression and hostility. This contradiction perpetuates a climate of despair for many LGBTIQ+ individuals, who yearn for consistent advocacy and protection from those in power.

House of Rainbow (HOR) serves as a sanctuary for those at the crossroads of faith, sexuality and identity. Our mission transcends mere advocacy; it seeks to create a community where black, minority ethnic and LGBTIQ+ individuals can reconcile their identities with societal and religious pressures. By providing critical support in areas such as asylum, sexual health, counselling and pastoral care, HOR empowers individuals to navigate the challenges of marginalization and exclusion.

However, the path to reconciliation is fraught with fear and complexity. Many participants in our programmes express profound anxiety about 'disappointing' their families. Within many cultures LGBTIQ+ identities are viewed as antithetical to familial honour, creating a painful tension between personal authenticity and communal expectations. Economic dependencies exacerbate these pressures, as well as the need to meet extended family obligations and concerns about career prospects. While these fears are deeply rooted, they cannot impede the transformative journey of reconciliation.

For many the journey begins with acknowledging the weight of negative perceptions surrounding their sexuality and gender identity. Religious communities have often been complicit in perpetuating these harmful narratives, dehumanizing LGBTIQ+ individuals through exclusion and condemnation. As a result many feel trapped – unable to embrace their identities fully or to confront the injustices they endure. This dynamic fosters a culture of silence, where victims of abuse prioritize survival over resistance, enabling perpetrators to continue their oppression unchecked.

The biblical call to justice offers a stark contrast to such collaboration. As the prophet Isaiah reminds us (Isa. 1.17), we are commanded to seek justice, defend the oppressed and also to plead for the vulnerable. This divine mandate to challenge injustice underscores the work of reconciliation, demanding that faith communities confront their roles in perpetuating harm.

## Paths to Reconciliation and Liberation

Faith can be both a barrier and a bridge in the reconciliation process. For many LGBTIQ+ individuals, faith communities have been sources of judgment and rejection. Yet these same individuals often hold a deep spiritual longing, seeking affirmation within the traditions they have been raised in.

The work of theologians such as James Cone (2011) and Marcella Althaus-Reid (2000) provides further insight into this dynamic. Cone's liberation theology emphasizes the importance of addressing systemic injustices, while Althaus-Reid challenges traditional interpretations of scripture and advocates for a more inclusive understanding of God's love.

Reconciliation is theologically central to the Christian narrative. In 2 Corinthians 5.18–19, Paul writes: 'All this is from God, who reconciled us to himself through Christ and gave us the ministry of reconciliation: that God was reconciling the world to himself in Christ, not counting people's sins against them.' This passage reminds us that reconciliation is not merely about resolving conflict but about restoring relationships and affirming the inherent dignity of every person.

The transformative power of House of Rainbow's interventions lies in their ability to shift participants from fear to empowerment. While many arrive with scepticism and trepidation, the programmes create a safe space for honest dialogue and exploration. Participants are encouraged to confront their doubts, fears and negative self-perceptions, considering theological teachings that affirm their worth.

'Coming out' – or the act of openly acknowledging one's sexual orientation or gender identity – is a profound and transformative experience for LGBTIQ+ individuals. It involves a journey of self-discovery and acceptance, often laden with significant emotional, social and spiritual challenges. Coming out has far-reaching implications – not just for the individual but also for their families, friends, colleagues and communities. For many the process is fraught with risk, potentially leading to losing familial support, societal acceptance, economic security and personal safety.

These disparities challenge the church's commitment to justice and equality. The Bible repeatedly calls for the defence of the marginalized and the oppressed. Isaiah 58.6 declares: 'Is not this the kind of fasting that I have chosen: to loose the chains of injustice and untie the cords of the yoke, to set the oppressed free and break every yoke?' This mandate calls on faith communities to confront systems of oppression, including those perpetuated by discriminatory laws and practices.

Marc Epprecht (2008a) underscores the economic and racial disparities that exacerbate the vulnerability of LGBTIQ+ individuals. At the heart of many faith-based objections to LGBTIQ+ inclusion is the traditional definition of love and marriage. Conservative interpretations often depict cis-heterosexual marriage as the sole legitimate expression of God's design. However, the work of historians such as John Boswell and Epprecht, as well as theologians such as Althaus-Reid, challenges this narrow understanding. Boswell (1980) traces historical evidence of same-sex unions within Christian traditions, while Epprecht (2008b) contests the misconception that homosexuality is a 'Western import' by documenting diverse expressions of same-sex relationships and gender variance in African traditions and histories.

On her part, Althaus-Reid (2000) calls for a radical rethinking of love and sexuality, grounded in God's boundless and inclusive love. Such a theology recognizes that human constructs do not confine God's love but are a dynamic and transformative force that affirms the diversity of human experiences. This profound truth echoes Paul's declaration in Galatians 3.28, where he insists that in Christ, all divisions – whether they are ethnic, social or gendered – are overcome in unity.

Faith-based discrimination is a theological issue and a human rights concern. The Yogyakarta Principles, a set of international principles on applying human rights law concerning sexual orientation and gender identity, emphasize that states cannot use religion to justify discriminatory laws or practices. These principles resonate with Jesus' teaching in Matthew 22.37–39: '"Love the Lord your God with all your heart and with all your soul and with all your mind." This is the first and greatest commandment. And the second is like it: "Love your neighbour as yourself."' True faith calls for love not judgement; inclusion not exclusion.

The Universal Declaration of Human Rights asserts the inherent dignity and equality of all individuals, irrespective of sexual orientation or gender identity. Article 18 guarantees freedom of thought, conscience and religion. However, these rights are often undermined by religious and cultural practices that discriminate against LGBTIQ+ individuals.

The work of queer theologians provides valuable insights for reconciling faith and identity. Alison (2001) reframes LGBTIQ+ experiences as integral to understanding God's grace and challenges the church to move beyond a theology of exclusion, urging believers to embrace the marginalized as reflections of Christ's presence.

Patriarchy, as Scott Siraj al-Haqq Kugle observes (2010), institutionalizes the dominance of elderly cis-heterosexual males over others – particularly women, younger men and non-conforming individuals. That system perpetuates power structures that marginalize LGBTIQ+ individuals, enforcing rigid gender norms and silencing alternative expressions of identity. Within many African contexts, patriarchy operates alongside cultural traditions, making rejection of these norms a path fraught with ostracism and violence.

Historical studies, such as *Boy-Wives and Female Husbands: Studies in African Homosexualities*, edited by Stephen O. Murray and Will Roscoe (1998), challenge the notion that same-sex relationships are a Western import. Concurrently, Epprecht (2008b) documents evidence of same-sex practices within traditional African societies, such as the

Bushman and Khoi in Southern Africa, and the linguistic expressions that described these relationships. Similarly, Rudolf Pell Gaudio (2009) highlights the coexistence of homosexual behaviours and orientations in Islamic northern Nigeria, offering a nuanced view of how these identities interact with religious and cultural norms.

These works collectively dismantle the narrative that homosexuality is 'un-African' or incompatible with traditional faith systems, affirming that diverse sexualities and identities have always existed within African cultures and histories.

The Bible provides numerous examples of God standing with the marginalized against systems of oppression. In Exodus 3.7–8, God speaks to Moses, saying: 'I have indeed seen the misery of my people in Egypt. I have heard them crying out because of their slave drivers, and I am concerned about their suffering. So I have come down to rescue them.'

The patriarchal structure of many African societies often instils a pervasive fear in LGBTIQ+ individuals, particularly within familial and religious contexts. This reflects a broader societal failure to provide safe spaces where LGBTIQ+ individuals can reconcile their identities with their faith and cultural backgrounds. The Bible offers many examples of transformation through learning and growth. In John 8.31–32, Jesus says: 'If you hold to my teaching, you are really my disciples. Then you will know the truth, and the truth will set you free.' The passage reminds us that education – spiritual, emotional and intellectual – has the power to liberate individuals from the chains of ignorance and fear.

This also aligns with the message of 2 Corinthians 5.18–19, which teaches that God reconciled the world through Christ and entrusted us with the ministry of reconciliation, 'reconciling the world to himself in Christ, not counting people's sins against them' (v. 19). Every ministry of reconciliation calls for dismantling oppressive systems and restoring relationships – both with God and one another.

Interpreting religious scriptures in a way that aligns with modern cultural and human rights perspectives presents a significant challenge. This task is even more complex for LGBTIQ+ individuals in faith communities where traditional interpretations often lead to marginalization and exclusion. For too many, religious texts are read within the historical and cultural contexts in which they were written without considering how these texts might speak to present-day realities of identity, sexuality and human dignity.

One of the fundamental questions surrounding the rejection of same-gender loving individuals is the imposition of colonial-era laws, particularly those introduced by Christian missionaries in Africa. Many of these laws continue to criminalize homosexuality, perpetuating a legacy of violence and marginalization. The colonial period left an indelible mark on African nations regarding governance and religious and cultural practices. The Christian church became a key agent of these colonial powers, reinforcing cis-heteronormative ideologies and demonizing alternative sexualities.

The ethical questions surrounding this process are profound. How can African nations, having inherited these colonial structures, address the harm caused by such laws? The failure to critically examine and challenge these legacies leaves LGBTIQ+ individuals exposed to systemic rejection, and the Christian church's complicity in this injustice is troubling. It becomes even more perplexing when we consider the core Christian commandment: 'Love your neighbour as yourself' (Matt. 22.39).

In the words of the prophet Micah, God commands us to act justly, love mercy and walk humbly with him (Micah 6.8). Yet the experience of LGBTIQ+ people in Africa is far from one of inclusion, justice or mercy. Instead these communities are often subjected to exclusion, violence and discrimination from religious institutions that profess love, kindness and humility. For LGBTIQ+ individuals this contradiction becomes painfully clear: religious communities that should offer sanctuary instead contribute to their suffering. This hypocrisy calls for urgent theological reflection and action.

## Envisioning Dignity and Decolonization

For many LGBTIQ+ individuals the moment they first encounter alternative theological interpretations of homosexuality is transformative. It is often an 'aha' moment that opens their eyes to the possibility of reconciling their faith with their identity. This realization is revolutionary, as it challenges the long-held beliefs that have led to their ostracization and self-rejection. For the first time LGBTIQ+ individuals begin to see themselves as beloved children of God, created in God's image and worthy of love and respect.

The Bible offers numerous passages that affirm the dignity of all human beings, regardless of their sexual orientation. We read: 'So God created humankind in his image, in the image of God he created them; male and female he created them' (Gen. 1.27, NRSV). This foundational scripture highlights the inherent dignity and worth of every human being, created in the image of a loving and inclusive God.

Additionally, in the story of the Ethiopian eunuch in Acts 8.26–40 we see a powerful narrative of inclusion. The Ethiopian eunuch, an outsider both ethnically and sexually, encounters Philip, who shares the good news of Jesus Christ with him. After hearing the gospel the eunuch is baptized, affirming that in Christ there is neither Jew nor Gentile, slave nor free, male nor female (Gal. 3.28). This radical inclusivity is a central theme of the New Testament and must shape our understanding of LGBTIQ+ persons within faith communities.

The challenge of reinterpreting religious scriptures – whether the Bible or the Quran – to align with modern concepts of human rights and LGBTIQ+ inclusion cannot be overstated. Religious doctrines, which for centuries have been used as instruments of oppression, continue to hold significant authority within communities. These texts, when misinterpreted or selectively applied, have been used to justify slavery, the subjugation of women and the marginalization of LGBTIQ+ individuals. The historical patterns of religious justification for slavery and the oppression of women serve as a grim reminder that religious authorities have often perpetuated injustice. It is therefore not surprising that LGBTIQ+ individuals now face similar struggles of exclusion and demonization.

This theological misapplication is not merely an accident but part of a broader, systemic pattern that spans centuries. The fundamental task for faith communities today is to reckon with these historical misapplications and reconsider how sacred texts should inform the ethics of human dignity, justice and love. Cone (2011) speaks to the need for a radical rethinking of Christian theology considering historical injustices. Just as he critiques the church's role in perpetuating racial injustice, we must critique how the church has perpetuated homophobia and transphobia through flawed interpretations of scripture.

As individuals begin to question the harmful theological conclusions that have been used to alienate minority groups, including LGBTIQ+ individuals, the Apostle Paul's words become significant: 'Then we will no longer be infants, tossed back and forth by the waves, and blown here and there by every wind of teaching and by the cunning and craftiness of people in their deceitful scheming' (Eph. 4.14). This verse serves as a guide for theological reflection, urging individuals to move beyond simplistic and harmful interpretations of scripture that have historically been used to justify oppression. Instead Paul calls for spiritual maturity, which requires a careful and thoughtful engagement with the faith, seeking truth even when it challenges traditional authority.

The tension between being LGBTIQ+ and being a person of faith is particularly pronounced for individuals in Africa. The confluence of African cultural norms and Western conservative ideologies has often led to the marginalization and persecution of LGBTIQ+ individuals within faith communities. The problem is not solely the result of indigenous African beliefs but also the legacy of colonialism, which imported rigid, often harmful theological and social frameworks regarding sexuality. Western missionaries and conservative religious ideologies imposed doctrines that framed homosexuality as a sin, perpetuating ideas that have endured for generations. As a result many LGBTIQ+ Africans have had to wrestle with the painful contradiction of living as both their authentic selves and faithful people in communities that reject or ostracize them.

The challenge for LGBTIQ+ people of faith in Africa is thus multifaceted. On the one hand there is the pressure of deeply ingrained African cultural values that often see same-sex attraction as a threat to traditional family structures and roles. On the other hand there is the imposition of Western conservative theological doctrines, which have become the dominant framework through which many African Christians and Muslims view homosexuality. The result is a complex and sometimes oppressive environment where LGBTIQ+ persons are made to feel that their faith and their sexuality are incompatible.

The task before us is not simply to accept or reject Western theological positions but to construct an African-centred theology that embraces faith and sexual diversity. As Gutiérrez (1973) and Cone (2011) articulated, liberation theology offers a way forward. Liberation theology emphasizes the importance of context and lived experience, which involves acknowledging the realities of LGBTIQ+ individuals in African contexts. African theologians and faith leaders must develop theological perspectives reflecting African cultural understanding and an inclusive reading of sacred texts.

An important starting point is recognizing that African spiritual traditions have long acknowledged gender fluidity and non-binary identities, even if they were suppressed or redefined under colonial rule. Scholars such as M. Jacqui Alexander (2005) have discussed how non-Western cultures have historically been more accepting of sexual and gender diversity. By reclaiming these traditions, African theologians can create spaces for LGBTIQ+ people of faith, drawing on indigenous ideas of identity, kinship and sexuality. This reclamation process involves looking at the historical context of African spiritual practices and reinterpreting scripture to honour African cultural values and human rights.

A key barrier to LGBTIQ+ inclusion within African faith communities lies in the theological interpretation of biblical and Quranic texts that are traditionally seen as condemning homosexuality. Often used to justify discrimination and exclusion, these passages must be carefully re-examined through critical biblical scholarship. Texts such as Leviticus 18.22 and Romans 1.26–27 have been wielded for centuries to argue against same-sex relations. However, as scholars such as Robert Gagnon (2001) and Deryn Guest et al. (2006) have pointed out, these passages must be understood within their historical, cultural and linguistic contexts.

For instance, Leviticus 18.22, which condemns a man lying with another man as with a woman, must be understood within the context of ancient Israelite purity laws, which are not universally applicable to modern Christians. Similarly, Romans 1.26–27, which describes women and men exchanging natural relations for unnatural ones, can be understood as a critique of idolatry and social excess, not a universal prohibition of same-sex love. These passages, when read through a modern, progressive lens, do not necessarily prohibit consensual same-sex relationships but instead speak to issues of power dynamics, exploitation and idolatry in the ancient world.

A crucial part of reconciling faith and sexuality for LGBTIQ+ individuals in Africa is understanding that the Bible, like all religious texts, is subject to interpretation and can be understood in ways that support justice and inclusion. In his work on biblical interpretation, Walter Brueggemann (1978, 1997) stresses that scripture should not be seen as static but as a living text that speaks to the realities of our times. This understanding of scripture allows us to reframe traditional teachings on sexuality in ways that affirm the dignity and humanity of LGBTIQ+ people.

Reconciliation for LGBTIQ+ individuals in Africa requires a nuanced understanding of human rights and their application in African contexts. Frameworks like the Universal Declaration of Human Rights and the Yogyakarta Principles (International Commission of Jurists, 2007) emphasize that sexual orientation and gender identity are integral to human dignity, advocating freedom from discrimination. However, many African nations fail to recognize these rights, with laws criminalizing same-sex relations remaining in force. Even where legal protections exist they are often inadequately enforced, leaving LGBTIQ+ individuals vulnerable.

Education about international and national human rights laws is essential to empower LGBTIQ+ individuals to advocate for themselves and their communities. This knowledge fosters resilience and facilitates the pursuit of dignity and safety. Inclusive theological education and faith-based advocacy are crucial in challenging discriminatory laws and attitudes. Religious leaders, particularly within Christian and Muslim communities, have the capacity to transform societal perceptions through sermons and activism. Integrating human rights principles into theological teachings can support the recognition of sexual orientation and gender identity as vital components of personal identity, paving the way for greater acceptance and equality.

## Conclusion

The reconciliation of faith and sexuality for LGBTIQ+ individuals involves navigating profound challenges yet offers opportunities for transformation and renewal within faith communities. These challenges, rooted in religious and cultural prejudices, call for reimagining theological practices to embrace justice, love and inclusion. Drawing from scriptural foundations, including Christ's call to love (John 13.35), the prophet Amos's advocacy for justice (Amos 5.24) and the ministry of reconciliation emphasized by Paul (2 Corinthians 5.18–19), this chapter underscores the responsibility of faith communities to reflect God's boundless love.

Theological movements like liberation and queer theology provide frameworks for inclusive interpretations of scripture, challenging colonial and patriarchal ideologies that have perpetuated exclusion. Resources such as *The Queer Bible Commentary* (Guest et al., 2006) and organizations like House of Rainbow exemplify efforts to create safe, affirming spaces where LGBTIQ+ individuals can reconcile their faith and identity. These efforts extend to addressing broader issues like HIV stigma and societal rejection, offering hope and empowerment.

Faith communities are called to move beyond the cycles of condemnation that have long excluded and marginalized LGBTIQ+ individuals. Instead they are urged to become agents of healing and transformation, embodying the radical inclusivity central to Jesus's teachings. This work envisions a world where theology is in harmony with human rights principles, creating spaces where every individual is fully affirmed in their inherent dignity and worth as bearers of God's image. In such a world, people are free to live authentically, embrace their identities without fear or shame, and experience the liberative power of the gospel. This vision calls for theological frameworks to shift, recognizing the profound value of every person, regardless of sexual orientation or gender identity.

## References

Alexander, M. Jacqui (2005), *Pedagogies of Crossing: Meditations on Feminism, Sexual Politics, Memory, and the Sacred*, Durham, NC: Duke University Press.

Alison, James (2001), *Faith Beyond Resentment: Fragments Catholic and Gay*, Spring Valley, NY: Crossroad.

Althaus-Reid, Marcella (2000), *Indecent Theology: Theological Perversions in Sex, Gender and Politics*, London: Routledge.

Althaus-Reid, Marcella (2003), *The Queer God*, London: Routledge.

Boswell, John (1980), *Christianity, Social Tolerance, and Homosexuality: Gay People in Western Europe from the Beginning of the Christian Era to the Fourteenth Century*, Chicago, IL: University of Chicago Press.

Brueggemann, Walter (1978), *The Prophetic Imagination*, Minneapolis, MN: Fortress Press.

Brueggemann, Walter (1997), *Theology of the Old Testament: Testimony, Dispute, Advocacy*, Minneapolis, MN: Fortress Press.

Cheng, Patrick S. (2011), *Radical Love: An Introduction to Queer Theology*, New York: Seabury Books.

Cheng, Patrick S. (2012), *From Sin to Amazing Grace: Discovering the Queer Christ*, New York: Seabury Books.

Cheng, Patrick S. (2013), *Rainbow Theology: Bridging Race, Sexuality, and Spirit*, New York: Seabury Books.

Cone, James (2011), *The Cross and the Lynching Tree*, Maryknoll, NY: Orbis Books.

Epprecht, Marc (2008a), *Heterosexual Africa? The History of an Idea from the Age of Exploration to the Age of AIDS*, Athens, OH: Ohio University Press.

Epprecht, Marc (2008b), *Unspoken Facts: A History of Homosexualities in Africa*, Harare: Gays and Lesbians of Zimbabwe.

Gagnon, Robert A. J. (2001), *The Bible and Homosexual Practice: Texts and Hermeneutics*, Nashville, TN: Abingdon Press.

Gaudio, Rudolf Pell (2009), *Allah Made Us: Sexual Outlaws in an Islamic African City*, Chichester: Wiley-Blackwell.

Guest, Deryn, Robert E. Shore-Goss, Mona West and Thomas Bohace, eds (2006), *The Queer Bible Commentary*, London: SCM Press.

Gutiérrez, Gustavo (1973), *A Theology of Liberation: History, Politics, and Salvation*, Maryknoll, NY: Orbis Books.

International Commission of Jurists (2007), 'The Yogyakarta Principles: Principles on the Application of International Human Rights Law in Relation to Sexual Orientation and Gender Identity', at www.yogyakartaprinciples.org, accessed 01.12.2024.

Kugle, Scott Siraj al-Haqq (2010), *Homosexuality in Islam: Critical Reflections on Gays, Lesbians, and Transgender Muslims*, Oxford: One-World Books.

Macupe, Bongekile (2024), 'Zuma under Fire for Remarks about "Anti-Democratic" Same-Sex Laws' (News 24, 24 January), at https://www.news24.com/news24/politics/zuma-under-fire-for-remarks-about-anti-democratic-same-sex-laws-20240124 accessed 01.12.2024.

Murray, Stephen O. and Will Roscoe, eds (1998), *Boy-Wives and Female Husbands: Studies in African Homosexualities*, New York: Palgrave.

# 9

# Towards a Healthy Pastoral Work

ADELARD KANANIRA

## Introduction

The Synodal approach that the Roman Catholic Church has been developing over the past few years suggests the possibility of a renewed pastoral work in which queer Christians play an integral role. This emphasis on the lived experiences of the faithful (Block, 2023) challenges the broader failure of Christianity to embrace LGBTIQ+ people fully. It confronts the perception of diversity as a threat rather than a foundational aspect of Christian values. An analysis of scriptural misinterpretations – such as the story of Sodom and Gomorrah, often weaponized against queer individuals – reveals that these biases arise not from authentic Christianity but from more ingrained cultural and historical influences. This chapter advocates for a transformative pastoral framework that fully accepts LGBTIQ+ Christians, highlighting the essential roles of parents and religious leaders in fostering meaningful dialogue. In doing so it envisions a Christianity that genuinely reflects Christ's message of unconditional love, offering a spiritual home for all, including LGBTIQ+ individuals.

By healthy pastoral work I mean a ministry that liberates Christians from superficial religiosity and the spiritual complacency that fosters ignorance and an unfruitful faith. Such a pastoral approach encourages believers to grow and mature both spiritually and in their faith journeys. Unfortunately, not everyone agrees that queer individuals and LGBTIQ+ Christians deserve inclusion in Christian communities. In some cases their very existence is denied. For example, in 2018, two African seminarians in Italy openly stated to their peers: 'These people need to be beaten up; they deserve death; there is no place for such nonsense in our country' (Reuters, 2023). Such a statement is deeply troubling, especially coming from future religious leaders, but it is also supported by political leaders. This perspective, however, is often defended by appealing to the Sodom and Gomorrah narrative (Gen. 19) in the Hebrew Bible – a text frequently misinterpreted and weaponized to justify exclusion, discrimination and even violence against queer individuals.

There are Christians who have transformed the Christian church into a congregation of self-proclaimed holy and pure individuals, using this as justification to discriminate against those they judge as 'unholy' and 'undeserving' of God's grace, such as queer people and queer Christians. This behaviour corrupts the Christian church, creating a toxic environment filled with unhealthy spirituality, hypocrisy and falsehoods. When a new generation of church leaders clings to outdated methods of shepherding the congregation, it signals that the Christian church is in a state of decline and its pastoral work is failing. As it is written: 'And no one puts new wine into old wineskins' (Mark 2.22, NRSV). This generation requires church leaders who are able to recognize and embrace reality and – in the light of the gospel – teach congregations to activate Godly love, fostering a community where everyone is valued, celebrated and fully integrated.

The talents and gifts of queer Christians are being wasted, as they are often labelled as sinful, which leads to the misconception that they cannot contribute to God's glory or the service of our Christian communities. As a result they often participate passively, merely fulfilling what they believe is expected of them. Yet every queer Christian harbours a deep desire to freely share their gifts without the constant fear of being judged, denied, rejected or discriminated against. Embracing a path towards queer acceptance within African churches is not only a step towards justice but also a vital move for creating a more harmonious and equitable society. Such acceptance involves fostering spaces where parents of queer individuals can deepen their love and understanding of their children. This is not limited to parents alone but extends to siblings and friends, building the groundwork for a healthier society where compassion, humanity and acceptance triumph over hatred and discrimination.

The experiences of queer Christians can offer much to the church today. They can amend and heal wounds in our Christian communities. The feeling of being hated, unfit and unwelcome, the sense of guilt they hold because of the cage their communities have put them in (in God's name), feels real. Listening should be the first move the church can make towards queer Christians. Queer Christian stories are stories of hope. Their stories are at the margins or the periphery, as are the Bible stories (Van Klinken et al., 2021). As Marc Epprecht (2013) states, LGBTIQ+ people in Africa are proudly, happily and deeply religious. This kind of faith and resilience profoundly challenges entrenched narratives about the queer lifestyle and queer spirituality, demonstrating that queer

Christians can embody deep, authentic spirituality. Their experiences push beyond traditional boundaries, questioning the rigidity of interpretations often used to marginalize them.

The new evangelization of the gospel refers to a transformative and contemporary approach to living and sharing its message. It moves beyond mere adherence to scripture towards fostering a deeper, more dynamic faith that transcends the spiritual complacency many Christians are trapped in, a state that often hardens hearts with pride and judgement, hindering the realization of God's inclusive love. The misinterpretation of the story of Sodom and Gomorrah will not hinder queer Christians from embracing their roles as the new disciples, evangelists and missionaries of God's grace and love – roles they are already living out.

## Sodom and Gomorrah

There are seven biblical texts commonly cited to condemn homosexuality and LGBTIQ+ people in general. These are often referred to as 'clobber texts'. Among them the story of Sodom and Gomorrah in Genesis 19 is the most frequently cited (Shore-Goss, 2002). This prominence is unsurprising, as the dramatic destruction of the two cities and the depiction of God's anger evoke a sense of terror. Such a narrative has placed Christians on the wrong side of history.

One day – while speaking with my brother – he asked me what I thought about homosexuality in the Bible. I inquired further about what he meant, and he cited the story of Sodom and Gomorrah. He then told me he loves me deeply but struggles to reconcile his understanding of the story with Christian morality. When I asked if he had read the entire chapter and reflected on it personally, he admitted he had not but insisted: 'Everyone knows about Sodom and Gomorrah, the city destroyed because of homosexuality.'

The story of Sodom and Gomorrah is almost always the first question raised by queer individuals who are struggling to reconcile their sexuality with their faith. They often fear that their sexual orientation and homo-affection might upset God, potentially putting their country or even the world in danger. However, the scenario described in the story is quite different. In it the entire city, including children, approached Lot and demanded that he hand over his angelic guests. I always ask these individuals the same question I once asked my brother: 'Have you read the story yourself?' The answer is invariably 'No'.

I was one of them in my early twenties, grappling with the same fear. Yet I could not stop questioning why God would punish me and the world for my feelings. In contrast, others committed atrocities – such as killing, perpetrating injustice or engaging in inhumane fraud – that caused generational harm. These individuals, paradoxically, often seemed to thrive, growing wealthier, occupying prominent places in churches and being granted significant authority as though they owned God. Why, then, would I deserve a worse fate than religious leaders who publicly lie in God's name, declaring that God told them certain events would occur within months or years – predictions that never materialize?

The truth is that the story is widely known, and many use it to dehumanize and shame LGBTIQ+ individuals. Yet very few take the time to sit down and read it with the guidance of the Holy Spirit. In an era dominated by misinformation, I would describe this as a 'blessed' form of fake news or perhaps a deliberate mistranslation intended for a specific purpose. Recently I came across an insightful article by a theological student and author, Grant Hartley (2022). His work has significantly deepened my understanding of the Sodom and Gomorrah narrative. Hartley skilfully articulates the actual sin of these cities, drawing on the powerful biblical passage from Ezekiel 16.49–50:

> This was the guilt of your sister Sodom: she and her daughters had pride, excess of food, and prosperous ease, but did not aid the poor and needy. They were haughty, and did abominable things before me; therefore I removed them when I saw it. (NRSV)

Hartley explains that the story is meant to teach us about God's righteous anger towards arrogance and violence and abundant hospitality towards us despite our weaknesses and failures. Unlike many Christians today – who feel entitled to be inhospitable, cruel and violent towards LGBTIQ+ people – this passage clearly emphasizes violent humiliation, not sexual intimacy or pleasure. The people of Sodom sought to brutalize and harm the angels, not to fall in love with or seduce them. The failure to consider the broader context of the scriptures suggests a conscious or unconscious willingness to commit evil in the name of defending God's reputation. The Bible repeatedly states that God is hospitable to all people and desires God's followers also to practise hospitality (Matt. 25.35–40; Rom. 15.7; Heb. 13.2). To use the story of Sodom and Gomorrah as a justification for inhospitable behaviour – and, in some cases, to push anti-LGBTIQ+ laws in countries like Uganda while using Christianity as a scapegoat (Sherwood, 2012) – illustrates how the Bible is being weaponized. Sadly this is not a new phenomenon. In the past the Bible was weaponized to justify slavery. As James Alison

(2017) – the prominent British Roman Catholic theologian, author and priest – affirms, the story repeats itself.

The story of Sodom and Gomorrah, along with Christianity and the Bible, serves as a perfect excuse for irresponsible, corrupt and unaccountable politicians and policymakers in Africa. These figures create terror and fear among the people, using faith and scriptures to divert attention from the real issues that should hold them accountable for their failures in serving their nations and countries. Cis-heterosexual Christians often believe that their sins are less significant, forgetting that the sins that upset God most are not 'homosexuality' but egoism, greed, inhospitality, lying, devising wicked schemes and shedding innocent blood. What angers God is not the existence of LGBTIQ+ individuals but rather the pride and greed of a heart that, in the name of God, believes itself to be rich, self-sufficient and lacking nothing while failing to recognize its own wretched, pitiable, poor, blind and naked state (Rev. 3.17). Tragically, religious leaders often engage in this game of determining which sins are more forgivable, choosing to rejoice in the dehumanization of particular groups of people (Martin, 2023). When the state and religion, especially in the case of Christianity, align in this way, it is never a positive sign.

Christianity is more than a judgemental mindset; it is meant to lead us in following the footsteps of Jesus, which we, as Christians, are failing to do today. Jesus never looked down on anyone because of who they were, what they did, or their sins. In contrast to many Christians today, who proudly look down on others and fellow believers based on what they deem 'disgusting' or 'unforgivable', Jesus always looked up to everyone, even when others called them 'sinners'. He looked up at Zacchaeus (Luke 19.1–10) when he called him from the tree and chose to be his guest. He looked up at the disciples while he washed their feet (John 13.1–17), and he looked up at the woman caught in adultery when she was brought before him (John 8.3–11). Jesus never viewed one sin as more significant than another. That is why, when people wanted to stone the woman, he told them that the one without sin should cast the first stone. Later he told her to go and sin no more. He had the opportunity to delve into the idea that sexuality is worse or more sinful than anything else, as Christianity often portrays today, but he did not.

## Queer Christians

A few months ago I had the opportunity to reconnect with a friend who – five years ago – reached out to Gay Christian Africa because he was struggling to reconcile his sexuality with his faith. Raised in a deeply

Christian household where the family prayed together every evening, he was confused about his spiritual identity and questioned whether God truly loved him. He was also terrified of how his family would react if they learned about his sexuality. After five years of an incredible and transformative journey, he shared with me how grateful he was for connecting with Gay Christian Africa and how much he values our friendship. Today he is free and confident in his faith and spirituality. He recently said: 'I was depressed; I was failing for the first time in my life to study and failing exams, but now I'm back on track. And guess what? I feel God's presence and have no shame – I know I am loved.'

Being an LGBTIQ+ person is challenging enough in Africa, but being both LGBTIQ+ and Christian is even more difficult. As humans we continually crave a sense of belonging. Scientists and researchers describe how rejection causes physical and emotional numbness (Gerber and Wheeler, 2009). It harms our well-being in many ways, and in trying to avoid it we often develop survival strategies. Undoubtedly, one might try to conform to fit in, driven by the fear of rejection or abandonment by the only community one has ever known. This leads to an endless internal battle to meet expectations and to be what is deemed acceptable and tolerable. My friend made that giant step but many others are still trapped in that bubble of fear and shame, unable to envision a way out. The unknown is always frightening; it forces you to confront yourself alone before facing others. The path of self-acceptance, especially when it involves coming out, may appear to be a lonely one, mainly because there is no guarantee that your friends, or Christian friends, will stand by you or remain in your life. Hence the queer community is not always a welcoming or supportive environment either. It is filled with hurt individuals who, often unconsciously, can hurt themselves and others. No one can blame us; we learn everything – from loving ourselves to accepting ourselves – later in life, struggling to develop a healthy mindset.

For many LGBTIQ+ Christians, the first experiences of embracing their identity can be a total shock or a severe disappointment, often turning into drama, trauma and heartbreak. The instinctive reaction is frequently to deny one's sexuality and retreat into the spiritual shell that one believes can be controlled, even though it comes at a tremendous emotional cost. It feels safer to deal with the known, even though it is not what is needed to find peace and freedom. Healing can be painful; it is not a joyful process but it ultimately leads you to a place of growth in all areas of your life. In contrast, the slavery of the old self and the surrounding environment may feel more comfortable and less frightening. This mechanism of sacrificing one's happiness out of fear that the authentic self might come at too great a cost can be both a conscious decision and an unconscious reaction to the trauma encountered while trying to live one's true self or follow one's calling. I met a gay couple in Kenya several years ago who openly told me that they were fine with not coming out and that they would never do so because of the risks they would face in their Christian communities and society. They chose to marry women and – with the pastor's blessing – consciously decided to keep their love a secret and their identity in the shadows to continue participating in the church activities they felt gifted to do.

Queer Christians are a symbol of hope – an active, tangible and fertile hope. They offer their hands, hearts and minds to this hope in order to bring about the change needed within the church. Many of us have faced discrimination, rejection and constant prejudice about who we are. During one of the spiritual retreats held by Gay Christian Africa earlier this year, a participant who is both trans and Muslim shared a message to support Christians who were feeling the pressure of being inclusive in their discussions about spirituality and the challenges of living their faith and identity. They said: 'Feel free and faithful to your personal experience; I can definitely relate. After all, we come from different religions, but we are facing the same struggle: hatred, rejection, and discrimination in our own churches and society based on our beliefs.'

We have been asked – directly and indirectly – to change to fit into our Christian communities. We have witnessed how our identities have been reduced solely to our sexuality while our faith and the beauty within us remain overlooked. All the gifts and talents we could contribute to uplift our communities are set aside. This behaviour has forced us to shrink our spirituality, essence and potential to the size of what others – particularly fellow Christians – can accommodate because our value is not recognized, as Revd Keion Henderson (2024) affirms. Our Christian journey has been marred by shame and an undeserving attitude. The feelings instilled in us by the environment we once trusted have led us to dim our light and disconnect from our true selves for the comfort of others. Queer Christians who have gathered the courage and strength to reconcile their faith and identity are leading us towards a new path – one that is unfamiliar to many queer Christians, especially those in Africa. Talking about faith, sexual orientation, gender identity and expression together is still a taboo, if not a scandal.

Reconciling faith and identity for queer people is not only an urgent need but also a necessary move to break the negative pattern of appearance and hypocrisy that exists in many Christian communities. Being able to mature our faith and our identity and reconciling them makes us feel not victims:

I'm still grateful for each mountain
And glad for each valley
Every song, every service
Every pulpit, every alley
... I'm grateful for the rainbow –
that shone after the storm
The cloud that kept me cool,
the fire that kept warm
(Pinnock, 2024)

Those are the poignant words of the Christian gospel singer Seth Pinnock in his evocative poem 'Night Watch'. Pinnock's poem reflects a deep sense of introspection and vigilance, themes that resonate even more profoundly following his public coming out. This pivotal moment in his life was highlighted in an interview featured in *The Guardian* (Sherwood, 2024).

No one can deny that LGBTIQ+ people exist within our churches. The attendees of the spiritual retreats organized by Gay Christian Africa in sub-Saharan Africa this year were all active servants in their churches – choir members, gospel singers, former or current altar boys, leaders of Christian movements or those leading small Christian communities, among others. That underscores a profound yearning for spaces where queer Christians – and those outside the community – can reconcile their faith and spirituality.

It is shameful that the evangelization of God often erases the presence and existence of LGBTIQ+ people from the Christian framework. The Bible says: 'The stone that the builders rejected has become the cornerstone' (Matt. 21.42, NRSV; Mark 12.10–11; Luke 20.17; Acts 4.11; 1 Peter 2.7). Throughout history, Christians have often perceived diversity as a threat. Even the disciples took time to understand that non-Jews could be called by God and fully integrated into the church's service (Acts 11.1). The resilience and strong faith of queer Christians will transform us into builders of hope, peace and bridges. We are the hope for constructive dialogue within our churches and beyond: within our religions, between religions and across cultures.

## Beyond Queerness

Last year an African public figure who identifies as Christian publicly declared that gay people should be taken to the stadium and stoned to death. Unfortunately it has become all too common to hear African policymakers, politicians and even religious leaders using Christianity to justify their homophobia and hostility towards LGBTIQ+ people. Given this understanding of Christianity, one might ask: What is at the core of Christian teaching if hatred is justified? If Christianity is truly a space where diversity is celebrated, why does dialogue with queer people appear to be a threat? Suppose Christianity is meant to be a place where pastoral work, spirituality and fraternity come together in harmony. What has led to such a rigid and unhealthy form of spirituality in Africa?

The Bible clearly states that Christians who are unable to love are liars (1 John 4.20). Indeed, how can anyone claim to love those they have not seen yet hate the people they have seen? Unfortunately the reception of the gospel in sub-Saharan African cultures following colonization has been dictated and manipulated to the point where one might ask, as the Kenyan theologian Nyambura Njoroge (2001) did: 'Is Christianity a curse or a blessing?'

While Africans have warmly embraced the gospel, early missionaries were also complicit in European imperialism. Their silence in the face of the atrocities happening on their watch – as well as their direct or indirect involvement in the exploitation of the Democratic Republic of the Congo and other colonies – has left a legacy of unhealthy Christianity. That is not to say that Christianity itself is inherently bad but rather to invite churches to critically engage in deconstructing the form of Christianity we live by today with a mature and responsible spirituality. Christianity must overcome its blindness, its silence and the political manipulation that has used the Bible to control people for specific commodities and comforts (Togarasei and Chitando, 2011). As the theologian SimonMary Asese Aihiokhai (2023) argues:

> The ongoing cultural wars that are playing out in some societies and that are given validity through an appeal to the Christian faith call for a deconstructive engagement. To do this well, a deliberate attempt is made to unpack the politics of hermeneutics and show how it can help Christians to refute the agenda of those who make one perspective on Christian teachings the only valid interpretation. (p. 382)

This highlights that the narrative promoted by some Christians and politicians to criminalize and discriminate against queer people using Christianity is a calculated and intentional mistranslation of the scriptures. It aims to incite hatred and harm, offering a sacrificial scapegoat to populist and nationalist sentiments.

In societies struggling with numerous vices and desperately seeking a way forward, queer people often become the convenient scapegoat. The hardships faced by citizens are frequently attributed to God's anger, allegedly provoked by the existence of LGBTIQ+ individuals. At the same time the real issues – such as systemic corruption, poor governance and a lack of accountability among national and local leaders – are conveniently ignored. After all, if God is punishing the nation(s) because of queer people, what could leaders possibly do to stop divine wrath? This misattribution has fuelled widespread societal violence against LGBTIQ+ individuals, masquerading as 'defending the Gospel of Jesus Christ' (Kaoma, 2009, p. 17).

Fortunately a few African queer individuals, religious LGBTIQ+ groups and organizations and theologians are taking the lead in uncovering pathways for authentic evangelization. The negative biases introduced during the early evangelization and proclamation of Christianity significantly influenced its reception, requiring the deconstruction of these narratives as an essential task today. The unhealthy contradictions within Christian spirituality in Africa are deeply rooted in this colonial approach, which often dismissed or devalued indigenous beliefs and practices.

Theologians and scholars – such as Matthew Michael (2013) and Laurenti Magesa (2014) – argue that African cultures and traditions have much to offer in enriching and deepening the understanding of Christianity today (Ogunleye, 2014). Similarly, Aihiokhai (2023) contends that what is truly needed is a robust theological engagement that integrates the wisdom of African spirituality with a decolonized approach to Christianity, emphasizing reconciliation, authenticity and mutual respect:

> The querying of proclamation to ensure that the inherent biases, positive or negative, are validated by the one proclaiming, is itself a pathway for a decolonial critique of proclamation. By decolonial critique, I mean an intentional evaluation of the hermeneutic and epistemic world from which the bearer and content of proclamation operate. Decolonial critique allows for the realization of diverse epistemic traditions to be encountered and received by the audience. It invalidates the hegemony of universalism and normativity that a single vision and experience tends to perpetuate. (pp. 6–7)

The absence of decolonial critiques in Christian discourse is causing significant harm to families and societies, as it prevents the development of strong, healthy relationships between LGBTIQ+ individuals and their families. At the heart of Christianity lies the concept of home and family

– God is often envisioned as 'our Father', and spirituality is deeply reflected in 'our familial relationships'. In African Christian communities, believers commonly refer to one another as 'brothers' and 'sisters' in Christ. This emphasis on familial bonds is deeply ingrained, which is why it is no surprise that:

> We value so much family, to the point of putting our lives on hold because of the family if we judge it necessary. We struggle to detach ourselves from it even when it is for our own good. However the value we give to family should be the value family gives to us. Not only the biological family, even the church family as well. The value we give to church is the value the church should give to us. An individual should not use more effort to go to the bigger community than the bigger community going to one individual. (Gay Christian Africa, 2022)

Unlike others, queer people in many sub-Saharan countries often feel unsafe and fearful in their own homes. They live with the constant fear of losing their value within their families, damaging their reputation in the community and forfeiting respect in their neighbourhoods. They also worry about jeopardizing their careers and futures if they come out. The fear of rejection, abandonment and loneliness is pervasive, profoundly affecting their psychological, social and spiritual well-being. Those considered fortunate have relocated to Western countries, hoping to live freely and authentically. However, the idea of paradise remains elusive. Anti-immigration sentiments prevalent in Western countries often target them as well, and these nations – and their religions – are still in the process of learning to truly value and affirm black lives.

Last year, during a meeting with a Christian LGBTIQ+ group in Milan, I was invited to share my experience as a gay person in Uganda. Although the world's attention was focused on Uganda at the time due to the anti-LGBTIQ+ law that had been approved, I emphasized that not everything about my experience was negative. Some of my best and most memorable moments as a gay person were during the four years I spent in Kampala from 2013 to 2017. This period coincided with the introduction of the first anti-gay bill in parliament.

While uncertainty and fear were palpable, it would be a disservice not to acknowledge the beauty of the LGBTIQ+ community and the joy we shared, even during such challenging times. Those years allowed me to understand myself better and to grasp the true meaning of community for LGBTIQ+ individuals. I remain deeply grateful for every person I met, the fun moments we shared, the parties that lifted our spirits and the enduring friendships and sense of brotherhood I cherish. I also shared with the group in Milan that while I can now openly express my feelings and sexuality without significant risks, I have encountered a new challenge: my flesh – the colour of my skin. In many circumstances, it has become problematic in ways I had never considered before. Black people are often required to demand respect in every space we occupy, and in most places our very presence must be justified. Sometimes even our spirituality is questioned.

This view of black bodies does not spare the white LGBTIQ+ communities that already know and experience discrimination. Jarel A. Robinson-Brown (2021) explains:

> Our Black LGBTQ+ bodies, even in Queer-affirming spaces, can elicit danger, abuse and risk. The Black body in the White imagination is fetishized and regularly used as that upon which White fantasies are played out. Even in pornography, the Black male body being fixed to notions of the 'thug' or 'beast' perpetuates this idea that the Black body is unfeeling, less than human, and made to be brutalized and brutalized. (p. 98)

This awareness takes on a different weight when you realize your sexual orientation or gender identity. For example, while you can learn to control or disguise certain aspects of yourself in spaces or communities to ensure your safety or maintain inner peace, this is not something you can do regarding your skin colour. Your body is the suit you present to the world, and the colour of your skin is simply the colour of that suit (Robinson-Brown, 2021). As I shared with my friends during that meeting in Milan, this new experience has challenged my sense of existence, dignity and value as a person more profoundly than my sexuality ever did when I was in Burundi or Uganda.

Queer Christians, like all Christians, have a unique relationship with the Bible. Their lived experiences, shaped by their sexual orientation, gender identity and personal journeys, have led them to engage with scripture through a distinct lens (Van Klinken et al., 2021). Their perspectives are valid and essential for understanding the full scope of Christian faith in today's world. By embracing the experiences of LGBTIQ+ Christians, religious groups and organizations such as the Nature Network (2024) and Gay Christian Africa (2024), Christianity has a powerful opportunity to learn from those who have been marginalized yet remain committed to living out the gospel in its most radical and inclusive form.

## Conclusion

LGBTIQ+ Christians in Africa offer invaluable contributions to the Christian community. They are living testimonies of compassion, resilience and faithfulness (Van Klinken et al., 2021). They provide food for the hungry, drink for the thirsty, welcome for the stranger, clothing for the naked, care for the sick and visits for those in prison. They embody the true spirit of service that the gospel calls for, yet their faith is often questioned or dismissed because of their sexual orientation or gender identity. However, the pastoral work required in today's Christian communities is not only for LGBTIQ+ Christians; it is a call for all Christians, parents and religious leaders to embark on a transformative journey towards true Christianity. This journey involves accepting and embracing the diversity of human experience and recognizing that one's sexuality, gender identity or expression is not an obstacle to faith or spirituality.

It is unfortunate that when the topic of homosexuality arises in Christian communities, LGBTIQ+ Christians are often excluded, their voices silenced and their spiritual lives diminished. Yet these queer Christians stand as profound reflections of the peripheries of Christianity. Their lives, dignity and spirituality, which should be valued and celebrated, are often overlooked or outright rejected. In doing so the church misses the opportunity to experience a fuller, richer expression of the Body of Christ. By marginalizing LGBTIQ+ Christians, Christian communities are not only neglecting those who are at the margins but also denying themselves the chance to witness the transformative power of inclusive faith and love.

Christian communities must reconsider their stance on queer Christians, particularly those who seek dialogue and deeper understanding. These individuals should not be seen as a threat to traditional values or beliefs; instead, they represent a resource – an opportunity for renewal and growth within the church. By welcoming LGBTIQ+ Christians and engaging in meaningful dialogue, Christian communities can begin to reflect the truly inclusive nature of Christ's teachings. As the Body of Christ, the church is called to embrace all its members, recognizing that each individual brings a unique and valuable contribution to the whole. Every part of the body must be appreciated and loved, and when all members are valued, the Body of Christ becomes genuinely whole.

The inclusion of queer Christians in the church is not merely a matter of justice or tolerance; it is a matter of faith. It is a step towards restoring the gospel's radical message of love, inclusivity and grace. A Christian community that embraces all its members, regardless of their sexual orientation or gender identity, is a community that is truly living out the example of Christ. Queer Christians, through their faith and perseverance, have much to offer – not just to the church but to the world. By recognizing their dignity and embracing their contributions, the church can move closer to becoming the home for everyone that Christ intended it to be.

## References


Aihiokhai, SimonMary Asese (2023), 'Where/How/For What Purpose is Christ Being Proclaimed Today: Rethinking Proclamation in the World of Peripheries', *Religions* 14, no. 3, pp. 1–14.

Alison, James (2017), 'Reading Scripture and the LGBT Question', lecture delivered at the Seminary of the Southwest (Episcopal), Austin, Texas, on 12 September, at https://www.youtube.com/watch?v=I-CLf9fqq5E, accessed 01.12.2024.

Block, Elizabeth Sweeny (2023), 'The Synod Emphasized the Lived Experience of the Faithful. This must include LGBTQ People', *Outreach: An LGBTQ Catholic Resource*, 5 December, at https://outreach.faith/2023/12/the-synod-emphasized-the-lived-experience-of-the-faithful-this-must-include-lgbtq-people/, accessed 01.12.2024.

Epprecht, Marc (2013), *Sexuality and Social Justice in Africa: Rethinking Homophobia and Forging Resistance* (African Arguments Series), London: Zed Books.

Gay Christian Africa (2022), 'African and Religious Family with LGBTQ+ Member(s): Is this Possible?' (video), *Facebook*, 29 September, at https://www.facebook.com/watch/live/?ref=watch_permalink&v=2343953469085233, accessed 01.12.2024.

Gay Christian Africa (2024), 'Gay Christian Africa. Who We Are?' at https://www.gaychristianafrica.org/gaychristianafrica-who-we-are/, accessed 01.12.2024.

Gerber, Jonathan and Ladd Wheeler (2009), 'On Being Rejected: A Meta-Analysis of Experimental Research on Rejection', *Perspectives on Psychological Science* 4, no. 5 (September), pp. 468–88.

Hartley, Grant (2022), 'The Story of Sodom and Gomorrah asks us to Consider our own Inhospitality', *Outreach: An LGBTQ Catholic Resource*, 11 December, at https://outreach.faith/2022/12/the-story-of-sodom-and-gomorrah-asks-us-to-consider-our-own-inhospitality/?utm_source=chatgpt.com, accessed 01.12.2024.

Henderson, Keion [@keionhenderson] (2024), 'Faith and Resilience' [video], *Instagram*, 11 November, at https://www.instagram.com/reel/DCO4edAI9L8/?igsh=ZjkxN3dyMWxlNW1w, accessed 01.12.2024.

Kaoma, Kapya (2009), *Globalizing the Culture Wars: U.S. Conservatives, African Churches and Homophobia*, Somerville, MA: Political Research Associates.

Magesa, Laurenti (2014), *What Is Not Sacred?: African Spirituality*, Maryknoll, NY: Orbis Books.

Martin, Francis (2023), 'Church of Uganda "grateful' as Harsh New Anti-homosexuality Law is Approved', *Church Times*, 30 May, at https://www.churchtimes.co.uk/articles/2023/2-june/news/world/church-of-uganda-grateful-as-harsh-new-anti-homosexuality-law-is-approved, accessed 01.12.2024.

Michael, Matthew (2013), *Christian Theology and African Traditions*, Cambridge: Lutterworth Press.

Nature Network (2024), 'About', at linkedin.com/in/the-nature-network-730a362b8, accessed 01.12.2024.

Njoroge, Nyambura J. (2001), 'The Bible and African Christianity: A Curse or a Blessing?', in *Other Ways of Reading: African Women and the Bible*, edited by Musa W. Dube, Atlanta, GA: Society of Biblical Literature, pp. 207–36.

Ogunleye, Richard Adetunbi (2014), 'Christian Theology and African Traditions by Matthew Michael, Lutterworth, 2013 (ISBN 978-0-7188-9294-4), xvi+ 259 pp., pb $27', *Reviews in Religion and Theology* 21, no. 3, pp. 367–70.

Pinnock, Seth (2024), 'Night Watch' (poem), *Inclusive Evangelicals*, 29 July, at https://www.inclusiveevangelicals.com/post/watch-night-a-poem-by-seth-pinnock, accessed 01.12.2024.

Reuters (2023), 'Burundi's President says Gay People should be Stoned', 30 December at https://www.reuters.com/world/africa/burundis-president-says-gay-people-should-be-stoned-2023-12-30/, accessed 01.12.2024.

Robinson-Brown, Jarel A. (2021), *Black, Gay, British, Christian, Queer: The Church and the Famine of Grace*, London: SCM Press.

Sherwood, Harriet (2024), '"This is Right, this is the Future of the Church": Gay Black Evangelist on Coming Out', *The Guardian*, 28 July, at https://www.theguardian.com/world/article/2024/jul/28/gay-black-evangelist-seth-pinnock-on-coming-out?, accessed 01.12.2024.

Sherwood, Yvonne (2012), *Biblical Blaspheming: Trials of the Sacred for a Secular Age*, Cambridge: Cambridge University Press.

Shore-Goss, Robert E. (2002), *Queering Christ: Beyond Jesus Acted Up*, New York: Pilgrim Press.

Togarasei, Lovemore and Ezra Chitando (2011), '"Beyond the Bible": Critical Reflections on the Contributions of Cultural and Postcolonial Studies on Same-sex Relationships in Africa', *Journal of Gender and Religion in Africa* 17, no. 2 (December), pp. 109–25.

Van Klinken, Adriaan S. and Johanna Stiebert with Sebyala Brian and Fredrick Hudson (2021), *Sacred Queer Stories: Ugandan LGBTQ+ Refugee Lives and the Bible* (Religion in Transforming Africa Series # 7), Melton: James Currey.

PART 4

# Christology and Embodied Theology

# 10

# Grace: Times of *Cuir* Alchemy

MARILÚ ROJAS SALAZAR
*(translated by Hugo Córdova Quero)*

## The Queer/*Cuir* Grace

'Grace' is a fluid and porous concept that flows through corporealities, transforming and intertwining with them. It is alchemized within the 'blessed mixture' (Gebara, 2022) that defines our existence as beings inhabiting this planet. Grace permeates our physical and spiritual selves, creating a dynamic and interconnected presence that binds us to one another and the world around us:

> today, we are trying to embrace the diversity and the mixture that we are, as a challenge and the only condition for life to express itself in its limitless multiplicity ... the mixture that we are appears in all sectors of life, in the forms of knowledge, in our beliefs and the meanderings of our psychism. (Gebara, 2022, p. 38)

It manifests itself primarily in the in-world bodies and transgresses all normativity or law just because it is grace. These times of feminist and LGBTIQ+ militancy are politically kairological in the consolidation of posthumanist *cuir* theologies. To recognize the mixture is also to realize that there are no pure queer theologies to embrace post-Christian and decolonial positions.

A gratuitous or generous presence does not seek to protect itself from anything and does not claim anything for itself. Free actions do not want anything in return for what they give; they do not seek a secure or fixed place (Alison, 2003). They are nomadic. They are borderline, mixed, mongrel, abject and bitchy (Meloni, 2021). They are not afraid of disappearing, ending or being destroyed, and they fight for their ideals. Grace as a gift of divinity is a promiscuous category since it is given to all people regardless of their condition, so it is anti-racist, anti-sexist and anti-classist. It decolonizes our prejudices of gender and sexuality because it inhabits unworldly bodies. I use the category of 'uncleanness' here in the sense that Jean-Luc Nancy (2000) uses it. The unclean is a way of entering this zone of non-recognition without even a horizon that allows its appearance. Nancy uses the expression to indicate those remnants of the world that remain outside, opaque and unabsorbable remnants, seen from the world we call filth.

However, these unworldly bodies are inhabited by the grace of the divinity that makes in them an epiphany of recognition and dignity. In-world can also be used as under or inside the world and associated with the incarnational category. Grace is, then, incarnated in the unworldly bodies – inside the world – or in what is expelled by the world, the twisted and non-heteronormalized bodies. Grace is contained in bodies considered unworldly. This alludes to Mark 12.10, where 'The stone that the builders rejected has become the cornerstone' (NRSV). The disposable bodies, discarded in clandestine graves, have become a source of subversion. Many women have positioned themselves in search of collectives, creating movements and militancy. These efforts denounce necro-states allied with death systems and the criminal organizations of drug trafficking. The discarded bodies now cry out for justice in the voices of women searching for their relatives.

In the Christian tradition, grace derives from the word *charis*, meaning 'gift', and it refers to the necessity of divine grace to do good and live in love. This divine grace is bestowed upon human beings gratuitously, without any merit on their part, which is precisely why it is named *gratia*. It is also understood as a consequence of the presence of the Holy Spirit – better known as *Ruâh* in the Hebrew Bible – interpreted as a trans identity since, in some traditions, it is associated with the feminine while, in others, with the masculine. I prefer to describe *Ruâh* as a fluid and mixed category that embodies both realities and many others. Moreover, the action of grace does not override human freedom, as it operates through attraction, love and mercy. This makes grace a fluid force that resists institutional control and the morality of religions. Instead, it freely offers love to those who receive it, transcending gender categories and embracing the diversity of corporealities and sexualities.

Grace is inherently promiscuous because it emanates from the divine and is bestowed upon all without regard to race, culture, sexuality or notions of good and evil. In this way grace shatters binary divisions and cis-heteronormative constraints. It is not contingent upon our human actions, nor can it be earned through our merits. Once we are enveloped in this love it is from this place of fullness that acts of kindness and love arise, fuelled by the erotic power that dwells within our bodies. This love flows outward, extending to other bodies and challenging the limits of our physicality. Doing so transcends egoism and fosters the creation of inclusive, diverse communities rooted in love – what Rosi Braidotti (2022) refers to as the bio-zoo-geo-techno-mediated bodies.

The guilt and sin that have served as the tools of control of patriarchal religions and homolesbotransphobic discourses are decolonized by grace, as the latter rests on a tripod, or premises, that I suggest below.

In the first place, guilt and sin came with colonizing Christianity to censor the corporeality and sexuality of the inhabitants of these lands and impose on their cultures, which had many other forms of fluid sexualities. While grace positions at its maximum expression the capacity for the goodness of all beings who inhabit this typical home or in the bio-geo-zoo-techno-mediated bodies, in a decolonizing act of cis-heteronormative and speciesist anthropocentrism. It goes further towards posthumanism (Braidotti, 2022). It overcomes anthropocentrism in its obscene, phallocratic and kyriocentric Capitalocene phase, in which merits are constituted in a market profit that exchanges bodies and guilty sexualities exhibiting them in pornographic acts. Meanwhile grace places eroticism as the force that empowers from divinity the capacity to love of diverse bodies and sexualities.

Second, many people in the LGBTIQ+ communities experience feelings of guilt and have been categorized as sinners for their sexual practices. Both categories of guilt and sin are based on the idea that God will never forgive them and will punish them, thus building a discourse of hatred that fills them with terror and fear. This discourse is used by many religious sectors who are interested in showing a punishing image of the monotheistic, patriarchal-machoist God, who is certainly not the God of Jesus of Nazareth but the God of their prejudices.

Third, in Mexico, in some places in the countryside, they ask you, 'What's your grace?', referring to your name or to the way others name you. I want to rescue this sense of grace to re-signify that it is the right to name ourselves and to perform our names as we best identify ourselves, or in other words, our right to enter into disidentifying processes. Grace exiles the guilty God and alchemizes the performativity of the divinity that inhabits our bodies and expresses itself in multiform expressions of love and sexuality.

Last, guilt and sin oppress sexually diverse people, censure them, exclude them from the realm of goodness and categorize and prejudice them as 'bad', sinful or dirty. Both categories cloud people's capacity for reflection, intelligence and discernment to make decisions and exercise their freedom of conscience. Guilt is a feeling inflicted, installed in our conscience by external agents. We were not born with guilt; we learned it through religious thought, which is why it is essential to deconstruct it. Guilt is an emotion constantly fed by the memory – an image – of an action, omission or thought that is outside the will of God or another person and harms others and oneself because it acts as a mechanism of self-loathing. This mechanism of self-deprecation in words such as 'I am worthless', 'I am not worthy', 'I do not deserve God's blessing', 'I am a bad person' or 'I am a despicable being', among others, constantly undermines the self-esteem of people until it annihilates their love for themselves and places them continually in beings for others, which ends up being a terrible violence against them. Guilt is a feeling learned and installed in our unconscious in childhood, and most of the time it is imaginary. Guilt prevents us from taking charge of the reality of the body and sexuality that inhabits us, and it is a feeling that hurts us. For Rocío Hernández Mella and Berenice Pacheco Salazar (2009):

> In a society based on unequal power relations between men and women and, likewise, on the logic of reward/punishment, guilt is based on the martyrological feeling that hinders us from assuming responsibility for our actions and omissions and, therefore, from being the builders of our own history and destiny. (pp. 150–1)

Therefore, recovering the category of grace in its broadest sense as a coven of queer/*cuir* alchemies is a bet to deconstruct guilt and sin as colonial categories and tools of control of abject bodies. To achieve my purpose in this chapter, I first make a feminist and ecofeminist theological proposal for the Kairos category. Then I analyse the painting *Tiempo de Mujer* [*Woman's Time*] by the artist Carlos Márquez Peralta (2024). Finally I place the category of erotic tension as an element of aesthetics from the feminist proposal to continue questioning our colonial aesthetic categories.

## Queer/*Cuir* Kairological Times

Kairos [*Καιρός*] in the Christian tradition is the opportune time that God has for each thing to happen, willing to give his grace. Kairos is the act of fissioning chronos as the linear and perfect time. The word is of Greek origin and found in the Bible, and is translated as 'the opportune time, the determinate time in which something happens', unlike Kronos [*Κρόνος*], which refers to sequential time and the way we humans measure it. Kairos is qualitative and Kronos is quantitative. Kairos is the qualitative time of life. The Greeks considered it the most suitable for novelty:

> The concept has its origins in the practice of Greek archery, representing the moment when the archer finds the perfect opening to shoot his arrow and hit his target. But Kairos (or Caerus) was also the Greek god of opportunity. He had wings on his feet and he ran a lot, but if you were paying attention, you could catch him by the long tail of hair hanging behind his bald head. (Mària, 2021)

What does this have to do with queer/*cuir* theology? From my point of view, these times are the opportune time, the precise moment in which the experiences of faith and the theological-spiritual reflection of the unworldly bodies embody a presupposition of sexual identity, as Marcella Althaus-Reid (2019) writes:

> I affirm that Christology and all doctrinal propositions – even the doctrine of Grace or Redemption – developed based on a presupposition of sexual identity. They function at the level of ontological 'pre-text' and determine the essence of the human being and their relationships with the world, be they affectional or economic exchanges. In other words, theology has made an idol of a sexual ideology like heterosexuality. (p. 35)

It is this time, the precise, opportune time, the time for the patriarchal idol to fall and for the queer Kairos to emerge as the opportune and dissident time of the 'indecencies' and sexual nomadisms. To make this truly liberating we must establish that time as the theological place or the queer theological corpus.

Grace is a matter of knowing how to give an account of love, but not of idealistic romantic love, nor colonial or naive love, but of the love that crosses our corporealities, our sexual caverns and our erotic strength; the love that experiences the sufferings and misunderstandings in the love of the in-world body we inhabit, for:

> The Christian Church has never heard people's sexual stories, and that is why theology knows so little about love. How will we talk about Grace – something that is free, God's free love – if we do not understand what lies behind the lives and loves of so many people, of so many theologians who hide behind idealistic rhetoric? (Althaus-Reid, 2019, p. 46)

Should we not start thinking about posthuman sexualities and not remain locked in the paradigm of human sexuality? What about the multiple forms of love, the multiple sexual expressions? That is, the forms of love of humans and the rest of the species? It is necessary to think that grace happens in the world and is not reduced to be experienced only by humans.

## Queer/*Cuir* Alchemies and Cross-Border Aquelarres of Grace

Grace is the alchemy of flows and diversities in a constant coven of border bodies. I explain it as alchemy: it is not that we always love well, nor perfectly, because our loves are always mixed of good and bad loves, of fulfilment and disappointment, of mistakes and successes. Love is not perfect, that is why it is alchemical. Grace is a coven because it converges in the meeting of dissident bodies considered unworldly, bodies that love each other, express their eroticism as the spiritual force that conspires to transgress colonial love in an orgiasmic subversive act. However, these bodies are at the frontiers of transsexuality, transcorporeality and the posthuman (Braidotti, 2022).

The concept of 'cross-border' or 'trans-borderization' seeks to transcend the restrictive confines of nationalistic ideals. It emphasizes the mobility, transformation and redefinition of zones, spaces and communities, considering cultural, historical, socio-economic, class, racial and gender dimensions. This approach highlights the fluidity and interconnectedness of these various factors. Focusing on gender studies, I position the transborder as going beyond fixed gender identities and allowing transsexual experiences to dislocate us to give way to bio-geo-zoo-techno-mediated epistemic categories of the unworldly bodies that are summoned to account for the loves and the precise times in which sexual dissidence occurs as epiphanies of grace and blessing and to make mention of a coven of grace or grace as a coven because the word 'coven' was used to denominate the groupings or meetings of witches and warlocks, where rituals and spells were performed. The word is of Basque origin. It comes from *akelarrre*, which means field or farmland. That happens in the LGBTIQ+ community; every time it convenes to express and think beyond the boundaries of bodies, sexualities and desires, Kairos occurs as the time of love.

The 'out of the closet' narrative is about unconventional thinking, away from the usual mental schemes and in line with new perspectives. It is an open way of thinking that produces insecurity and vertigo. Thinking out of the closet makes us lose security, but we gain vision and perspective. Events of an international nature allow us to 'come out of the closet' and free ourselves from some of the burdens of 'thinking in the closet', using 'thinking in a cross-border mode'. We can speak of cross-border thinking using the categories of gender as thinking outside the cis-heteronorms of colonial Christianity to give way to post-Christian and even post-theological thinking.

Grace is then a transboundary episteme because it escapes any norm or structure and is uncontainable, for in theological thought we say that grace is 'poured out', it is uncontainable in a single bodily and sexual model, it is superabundance and not scarcity. It is poured out to all sexualities, corporealities and modes of affection in polyamorous acts in all creation to empower multiple forms of relationship, making the outpouring of grace a kenotic and kairological coven. Grace as love of the divinity is then a transborder erotic act that occurs in every act of love of the creatures that inhabit this cosmos.

While the colonial and fundamentalist Christian tradition condemned and exiled diverse sexualities and corporealities from grace and redemption, feminist and queer theologies now recognize the superabundance of grace and kairological redemption. These are understood as times of opportunity, dissent and fissure against patriarchal systems that exiled our bodies and sexualities by denigrating or condemning them as outside redemption. Redemption is not understood, then, as maintaining a particular condition placed as 'abstentionism of the sex-affective-erotic praxis'. On the contrary, redemption implies recognizing ourselves from the depth of our erotic-affective-sexual and corporeal realities as the theological space of the diverse love of the divine superabundance that is incarnated in the dissident corporealities and the fissures of our bodies and daily relationships.

## Feminist Kairos Times: An Aesthetic Interpellation from Dissident Corporealities[1]

The emergence of multiple contemporary feminist movements, the dissidences and theoretical-epistemological discussions among feminist activists and academics, the criticality of feminisms, transfeminisms, cyberfeminisms, posthumanist feminisms, queer/queer feminisms, community feminisms, black feminisms, lesbofeminism and ecofeminists, among other various currents, place us in a Kairos as a time of grace or times of opportunity for all of us who call ourselves women. They are prophetic times since, if we understand that prophetic movements emerged in times of political crisis as an irresistible force of the world with the strength to change or transform history, then feminist movements and their various currents are an attack on the neocolonial patriarchal system called Capitalocene.

At the time of writing this chapter, the 4B feminist movement is gaining strength, which arose in Korea and maintains four principles: no children, no marriage with men, no dating men and no sex with men, especially with men with macho characteristics (Rashid, 2024). The context in which it arises is because South Korea is the country that has the most significant wage gap in the world between men and women. It has not wanted to recognize the issue of rape as sexual violence legally, it is a highly patriarchal society, and the incidence of violence against women has increased more and more. It is an emancipatory movement against social, corporeal and psychological sexual oppression. The movement has gained strength now with the election of Donald Trump and the positions of the extreme right that has made highly violent statements against women's sexual rights and against the right to decide. From my point of view, it is a feminist movement fed up with political, social and religious fundamentalisms that seek to roll back the achievements of the waves of feminism (Refuge, 2024).

The movement is more among girls and some intellectuals or academics who no longer tolerate the patriarchal machoist camouflage of many men:

- 'Pretend to be feminists' as a means of pleasing women and being more successful with them.
- Men who perform so-called studies of 'new masculinities' as chameleon-like acts appear to be 'new men' yet they retain the same privileges.
- Men who pretend to be 'experts' in feminism and gender studies and are going to teach us women how they can 'cook', 'wash', do care work, but as a heroic act that we women have to recognize and give them a red carpet and applaud them as extraordinary men.
- Men who want to appear progressive and open-minded, and to make a good impression.
- Sexual diversity partners who are misogynistic reject feminists because they are more assertive and creative and confront them in their practices of power, domination or control.

The 4B feminist movement is a way of expressing the weariness of women against the purported colonization of bodies and sexualities. It also challenges the stubbornness of public policies that want to see us as a political 'agenda' because it sells well or to place us as a 'gender quota' without a critical feminist perspective.

Some have called this emergence of activisms and theories the fourth wave of feminism, and I agree. However, my position, drawing from my lexicon as a feminist theologian, impels me to place the category of feminist kairological times: the times of women, the times of dissidence, and the recreation of many other ways of conceiving the world, relationships, politics and love.

## Analysis of the Painting *Tiempo de Mujer* (*Woman's Time*)

*Figure 1:* Tiempo de Mujer *by Carlos Márquez Peralta, 2024. Reproduced by permission of the artist.*

I commissioned the work from the artist during a particular crisis: both the artist and I were experiencing personal mourning, each in our own way. When the work reached my hands it was an opportune moment to begin a new stage in my life. The hermeneutic I will make of *Tiempo de*

*Mujer* (Márquez Peralta, 2024) has that slant, but it could have many other views; that is just what art allows us. Art questions us and moves us internally to the point of causing a revolution of affection and knowledge. This work provokes me to reflect on the exaltation of the senses, on the stirred interiority and on subversive movements.

The work shows a kind of uterus, which at first glance also appears as a biological hourglass between muscles and flesh in upward and downward movements. It is in dynamic flux wrapped in flesh and blood that pulsate and express the life, drive and passion where feminist movements are gestated. It clearly shows several layers of muscle or flesh, at least four very defined, which leads me to associate them with the four waves of feminism. The upper left side culminates with a golden sunrise and the upper right side with a hint of hopeful nostalgia. The whole work is accompanied from bottom to top and from top to bottom by a faint greenness that awakens me to think of the critical and creative hope typical of feminist movements. The whites and greys appear as interstices, as small times of fissure or light that accompany the entire work. The light fills the spaces and opens them to other multiple dimensions. The work is embodied in a body; it is the inner part of a body, and it shows us brazenly the deepest interior of that corporeality, as well as its most precious treasure.

The fourth wave of feminist movements has been characterized by its intentional rupture of political systems, prolific creative and dissident literature, the defence of trans rights overcoming gender binarism, and an intersectional bet. The work moves us to think of the category of Kairos as the precise opportune time to transform everything, the times of feminism as times of grace and conversion to transform patriarchal structures and begin a new era: posthuman feminisms.

These troubled times have become a time of opportunity for women. It is the era of women and feminisms. Women are bringing creativity, struggles and activism, and we are building a world that can be liveable from the *entrecuido* [interweaving],[2] making a mutual agreement connecting with the bio-zoe-geo-techno-mediated bodies, as Braidotti (2022) calls them. This is not without limits, as we struggle with our own internalized patriarchy that has often led us to rethink when we are victims of our aggressions. Recognizing the grace that inhabits us has required feminist movements to rethink salvation as clandestine freedom (Rojas Salazar, 2023), as everything that happens in women's desires and bodies, passing through the pain that crosses our tight skins and bodies:

> Pain ... to define a place of affection and reason, emotion, and reflection and to point out what we can give to each other (I include here all of humanity in a new and more complete idea of community) in the scenario of spiritual and material misery that hangs over all of us today. (Piedade, 2021, p. 8)

The grace that happens in the fat bodies, in the bodies of bastard origin (Galindo, 2022), in cyborg bodies (Haraway, 2020). The grace that happens in my old age (Gebara, 2022), in the bodies that live with a disability (Taylor, 2021) or in the bodies considered monstrous. To recognize grace or the opportune time is not to return to the 'normality' of violence, homolesbotransphobia and fatphobia. The trinomial of grace, salvation and redemption invites us to recognize crises and desires as theological loci, prompting questions like: What do women desire? Or – as Lucía Ramón Carbonell (2021) asks – must women rethink salvation in 'green and violet'? This reimagining demands that we consider grace and salvation within corporealities beyond the human: the bodies of plants, animals, the Earth itself and even unworldly corporealities. It urges us to see divine grace manifest in the human realm, the world's interconnected ecologies and posthuman and transcendent corporeal expressions.

Colonialism based on racism, sexism and classism continues to look at knowledge often without bodies or with stereotyped bodies. The question arises: If decolonial studies emanate from critical thinking, how can we achieve the deconstruction of knowledge and take seriously the critique of social movements such as migration, especially theology, as an ally of coloniality? In other words, how do we decolonize theology from the so-called colonial flaw (Walsh, 2005)? The recovery of the incarnation of bodies is undoubtedly a means. However, within the category of incarnation, we must re-feel and re-think which bodies, corporealities and sexualities are represented in the very concepts of Christianity. That is why I place the corporealities categorized as 'unclean' in the framework of the terrible reality that Mexico has been living for some years and more than a decade: forced disappearance.

More than 112,000 people have disappeared, according to the official figures of the UN experts (Shailer, 2023). However, those are the official figures, and unofficially at least 200,000 to 250,000 people have disappeared in the country since the 'war against drug trafficking' started by President Felipe Calderón in 2006 (Reed-Sandoval, 2024). The number of migrants entering, residing or continuing their journey to the USA can be counted in the millions each month (Secretaría de Gobernación, 2022). Furthermore, the entire country has become a vast clandestine grave for discarded bodies – bodies thrown into dumps, mutilated, tortured, raped and dismembered. Bodies without names or identities are discarded into sewage canals, mingling with faeces, industrial waste and the toxic chemicals and pollutants emitted by factories, or they are dumped in clandestine pits. Among these dehumanized remains lie the bodies of migrants. In the face of such degradation, how do we define filth?

The category of 'filth' comes from the work of Jean-Luc Nancy (2000). For this author, the unclean is a way of entering this zone of non-recognition without even a horizon that allows its appearance. Nancy (2000) employs the term to refer to the residual elements of existence that persist beyond the boundaries of comprehension. These remnants are opaque, resistant to assimilation, and exist as fragments that the world often disregards or labels as refuse. From this perspective they are the 'filth' – the unintegrated and unacknowledged aspects of the world: 'The unclean is what remains outside, expelled from the world in the midst of the world, the foul-smelling, putrefying' (Nancy, 2000, p. 60). Malodorous, decaying bodies that are not reclaimed because they are considered nobodies are expelled from the neoliberal capitalist political systems. We are facing the globalization of (un)worldliness [*in-mundicia*].

*In-mundicia* in the Bible refers to contamination; that is, to the non-purity of a body, and in our contexts to impure bodies, garbage and the non-decency of bodies. And theology has spoken of bodies, but of the bodies that Judith Butler (2020) calls 'the weepable', those that 'deserve to be mourned'; but there are other corporealities that do not have such merits. Thus, Mexico is now full of filth: of unrecognized bodies, human remains of the world left outside, bodies that stink, bodies in corruption or in a state of putrefaction whose unbearable odour reminds us that the colonialist system, along with its prevailing institutions, stink. These bodies remind us that capitalism in its neoliberal phase is a predatory system of the human species itself, for according to Claudia von Werlhof (2015), the task of patriarchy is to break with the power of feelings to get rid of the power of the body in its totality, the power of life and along with it, all emotions and sensibilities that feast with it. What is intended is a dulling of the senses and the replacement of the world of the sensual and betting on an a-sensual world, without senses, betting on a world of the senseless (Von Werlhof, 2015). We are facing the sacrifice of the erotics of the body, understood as the ability to position oneself politically with the whole body and the senses in the face of the challenges of everyday life to confront or transgress. Migration is a transgressive act of the neoliberal capitalist patriarchal systems, and it is a transgressive act of epistemologies since it leads us to leave the theories and ways of thinking about migrant in-world corporealities to place ourselves before nomadic ways of thinking as suggested by Braidotti (2022).

From theological reflection we are faced with a significant problem since Christianity, like theology, is a colonial institution, and one might ask: Is decoloniality possible without having to shoot ourselves in our own feet? Or perhaps we would have to recover the incarnation in the unclean corporealities? How do we migrate from our Christian colonial concepts? What about the incarnation of Jesus in the unclean corporealities of women, children and LGBTIQ+ persons? That is, theology and Christianity must assume being the remains left out: to be impure and trashed, opaque and unabsorbable, indecent, migratory and exiled theologies, as Althaus-Reid (2022, p. 45) asserts. They must also assume being expelled from the colonial, cis-heteronormative, racialized and classist world. Even more: to be expelled from institutions. Specifically, to question the metaphor of the monolatrous, patriarchal, white, male and heterosexual God, sedentarized and immobile.

It is the voices of unclean bodies and sexualities that cry out for justice. These echoes arise from the clandestinity of the migrant checkpoints, from dangerous roads, from exhaustive journeys, from lives exposed to any violation and from the clandestine graves where the unclean bodies of those who migrate are thrown. These voices are manifested through the Kairos of eroticism, understood as the ability to leave oneself to donate oneself to others, overcoming our egomaniacal narcissism and revealing the pornographic act of only exhibiting bodies as a result of social decomposition or sustaining the pedagogy of violence and cruelty, as Rita Laura Segato (2018) has called it. To speak of the erotic is to recognize the inner strength of corporealities that exert subversion and resistance to domination through forced mobility.

## Feminist Aesthetics and Erotic Tension

Aesthetics and feminisms have not journeyed well together. At the same time, feminist theories have challenged the conception of 'aesthetic' or stylized bodies and have placed gender as a category that influences the formation of ideas about art, artists and aesthetic value. The word *aisthesis*, origin of 'aesthetics', has been translated as 'sensibility' to denote philosophical reflection on art. It has placed women as inspiring art muses but not as art generators. Aesthetics and feminisms are fostering discussions about creating epistemological bridges that support the development of feminist aesthetics. In this context, I follow the proposal of María Isabel Peña Aguado (1999), which I briefly address below.

### *The Way we Conceive the Body*

Aesthetics and feminist theory have emphasized the significance of understanding the body as a powerful metaphor. The body is a dynamic site where stories unfold, emotions and feelings shape, and rationality intersects with desire, sex and love. This perspective highlights the body not merely as a biological entity but as a canvas of lived experiences, cultural narratives and personal expressions, underscoring the need for a discourse that captures its multifaceted and significant nature.

### *Rational Sensibility and Sensible Reason as Cognitive Value*

Aesthetics, therefore, explores the rationality of the sensible and its cognitive significance. Feminist theory, meanwhile, introduces the issue of sexual difference. It exposes how traditional reason subordinates feminine experience to mere sensuality while simultaneously rejecting and relegating this sensuality to the realm of the irrational. The goal is to challenge and revise Cartesian rationalism. Feminist theory, as we will see below, proposes a sexed reason that incorporates erotic tension into its framework.

### *The Emancipatory Potential Contained in Feminist Theory*

This is powerfully expressed through aesthetics. This is seen in a subject who rejects God as the sole guarantor of truth, instead reclaiming the divine wisdom. This wisdom is embodied in the metaphor of a street woman who seeks knowledge in the everyday life of towns, cities and nature. She acknowledges the limitations imposed by her sensory experience yet places her trust in her creative power. Through this she proposes ero-eco-sophianic pathways that bridge eroticism, ecology and wisdom in transformative ways.

### *Disruptive Art of Denunciation and Subversion*

Women are creating disruptive art that serves both as a denunciation and a form of subversion. They express powerful messages that challenge societal norms through murals, poetry, dance, music, sculpture, weaving and ceramics. These artistic practices act as forms of resistance and provide a foundation for epistemic, economic and ecological sustainability, allowing women to reclaim their voices and craft new spaces of empowerment and survival.

## *Proposed Geo-corpo-territorial Aesthetics*

Feminist and ecofeminist movements advocate for geo-corpo-territorial aesthetics, which are deeply rooted in the survival of communities and the defence of vital spaces. These movements emphasize the importance of protecting the land, body and territory from the harmful effects of extractivism. They propose a vision that subverts abusive and predatory practices, aiming to restore balance and honour the interconnectedness of nature, culture and the human body. Through these aesthetics they challenge systems that exploit and destroy people and the environment.

Finally, I want to approach feminist aesthetics as an 'erotic tension'. This concept has allowed me to delve deeper into the intersections of passion, desire and activism. My exploration of this idea has been greatly facilitated by my involvement in the ReGeSex research group, coordinated by André S. Musskopf at the Ruiz de Fora University, where I am also a member. The concept of 'erotic tension' emerges from a colloquial Brazilian expression that speaks to intense passion, burning desire and a fervent commitment to a person or, in some cases, to a cause. The erotic tension I refer to here is the burning passion that women feel for feminist and ecofeminist causes – an urgency and drive that fuels the continued struggle for gender equality, ecological justice and the protection of life. In this sense, erotic tension becomes a powerful metaphor for the sustained and overwhelming force of women's struggles.

If we lose the struggles of women and the ecological movements that work to protect the environment, we will have lost everything. The forces of oppression and exploitation that affect both women and the planet are intricately connected, and to ignore one is to ignore the other. The passionate drive behind these movements is not just about securing rights or environmental protections but about creating a liveable, sustainable and just world for all. This idea is exemplified in the work *Tiempo de Mujer* (Márquez Peralta, 2024), which I analyse in the final section of this chapter. This work continues to ignite reflection on what stirs women to act – to build a world that is not only survivable but also enjoyable, meaningful and equitable. The passion behind these efforts is not simply an emotional outburst but a sustained, deliberate engagement with the world and its injustices.

We live in kairological times. They are often described in theological discourse as times of divine opportunity. For women, these are kairological moments in aesthetics, theology, philosophy and politics. In these moments we are called to act, engage, challenge the status quo and demand new ways of thinking and living. Women are increasingly being called upon to govern in decolonial, non-hegemonic ways, offering alternatives to the patriarchal structures that have dominated political, social and cultural life for centuries. This is a time when women's leadership, creativity and activism are not just essential but vital for the future of humanity and the planet.

But what about love? What about sexuality? These two concepts are at the heart of the 'erotic tension' that I am discussing. Erotic tension is not positioned as the antithesis of pornography, as some might assume. Instead, following the insights of post-porn studies, it is seen as a movement that transcends the commercialized and objectifying portrayals of sexuality in mainstream pornography. Erotic tension, in this context, is understood as an artistic, activist and political force that challenges and subverts the dominant narratives surrounding the body, love and sexuality. It offers a counterpoint to the commodified images of desire that permeate the media and popular culture.

Erotic tension is about reclaiming and reimagining sexuality and the body as sites of empowerment, resistance and expression. It moves away from the shallow, market-driven portrayals of sex and instead embraces a more nuanced, multifaceted view of human desire and intimacy. This form of eroticism is political, marked by performance and public art that resists the dominant norms of sexuality, challenging societal expectations and offering new, liberatory possibilities.

Undoubtedly, we must recognize that sexuality is not a neutral or apolitical space. It is, instead, a profoundly political and artistic positioning – one that is always marked by Kairos, the opportune moment. For women and all those who identify with or as women, this is a time of grace and salvation, a time of reckoning, a time of opportunity. Erotic tension, in its full manifestation, is not just about individual pleasure or personal liberation; it is about collective transformation. It is about seizing the moment to reshape the world, to bring about justice, to redefine love and to reclaim the power of the body in all its forms. This is 'woman's time', but it is also the time for all of us who are invested in creating a world that honours life, love and liberation.

## Conclusion

The work *Tiempo de Mujer* (Márquez Peralta, 2024), which expresses the times of feminisms, prompts us to rethink feminist aesthetics in other categories and decolonize it, starting from our understanding of 'other' bodies: large and 'fat' bodies, bodies of 'tight' skins, bodies of plants, bodies of animals, 'earth' bodies, bodies that live with disabilities to break with the colonial aestheticism of 'white' bodies, thin, subjected to cis-heteronormative standards and gender binarisms.

It is necessary to recognize that grace occurs in erotic tension and takes desiring bodies as theological sites of revelation. It challenges theology to live in constant 'exile' with a nomadic attitude of its epistemic securities, leaving its truths of faith to move in a disruptive act towards the Kairos as new times of opportunity for women and LGBTIQ+ diversities to renew themselves and let themselves be questioned by feminist theologies. Theology is invited to carry out in itself processes of conversion to leave the hierarchical, patriarchal-neo-colonial models in which it has been structured and give way to a new era of critical-political and creative thinking that allows it to be not only good news but an event of grace and salvation in all the *cuir* dimension that exposes us in LGBTIQ+ bodies and sexualities.

In times as insensitive as the ones we now live in, in which we have become accustomed to violence, even in academic and religious spaces, we need to recover the erotic, sophianic and ecologically sensitive reason as an opportunity to overcome the exacerbated anthropocentrism of the Anthropocene and Capitalocene and give way to the decolonial processes of erotic tension that occur as *ékstasis* in a constant coming out of oneself to recreate other and multiple ways of loving, being and thinking life: different ways of inhabiting this world so that it is possible to live it.

Mysticism and eroticism kiss in a subversive act of divine grace in what we would call a theo-erotic coven of bodies and diverse sexualities that make visible the cures of grace poured into all the reality that surrounds and embraces us.

## *Notes*

1 A portion of this chapter subsection is set to be published in Rojas Salazar (2025, forthcoming in *RIBET: Revista Iberoamericana de Teología*). However, the article has been revised to differ significantly from this chapter.

2 *Entrecuido* is a neologism coined by the Illé collective in Puerto Rico and used by Margarita Sánchez de León (2023) in her doctoral thesis to refer to the various forms of care that women provide to each other in collectives.

## References

Alison, James (2003), *Una fe más allá del resentimiento: Fragmentos católicos en clave gay*, Barcelona: Herder Editorial.

Althaus-Reid, Marcella (2019), 'Marx in a Gay Bar: Indecent Theology as a Reflection on the Theology of Liberation and Sexuality', translated by Hugo Córdova Quero, *Conexión Queer: Revista Latinoamericana y Caribeña de Teologías Queer* 2, pp. 29–48.

Althaus-Reid, Marcella (2022), *Dios Cuir*, Ciudad de México: Universidad Inter Americana.

Braidotti, Rosi (2022), *Feminismo Posthumano*, Barcelona: Editorial Gedisa.

Butler, Judith (2020), *Sin miedo: Formas de resistencia a la violencia de hoy*, Ciudad de México: Taurus.

Galindo, María (2022), *Feminismo Bastardo*, Ciudad de México: Siglo XXI Editores.

Gebara, Ivonne (2022), *La vejez que yo habito*, Montevideo: Doble Clic.

Haraway, Donna (2020), *Manifiesto Cíborg*, Madrid: Kaótica Libros.

Hernández Mella, Rocío and Berenice Pacheco Salazar (2009), 'De la culpa a la redención: Hacia una nueva psicología', *Ciencia y Sociedad* 34, no. 2, pp. 145–58.

Mària, Josep F. (2021), 'Chronos and Kairos: How We Measure Our Days and Our Lives', *Do Better*, 1 April, at https://dobetter.esade.edu/en/time-kronos-kairos, accessed 01.12.2024.

Márquez Peralta, Carlos (2024), *Tiempo de Mujer* (painting). Private collection, Ciudad de México, Mexico.

Meloni, Carolina (2021), *Feminismos Fronterizos: Mestizas, abyectas y perras*, Madrid: Kaótica Libros.

Nancy, Jean-Luc (2000), *Corpus*, Paris: Éditions Métailié.

Peña Aguado, María Isabel (1999), 'Estética y feminismo como paradigmas alternativos de la racionalidad', *Hiparquía* 10, 15 September, at http://www.hiparquia.fahce.unlp.edu.ar/numeros/volx/estetica-y-feminismo-como-paradigmas-alternativos-de-racionalidad, accessed 01.12.2024.

Piedade, Vilma (2021), *Doloridad*, Ciudad Autónoma de Buenos Aires: Mandacarú.

Ramón Carbonell, Lucía (2021), 'Repensar la salvación Cristiana en verde y violeta', in *¿Eres tú o esperamos a otro? (Lc. 7,19): La salvación en la que creemos las mujeres*, edited by María Belén Brezmes Alonso and Mónica Díaz Álamo, Estella: Editorial Verbo Divino, pp. 103–50.

Rashid, Raphael (2024), 'As 4B takes the world by storm, South Korea is grappling with a backlash against feminism', *The Guardian*, 15 November, at https://www.theguardian.com/world/2024/nov/15/4b-south-korea-feminist-movement-donald-trump-election-backlash?utm_source=chatgpt.com, accessed 01.12.2024.

Reed-Sandoval, Amy (2024), 'The Struggle to Identify all the Dead Bodies in Mexico', *The New Yorker*, 25 July, at https://www.newyorker.com/news/dispatch/the-struggle-to-identify-all-the-dead-bodies-in-mexico, accessed 01.12.2024.

Refuge, Paul (2024), *The 4B Movement: Who They Are, What They Stand For, and How Trump's Victory Ignited Global Interest*, Seattle, WA: Amazon Digital Services.

Rojas Salazar, Marilú (2023), 'Libertades Clandestinas: Hacia la elaboración de una teología queer encarnacional', *Conexión Queer: Revista Latinoamericana y Caribeña de Teologías Queer* 6, pp. 127–50.

Rojas Salazar, Marilú (2025, forthcoming), 'Tiempos de Kairós feministas: Una interpelación estética desde las corporalidades disidentes', *RIBET: Revista Iberoamericana de Teología* 21, no. 41 (January-June).

Sánchez de León, Carmen Margarita (2023), 'Transpaz(c)es y vulnerabilidad: Sintiendo los latidos de las activistas antirracistas del colectivo Ilé y dos de las co-fundadoras de Black Lives Matter"', doctoral dissertation, Ciudad de México: Departamento de Ciencias Sociales y Políticas, Universidad Iberoamericana.

Secretaría de Gobernación (2022), 'Durante el primer trimestre de 2022 ingresaron a México cerca de 9 millones de personas nacionales y extranjeras', Gobierno de México, 4 June, at https://www.gob.mx/segob/prensa/durante-el-primer-trimestre-de-2022-ingresaron-a-mexico-cerca-de-9-millones-de-personas-nacionales-y-extranjeras, accessed 01.12.2024.

Segato, Rita Laura (2018), *Contra-pedagogías de la Crueldad*, Ciudad Autónoma de Buenos Aires: Editorial Prometeo.

Shailer, Daniel (2023), 'The official count of disappeared people in Mexico could be an underestimate, say UN and advocates', Associated Press, 3 October, at https://apnews.com/article/mexico-missing-disappearances-united-nations-147b08e445c715fe0ee487a5b07287288, accessed 01.12.2024.

Taylor, Sanaura (2021), *CRPI: Liberación animal y liberación disca*, Madrid: Ochodoscuatro.

Von Werlhof, Claudia (2015), *¡Madre Tierra o muerte! Reflexiones para una teoría del Patriarcado*, Ciudad de México: El Rebozo.

Walsh, Catherine (2005), *Pensamiento crítico y matriz (de)colonial: Reflexiones latinoamericanas*, Quito: Ediciones Abya Yala.

11

# Embodied Theology of Liberation: Intersecting Violence on Dalit and Queer Bodies

SAMUEL MALL

## Introduction

Why do queer voices or theology remain neglected in Indian theological and ecclesial circles? This question becomes significant because India is a place where many contextual theologies have emerged over time. Despite the diversity of contextual theologies, queer theology continues to be ignored and even discouraged. There might be many reasons for it. A dominant one has been the assumption that conversations about human sexuality reflect a Western agenda. This is because most non-Western queer people are preoccupied not with the politics of identity but with equating their sexuality with culture, religion or nation (Dave, 2012, p. 16). In other words, queer issues are not significant in the Indian context. Such categorization makes it visible to us that the theological and ecclesial world has not questioned its cis-heterosexual orientation and learning. Despite the vibrant visibility of queer bodies and experiences, we have resisted in not recognizing the authenticity of queer sexual orientation and experiences.

While queer experiences continue to be neglected, various contextual theologies in India – Dalit, Tribal, Adivasi and feminist – continue to explore partnerships in realizing the vision of liberation. These partnerships among contextual theologies in India have made us realize that the liberations of different communities cannot advance in isolation from each other. We are increasingly becoming aware of the interrelatedness of liberation and how significant it is for the discriminated to live in solidarity with each other and work collectively towards transforming structures that perpetuate discrimination. Therefore, neglecting queer experiences would not make liberation theology in India holistic. Recognizing the neglected experiences of the queer community and the urgency of including it in the process of theologizing, this chapter focuses on intersecting violence on Dalit and queer bodies. The effort to intersect bodily violence will help us realize that when we explore the experiences of both these communities, we become aware of the commonalities of their oppressive experiences.

Exploring such commonalities is essential because it will provide us with opportunities to build liberative partnerships, and the liberation agenda will no longer move in exclusive ways. In other words, this chapter is an attempt towards queering Dalit theology where Dalits become an ally of the queer community by recognizing the similarity of bodily experience. In addition, it will explore how we can look at God from the perspective of bodily experiences of Dalit and queer bodies and arrive at an embodied theology of liberation that builds on justice for the marginalized. As a result, both queer and Dalit theology will not only envision their liberation but will also develop liberating partnerships with other marginalized groups.

The chapter is divided into three sections. The first deals with intersecting natures of bodily violence on Dalit and queer bodies. It aims to locate the similarities of bodily oppression. The second section deals with the positive meaning of Dalit and queer bodies and how they become essential to reimagining liberation from the perspective of bodies. The last section develops an embodied theology of liberation that highlights that the bodies of the marginalized become significant in the message of the Kingdom of God. Roman imperialism is analysed through the bodily experience of the marginalized. This further highlights that Jesus never neglected the bodies of the marginalized and formed a movement of solidarity to challenge the imperialism of the Roman Empire (Horsley and Hanson, 1985).

## Violence on Dalit and Queer Bodies

Why do bodies become very significant in the process of theologizing? For a long time bodily experiences have been neglected in theology because they have been viewed negatively as against the spirit. The 'body' and 'spirit' binary accorded negative value to the body because it was seen as a site of sinful desires. Such sinfulness had to be controlled, and therefore theology was concerned about disciplining the body rather than affirming the human body. It is because of such an understanding that queer bodies are seen negatively as aspects of sexuality, are seen as the sources of sinful desires. Because of the caste structure, Dalit bodies are also viewed negatively as they fall outside the structure of *Varna*, the fourfold hierarchical division of the Hindu society. Both Dalit and queer bodies are thus discriminated against and dehumanized in society. They have to be controlled, disciplined and further assimilated into the dominant structures of sexuality and society. If bodies are not regulated, assaulting them becomes the strategy of preserving the power of the dominant. Dalit and queer bodies become a site of assault. It is the aspect of suffering that defines Dalit and queer bodies. However, such an attitude towards the body has now been challenged.

Recognizing the significance of bodily experience in theology has accorded positive meaning to the body. It is because bodies represent the context and life setting of the people with whom and for whom we articulate the liberative aspect of theology. Bodies are essential because they relate to the materiality of the world. Joshua Samuel (2019, p. 155) rightly points out that in queer Dalit theology, the body is the key, and there is a need to affirm the bodies of those who identify as Dalits and queer, as these bodies are continually marginalized and made invisible.

Sexuality and gender understanding play a significant role in the violence that is committed on queer bodies. Cis-heterosexuality is considered the norm, and only male and female genders are socially recognized as standard. This normativity is further authenticated to be divine based on creation narratives of the Bible. Cis-heterosexuality and the two-gender theory thus become the foundations for the social and ecclesial body. Any deviation from it becomes unholy and is looked at with contempt. Queer bodies face discrimination not only in the broader social body but also in their homes because deviant sexualities are considered to be unholy and unacceptable. The church has been guilty of promoting cis-heterosexuality as divine, thereby marginalizing queer bodies, sexuality and experiences.

Queer identities are forced to live closeted lives, and the fear of rejection continually haunts them if they become open about their sexuality. They also become victims of hate and violence. When the church questions or demonizes people based on the cis-heterosexual understanding of sexuality, the church abuses people, spiritually and sexually, and further dismembers them from the body of Christ (Theodore, 2020, p. 43). This produces a double epistemological othering of queer bodies. They are separated from the social body and Christ's body. This marginalization affects them physically and psychologically. They are punished simply for being who they are. Families go to the extent of corrective rapes, conversion therapies to straighten deviant sexualities. Almost 80 per cent of queer communities go through such conversion therapies and corrective rapes (Minj, 2020). This is so because queer bodies are seen as unworthy and sick bodies that can never be autochthonous (Shahani, 2021, p. 171).

The bodily oppression of queers and Dalits make it visible to us that power rests with the dominant in the society. As a consequence, Dalit and queer bodies become the leading site for executing violence and oppression. The binary of body and spirit adds to the violence, as the violence upon the body is aimed at maintaining acceptable spirituality in the hierarchical social body. In other words, Dalit and queer bodies are considered to be unspiritual, polluted and thus worthy of violence by the dominant. Such bodily violence affects the whole identity of Dalits and queers. Hence, the bodies become a site on which hatred and contempt are erected. In light of all bodily oppression, the bodies of Dalits and queers should not only be looked upon as mere victimized bodies. Bodies must not be limited to understanding oppression, exclusion and abuse. They should become central to the programme of liberation. Therefore, there is a need to reinterpret bodies positively.

Both Dalit and queer bodies, which are dominated, should be used as agents of resistance in challenging the identities ascribed to them by the dominant. While both Dalit and queer bodies are victimized, the aspect of suffering cannot become the only identity marker because there is a risk of romanticizing suffering involved.

Dalit theology initially developed on the aspects of 'pain' and 'pathos', as they were the first-hand experience for most Dalit people. 'Pain' and 'pathos' became a standard identity marker and were further used as an interpretative lens for developing Dalit Christology. As a result, the servanthood of Jesus Christ became the foundation for Dalit Christology. Critiquing such an approach, Peniel Rajkumar (2010) observed that the paradigm of 'pain' and 'pathos' and the servanthood of Jesus Christ becomes counterproductive for Dalit liberation, as there is a risk of romanticizing suffering (p. 64). Such an understanding of identity encourages most Dalits to suffer so that liberation takes place at a later stage. Rajkumar further observes that:

> the *servant* nature of God suffers the risky possibility of reinforcing the deeply inculcated sense of inferiority of the Dalits, rather than helping the Dalits to transcend this Dalitness. By the glorification of suffering and re-creation of Jesus in the image of the Dalits ... Dalit theology contributes to the reinforcement of the status quo rather than challenging it. (p. 67; emphasis original)

Therefore, by focusing only on pathos as a common identity marker, broken and crushed identities cannot be healed or mobilized by positing a common Dalit identity (Clarke, Manchala and Peacock, 2010, p. 12). To reimagine Dalit and queer identity, we need to go beyond the experience of suffering and infuse a sense of positivity in the identity so that it becomes affirmative in the process of liberation. Arvind Narraian and Gautam Bhan (2005) argue that the focus of queer identities should be to challenge all hierarchies and power structures, not only those where queer individuals find themselves disadvantaged. Within this framework, intersections emerge between queer movements and the deeply ingrained sense of inferiority experienced by Dalits and other marginalized groups. Intersecting bodily violence of queers and Dalits aims at developing Dalit and queer solidarity that challenges all hierarchies.

## Dalit and Queer Identities Question Binaries

Patrick S. Cheng defines 'queer' in three possible ways. First, 'queer' as an umbrella term refers collectively to lesbian, gay, bisexual, transgender, intersex, questioning and other individuals who identify with non-normative sexualities and/or gender identities. The term can also include 'allies' who may not themselves identify as LGBTIQ+ but stand in solidarity with their queer community (Cheng, 2011, p. 3). While this meaning focuses on the aspect of marginalization according to sexualities and gender identities, the second meaning focuses on the positive aspect of the word, which has been used by many LGBTIQ+ people as a positive label that proudly embraces all that is transgressive or opposed to societal norms, particularly concerning sexuality and gender identity (Cheng, 2011, p. 5). Therefore, it's an action-orientated term that seeks to challenge and dismantle the status quo. It also disrupts the negative aspect of identity ascribed by the dominant. The third usage deals with the question of boundaries in understanding sexuality and gender. Cheng points out that queer theory challenges and disrupts the traditional notions that sexuality and gender identity are simply questions of scientific fact or that such concepts can be reduced to fixed binary categories such as 'homosexual' vs 'heterosexual' or 'female' vs 'male' (p. 7).

Those understandings highlight that sexualities and gender identities are often constructed by society to fall into binaries that are opposing and oppressive. It is these binaries that the term 'queer' seeks to deconstruct and erase. Developing from these positive meanings, Cheng defines queer theology as LGBTIQ+ people 'talking about God', and this 'talking about God' is done in a self-consciously transgressive manner that challenges societal norms about sexuality and gender (p. 9). Furthermore, queer theology is 'talk about God' that challenges and deconstructs the natural binary categories of sexual and gender identity. We can observe that even though queer identity highlights the aspect of suffering, it does not limit itself to it. It goes further and points out that the primary goal of queer identity is to analyse and expose the structures of oppression from the perspective of the queer and overcome marginalization. Therefore, queer identity is a fluid identity that does not confine itself to the sexual binaries created by cis-heterosexual understanding, and this fluid nature makes queer identity liberation-orientated.

Dalit identities also challenge and deconstruct binaries that are based on caste. The census projects that the British undertook in India to streamline the population for effective management were based on the Western understanding of religion, which considered every religion a watertight compartment. Thus, the census proclaimed that India comprised a multiplicity of groups that could be defined and demarcated by religion and caste. As a result, identities of Dalits and other marginal groups have been constructed in singular notions. Every religion and caste is located in a singular space. We are increasingly becoming aware that the dominant often construct and reinforce the singular notion of identity to protect their privilege and sustain their dominance. The postcolonial political system in India has inherited such an understanding of identity because Dalits belonging to Christianity and Islam are not eligible for affirmative action by the government. Therefore, the needs and aspirations of different communities are considered to be different from each other.

Contrary to such a singular identity construct, Dalit theologians have stressed the fluid nature of Dalit identities that deconstruct the singular notion of identity. This fluid nature of Dalits is expressed in the name 'Dalit' that the community chose for itself, which comes from the root word *dal* meaning 'oppressed', broken and crushed. It thus addresses the context of discrimination and incorporates elements of pride and resistive strategy for combating caste oppression (Clarke, 2002, p. 199). Philip Vinod Peacock points out that such a notion of identity signifies the aspect of non-belongingness to a fixed space (Peacock, 2020, p. 122). He therefore asserts that Dalit identity:

> is permanently seen as occupying a marginal position with reference to all systems of domination. The identity of Dalit is not just perceived as an advocacy position that foregrounds the construct of caste, but becomes the interpretative lens to analyse all of society. Dalit, then, is conceived in terms of what destabilizes the centre; it exposes all power equations while imagining an alternative reality of justice and equality. (p. 123)

It can be observed that Dalit and queer identities are fluid in the way that they displace binary identities. While queer identities displace sexual and gender binaries and expose the victimization of sexual minorities, Dalit identity displaces the fixed nature of caste identities while exposing the victimization of Dalits and similarly oppressed groups. Both Dalit and queer identities were used in a negative sense to shame people who belong to these communities. Still, the people within these communities have reinterpreted these identity markers positively. This aspect of fluidity that entails positivity can provide both communities with an opportunity to form resistive, radical and liberative partnerships. In other words, it is of paramount importance that partnerships between marginalized groups that extend beyond religion, caste and sexuality be established because such collective resistance can effectively counter the hegemony of the dominant.

Furthermore, both identities become interpretative lenses for analysing society's oppressive structures. They both expose power and domination while envisioning a liberation grounded in justice and freedom. Such an understanding of bodies becomes essential for an embodied theology of liberation.

## Embodied Theology of Liberation

In an embodied theology of liberation, bodies become the source of theologizing. We no more remain limited to the identities ascribed by the dominant but reimagine the bodies of Dalits and queer positively. Such positive reconstruction of bodies reconstructs not only the social body but also the ecclesial bodies. Stressing the aspect of the body helps us to critically view how dominance was constructed historically and how social institutions, informed by such dominant ideology, oppress the marginalized. Homophobia, sexuality and patriarchy have led to the marginalization of the queer community.

On the other hand, caste, sexuality and cis-heteropatriarchy have marginalized the Dalit community within the church and beyond. My intention behind mentioning just a few oppressive tendencies is not to limit the experience of oppression to a handful of oppressive strategies but to point out that oppressive strategies not only intersect each other but also construct social institutions in which Dalits and queer people are marginalized. We thus need to reconstruct bodies with a new approach.

Dalit and queer identity should be reimagined as agents of social change. The continued oppression of Dalit and queer bodies invites us to look at these bodies from a democratic outlook because when the oppressed talk about democracy, they speak about inclusion, justice, fraternity and equality. When the dominant talk about democracy, they will talk about development, and this development would be based on uncontrolled capitalism. In capitalism, bodies are tied to profit, and social institutions are erected to dominate and extract profit from the working class. In a democracy, bodies experience freedom, and social institutions aim for equality. Body as a hermeneutical tool helps us to create a dialogue of solidarity among the Dalits and queer community. In such a way, the spirituality of Dalit and queer bodies is defined by challenging the hierarchal and hegemonic structures. The spirituality of the body listens to bodily experiences to transform the oppressive structures of the social body, and embodied theology develops how bodies become significant in the understanding of the politics of liberation and transforming ecclesial structures.

We have observed that Dalit and queer identities intersect each other as they both are fluid and do not fit into the binary identity markers constructed by the dominant. In other words, Dalit and queer identities entail in themselves a sense of non-belongingness. This aspect of non-belongingness does not mean that the critical differences between these communities are glossed over to establish partnerships. Instead, this chapter focuses on developing the shared experiences of oppression while maintaining differences. Jesus displayed the importance of establishing alliances while maintaining differences in his opposition to the Roman Empire. Jesus worked hard to weave partnerships across different identities and established an inclusive community that resisted the empire. He brought people with various identities together, valued differences, and worked to bring these differences together to resist the imperialism of the Roman Empire.

Jesus' twelve disciples were from diverse backgrounds and represented different identities, such as fishermen, zealots and tax collectors. Only those with dominant identities had high social standing in the Roman Empire. The whole apparatus of the empire was dedicated to their benefit and progress. Hence, the oppressed had no place in the society as their identity was constructed in such a way that they experienced non-belongingness in the empire. Their identity, body and spirituality were not necessary, as they were considered to be polluting. The social body constructed by the Roman Empire was oppressive, closed, and lacked diversity. The marginalized communities were kept out of it because they were polluted. The marginalized experienced a sense of non-belongingness.

In the practice of the Kingdom of God, bodies become very significant, as it was in the experience of non-belongingness in the Roman Empire that Jesus envisioned God's Kingdom. God's Kingdom belonged to polluting, oppressed and unclean identities, who had no sense of belonging (Crossan, 1991, p. 273). All such identities were not subjugated but free in God's Kingdom. It was an alternative to the Roman kingdom because it provided space for the destitute. Robert E. Shore-Goss (1993) points out that:

> Jesus' *basileia* message and praxis signified the political transformation of his society into a radically egalitarian, new age, where sexual, social, religious, and political distinction would be irrelevant. Jesus struggled for *basileia* liberation in his siding with the humiliated, the oppressed, and the throw-away people of the first-century Jewish society. (p. 73)

The Kingdom of God also became an analytical lens through which imperial domination was analysed and resisted. It is only after one has understood what Kingdom meant that one can critically assess the exploitation in the Roman imperial world. By resisting the empire, the Kingdom of God aimed at creating inclusive communities where justice would rule by displacing the centres of power. God's Kingdom was to be characterized not by singular notions of identity but by the coming together of various identities that the empire worked to destroy, be it women, Samaritans, lepers, prostitutes, children, for example. It aimed at rebuilding oppressed communities. Thus, Jesus' programme was not just a religious revival of Jewish society but included political, social and economic aspects of life. This sense of non-belonging to a fixed space makes it possible to forge effective partnerships in challenging the empire. The resistance that Jesus explained towards the empire was signified by cooperation, unity and the bringing together of different identities, not the harmony of everyone into one dominant identity. In understanding the Triune God, differences are recognized and held distinctive while explicating one-ness.

The intersectionality of Dalit and queer bodily experiences of discrimination points out that their experience of marginalization is a 'material reality'. In other words, violence on bodies is a means to create dominance that is based on access to material resources. Bodily violence against the Dalits and queer ascribes power and resources to the dominant. The notion of purity and pollution is used to codify relations of domination. Dalits' bodies are considered to be ritually polluted, and violence against them is aimed at denying material benefits to them. It is also directed at confining them to menial and underpaid jobs. In a world defined by capitalism, the dominant needs to control material wealth to preserve its privileged position, and violence against Dalits performs this function. Violence against the queer community is aimed at excluding them from the social body because their sexuality is seen as polluting. Therefore, queer liberation is aimed at the affirmation of life in their bodies. Highlighting this aspect, Laurel C. Schneider and Thelathia Nikki Young (2021) point out that:

> Living fully into the multivalent and ever changing, ever mixing measures of bodily desire, connection, and expression is a key, hard-won and still winning queer virtue. This is because one of the principal conduits for queer oppression runs through 'the body' – social, material, erotic, and gendered. Contemporary queer theologies have consistently taken stands against an ancient, medieval, and modern Western bifurcation of spirit and body that has manifested in a hierarchy not only of genders (male over female) but of races, religions, and all orders of nature. (p. 50)

This alienation from the social body not only brings mental trauma but also material marginalization. Therefore, sexual violence against the queer and caste violence against the Dalits have a material base. Violence against these communities is committed to hampering their social progress by denying them material benefits. In her analysis of queer politics, Shraddha Chatterjee (2018) points out that:

> Critique emerging in parts of the world where queer politics has fallen prey to homonormative tendencies reveals clear fulfillments of homonationalist moments, and the assimilation of middle- or upper-class, able-bodied, mostly White queer subjects into the logic of nationhood, neoliberalism and capitalism demonstrates how such projects of inclusion are built at the cost of excluding queer subjects who are poor, disabled, and people of colour. (p. 46)

Similarly, Dalits continue to be excluded from neoliberalism. They are more prone to the adverse effects of globalization because the caste context of their lives has always been oppressive (Massey, 2014, p. 116). The lie of globalization offering economic uplift of the underprivileged has been busted. Education, health, land reform, secure jobs, democracy and modernity, the parameters that can result in Dalit empowerment, are all destroyed by globalization's impact (Teltumbde, 2017). Therefore, the material aspect of bodily violence helps us to comprehend that material propositions are the ones that define bodily violence. The struggle against discrimination requires unity and solidarity among marginalized groups that extend beyond caste, gender and sexuality. Such solidarity must be based on how the subalterns are placed in the world settings characterized by access to material resources.

Material considerations were significant in Jesus's resistance to the empire. Palestine in the Roman Empire was a peasant society (Horsley, 1989, p. 2). The societies were divided into two groups, the ruler and the ruled (Crossan, 1994, p. 24). The ruler group, even though in the minority, controlled political-military power and oppressed the vast majority of people (Crossan, 2007). Palestine was an agrarian society where the minority wealthy exploited the labour of the poor. The confluence of political and religious concerns signified the imperial characteristics of the Roman Empire. Politics and religion – the Temple and the High Priest – worked together to support the colonial process through economic exploitation (Horsley, 2009, p. 86). In the Gospels we can see that Jesus stood against the Temple and High Priests and frequently clashed with those in a dominant position. In doing so he resisted the empire. On the other hand, his followers were peasants, including fishermen, craftspeople, tax collectors and prostitutes (Horsley, 1989, p. 120). Thus, in an imperial context, Jesus could form resistive partnerships among the oppressed in an imperial society.

In this context of Roman imperialism, Jesus' authority was attacked by imperial powers, as signified by Jewish leaders, Herod Antipas and Roman officials (Seo, 2015, pp. 30–1). Thus, the Bible presents God's religion, justice and peace programme. The material base was significantly crucial for Jesus in his resistance to empire. The poor families began to disintegrate in the Roman Empire, and Jesus called the people to embody God's justice in their social-economic relations for resistance to Rome; Jesus collaborated with materially poor village communities. Such materialism is the key to understanding Jesus' messianism. Jesus became Christ through his interactions with others; his relationship with people around him was reciprocal. He touched people with his message and they responded by participating in his ministry (Schweitzer, 2012, pp. 184–5). The solidarity of the poor families in the programme of Jesus becomes essential for Dalit queer solidarity as it reimagines a radical world. Radical worlds are always evolving, linked through shared existence. Activism then enables actions within the processes by which liberation is approached and achieved (Dave, 2012, p. 14).

## Conclusion

This chapter has observed that when we apply intersectionality to queer and Dalit bodily experiences, we realize that both these communities share similarities in the way they experience discrimination. It was also observed that theology has continued to marginalize human bodies by neglecting the aspects of bodily experience. Such marginalization has served the interest of the dominant as they erect structures and hierarchies into which the subalterns are forced to assimilate. Queer bodies are forced to assimilate into cis-heteronormativity, and Dalits are forced to surrender to the caste structure of the society. In other words, discrimination of Dalit and queer bodies is aimed at dismembering them from the social body, which is constructed on the dominant understanding of sexuality and caste. Therefore, the bodies and voices of the subalterns become crucial to analysing and dismantling the oppressive structures of society. It is in the experience of subalternity that Dalits and queers can come together to challenge the hegemony of the powerful. Such solidarities maintain the distinctiveness of the experience of each community, but at the same time realize the commonality of suffering. This further leads to a realization that our liberation is tied to the liberation of others. Such partnership accords positive understanding to bodily experiences, and the body becomes a source of theologizing.

Jesus, in his ministry, worked with the bodies of the subalterns, and he formed resistive partnerships among diverse identities to challenge the hegemony of the Roman Empire. Therefore, Jesus' message of the Kingdom of God, when interpreted in the context of Roman imperialism, becomes a valuable source. Jesus challenged the Roman Empire by building a movement of solidarity among various marginalized groups. Through his actions and message, Jesus highlighted the importance of cooperation among the marginalized in building resistance to the empire. Jesus' life during the empire and the context of Dalit and queer bodies point out that the resistance towards the hegemony of the dominant should be done collectively by the oppressed from the perspective of equality and justice.

## References

Chatterjee, Shraddha (2018), *Queer Politics in India: Towards Sexual Subaltern Subjects*, London: Routledge.

Cheng, Patrick S. (2011), *An Introduction to Queer Theology: Radical Love*, New York: Seabury Press.

Clarke, Sathianathan (2002), 'Hindutva, Religious and Ethnocultural Minorities, and Indian-Christian Theology', *Harvard Theological Review* 95, no. 2, pp. 197–226.

Clarke, Sathianathan, Denabandhu Manchala and Philip Vinod Peacock (2010), 'Introduction: Enflamed Words, Engaging Worlds, Embryonic Word-Worlds', in *Dalit Theology in Twenty-First Century: Discordant Voices, Discerning Pathways*, edited by Sathianathan Clarke, Denabandhu Manchala and Philip Vinod Peacock, New Delhi: Oxford University Press, pp. 1–16.

Crossan, John Dominic (1991), *The Historical Jesus: The Life of a Mediterranean Jewish Peasant*, Edinburgh: T&T Clark.

Crossan, John Dominic (1994), *Jesus: A Revolutionary Biography*, New York: HarperCollins.

Crossan, John Dominic (2007), *God and Empire: Jesus Against Rome, Then and Now*, New York: HarperCollins.

Dave, Naisargi (2012), *Queer Activism in India: A Story in the Anthropology of Ethics*, Durham, NC: Duke University Press.

Horsley, Richard A. (1989), *Sociology and the Jesus Movement*, New York: Crossroad.

Horsley, Richard A. (2009), *Covenant Economics*, Louisville, KY: Westminster John Knox Press.

Horsley, Richard A. and John S. Hanson (1985), *Bandits, Prophets, and Messiahs: Popular Movements in the Time of Jesus*, San Francisco, CA: Harper & Row.

Massey, James (2014), *Dalit Theology: History, Context, Text, and Whole Salvation*, Delhi: Manohar Publishers.

Minj, Nolina (2020), 'The Horrors of Queer Conversion in India', *Scroll.in*, 7 September, at https://scroll.in/article/1032115/the-horrors-of-queer-conversion-therapy-in-india, accessed 01.12.2024.

Naraian, Arvind and Gautam Bhan (2005), *Because I have a Voice: Queer Politics in India*, New Delhi: Yoda Press.

Peacock, Philip Vinod (2020), 'Now we will Have the Dalit Perspective', *Ecumenical Review* 72, no. 1, pp. 116–27.

Rajkumar, Peniel (2010), *Dalit Theology and Dalit Liberation: Problems, Paradigms and Possibilities*, Aldershot: Ashgate.

Samuel, Joshua (2019), 'Towards Queer Dalit Theology: Dialogue and Solidarity Among the Margins', *Bangalore Theological Forum* 51, no. 2, pp. 142–67.

Schneider, Laurel C. and Thelathia Nikki Young (2021), *Queer Soul and Queer Theology: Ethics and Redemption in Real Life*, London: Routledge.

Schweitzer, Don (2012), *Jesus Christ for Contemporary Life*, Eugene, OR: Cascade Books.

Seo, Pyung Soo (2015), *Luke's Jesus in the Roman Empire and the Emperor in the Gospel of Luke*, Eugene, OR: Pickwick Publications.

Shahani, Nishant (2021), *Pink Revolution: Globalization, Hindutva, and Queer Triangles in Contemporary India*, Evanston, IL: Northwestern University Press.

Shore-Goss, Robert E. (1993), *Jesus Acted Up: A Gay and Lesbian Manifesto*, New York: HarperCollins.

Teltumbde, Anand (2017), *Dalits: Past, Present and Future*, London: Routledge.

Theodore, Arvind (2020), *Church and Human Sexuality*, New Delhi: ISPCK & CWM.

12

# *Izitabane Zingabantu* Ubuntu Theology: Amplifying Voices of South African *Izitabane*

TRACEY MASWAZI GUMEDE

## Introduction: Reclaiming Queer Narratives in African Faith Contexts

The battle over one's sexuality, gender and faith has been a longstanding and deeply personal struggle for lesbian, gay, bisexual, transgender, intersex, queer and other (LGBTIQ+) individuals of faith within the African context, often referred to as *Izitabane* within the South African landscape, 'a derogatory label used in the African context to mark LGBTIQ+ people as the "other" and "outside" the norm prescribed by' patriarchal standards (Reygan and Lynette, 2014, p. 713; Davids et al., 2019, p. 10; Sibisi and Van der Walt, 2021, p. 67). This conflicting reality requires constant negotiation – within oneself and a society that persistently polices bodies that deviate from its rigid norms. It is important to note that issues of sex, sexuality and gender are deeply rooted in the systemic foundations of cis-heteropatriarchy globally. In the South African context this reinforces the marginalization and silencing of diverse queer identities.

This systemic struggle is rooted and sustained within African cultures, religions and social and political landscapes. However, it is crucial to recognize that this struggle lacks an authentic identity within this context, as it has been heavily influenced and shaped by Western narratives and interests that have long imposed shame on African bodies. As a result, no explicit language, vocabulary or framework genuinely resonates when addressing these issues within the African context. Consequently, the battle, the constant negotiation of one's sexuality and gender identity concerning faith, is not merely a fight for belonging but also a deeper interrogation of identity, historical loss and systemic exclusion, as this testimony demonstrates:

> I was a Sunday School teacher ... I enjoyed being part of Sunday school with the kids because they do not judge. Someone found out about my sexuality, and I was reported to the elders, and they prayed for me. They did not chase me out, but they treated me differently. It changed the love of God for me. I became a demon. My excellent work did not matter, so I decided to leave. – Participant. (Sibisi and Van der Walt, 2021, p. 78)

The Western narrative of 'faith' and its interpretation of scripture concerning sex, gender and sexuality have deeply influenced how Africans, particularly those in the global South, perceive their bodies and navigate their sexuality and gender identities. The West has long understood that 'faith is a powerful shaper of identity and meaning that influences social norms, values, ethics, and behavior' (Judge, 2020, p. 1), a reality that resonates profoundly in this context. This influence is a daunting force that has not only shaped the lives of African people but has also left irreversible marks on the lives of *Izitabane* of faith, who have and continue to face the harsh repercussions of these imposed narratives. These narratives have systematically silenced bodies that do not conform to their rigid expectations.

Carla Wilson (2001) states that 'Ideas about gender difference, sexuality, and their implications for society can be traced back to the fragmented artifacts and representations of Western culture and the varied traditions of knowledge it has produced' (p. 47). This perspective often degrades and sidelines African indigenous knowledge systems, cultures, traditions, religions and spiritualities as inferior and barbaric, reinforcing an arrogant stance that fuels homophobic narratives 'driven by a conservative Western agenda to queer identities elsewhere' (Ntombana and Sibanda, 2024, p. 4). Such systematization of knowledge, including theology and biblical studies rooted in a Western world view, must be disrupted and dismantled for *Izitabane* of faith in the African context to redefine themselves within the principles of Ubuntu to reclaim their distinct identities (Bishop, 2022, p. 72). To achieve this, there is a need for a theological framework developed from within the African context that not only considers the contextual realities shaping the experiences of *Izitabane* of faith but also adopts an intersectional approach to discussing sex, sexuality and gender within the African faith landscape.

This chapter aims to contribute to the larger discourse on global queer theologies by centring the narratives of Christian *Izitabane*, queer bodies from the South, who have been marginalized, oppressed and silenced within the African faith landscape through Western-imposed cis-heteropatriarchal structures, which devalue *Izitabane* in both church and theological contexts, systematically excluding them based on rigid ideas of gender and sexuality. Written from a queer activist perspective, it employs Ujamaa's Contextual Bible Study (CBS) methodology as a practical tool for engaging and disrupting these exclusionary narratives. Using *Izitabane Zingabantu* Ubuntu Theology, an African-developed queer theological framework, the chapter examines how CBS amplifies the voices of Christian *Izitabane*, reclaiming life-affirming aspects within African spirituality and fostering a more inclusive and intersectional understanding of faith, sexuality and gender through a continued act of praxis and reflection. This aligns with the volume's aim to develop liberating and contextual theologies that resonate with local diversities and embody a more inclusive Christian faith.

## Marginalization of Christian *Izitabane*: African Realities

According to the UN, 'many African countries still have many cases of open condemnation of same-sex relationships' (Ntombana, Toa and Phuza, 2020, p. 77). In countries like Kenya, Uganda and Somalia, individuals who are either caught engaging in same-sex acts or merely suspected of being *Izitabane* face severe forms of violence and persecution, with punishments ranging from imprisonment to the death penalty (Makhaye, 2024, p. 46). Even in regions where legal frameworks recognize LGBTIQ+ rights, societal attitudes often exhibit significant intolerance towards *Izitabane* and sexual and gender diversity. This intolerance is rooted in rigid and deeply entrenched understandings of sex, gender and sexuality. As a result, *Izitabane* continues to be marginalized and perceived as existing outside of, and in opposition to, so-called African values, systems and beliefs (Brown, 2012, p. 51).

The understanding of African values and beliefs, often engaged in this conversation, are shaped by narrow notions of family structure, influencing ideas about cultural identity and the roles different bodies are expected to play within this context. These value systems are supported by patriarchal expectations that normalize cis-heterosexual ideologies, which are used to control bodies and dictate that anything outside this norm is a threat to African traditions and cis-heteronormative family values (Sibisi and Van der Walt, 2021, p. 68). Such frameworks 'stigmatize, marginalize, subordinate, oppress, and regulate' alternative identities and realities, particularly those of *Izitabane*, forcing them to the margins of society (Makhaye, 2024, p. 46). This regulation is deeply embedded in African culture, traditions and religious practices, which are complex and multifaceted.

African societies have actively sought to exclude and condemn *Izitabane* through overt and covert means. Overtly, this is achieved by enacting laws and policies that criminalize queer bodies. Covertly, it is maintained through the daily reinforcement of systemic binaries that are solidified by structural separation and discrimination (OutRight Action International, 2022, p. 6). Even in countries like South Africa, where legal protections exist, the marginalization of *Izitabane* is evident in the lived experiences of those who deviate from perceived societal norms. This marginalization manifests in the denial of their existence, the shaming and othering of individuals whose sexual and gender identities are seen as different, and the persistent efforts to erase queer bodies through violence. Such actions reveal deep-seated intolerance towards *Izitabane* within the South African context (Morrell, Jewkes and Lindegger, 2012, p. 14; Van der Walt and Davids, 2022, p. 36).

Despite being celebrated as one of the most progressive countries in the world concerning the recognition of LGBTIQ+ rights, South Africa presents a complex difference between its legal frameworks and the lived realities of *Izitabane*: 'In 1996, South Africa added an anti-discrimination clause to the Constitution, which stated that "no one may discriminate against anyone because of their sexual orientation"' (Ntombana and Sibanda, 2024, p. 2), marking a significant victory for *Izitabane*. Moreover, 'a 2005 parliamentary order recognized relationship law discrimination as unconstitutional – leading to marriage equality and cohabitation protections for same-sex couples in 2006' (Jones, 2019, p. 456). However, these legal wins have been met with a tremendous backlash from faith communities, traditional leadership and the general population in South Africa, reflecting persistent intolerance that remains evident to this day.

Recent reports highlight this ongoing struggle. In 2021 the South African Government News Agency indicated that there were 12 pending cases of rape specifically targeting *Izitabane* that were reported as hate crime cases. This number saw a daunting increase by August 2024, with the murders of four *Izitabane* individuals. Notably, Nombulelo Bhixa (aged 28) and Minenhle Ngcobo (aged 22), a lesbian couple, were shot in the head in a public space by a known assailant in Pietermaritzburg, KwaZulu-Natal, on 27 August 2024 (Myeza, 2024). Another case involved Clement Hadebe (aged 22), who was shot by an unknown assailant while walking home in Johannesburg on 9 August 2024 (Igual, 2024). Lastly, Xolani Xaka (aged 32) was repeatedly stabbed to death by a group of men at the gate of his home on 18 August 2024 in the Eastern Cape (Igual, 2024). Such incidents are becoming widespread, creating a pervasive culture of fear and anxiety within South Africa's

*Izitabane* community, compelling them to mobilize and raise awareness of the surge in hate crime, defined as 'a criminal offense committed against a person, property, or society because of [their] actual or perceived membership in any particular group or identifying class, such as race, sexual orientation, gender or ethnicity ... because of the perpetrator's bias, prejudice or hate' (Brown, 2012, p. 63).

There is a noticeable gap between the rights of *Izitabane* and their lived realities in South Africa. This gap is regrettably visible in the experiences inscribed on the bodies of *Izitabane* and in the systems that pervade the lives of queer individuals, systems that are deeply engraved into the societal and cultural landscape. These harsh realities are not merely products of isolated acts of prejudice; they are symptoms of a much larger and deeply entrenched system of oppression known as cis-heteropatriarchy. This system enforces a hierarchical structure that privileges heterosexual, cisgender men while systematically excluding and marginalizing those who do not conform to these norms. Understanding the intersection of structural and theological exclusion is crucial in unpacking how deeply embedded ideologies within religious and cultural frameworks perpetuate the marginalization of *Izitabane*.

## Cis-heteropatriarchy: Structural and Theological Exclusion

The systemic exclusion of *Izitabane* (queer individuals) takes many forms, but at its core lies the pervasiveness of patriarchy and cis-heteronormativity. Patriarchy, defined as 'a system of social structures and practices in which men dominate, oppress, and exploit women' (Vaka'uta, 2022, p. 164), and bodies deemed weaker or subordinate, has contributed significantly to the marginalization of *Izitabane* within the African context. It thrives by socializing men and masculine-presenting bodies into believing they hold power over the 'other', a power reinforced through upholding imposed norms like cis-heteronormativity (Sibisi and Van der Walt, 2021, p. 73). This system elevates those viewed as the 'perfect being', the cisgender man. It seeks to silence or erase those who do not fit within its boundaries.

Bodies that conform to these patriarchal norms may exist in silence, but for those who cannot align themselves with such standards, exclusion and erasure are inevitable. Melissa M. Wilcox (2020, p. 20) argues that bodies do not exist in isolation; they exist within a complex environment that reproduces and reinforces norms, often unknowingly. These norms, such as patriarchy, are performed and upheld not only in public life but also in intimate relationships, dictating how bodies should interact with one another. The failure to conform results in violence, othering and shame. These systems are deeply inscribed in our lives, with patriarchy and power emerging as two of the cruellest and most persistent factors in the oppression of women and marginalized sexual and gender minorities (Siwila, 2021, p. 188). Such oppression continues to shape African social realities, further entrenched through the pervasive enforcement of cis-heteronormativity.

Cis-heteronormativity, as Julie Beth Tilsen (2021) defines it, is 'a set of practices and institutions that legitimizes heterosexuality as the only "natural" and legitimate sexual orientation' (p. 41). It reinforces the binary of the 'us', the so-called normal, and the 'them', those who are deemed as deviant in terms of sex, sexuality and gender. This framework silences *Izitabane* and dismisses *ubutabane* (queerness) as both un-African and ungodly (Makhaye, 2024, p. 42), sanctioning their exclusion and alienation. This life-denying system sustains a binary norm that leaves those who resist conforming to it on the margins of African societies. Importantly, these structures are not only embedded in African cultures but are also perpetuated by the Christian church in South Africa, affecting *Izitabane* of faith in harmful ways.

The Christian church, with its influential role in shaping societal values, has been complicit in the othering of *Izitabane*, labelling them as 'unnatural, ungodly, and sinful' (Judge, 2020, p. 3). This condemnation pushes them to the margins of Christianity, even as many strive to remain faithful to both their faith and their authentic selves. As a result, *Izitabane* often carry deep wounds from their church experiences, forcing them to hide aspects of their identity to participate in spaces of worship and to draw closer to God's love (Palm and Gaum, 2021, p. 216).

This brings us to a crucial conversation about theological exclusion. The Christian faith, which is meant to embody love, acceptance and inclusion, has historically been a source of great pain for queer individuals. The systemic enforcement of cis-heteronormativity and patriarchy within the church not only perpetuates exclusion but also denies the spiritual agency and belonging of queer people. For *Izitabane*, this exclusion is not just a matter of social alienation; it touches the deepest parts of their spiritual identity, often leaving them in a profound state of struggle between faith and identity.

Through scripture and theological reflection, the Christian church in South Africa has wielded immense power in shaping and enforcing interpretations of 'God's word' that uphold dominant norms and standards. Heavily influenced by colonial-era ideologies, the church has played a central role in controlling and policing bodies, mainly through its regulation of sexuality and gender, positioning itself as an enforcer of a heteropatriarchal system (Davids et al., 2019, p. 30). This system, reinforced by church structures and biblical interpretations, often presents a single narrative that is life-denying to those who fall outside cis-heteronormative boundaries. It has been driven by a theology that engages with sex, sexuality and gender in disembodied, contextually ignorant ways. Such theology constructs reality from a cis-heteropatriarchal position, a framework identified as one of the key drivers of LGBTIQ+ discrimination and exclusion within African faith landscapes (Van der Walt, 2021, p. 402).

As Jione Havea (2022) rightly points out, these theologies fail to acknowledge that 'theology is a human project, and humans come in many sizes and shapes, out of many closets with many blind spots' (p. 1). Therefore, the notion of a one-size-fits-all theology is both unreasonable and unjust, as it ignores the diversity of human experience and the complexity of embodiment. The exclusionary nature of such theology underscores the urgent need for alternative approaches that consider lived realities, especially for marginalized communities like *Izitabane*. One such approach is Contextual Bible Study (CBS), a methodology developed by the Ujamaa Centre for Biblical and Theological Community Development and Research, a theological research community centre based in Pietermaritzburg, South Africa. This tool offers a way to engage with scripture in life-giving and liberating ways. Rather than imposing fixed interpretations, CBS encourages reading scripture rooted in context, allowing for reflection on the specific social, political and cultural conditions that shape people's lives.

## Contextual Bible Study as a Tool for Liberation: The Ujamaa Methodology

Contextual Bible Study is a transformative method of biblical interpretation that starts the process of decolonizing traditional, rigid ways of reading scripture. It challenges the centring of biblical interpretations within the African faith landscape, often monopolized by church hierarchies. The CBS methodology amplifies the voices and lived experiences of those who have long been silenced and marginalized, specifically, bodies at the margins of faith spaces. By engaging these diverse perspectives, CBS reimagines the process of reading and interpreting the Bible. This approach is vital to creating a culture of inclusivity and justice within theological reflection. In this methodology, good theological processes are understood as 'restless', constantly shifting and expanding to accommodate new insights. These processes are not fixed or static, allowing for welcoming, hospitable and life-affirming interpretations for all bodies (Havea, 2022, p. 7). Therefore, CBS opens spaces for theologies that affirm the humanity of marginalized groups, ensuring that engaging scripture becomes an inclusive and progressive process.

CBS also dismantles the idea that biblical interpretation should remain the exclusive responsibility of a privileged minority within church leadership. Instead it promotes a communal approach to reading scripture that is contextual and grounded in the realities of everyday life. This collective process draws on the experiences of all participants, particularly those whose voices have historically been excluded. As Davids et al. (2019) note, CBS is a method based on the foundations of 'reading together'. It engages the embodied realities of marginalized communities and acknowledges the diversity of voices within both the biblical text and the faith community (Davids et al., 2019, p. 35). In line with this, CBS challenges the misconception that the Bible contains a single narrative, a dominant message, pushing the agenda of those in positions of power. CBS recognizes the diverse number of voices within scripture, some of which have been silenced or misrepresented through traditional modes of interpretation. As Gerald O. West (2021, p. 132) points out, the Bible carries 'many voices', some silent, some spoken about and some spoken for. CBS thus becomes a powerful tool for uncovering these hidden voices and exposing how dominant discourses have often promoted a singular agenda that erases and marginalizes Christian individuals, particularly those whose expressions of faith do not conform to normative ideals.

Just like queer theology and other liberation theologies and practices, the CBS methodology seeks to interrogate and dismantle oppressive power structures; it requires us to problematize the dominant discourses that have historically controlled biblical interpretation. These discourses, administered by theological elites, are often used to protect systemic privileges that uphold the needs of an oppressive majority. In doing so they exclude and marginalize minority groups, such as *Izitabane* of faith, who do not conform to normative standards of gender and sexuality. CBS calls for a radical deconstruction of these narratives, exposing how they harm marginalized bodies and limit the potential for life-affirming theological engagement. By challenging these exclusionary interpretations, CBS makes room for the lived realities of *Izitabane* and other marginalized groups, allowing them to take their rightful place in the faith community.

For Christian *Izitabane*, the exclusion they face is often perpetuated by a combination of exclusivist biblical interpretation and cultural conservatism. Van der Walt and Davids (2022, p. 399) argue that in many African contexts, any form of sexual diversity is constructed as both un-African and un-Christian. This dominant discourse shapes the way *Izitabane* experience their faith, as their bodies and identities are deemed illegitimate in both cultural and religious spaces. The cis-heteropatriarchal norms that inform this exclusion are deeply ingrained, positioning *Izitabane* at the margins of both faith and society. In this context CBS becomes vital for dismantling these harmful narratives. It exposes the exclusionary logic that privileges one story, one interpretation over others, and it creates space for the diverse stories and experiences of *Izitabane* to be heard and valued. By making room for previously marginalized ideas, CBS offers an opportunity to transform faith spaces into places of radical inclusion where all bodies matter (Tilsen, 2021, p. 37).

CBS draws on the principles of liberation theology, which emphasizes the 'liberating potential that responsible and accountable bible engagement and religious acts of care hold for the poor and marginalised' (Van der Walt and Davids, 2022, p. 39). Through its See–Judge–Act methodology, CBS begins with a reflection on the lived realities of marginalized communities, using these experiences as the foundation for engaging with scripture. They are followed by a process of theological reflection that engages scripture while carrying the realities identified within the context of reflection. This reflective process is followed by deliberate action, where participants work together to address the injustices exposed through biblical interpretation (Van der Walt and Davids, 2022, p. 40). By centring the experiences of *Izitabane* and other marginalized groups, CBS not only exposes the exclusionary practices that have historically silenced these voices but also calls for action to affirm their dignity and humanity. This process of reading and reflection is life-giving and affirming, as it challenges theological practices that marginalize and oppress. By engaging the embodied stories of those on the margins, CBS opens new possibilities for inclusive, life-affirming theological engagement.

The liberatory process that CBS facilitates is one of both action and reflection, a constant cycle of critical engagement with scripture and the lived realities of the individuals who engage in the reading process together. For *Izitabane* of faith, this process is transformative, as it resuscitates life and affirms the value of their stories and experiences. By bringing the 'embodied stories of our own lives into conversation with the stories of the Bible', CBS helps clarify how scripture can be used to affirm rather than marginalize (Davids et al., 2019, p. 35). It is a process that seeks to disrupt systems of exclusion and violence, offering a path towards justice, dignity and radical inclusion for all bodies, especially those who have been pushed to the margins.

In this context the theological lens offered by *Izitabane Zingabantu* comes into focus as a powerful tool for strengthening CBS. *Izitabane Zingabantu* – which translates as 'queer people are human' – is a theological framework that intersects with the values of Ubuntu theology, emphasizing the inherent dignity and interconnectedness of all people (Davids et al., 2019, p. 12). This theology challenges the exclusionary practices of the church and society, asserting that *Izitabane* are fully human and deserving of love, respect and inclusion. It draws on the principles of Ubuntu, which teaches that 'a person is a person through others' (Davids et al., 2019, p. 12), calling for a more inclusive understanding of the community that centres on the dignity of every person. When integrated into CBS, *Izitabane Zingabantu* Ubuntu theology strengthens the process of reclaiming the life-affirming aspects of faith by offering a theological vision that affirms the humanity of *Izitabane* and other marginalized bodies. It insists that all people, regardless of their sexuality or gender identity, are worthy of being fully embraced within the faith community.

## *Izitabane Zingabantu* Ubuntu Theology: Reclaiming Life Affirming Aspects of Faith

*Izitabane Zingabantu* Ubuntu theology – also known as Stabanization – is a uniquely South African theology that centres on the lived experiences of *Izitabane*, or queered bodies, within the South African context. This theology acknowledges the embodied impact of traditional theologies on these bodies, drawing on the language used to describe and marginalize them as crucial starting points for engagement. It is a theology that 'calls for a theology by Izitabane people, for Izitabane people in Africa' (Makhaye, 2024, p. 51). The framework emphasizes the need for an 'embodied reclaiming of what is good and life-affirming within faith landscapes', with a focus on reimagining community and reconnecting with faith to 'remember our communal and sacramental identity' (Davids et al., 2019, p. 29).

Like the methodology used in CBS, *Izitabane Zingabantu* Ubuntu theology advocates dismantling rigid, fixed scripture interpretations. It starts from the body, recognizing the contextual realities that shape individuals' faith experiences and God's love. Central to this theology is the belief in 'the body as a site of experience, connection, and meaning making' (Davids et al., 2019, p. 30), which positions the body as the focal point of theological reflection.

Constance M. Furey (2012) argues that 'the body is coincident with identity, selfhood, and being' (p. 12). We engage with the world through our bodies, feel, love and navigate our context's systemic realities. Therefore, meaningful engagement with faith and spirituality requires recognizing that we are deeply connected to and transformed by our embodied experiences (Furey, 2012, p. 13). The body is 'deeply symbolic in human culture'. It serves as the medium through which individuals and communities express themselves (Isherwood and Stuart, 1998, p. 10). As the tool to comprehend the contextual realities around us, the body must be included in any theological reflection. This is the unique contribution of *Izitabane Zingabantu* Ubuntu theology to Contextual Bible Study: it creates a space where bodies matter, allowing for engagement based on lived, embodied experiences influenced by an intersectional array of issues.

In tune with the process of CBS, *Izitabane Zingabantu* Ubuntu theology emphasizes beginning with the contextual realities of the community. It recognizes that 'our bodies create the landscape from which we interpret our lived realities' (Davids et al., 2019, p. 30), fostering human connectedness and the possibility of true community. By drawing from individual experiences of gender, sex and sexuality, this theology allows for a collective reflection on the systemic challenges posed by cis-heteropatriarchy and harmful theological narratives. It advocates for communal scripture reading that is honest about the terms historically used to degrade, shame and erase queer bodies. These terms are reclaimed to affirm *Izitabane*, allowing them to engage these issues from a place of pride and belonging.

*Izitabane Zingabantu* Ubuntu theology offers the gift of reclaiming language. It fosters an in-depth engagement with the body that ultimately contributes to communal reflection on toxic theologies, helping to restore dignity and a sense of belonging to marginalized bodies. Building on the conversation about *Izitabane Zingabantu* Ubuntu theology and its transformative role in reclaiming the embodied experiences of *Izitabane*, we can now explore how this framework can serve as the foundation for a broader move towards an inclusive African faith landscape.

By placing the body, language and context at the centre of theological reflection, *Izitabane Zingabantu* Ubuntu theology challenges traditional, exclusionary interpretations of scripture. This shift encourages a more profound, communal engagement with faith through CBS, where marginalized bodies' lived realities are acknowledged and celebrated. This theology opens the door to reimagining faith spaces where diversity is embraced, harmful narratives are dismantled and all bodies are affirmed in their sacredness. As we consider this move towards inclusivity, what are the necessary steps to ensure that this theological framework not only reshapes Bible study but also leads to tangible changes in African faith communities? How can we ensure that this vision of inclusivity takes root and thrives?

## Towards an Inclusive African Faith Landscape

Davids et al. (2019) argue that 'We encounter injustice, stigma and discrimination fundamentally in our bodies' (p. 32). In agreement with this perspective, I contend that we also experience and understand the impacts of theological ideologies through our embodied experiences. For *Izitabane* of faith, their lived and embodied realities are crucial to recognizing the need for transformative theologies. These theologies must liberate the bodies they address. One such theology, *Izitabane Zingabantu* Ubuntu theology, is a foundational lens when engaging in CBS, particularly when exposing and challenging the toxic theologies in the South African faith landscape. These toxic theologies often enforce harmful interpretations of sex, gender and sexuality and oppress individuals whose identities do not align with traditional cis-heteronormative expectations. Liberation, in this sense, must address the systemic realities embedded within the faith context that impact *Izitabane* bodies. Through this recognition we can begin to apply theologies that affirm the dignity and humanity of *Izitabane* and liberate them from oppressive frameworks.

We must engage with theologies that resist exclusion and violence to move towards an inclusive and affirming faith landscape. It is imperative to disrupt dominant theological discourses that perpetuate narratives of marginalization and erasure. To achieve this we must bring the stories and lived experiences of *Izitabane*, bodies that exist at the peripheries of these theological narratives, into focus. This process requires that we expose the theological frameworks contributing to their marginalization by interrogating the structures that produce and uphold these harmful ideologies. As Wilcox (2020) insightfully states, it is essential to ask 'who produced a story, who gets to define the "true" version of it, and who benefits (and who loses) from the way the story is told' (p. 61). By interrogating these questions we can initiate the process of dismantling oppressive theologies and the systemic forces that support them. This in turn will expose the mechanisms of power that continue to exert control over the bodies of *Izitabane* within faith communities.

I align with Wilcox (2020) when she asserts that 'the most profound wisdom comes from living and reflecting on life' (p. 84). This profound wisdom, cultivated from lived experience, offers critical insights for developing inclusive, life-giving theologies. To create these theologies we must root our theological reflections in the everyday realities of people, particularly those marginalized by dominant discourses. *Izitabane* of faith, through their intersectional and embodied realities, offer vital perspectives that challenge static and oppressive theologies. By embracing their experiences and insights we can begin to imagine theological frameworks that are genuinely transformative. These theologies must recognize and honour the complex and nuanced ways sex, gender and sexuality intersect in African contexts. When theology engages deeply with these embodied realities it becomes a tool for liberation rather than oppression.

The lived experiences of *Izitabane* not only challenge existing theological norms but also illuminate the potential for queer traditional understandings of sex, gender and sexuality. *Izitabane* embody the capacity to disrupt and subvert rigid and fixed norms by demonstrating the fluidity of roles, identities and sexualities. By doing so they expose the shakeable nature of systems that present themselves as immovable and unchangeable. Through the embodied realities of *Izitabane* we can begin to reimagine and transform the African faith landscape into one that is more inclusive, affirming and reflective of the diversity of human experience. As Van der Walt (2021) argues: 'It is important to do theology from the body and take seriously how we know the world through our bodies' (p. 409). Our bodies, as sites of knowledge and experience, are critical to interpreting our lived realities.

Furthermore, our bodies facilitate human connectedness and are integral to forming an authentic community. Theology must start from the body to truly engage with the complexities of human existence. As Van der Walt (2021) notes: 'Our bodies create the landscape from which we interpret our lived realities and enable the possibility of human connectedness' (p. 409).

## Conclusion: Reimagining a Liberative Future for Christian *Izitabane*

In reimagining a liberating future for Christian *Izitabane* we must draw from their lived realities and amplify their voices in theological transformation within the African faith context. We must centre their contextual realities when engaging in theological practices impacting their bodies. It is essential to understand that theological transformation concerning issues of sex, gender and sexuality will not be achieved through abstract theorizing alone but through a deep engagement with the lived experiences of *Izitabane*, who challenge and disrupt traditional norms by their very existence.

Transformative theologies that amplify the voices of *Izitabane* of faith and illuminate their embodied truth must first admit that conversations about sex, gender, and sexuality are complex. These are rooted in an environment that enables the maintenance of cis-heteropatriarchy and sustains it in its cultures, traditions and everyday socialization. Being truthful about this reality will allow us to expose and dismantle toxic theologies perpetuating harm and marginalization through frameworks such as *Izitabane Zingabantu* Ubuntu theology and methodologies like Contextual Bible Study.

Such frameworks and theological practices will challenge the systems that continue to oppress *Izitabane* bodies and empower these individuals as agents of change within the faith community. The journey towards transformation is not merely an academic exercise but embodied and lived. It requires us to embrace the fullness of human diversity, recognizing the sacred worth of all bodies, particularly those at the margins. Through this we can move towards a future where *Izitabane* are not placed at the margins but at the centre of the transformation process to fully challenge injustices, creating hospitable, compassionate and inclusive spaces. In this liberating future, *Izitabane* are affirmed in their identities and experiences, and theology becomes a tool for affirming life, dignity and community.

## References

Bishop, Sara S. V. (2022), 'Hospitality, Othering, and the Infinity of Worlds', in *Bordered Bodies, Bothered Voices: Native and Migrant Theologies*, edited by Jione Havea (Intersectionality and Theology Series), Eugene, OR: Wipf & Stock, pp. 66–80.

Brown, Roderick (2012), 'Corrective Rape in South Africa: A Continuing Plight Despite an International Human Rights Response', *Annual Survey of International & Comparative Law* 18, pp. 45–66.

Davids, Hanzline R., Abongile Matyila, Sindi Sithole and Charlene van der Walt (2019), 'Stabanisation: A Discussion Paper about Disrupting Backlash by Reclaiming LGBTI Voices in the African Church Landscape', Johannesburg: The Other Foundation.

Furey, Constance M. (2012), 'Body, Society, and Subjectivity in Religious Studies', *Journal of the American Academy of Religion* 80, no. 1, pp. 7–33.

Havea, Jione, ed. (2022), *Bordered Bodies, Bothered Voices: Native and Migrant Theologies* (Intersectionality and Theology Series), Eugene, OR: Wipf & Stock.

Igual, Roberto (2024), 'Murder of Lesbian Couple in KZN Highlights Persistent

LGBTIQ+ Hate Crimes', *Mamba Online.com*, 3 September, at https://www.mambaonline.com/2024/09/03/murder-of-lesbian-couple-in-kzn-highlights-persistent-lgbtiq-hate-crimes, accessed 01.12.2024.

Isherwood, Lisa and Elizabeth Stuart (1998), *Introducing Body Theology*, Sheffield: Sheffield Academic Press.

Jones, Tiffany (2019), 'South African Contributions to LGBTI Education Issues', *Sex Education* 19, no. 4, pp. 455–71.

Judge, Melanie (2020), 'Navigating Paradox: Towards a Conceptual Framework for Activism at the Intersection of Religion and Sexuality', *HTS Teologiese Studies/Theological Studies* 76, no. 3, pp. 1–10.

Makhaye, Nandi (2024), 'Condemned Bodies: Experiences of Homophobic Hatred and Violence in Pietermaritzburg, South Africa', *Revista Sacrilegens* 21, no. 1 (January–June), pp. 39–72.

Morrell, Robert, Rachel Jewkes and Graham Lindegger (2012), 'Hegemonic Masculinity/Masculinities in South Africa: Culture, Power, and Gender Politics', *Men and Masculinities* 15, no. 1, pp. 11–30.

Myeza, Zama (2024), 'LGBTQI+ Community Reels from Brutal Murder of Same-sex Couple', *The Witness*, 29 August, at https://witness.co.za/news/kzn/2024/08/29/lgbtqi-community-reels-from-brutal-murder-of-same-sex-couple/, accessed 01.12.2024.

Ntombana, Luvuyo, Nombulelo Towa and Nobubele Phuza (2020), 'Queer Spirituality of Black Lesbians in Bloemfontein, South Africa', *International Journal of Sociology and Anthropology*, 12, no. 3, pp. 76–84.

Ntombana, Luvuyo and Francis Sibanda (2024), 'The God of the Ostracised: The Use of Lived Religion Theory in Advancing Queer Spirituality', *Pharos Journal of Theology* 105, no. 2, pp. 1–11.

OutRight Action International (2022), 'Converting Mindsets, not our Identities: Summary of the Research Findings on the Nature, Extent, and Impact of Conversion Practices in Kenya, Nigeria, and South Africa', New York: OutRight Action International.

Palm, Selina and Laurie Gaum (2021), 'Engaging Human Sexuality: Creating Safe Spaces for LGBTIQ+ and Straight Believers in South Africa', *Theologia in Loco* 3, no. 2, pp. 205–30.

Reygan, Finn and Ashley Lynette (2014), 'Heteronormativity, Homophobia and "Culture Arguments" in KwaZulu-Natal, South Africa', *Sexualities* 17, nos 5–6, pp. 707–23.

Sibisi, Tracey and Charlene van der Walt (2021), 'Queering the Queer: Engaging Black Queer Christian Bodies in African Faith Spaces', *African Journal of Gender and Religion* 27, no. 2 (December), pp. 67–91.

Siwila, Lilian Cheelo (2021), 'Speaking with Silenced Bruised Bodies: Feminist Reflection on Atlantic Slave Trade and Colonial Empire', in *Religion, Patriarchy and Empire: Festschrift in Honour of Mercy Amba Oduyoye*, edited by Lilian Cheelo Siwila and Fundiswa A. Kobo, Pietermaritzburg: Cluster Publications, pp. 186–209.

South African Government News Agency (2021), 'Spate of Attacks on the LGBTQI+ Community in SA', *SAnews.gov.za*, 1 July, at https://www.sanews.gov.za/south-africa/spate-attacks-lgbtqi-community-sa, accessed 01.12.2024.

Tilsen, Julie Beth (2021), *Queering Your Therapy Practice: Queer Theory, Narrative Therapy, and Imagining New Identities*, London: Routledge.

Vaka'uta, Nāsili (2022), '*Kalanga*: (Sh)Outing Bodily Abuse in the Bible, Society, and Churches', in *Bordered Bodies, Bothered Voices: Native and Migrant Theologies*, edited by Jione Havea (Intersectionality and Theology Series), Eugene, OR: Wipf & Stock, pp. 162–72.

Van der Walt, Charlene (2021), 'Better is Never Better for Everyone, it Always Means Worse for Some: Could there be Space in an African Woman's Theology for Those Known as *Izitabane*?', in *Religion, Patriarchy and Empire: Festschrift in Honour of Mercy Amba Oduyoye*, edited by Lilian Cheelo Siwila and Fundiswa A. Kobo, Pietermaritzburg: Cluster Publications, pp. 389–414.

Van der Walt, Charlene and Hanzline R. Davids (2022), 'Heteropatriarchy's Blame Game: Reading Genesis 37 with Izitabane during COVID-19', *Old Testament Essays* 35, no. 1, pp. 32–50.

West, Gerald. O. (2021), 'Phantsi Patriarchy, Talitha Cum! The Quest for Post-Patriarchal Biblical Resources', in *Religion, Patriarchy and Empire: Festschrift in Honour of Mercy Amba Oduyoye*, edited by Lilian Cheelo Siwila and Fundiswa A. Kobo, Pietermaritzburg: Cluster Publications, pp. 123–45.

Wilcox, Melissa M. (2020), *Queer Religiosities: An Introduction to Queer and Transgender Studies in Religion*, Lanham, MD: Rowman & Littlefield Publishers.

Wilson, Carla (2001), 'Decolonizing Methodologies: Research and Indigenous Peoples by Linda Tuhiwai Smith, 1999, Zed Books, London' (book review), *Social Policy Journal of New Zealand* 17 (December), pp. 214–18.

# PART 5

# Soteriology and Eschatology

# 13

# (W)hol(e)y Saved: Queering Constructs of Salvation from a Naga Perspective

INATOLI AYE

## Introduction

On a busy Wednesday in the supermarket of Dimapur town in Nagaland, India, the air was alive with the sounds of vendors selling fresh vegetables, meat, insects and secondhand clothes. Amid this vibrant scene a small group of mainstream Indians, non-Naga evangelists, stood near the market's edge. Their voices rose above the hustle of vendors and customers bargaining for the best price. With a guitar in hand they sang songs of God's love and salvation, hoping to bring the good news of Jesus to the shoppers and vendors passing by. They held a signboard that asked: 'Are you saved?' To the Naga onlookers this was a curious sight. In a region where most identify as Baptist Christians, seeing non-Naga evangelists preach felt disorientating. For many Nagas, mainland India is seen as predominantly Hindu, Muslim or Sikh. Christianity is only heard of in connection with persecution. The presence of these outsiders, passionately proclaiming a message of salvation, raised questions: What does salvation mean to the Naga people, who already consider themselves Christian? To me it asked a further question: Can Naga indigenous Christianity be reimagined to honour both their indigenous identity and the queerness that has long been hidden in plain sight?

Yet beneath the surface a more profound tension emerges. Colonial Christianity and modernity have systematically demonized Naga indigenous traditions, pushing them to the margins of religious practice, such as specific traditional clothing, once integral to Naga identity, being now forbidden within church walls. Meanwhile issues of gender and sexuality remain primarily unspoken, leaving queer Nagas marginalized within their spiritual communities. For centuries, Christian theology has conceptualized salvation as an individual endeavour, personal, detached from one's relationships with community, environment and even body. This framework, rooted in Western Christian thought, is individualistic, anthropocentric and often cis-heteronormative, neglecting the interconnected web of life emphasized in indigenous theologies.

Naga indigenous traditions, when seen through a queer lens, challenge these dominant theological paradigms. Salvation cannot be understood in isolation from the marginalized, particularly queer indigenous peoples whose identities have been rendered invisible by colonial, nationalist and cis-heteropatriarchal structures. This chapter reimagines salvation as an inclusive, relational and decolonial process by exploring bodily fluids, pollution and salvation. It argues that salvation, ecological, spiritual and communal, cannot be achieved without the liberation of queer indigenous peoples.

## Colonialism, Nationalism in India and Christian Salvation

In this section I briefly situate Christian belief in the socio-economic-political context of the Nagas, whose identity has long been shaped by the intersections of colonialism and Christianity and the nationalist politics of India. The Indian nation state has historically relied on the construction of purity based on the caste system, framing particular religious and cultural identities, such as Muslims, Christians and indigenous peoples, at once as impure and anti-national. The Naga people, being both indigenous and predominantly Christian, are marginalized in this narrative and further oppressed for their demand for a self-determined nation, as they were never historically part of India (Iralu, 2003). For queer Nagas, this exclusion extends even further, as their queerness, alongside their indigenous identity, positions them as impure within both dominant theological and cultural frameworks.

In this colonial context Christian salvation has often been framed through binaries of holy/unholy, saved/unsaved and clean/polluted. These binaries, imposed by colonial missionaries, demanded the abandoning of indigenous spiritualities, cultural ethics and bodily practices. Queer indigenous bodies, already excluded as 'polluted' within cis-heteronormative Christian spaces, are further marginalized by these frameworks, making salvation not only inaccessible but also a site of violence and exclusion.

The colonial American Baptist missionaries, shaped by the pietist and puritanical movements of Europe and America, brought a salvation narrative that demanded the erasure of indigenous-embodied practices. To 'be saved' meant to abandon traditional ways, to reject indigenous relational ethics and to adopt a Christianized, sanitized identity. This understanding of salvation persists in many Naga churches today, where teachings emphasize that salvation is only attainable through accepting Jesus Christ as one's personal Lord and Saviour. This view is reinforced among Naga Baptists. The youth Bible study booklet *Starting New Life in Christ* (Nagaland Baptist Church Council, 2023), describes it:

> We are sinners who are condemned to eternal death and cannot save ourselves. It is only through God's love and grace that we can be saved. God sent His only son Jesus Christ to the earth to save men from this eternal death. Jesus, who is sinless, died on the cross and resurrected to pay for our sins and give us eternal life. (p. 6)

This theology frames salvation as a profoundly personal decision: 'To believe and accept Christ as our personal Lord and Savior is the most important decision in our life' (Nagaland Baptist Church Council, 2023, p. 6). Even those born and raised in Christian families are not exempt. Being a Christian and going to church alone will not guarantee salvation. One must repent of one's sins, ask God for forgiveness and believe Jesus died on the cross and was resurrected.

While this narrative emphasizes grace, it often translates into a transactional theology or the atonement theories of Anselm, where God requires the sacrifice and death of Jesus to pay the debt for the sake of humanity's sin (Althaus-Reid, 2007, p. 292; Weaver, 2011, p. 298; Johnson, 2018). This understanding of retributive violence in salvation should be decisively rejected, as it impacts the marginalized (Weaver, 2011, p. 298). In practice we find that the prevalent notions of salvation are tied to moralistic and cis-heteronormative ideals, such as 'sinner', 'transgender thoughts' or 'unnatural' (Malhotra, 2009). These moralistic and cis-heteronormative ideals impact the marginalized, as they face violence because of it.

These church teachings among the youth reinforce homophobia through the teaching of purity culture in the Naga churches ('Churches Protest Against Homosexuality', 2018). It is most prevalent in the manner in which Naga churches have adopted the True Love Waits programme (2006). That is primarily a North American agenda that calls young people to pledge sexual abstinence until marriage. Apart from its colonial origins, this programme not only implicitly values a purity culture that denigrates an embodied sexuality, thereby creating a guilt complex among younger people, but True Love Waits is also decisively cis-heteronormative and homophobic and explicitly condemns same-sex relationships.

What is required is a rethinking of atonement towards one that lies beyond theories vested in guilt and condemnation. The embodied realities of Naga life, its interdependence, ecological wisdom and queer possibilities are excluded from such frameworks (Keneipfenuo, 2018). Salvation becomes a moralistic endeavour, measured by adherence to purity codes and neoliberal ethics, where failure is seen as a lack of faith or work ethic. This theology reinforces polluted anthropology: bodies marked as queer, poor or indigenous are cast as failures, incapable of achieving salvation. Queer indigenous bodies then are sites of failures (Goh, 2021), showing new or alternative ways of knowing, and are sites of rupture, challenging the theological domestication that renders them invisible.

This understanding of salvation, which avoids talking about bodies but instead considers them dangerous, is reflected by Hugo Córdova Quero (2020):

> Most Christian churches perceive bodies, gender, and sexuality as dangerous areas that need to be controlled to achieve holiness or salvation. From spiritual practices that censor bodies as negative – thus, for example, encouraging self-flagellations – to systems of hierarchies based on gender, sexual orientation, color of skin, class, or nationality, among many other instruments, Christian churches have obtained their power to legislate which bodies are fit to 'God's grace' and which ones are not. (p. 155)

Córdova Quero's analysis highlights how these theological frameworks marginalize certain bodies, reinforcing the harmful cycle of exclusion and violence.

In such a context the question posed by Marcella Althaus-Reid (2001, p. 243), 'What do we want to be "saved" from in our lives?', is urgent. For the Naga people, salvation must include liberation from Indian state oppression and the realization of a self-determined nation. For queer indigenous peoples, salvation must go further, liberating them from theological domestication and cultural erasure. Salvation cannot be confined to the binaries of pure and impure, saved and unsaved; it must embrace the dirty, the polluted and the embodied as sites of transformation. Salvation must rupture the systems that exclude (Althaus-Reid, 2001). It must dismantle the colonial and cis-heteronormative frameworks that mark queer indigenous bodies as unworthy. As Althaus-Reid (2001) argues, salvation comes from the margins, from the polluted and excluded bodies that refuse domestication. That is not a salvation of restoration, of returning to an idealized order but a salvation of rupture, breaking open theological and ideological systems to make space for embodied liberation.

Naga Baptist theology, like much of evangelical Christianity – in general – remains profoundly anthropocentric and androcentric (Longchar, 2012, p. 49). Salvation is framed as an individual endeavour, often tied to cis-heteronormative morality and economic success. This theology mirrors the prosperity gospel, where poverty or illness is seen as a failure of faith (Wrenn, 2021, p. 303). Such teachings reinforce neoliberal ethics, where salvation is contractual, contingent on one's ability to perform faith and morality.

Yet salvation cannot remain confined to human-centred narratives. Feminist theologians like Rosemary Radford Ruether (1983, p. 25) and Rüpreo Angami Keneipfenuo (2018, p. 251) remind us that Jesus' prophetic mission was to liberate the oppressed; this means women, children, queer lives and the earth itself. For queer indigenous peoples, salvation is deeply ecological, spiritual and communal (Longchar, 2012, p. 57). It is not about escaping the pollution of the body but reclaiming it as sacred, interconnected and life-giving. The colonial theology of salvation has no liberatory potential for queer indigenous peoples. Instead, salvation must be disrupted and reclaimed as a queer, embodied rupture that confronts systems of oppression and exclusion.

In a context where cis-heteronormative theology excludes queer bodies from salvation, it is queer bodies that hold the potential for liberating salvation. Salvation comes not from the centre but from the margins, from the polluted and excluded bodies that refuse to conform. It is a salvation that liberates theology from 'ideological domestication and theological somnolence' (Althaus-Reid, 2001, p. 243). For the Naga people and queer indigenous peoples everywhere, salvation must mean liberation: liberation from colonialism, from androcentric theology, from the binaries of purity and pollution. It must mean creating just, loving and embodied communities where all bodies are sacred and all lives are interconnected. Only then can salvation be truly liberative, for there can be no salvation for anyone without the salvation of queer indigenous people.

## Queering Salvation: A Theological Reinterpretation

Salvation within traditional Christian frameworks is often linked to bodily fluids, such as Christ's blood, the water from his side and the womb of Mary. All are seen as symbols of purity and life. Yet these same fluids, particularly within patriarchal religious systems, are paradoxically associated with pollution. Churches talk about bodies but in sanitized and non-sexual ways, such as churches saying 'womb' but not 'vagina' or 'menstrual blood' or being willing to embrace the messiness of the blood or woundedness, reinforcing cis-heteropatriarchal systems of exclusion (Althaus-Reid, 2000). This duality reinforces cis-heteropatriarchal exclusions that queer bodies disrupt.

A queer reimagining of salvation subverts this purity-pollution binary. Queer bodies, often regarded as polluted or impure, hold the potential for salvation precisely because of their exclusion. Drawing from Naga indigenous epistemologies, this chapter examines salvation through two lenses: an indigenous folk story and the lived experience of queer indigenous bodies. These perspectives reveal how sites of pollution – blood, graves and the queer body itself – become transformative spaces of liberation.

## Indigenous Perspective: The Redemption of Ruptures and Reclaiming the Sacred Web

Naga folklore, particularly the story of the three brothers (a tiger, a spirit and a human), provides a profound metaphor for rethinking salvation as relational rather than individualistic. The tale of three brothers is a case in point. They were born to the same mother. It presents us with an unusual story beyond the constraints of cis-heteronormativity. It also presents the brothers' relationships as rupturing, reflecting the breakdown of the division between humans, animals and spirits. Here is the story of the three brothers as told by Joseph S. Thong and Phanenmo Kath (2011):

> In olden days, the mythology says that a spirit, tiger and man were born of the same mother. Their mother became old with age and the three brothers had to take turns to look after her. When the spirit looked after her mother, he washed her, fed her with rice and gave her rice-beer to drink, so his mother fared well. When the man looked after her, she was okay, but when the tiger looked after her, he scratched her and licked his own mother's blood, so that she withered with the passage of time.
>
> One day, the mother said to the spirit and man that she would die that day and that they were to send the tiger to their field. She further instructed them to bury her when she was dead, and to cook and eat their meal on top of her grave.

> After the tiger had gone to the field, their mother died. They buried her as per her wishes and began to cook their food at the top of her grave and took their meal there. After some time, the tiger arrived from the field and began to search for his mother. When he could not find her, he started wailing for her and scratched around his mother's grave, but not able to find her, fled away to the jungles. (p. 192)

In another account by Esther Jish Rengma and Phanenmo Kath (2023):

> When their mother passed away, man and tiger quarrelled over who would receive their mother's worldly possessions. They decided to hold a competition to settle the matter. Man, with his guile, eventually beat the tiger, who then went to dwell in the forest. The spirit, angered by man's deception, cursed him so that he'd never see the spirit again. Later, when the man began to miss his brothers, he came up with an array of rituals to appease them. In due course these ceremonies became a part of Naga culture. (p. 202)

In this story, animals, spirits and humans once lived in harmony, connected by their shared origin and kinship. The rupture between them symbolizes the breakdown of the interconnected web of life, a rupture that requires mending for salvation to occur. This story resists cis-heteronormative familial structures, presenting a 'queer family' that challenges binaries. That is not unusual for indigenous peoples. Many indigenous peoples also consider that we are all related to the earth and all our kin (Vashum, 2009). This alternative familial bond highlights not only the interconnected web of all life forms but also the complexity of relationships and, most importantly, a move to the restoration of just relationships, a move towards the communion of humans, nature, spirits and animals.

In contrast to the Western Christian model of salvation, which is often anthropocentric and centred on the individual, indigenous perspectives emphasize relationality. From a Naga indigenous standpoint, salvation involves restoring the relationships between animals, spirits, humans and the earth. This relational understanding of salvation offers a model that embraces queer siblings, whose identities often defy rigid binaries. The folk story vividly illustrates this understanding, which lends itself to two distinct interpretations. On one hand, the image of the tiger licking the mother's blood symbolizes a primal connection, a visceral intertwining of life and death. On the other hand, the shared meal atop the mother's grave reflects a ritualistic act of remembrance, a communal acknowledgment of loss, and the continuation of life through shared bonds. Both interpretations offer profound insights into themes of sacrifice, legacy and the cycles of existence.

## *The Mother's Blood: Pollution as Life*

In patriarchal systems, bodily fluids, blood, especially menstrual blood, are often stigmatized as impure. Similarly, in the story, the tiger's act of licking the mother's blood causes her to wither, marking blood as a site of death and decay. Yet blood also holds life-giving power. Christian theology considers Christ's blood redemptive and enacted in every Eucharist. Yet we must not forget the gender and sexuality of the mother and her children presented as male. The male taking care of the mother or nature is also subversive in our present masochistic ideology.

Here, the tiger's relationship with blood can be seen as ambiguous: it causes the mother to weaken yet it also binds the tiger to the mother through an intimate, corporeal act. Blood, often perceived as polluting, becomes a site of deep connection, a marker of kinship and shared existence. The tiger licking the mother's blood is indeed destructive; her body withers over time. At first glance this could be seen as a toxic relationship or violent, and we should not shy away from acknowledging that tension. Though destructive, the tiger's action reminds us of life's fragility and the interconnectedness of relationships. Just as queer bodies disrupt cis-heteropatriarchal purity systems, the tiger's interaction with the mother's blood disrupts the boundaries between life and death, care and harm. The tiger's relationship with the mother's blood reveals a tension that mirrors real-world complexities, intimate yet imperfect relationships, loving yet damaging. This ambiguity resonates deeply with queer and indigenous theological frameworks, which challenge rigid binaries and embrace liminality.

Queer salvation, then, embraces these liminal spaces, reclaiming pollution as a site of potential healing and relational restoration. The tiger's actions challenge the idea that relationships must be free from tension to hold meaning. Whether human, animal or spiritual, relationships are never without struggle. It is often through engaging with this struggle that restoration and transformation become possible. The tiger's licking blood reminds us that what society deems polluting or harmful can also hold the potential for connection and redemption. The tiger's action reminds us that, like care, salvation is not always clean or straightforward. It involves confronting pain, rupture and messiness. Just as the tiger's care reveals the fragility of life, salvation demands we face the uncomfortable truths of exclusion and harm, especially the damage done to queer bodies. This disruptive process, though painful, is necessary for restoration and healing.

### *The Mother's Grave: Pollution and Communion*

The brothers' act of eating atop their mother's grave transforms the site of death into one of communion. Graves, associated with death and decay, are traditionally seen as impure spaces in many cultures (Clark, 1907, p. 59; Douglas, 1984, p. 35). It becomes a ritual of connection between the brothers and their mother, between the living and the dead. This ritual can be interpreted as an indigenous model of salvation rooted in relationality. Salvation is not about escaping polluted spaces but engaging them to restore balance. For the brothers, the meal signifies a return to their shared origin, their mother and an acknowledgement of the rupture caused by their differences. In this act the grave becomes a site of reconciliation, where pollution – death and decay – coexists with nourishment and life.

From a queer theology perspective this challenges the purity-pollution binary. Queer bodies, like the grave, are often marked as polluted by dominant cis-heteronormative systems. Yet just as the meal atop the grave signifies communion and restoration, queer bodies embody the potential for healing and liberation. They offer spaces where binaries, pure and impure, life and death, saved and unsaved, are dissolved.

From the perspective of traditional theology, this folk story may seem unauthorized or non-canonical. Yet this is precisely why theology must be destabilized and freed from fixed, exclusionary doctrines. The folk story reimagines salvation in new ways and invites us to relate to the divine through diverse, embodied and relational experiences. The indigenous perspective offers epistemologies that are embodied, relational and subversive, aligning with the tenets of queer theology. It dismantles colonial and cis-heteronormative frameworks, favouring localized, community-based theologies that honour diversity and interconnectedness.

## Queer Indigenous Bodies

Colonialism and cis-heteropatriarchy imposed rigid hierarchies that fractured indigenous relationality, particularly for queer bodies (Driskill, 2016). Missionary archives from the Lushai Hills reveal colonial astonishment at indigenous gender fluidity, describing individuals who defied Western norms of male and female roles (Lorrain and Savidge, 1898). Queer indigenous peoples were often feminized or desexualized (Finley, 2011), positioned as both impure and spiritually liminal. The story of the 'man-woman' from the Lushai Hills in the Northeast part of India reflects this colonial gaze, where queer indigenous peoples were simultaneously marginalized.

In the colonial missionary archives documenting the people of the Lushai Hills, present-day Mizoram, inhabited mainly by Mizo indigenous peoples, the missionaries provide striking descriptions. They note that the Lushai people are 'by no means a type of beauty' (Lorrain and Savidge, 1898, p. 479) and are generally not known for their cleanliness, whether as children or adults. However, an exception is found in their description of a 'man-woman', as they referred to this person without more appropriate terminology. This individual, dressed in female clothing and performing tasks traditionally assigned to women, was regarded as 'by far the neatest and cleanest person in the village' (Lorrain and Savidge, 1898, p. 482).

The missionaries describe this person as having a deep voice and pulling out facial hair, remarking on their 'troublesome mustache' being plucked. They also found this individual's existence, along with a 'curious' community of others like them, mysterious. The archive notes that among this group, women dressed as men performed men's work and smoked pipes typically used by men. The missionaries' observations reflect their astonishment at the apparent fluidity in gender roles. They express surprise that in a society where women's labour was described as 'the lion's share', individuals like the 'man-woman' would prefer to engage in women's work. They go on to explain that the indigenous men and women had such similar appearances – both parting their hair in the middle, tying it in a knot at the back, and wearing long clothes woven by women – that at first the missionaries could not distinguish between the sexes (Lorrain and Savidge, 1898, p. 482).

In this colonial lens, indigenous people of the Lushai Hills were perceived as transgressing Western norms of cis-heteronormativity. Indigenous men were feminized, and women appeared to blur the boundaries of male and female, leaving the missionaries unable to discern clear gender distinctions. That mirrors broader colonial interpretations of indigenous peoples throughout the region.

Queer bodies are subjected to ideological warfare, causing harm to them, yet these bodies embody salvific potential. Queer bodies are considered indecent, impure. However, in the biblical tradition Christ's incarnation affirms the body as a site or the *locus* of divine revelation (Córdova Quero, 2020, p. 166). For queer people, whose bodies are often humiliated, this incarnational theology offers profound affirmation: queer bodies are not only sacred but also sites of salvation. The touch, love and desire of queer bodies disrupt binaries of purity and impurity, revealing the goodness and holiness of queer existence. Justin Tanis (2006) also points this out:

> One of the powerful messages of the incarnation of Christ is the blessing of the body as a source of salvation and the revelation of God. Queer people know that our bodies are not like other bodies – especially those of us who are transgender. And yet, through the revelation of our bodies, we experience liberation and personal salvation. Gay, lesbian and bi people know the power of touching bodies that are like our own, affirming in the flesh of another the goodness of our own gendered, queer bodies, finding beauty in bodies that are like our own and yet different as well. Part of the development of queer sexual culture rests on an enjoyment of bodies for their own sake.

This understanding starkly contrasts with the colonial ideologies imposed by missionaries, who defined cleanliness and uncleanliness through arbitrary power dynamics. This same arbitrary power shapes ideas of purity and impurity, often rooted in a binary logic that upholds domination. The absurdity of such classifications becomes evident when considering the biblical tradition that frequently positions impurity or marginalization as a site for salvation (Isherwood and Stuart, 1998; Melanchthon and Varkey, 2020). If salvation can emerge from what is deemed impure, as suggested by these fixed binaries, then our contemporary understanding of purity must be challenged. From this perspective, there is salvific value in breaking these rigid categories, revealing a deeper connection between impurity and redemption in our current societal context.

## Towards a Queer Indigenous Theology of Salvation

Salvation, from a queer Naga perspective, is about restoring relationships fractured by colonialism and cis-heteropatriarchy. For many Nagas, salvation has been domesticated into a cis-heteronormative framework, ingrained as an exclusionary ideal. The folk story and queer indigenous bodies disrupt this domesticated vision of salvation, challenging the notion that salvation can ever be exclusionary. Salvation, as grace from God – as Althaus-Reid (2001) reminds us – cannot be confined by human manipulation. However, cis-heterosexual theology has often subverted this grace to create exclusionary doctrines. If we assume there is no grace, humans are left only with the wrath of God. The folk story of the three queer siblings shows us another way: a relational and reparative understanding of salvation, where differences are reconciled and justice is restored. This indigenous understanding of salvation, rooted in relationality and justice, is essential for addressing those wronged by the church. The church must repent and strive for just relationships between humans, animals, spirits and the earth.

Modern Naga Christianity often reduces salvation to a personal, individualized experience – 'me and Jesus'. This perspective aligns with a capitalistic world view that prioritizes individualism over community. Yet indigenous spirituality offers a counter-narrative: salvation is inherently relational. It involves not just relationships but just and proper relationships with the whole creation. Indigenous values reveal that salvation is not limited to individuals but encompasses creation. If the tiger, spirit and human brothers emerged from the same womb, as Naga traditions tell us, then life is interconnected. Salvation cannot be exclusive to a few selected cis-heterosexuals; it must embrace all beings and the earth itself. Furthermore, salvation is not confined to Jesus' work on the cross but is part of God's ongoing divine activity, beginning with creation.

Queer bodies, often vilified as impure or sinful, embody the paradox of salvation. In the incarnation of Christ, the body becomes a holy site of divine revelation. For queer people whose bodies have been humiliated and excluded, this incarnational theology offers a profound affirmation: our bodies are not only sacred but also sites of salvation. The touch of queer bodies – affirming, loving and desiring – challenges the binaries of purity and impurity, revealing the goodness and holiness of queer existence.

Salvation is not a sanitized process. It is embodied, messy and deeply relational. Queer bodies – with their transgressive beauty – disrupt and redefine spaces moulded by cis-heteronormative ideals. Lorina Muñoz's (2016) concept of 'pseudo-heteronormative spaces' highlights how queerness persists even in contexts dominated by normative structures, creating opportunities for disruption and transformation. This disruption reflects the salvific potential of queer bodies as they resist erasure and oppression. While Muñoz (2016) proceeds with caution not to suggest that everything is queer, the author suggests that 'heteronormative spaces are not absent of queer social constructions' (p. 66). There exists queerness in perceived cis-heteronormative spaces, thereby creating a space that is pseudo-heteronormative. Perhaps this is what Philip Vinod Peacock (2017, p. 263) calls us to do, to disrupt these cis-heteronormative spaces by living transgressively, for it is an act of resistance and liberation. Queer indigenous people disrupt these spaces, embodying a salvific defiance against colonial and theological oppression.

Salvation is the flourishing of life – a flourishing denied to queer indigenous people by the violence of colonialism, cis-heteronormativity and exclusionary theology. God wills wholeness, an interconnectedness that embraces all bodies, relationships and creation. In the Gospels tradition, Jesus heals physical ailments and restores humanity within the community, challenging the sociopolitical norms of his day (Peacock, 2007). That is salvation: the restoration of relationships, the mending of ruptures and the liberation of all excluded.

Gustavo Gutiérrez (1973, p. 83) argues that liberation and salvation are inseparable. James H. Cone (1997) also sees liberation as integral to salvation: 'Any starting point that ignores God in Christ as the Liberator of the oppressed or that makes salvation as liberation secondary is *ipso facto* [by the fact] invalid and thus heretical' (p. 75). Both recognize the seriousness of sin and immorality in human society. Sin is not merely personal but systemic, embedded in the fractures caused by colonialism, patriarchy and cis-heteronormativity. Resistance and struggle against these oppressive forces are integral to Jesus' mission. The Naga indigenous theologian Yangkahao Vashum (2020, p. 178) reminds us that Jesus Christ is the ground of liberation; we extend God's Kingdom on earth in our struggle for justice and liberation.

In this queer indigenous theology of salvation we are called to embrace the sacredness of the polluted, the transgressive and the liminal. To embrace salvation is to dismantle oppressive systems, to challenge purity culture and cis-heteronormativity and to affirm the holiness of queer bodies and the wholeness of creation. Queer indigenous theology calls us to reimagine salvation as a communal act of mending ruptures and restoring the sacred web of life.

## Conclusion

A queer indigenous theology of salvation provides a unique framework that honours both indigenous identity and the queerness that has long been hidden in plain sight. In doing so it reimagines alternative trajectories for Naga Christianity. By centring relationality, communion, justice and the sacredness of all bodies, this theology disrupts colonial and cis-heteronormative frameworks that have fractured communities. It calls for the church to repent of its complicity in exclusion and embrace a communal vision of salvation.

The Naga story of the tiger, spirit and human brothers illustrates that salvation is relational, addressing ruptures caused by exclusion and pollution. Similarly, the marginalization of queer people fractures the interconnected web of life, making their liberation essential for salvation. This vision transcends binaries of purity and pollution, embracing complexity and diversity. By centring queer indigenous bodies in the restoration of relationships, salvation becomes an act of communal and ecological healing, affirming the sacredness of all life and reweaving the web of creation.

Salvation is a matter of individual faith and a communal act restoring the interconnected relationships that sustain life. This is the essence of a queer indigenous theology of salvation, a vision of wholeness, justice and liberation for all.

## References

Althaus-Reid, Marcella (2000), *Indecent Theology: Theological Perversions in Sex, Gender and Politics*, London: Routledge.

Althaus-Reid, Marcella (2001), 'Sexual Salvation: The Theological Grammar of Voyeurism and Permutations', *Literature and Theology* 15, no. 3, pp. 241–8.

Althaus-Reid, Marcella (2007), 'Queering the Cross: The Politics of Redemption and the External Debt', *Feminist Theology* 15, no. 3, pp. 289–301.

'Churches Protest Against Homosexuality' (2018), *Nagaland Post*, 23 October, at https://nagalandpost.com/index.php/churches-protest-against-homosexuality, accessed 24.05.2023.

Clark, Mary Mead (1907), *A Corner in India*, Boston, MA: American Baptist Publication Society.

Cone, James H. (1997), *God of the Oppressed*, Maryknoll, NY: Orbis Books.

Córdova Quero, Hugo (2020), 'Unfaithful Noxious Sexuality: Body, Incarnation, and Ecclesiology in Dispute', in *Unlocking Orthodoxies for Inclusive Theologies: Queer Alternatives*, edited by Robert E. Shore-Goss and Joseph N. Goh (Gender, Theology and Spirituality Series), New York: Routledge, pp. 154–73.

Douglas, Mary (1984), *Purity and Danger: An Analysis of the Concepts of Pollution and Taboo*, London: Routledge.

Driskill, Qwo-Li (2016), *Asegi Stories: Cherokee Queer and Two-Spirit Memory*, Tucson, AZ: University of Arizona Press.

Finley, Chris (2011), 'Decolonizing the Queer Native Body (and Recovering the Native Bull-Dyke): Bringing "'Sexy Back" and Out of Native Studies' Closet', in *Queer Indigenous Studies: Critical Interventions in Theory, Politics and Literature*, edited by Qwo-Li Driskill, Chris Finley, Brian Joseph Gilley and Scott Lauria Morgensen, Tucson, AZ: University of Arizona Press, pp. 31–42.

Goh, Joseph N. (2021), 'Manang Bali, Indecent Interweavings and Healing Spaces in Contemporary Malaysian Trans and Queer Theo-Pastoralities', in *The Indecent Theologies of Marcella Althaus-Reid: Voices from Asia and Latin America*, edited by Lisa Isherwood and Hugo Córdova Quero (Gender, Theology, and Spirituality Series), London: Routledge, pp. 70–91.

Gutiérrez, Gustavo (1973), *A Theology of Liberation: History, Politics, and Salvation*, translated by Caridad Inda and John Eagleson, Maryknoll, NY: Orbis Books.

Iralu, Kaka D. (2003), *Nagaland and India. The Blood and the Tears: A Historical*

*Account of the Fifty-Two Year Indo-Naga War and the Story of Those Who Were Never Allowed to Tell It*, NP: Kaka D. Iralu.

Isherwood, Lisa and Elizabeth Stuart (1998), *Introducing Body Theology*, Trowbridge: Sheffield Academic Press.

Johnson, Elizabeth A. (2018), *Creation and the Cross: The Mercy of God for a Planet in Peril*, Maryknoll, NY: Orbis Books.

Keneipfenuo, Rüpreo Angami (2018), 'Copious amidst Chaos: A Tribal Postcolonial Feminist God-Talk from Northeast Indian Perspective', doctoral dissertation, Nijmegen: Radboud University.

Longchar, A. Wati (2012), *Returning to Mother Earth: Theology, Christian Witness and Theological Education. An Indigenous Perspective*, Kolkata, West Bengal: Programme for Theology and Cultures in Asia.

Lorrain, J. Herbert and Fred W. Savidge (1898), 'Among the Head-Hunters of Lushai', *Wide World Magazine* 4 (November 1899 – April 1900), pp. 474–83.

Malhotra, John (2009), 'Nagaland Pastors Blow Whistle on Gay Judgment', *Christian Today*, 13 July, at http://www.christiantoday.co.in/article/nagaland.pastors.blow.whistle.on.gay.judgment/4209.htm, accessed 01.12.2024.

Melanchthon, Monica J. and Mothy Varkey (2020), 'Teaching Biblical Studies in a Pandemic: India', *Journal of Biblical Literature* 139, no. 3, pp. 613–18.

Muñoz, Lorena (2016), 'Brown, Queer and Gendered: Queering the Latina/o "Street-Scapes" in Los Angeles', in *Queer Methods and Methodologies: Intersecting Queer Theories and Social Science Research*, edited by Kath Browne and Catherine J. Nash, London: Routledge, pp. 55–66.

Nagaland Baptist Church Council (2023), *Starting New Life in Christ*, Guwahati: Nagaland Baptist Church Council (NBCC).

Peacock, Philip V. (2007), 'Untouchability is the Key', *In God's Image: Journal of Asian Women's Resource Centre for Culture and Theology* 26, no. 3, pp. 55–7.

Peacock, Philip Vinod (2017), 'Masculinity and Justice', in *A Theological Reader on Human Sexuality and Gender Diversities: Envisioning Inclusivity*, edited by Roger Gaikwad and Thomas Ninan, Delhi: NCCI and ISPCK, pp. 258–63.

Radford Ruether, Rosemary (1983), *Sexism and God-Talk: Toward a Feminist Theology*, Boston, MA: Beacon Press.

Rengma, Esther Jish and Phanenmo Kath (2023), *Retelling Our Stories: Once Upon a Time ...: Fables, Folktales and Folklore. Narrating Indigenous Tales of North East India*, Culture/Religion/Society, Jorhat, Assam: The Tribal Development and Communication Centre.

Tanis, Justin (2006), 'Philippians', in *The Queer Bible Commentary*, edited by Deryn Guest, Robert E. Goss, Mona West and Thomas Bohache, London: SCM Press, pp. 650–1.

Thong, Joseph S. and Phanenmo Kath (2011), *Glimpses of Naga Legacy and Culture*, Kottayam, Kerala: Society of Naga Student's Welfare.

'True Love Waits' (2006), *Morung Express*, 11 February, at https://www.morungexpress.com/true-love-waits, accessed 01.12.2024.

Vashum, Yangkahao (2009), 'The Stars Are Our Relatives: Tribal/Indigenous People's Stellar Theology', in *Doing Tribal Christian Theology with Tribal Resources: Cultural Resources from North East India*, edited by Razouselie Laseto and Eyingbeni Hümtsoe (Tribal Studies Series #18), Jorhat, Assam: Eastern Theological College, pp. 169–88.

Vashum, Yangkahao (2020), *Faith Seeking Transformation: Rethinking Faith, Theology and Mission in North East India*, Delhi: Christian World Imprints.

Weaver, J. Denny (2011), *The Nonviolent Atonement*, 2nd edn, Grand Rapids, MI: William B. Eerdmans.

Wrenn, Mary V. (2021), 'Selling Salvation, Selling Success: Neoliberalism and the US Prosperity Gospel', *Cambridge Journal of Economics* 45, no. 2, pp. 295–311.

# 14

# A Queer Trinitarian Reading of Communion and Otherness

MIGUEL H. DÍAZ

## Introduction

At the 2006 annual meeting of the Academy of Catholic Hispanic Theologians of the United States (ACHTUS) I delivered my presidential acceptance speech titled: 'Human Beings at the Crossroads of Divine Self-Disclosure: Otherness in Black Catholic and Latino/a Catholic Theologies and the Otherness of God'. At that time I explored the question of human identity, considering ethnocentric and racist experiences within the United States that undermine, marginalize and erase Latinx and Black identities. To provide a theological reading of this question I turned to the doctrine of the Trinity, particularly the theology of the contemporary Orthodox theologian John Zizioulas. Drawing from early Greek Christian writers, he proposes a relational and dynamic approach to human and divine persons. His theological contributions have been taken up by leading Christian theologians in the global North, including key feminist Trinitarian theologians (LaCugna, 1991; Fox, 2001). I believe that his relational ontology, and more specifically his focus on the interpersonal otherness that constitutes divine life, also speaks to queer theologians highly critical of essentialism, the denial of gender and sexual differences, and the idolatrous ways that cis-heterosexist constructions of the mystery of God have been deployed against LGBTIQ+ persons. As a verb I use the word 'queer' methodologically to disrupt cis-heteronormative theological constructs. As a noun I use it in reference to something or someone disruptive, as is the case with God as the exemplary disruptor of the status quo and LGBTIQ+ persons who disrupt because of their gender identities and sexual orientations.

This chapter explores and queers two building blocks in Trinitarian theologies, namely divine otherness and communion. These theological constructs, which tap into central Christian understandings of the mystery of God, provide theoretical tools that challenge the otrocide that queer bodies often experience. Borrowing from and building upon Carmen Nanko-Fernández (2010, p. 55), I understand otrocide as a socially constructed and life-threatening cis-heteronormative othering that leads to the erasure, suicide and at times targeted killing of queer bodies. First, I offer some brief remarks drawn from the Judaeo-Christian creation narratives (Gen. 1—3). These narratives speak not only to the erotic nature of creation – that is, life-giving/-saving and divinely willed communion among diverse creatures – they also offer signposts to understand how we have rejected this divine scripting to turn creaturely communion into othering and division. Second, I will summarize Zizioulas's central theological arguments concerning communion and otherness in the life of God. Third, Zizioulas's arguments will be critically engaged from queer and US Latinx Trinitarian perspectives.

Queering communion and otherness challenges and deepens these fundamental building blocks associated with the doctrine of the Trinity. My central aim is to expand from a queer lens what Ignacio Ellacuría invited us to ponder, namely that 'creation can be seen as the grafting *ad extra* of the trinitarian life itself, a freely desired grafting' (Ellacuría and Sobrino, 1993, p. 276). To paraphrase his argument from the perspective of LGBTIQ+ persons, it is not enough to argue that creation, in general, has been grafted to reflect God's life, but that LGBTIQ+ persons – each in their own and distinct queer way of being human – have been grafted with divine life to refract the divine mystery of communion and otherness.[1]

## Communion and Otherness in the Judaeo-Christian Creation Narratives (Gen. 1—3)

Two creation narratives in the Hebrew and Christian scriptures (Gen. 1.1—2.4a; 2.4b—3.24) have profoundly impacted how we understand the relationship between divine and human life. At their best the stories speak to divinely willed mutuality and interdependence among all creatures. At their worst these stories have been misinterpreted and weaponized in ways that have unnaturally engendered sexism, cis-heterosexism and anthropocentrism. Chronologically speaking, Genesis 1.1—2.4a appears first in Hebrew and Christian Bibles. Following the documentary hypothesis theory, biblical scholars attribute its composition to the Elohist or 'E' source some time in the sixth century BCE. The story breaks up the creation of earthly creatures into seven days, culminating with the creation of human persons on the sixth day and divine rest on the seventh day. Genesis 2.4b—3.24, or the second creation narrative, immediately follows this first and chronological account of creation. It is attributed to the Yahwist or 'J' source and was probably composed in the eighth or ninth century BCE. This story of creation offers much wisdom about the divine will to create creaturely differences and the life-threatening misuse of human power that undermines communion among persons and care for all of creation.

Phyllis Trible (1978) maps the literary landscape of Genesis 2.4b—3.24 into three scenes: 1) the emergence, development and diversification of *eros* [life]; 2) the contamination and disintegration of life brought about by the abuse of power that turns difference into division and human interdependence into isolation; and 3) the divine condemnation for these human actions (pp. 72–143). I will limit my observations to how Trible interprets three key passages in the second creation narrative: Genesis 2.7, 23 and 3.20. These passages capture God's will for creation to exist in interdependence and the dire consequences humans usher in when we fail to live up to the divine will. God wills the affirmation of otherness and communion to rule creation. Conversely, humans' rejection of the divine plan and order of creation results in othering and alienation.

Trible's translation of Genesis 2.7 from the Hebrew scriptures and the theological implications that follow from her literary analysis paves the way to rescue this creation narrative from its theological ruins. Her feminist interpretation not only frees the narrative from gender biases but also carries implications concerning questions of life related to human sexuality and the environment. Let us consider Trible's translation of Genesis 2.7:

> Then Yahweh God formed the earth creature [*hā-'ādām*] dust from the earth [*hā-'ᵃdāmâ*] and breathed into its nostrils the breath of life. and the earth creature [*hā-'ādām*] became a living ***nephesh***. (p. 78)

Parting from traditional translations that presume that God first creates a male creature, that is, the man 'Adam', Trible argues that the word *hā-'ādām* in fact contains three understandings in the story. In this first episode that introduces the term, she argues that *hā-'ādām* connotes an androgynous or gender and sexually undifferentiated earth creature. Thus, Trible's argument invites consideration of all human persons' divine – and earthly – common origin and egalitarian status regardless of their gender identities and sexual orientations.

As the second creation story unfolds we learn that creation is never a fait accompli but entails a dynamic process of ongoing differentiation and development. Here Trible's exegesis underscores the diverse, dynamic, interdependent and fluid character of all creatures, including humans. After the creation of plants (Gen. 2.9–17) and animals (Gen. 2.18–20), the story introduces another kind of creaturely otherness with the differentiation of the earth creature into male and female persons. God causes the earth creature to fall into a deep sleep, and from the earth creature creates human sexuality. The parallel and playful use of terms for the differentiated earth creature, *'îš* [male] and *'iššâ* [female], suggest the fundamental dignity, equality and commonality of human persons. Trible argues (pp. 97–8) that at this point in the story the word *hā-'ādām* becomes exclusively identified with the proper name of the male creature.

Adam, the differentiated male earth creature, speaks for the first time and recognizes his equal partner within the divine order of creation: 'And *hā-'ādām* said: This, finally, bone of my bones and flesh of my flesh. This shall be called woman [*'iššâ*] because from man [*'îš*] was taken this [Gen. 2.23]' ( Trible, 1978, p. 97). Despite a long history of oppressive, sexist interpretations related to the expression that *'iššâ* was taken from *'îš*, the biblical text neither supports subordinating the female to the male nor falsely concludes that first means superior and second inferior. As Trible argues, God forms the female creature from a rib, 'the rib is raw material, comparable to the dust of the earth ... Clearly in the prose account [of creation], then, it is the raw material, not the woman herself, that is taken from the earth creature' (pp. 100–1). Moreover, I would underscore that the play of words between 'man' and 'woman' in the text does not support an essentialized and binary relationship between two rigidly defined human beings. Instead, it invites us to conceive the radical equality and mutuality that God intends for all human persons and their relationships.

The word that Adam uses to recognize his partner *'iššâ* reinforces the radical mutuality of sexed and gendered bodies. At this point in the story, Adam 'calls' her 'woman', but he does not 'call her' using a proper name. 'Calling' simply acknowledges the equality of his partner within the unfolding story of creation that affirms the value of creaturely differences. Later in the story, because humans turn away from divine intentionality (Gen. 2.25—3.7), creative communion and the affirmation of otherness turn to destructive othering. The words that Adam now uses signify the human misuse of power and the failure to embrace diversity. As the creation narrative progresses the reader transitions from life-sustaining relationships willed by God to unnatural relations that carry profound consequences for all of God's creation. *Eros* becomes marred when humans pursue unnatural relations. These distorted relations contaminate the mutuality and interdependence of human persons with one another and human persons with the rest of creation. Trible argues that such contamination precipitates a hierarchical ordering that socializes some humans above others. And this unnatural condition, we might surmise, points to the 'beginning' of the anthropocentric, sexist and cis-heterosexist rendering of creation that erases and subordinates some gender and sexual differences.

For Trible, Adam's expression in this state of disorientation crystallizes what Christian traditions refer to as the 'Fall' from grace: 'Now *hā-'ādām* called the name of his woman Eve.' Genesis 3.20–21 succinctly expresses the human shift from life-giving to life-threatening relationships (Trible, 1978, p. 133). As opposed to the first time he speaks when Adam, the male creature [*'īš*,] simply called or recognized his equal partner as female [*'iššâ*], he now calls his female partner by the proper name of Eve. The Bible often uses the phrase to 'call the name' to express power over another. Thus, using these words Adam symbolically embodies the human turn from divinely willed otherness into othering and from communion to separation. We might theologize Adam's rhetoric to characterize the 'beginning' of words deployed to advance sexism and cis-heterosexism and the cis-hetero narratives and theologies from which they have been birthed in service to these words. Simply stated, these and other -ism words – such as racism and ableism – offer historical glimpses of our 'original sin'.

## The Trinity: The Divine Being Who Exists as a Communion of Distinct Others

While the Bible does not serve as a blueprint to map the mystery of God, its stories can nourish the theological imagination, inviting critical reflections on this mystery and the ways that divine life is grafted within human experiences and all of creation. In underscoring creaturely diversity and God's intention for this diversity to exist in playful and life-sustaining relationships, the two creation stories provide key building blocks to revise theologies that contrast cis-heteronormative approaches to the mystery of God. In this sense, the second story of creation (Gen. 2.4b—3.24) offers a Judaeo-Christian biblical foundation for understanding a God who creates and delights in human differences and invites us to reject gender and sex-based othering as a disruption of our human capacity to embrace communion with one another in the image of God.

Few have offered a more persuasive Trinitarian approach to this biblical vision in contemporary theological reflections than the Greek Orthodox theologian John Zizioulas. His central contribution hovers around a critique of essentialism in Latin Trinitarian theologies that heavily rely on Augustine. Instead Zizioulas turns to early Greek Christian voices, especially Athanasius of Alexandria and the Cappadocian Fathers, to propose a relational ontology rooted in the Trinitarian affirmation of communion and otherness. Echoing ancient philosophical (e.g. the 'One with the Many') and theological arguments (e.g. *mia ousia, treis hypostaseis*), he grounds a Christian understanding of human differences in the very Triune mystery of God. Zizioulas (1985) argues that the divine-to-be is utterly and dynamically relational. Being in communion and diversity with respect to divine life is not a hindrance to divine unity but, rather, its essential ingredient. Zizioulas (2006) writes:

> The theme of otherness is a fundamental aspect of theology. Being 'other' is part of what it means to be oneself, and therefore to be at all, whether reference is made to God or to humanity or to anything that is said to exist. (p. 1)

Furthermore, he argues that:

> The fact that the fear of the other is pathologically inherent in our existence results in the fear not only of the other but of *all otherness*. This is a delicate point requiring careful consideration, for it shows how deep and widespread fear of the other is: we are not afraid simply of certain others, but even if we accept them, it is on condition that they are somehow like ourselves. Radical otherness is an anathema. Difference itself is a threat ... When the fear of the other is shown to be fear of otherness, we come to the point of identifying difference with division. (p. 2)

The life-threatening and sinful othering that LGBTIQ+ persons frequently experience from failures to encounter our humanity speaks to this human polarization. It also raises an existential and theological question, particularly for those who have experienced othering and various forms of otrocide. Recalling the words of Jean-Paul Sartre, Zizioulas (2006) asks: 'Is it not true that, by definition, the other is my enemy and my "original sin"?' (p. 1).

Zizioulas's Christian theological response to this conundrum affirms that otherness – difference – and communion have united in the most radical sense in the Triune mystery of God. In other words, in God, difference does not result in division but instead in radical communion. It is beyond the scope of this chapter to discuss the wide range of arguments from both Greek and Latin theological traditions that he engages

(Zizioulas, 1985, pp. 155–77). My intention is to highlight some of his main arguments so that I can bring them into fruitful conversation with queer and Latinx approaches. I will limit my observations to the following two things: 1) summarizing Zizioulas's key argument concerning Trinitarian theology and its existential anthropological implications; and 2) discussing how he theologically constructs the notion of persons (divine or human). We could summarize that, for Zizioulas, we are ecstatic beings constituted and sustained in relation to the diversity of the Other (divinity) and called to participate in the divine life through communal relations with others (humanity).

Zizioulas strongly critiques essentialism or what he terms a Latin metaphysics of substance. In his view this metaphysics undermines our capacity to embrace human differences, turning difference into division and engendering the fear of others. For Zizioulas, Western cultures have been heavily shaped by Latin (Augustinian) conceptions of the Trinity. These cultures have often emphasized a monolithic unity over the diversity of divine and human life. Furthermore they promote intrapersonal rather than interpersonal, individualistic rather than communal and psychological rather than social understandings of divine and human persons. In contrast to this approach, Zizioulas retrieves the theology of early Greek voices, particularly the Cappadocian theologians (Zizioulas, 1985, pp. 15–65; LaCugna, 1991, pp. 53–79). Summarizing what he sees as the central difference between Greek and Latin Trinitarian theologies, Zizioulas (1985) writes:

> The basic ontological position of the theology of the Greek Fathers might be set out briefly as follows: No substance or nature exists without person or hypostasis or mode of existence. No person exists without substance or nature, *but* the ontological 'principle' or 'cause' of being – i.e. that which makes a thing to exist – is not the substance or nature but the person or hypostasis. Therefore, being is traced back not to substance but to person. (pp. 41–2, n. 37; emphasis original)

While his approach is undoubtedly theocentric (e.g. Trinitarian), conceiving his theocentric construction as a theological abstraction would be a mistake. As Patricia Fox (2001) points out, 'a catch phrase that echoes throughout Zizioulas's work both explicitly and implicitly is that "Trinitarian theology has profound existential consequences"' (p. 9).

In our times, metaphysical constructions have come under suspicion. This turn from metaphysics has given rise to queer and liberative epistemologies that reject essentialized constructions of divine and human life. From this perspective we can easily dismiss metaphysical approaches to divine life for their perpetuation of naturalizing and normatizing meta-narratives associated with oppressed and marginalized communities, especially LGBTIQ+ persons. However, Zizioulas's reappropriation of ancient theological sources and his contemporary implications deserve a hearing. A metaphysics rooted in the relational, diverse and dynamic nature of divine life paves the way to explore how queer persons qua persons in all their rainbow of LGBTIQ+ expressions can be theologically constructed as an expression of divine life.

For Zizioulas, the fundamental questions related to God and human persons are: Who is God? Who are we as human persons? He rejects all efforts to reduce divine or human persons to a 'what' question. In his view, an approach to God that understands divine life in terms of a 'what' question rather than a 'who' question carries implications concerning how we theorize human persons. He critiques an exclusive anthropological focus on human qualities and attributes – such as gay, straight, black, brown, white – not because they are unimportant markers of human existence but because they can become reductionistic and fail to situate persons about the mystery of God *ultimately*. Here Zizioulas points to an argument raised by several theological giants: we can know who God is and how God is but we cannot know what God is (Aquinas, *ST* I, 12, 12 ad. 1). Similarly we cannot closet persons into their human qualities and attributes. Thus, in his view essentialist constructions of divinity – the 'what' question – and the corollary focus on divine qualities lead to anthropological projections that result in the otrocide of human diversity and impede embracing the radical affirmation that otherness – that is, that human difference – reflects the life of God. In other words, the human person, like God, is a mystery and – as such – cannot be reduced to qualities, stereotypes and ideological constructions.

The divine and personal existence of the Creator-God, this metaphysical reality on which Zizioulas bases his theological construction, is the generator of divine and human life. 'T-theology', as Marcella Althaus-Reid (2003, pp. 7–22) would say, refers to this person as the 'Father' of Jesus Christ. Setting temporarily aside issues related to God-talk concerning sexist and cis-heterosexist language, I believe there is much value to Zizioulas's metaphysical approach when it comes to grounding all of reality in a relational or, to be more precise, an interpersonal divine being. It is important to note that by tracing the origin of all life – divine and human – to the personal divine being of the 'Father', Zizioulas unequivocally rejects individualism and all its manifestations as the building block for any social order. Opting instead for a relational and communal understating of divine personhood, he provides a theological foundation to critique all forms of human othering and hierarchical arrangements. While he stops short of exploring social, cultural, economic and political expressions of individualism and othering, his Trinitarian argument offers a valuable source to critique capitalist, sexist and cis-heterosexist ideologies that cause the erasure of human persons. Zizioulas (2006) makes three key observations related to the triune mystery of God that merit attention:

> The first thing that emerges from a study of the doctrine of the Trinity is that otherness is *constitutive* of unity, and not consequent upon it. God is not first one and then three, but simultaneously one and three ... Secondly, a study of the Trinity reveals that otherness is *absolute*. The Father, the Son, and the Spirit are absolutely different (*diaphora*), none of them being subject to confusion with the other two. Thirdly, and most significantly, otherness is not moral or psychological but *ontological*. We cannot tell *what* each person is; we can only say *who* he is. Each person in the holy Trinity is different not by way of difference of natural qualities (such qualities are all common to the three persons), but by way of the simple affirmation of being who he is. As a result, finally, otherness is inconceivable apart from *relationship*. Father, Son and Spirit are all names indicating relationship. No person can be different unless he is related. Communion does not threaten otherness; it generates it. (p. 5; emphases original)

This Trinitarian ontology provides the basis for Zizioulas's argument that persons, whether divine or human, can be best conceived as an openness to another, an *ek-stasis* of being that rejects and transcends all socially established boundaries, individual qualities and social constructions (Zizioulas, 1985, p. 213). Following Zizioulas, we cannot conceive divine or human nature apart from personal existence, and we cannot conceive persons apart from our relationship with and communion with others. This also means that because socialization with others is indispensable, radical otherness is essential in the 'performance' of divine and human life. Consequently, *ek-stasis* – understood as the nomadic movement towards distinct others – is how we exist in the divine image. Zizioulas writes (2006):

> The combination of the notion *ektasis* with that of *hypostasis* in the idea of person reveals that personhood is directly related to ontology – it is not a quality added, as it were, to beings, something that beings 'have' or 'have not', but it is constitutive of what can be ultimately called a 'being'. (p. 213)

Put succinctly: 'being a person is basically different from being an individual or "personality" in that the person cannot be conceived in itself as a static entity, but only as it *relates to*' (Zizioulas, 2006, p. 212; emphasis original). In this sense, Zizioulas (2006) would say that our individual and collective human markers include our gender identities and sexual orientations:

> Such qualities, important as they are for personal identity, become ontologically personal only through the hypostasis to which they belong: only by being *my* qualities are they personal, but the ingredient 'me' is a claim to absolute uniqueness which is not granted by these qualities constituting my 'what,' but by something else. (p. 111; emphasis original)

Ontologically speaking, something that exists is ultimately and *theologically* attributable to someone else. Zizioulas would argue that someone else is the divine Being who exists as communion in otherness. God, who eternally exists in interpersonal, perpetual and dynamic differentiation, has created us in rich human diversity to exist to and from others. Or to be more precise, in the distinct persons of the Trinity we find the source of creation and the sustenance of our distinct ways of being human. Stated from an LGBTIQ+ theological perspective, only in divine life can we ultimately ground and realize the saving significance of our gendered and sexually diverse personhood. The erasure of LGBTIQ+ lives perpetuated by cis-heterosexist ideologies is idolatrous and symptomatic of an individualistic mindset that stubbornly refuses to accept divine-intended differences reflected in 'Adam's' words and actions. As Zizioulas (2006) maintains: 'The rejection of God by Adam signified the rejection of otherness as constitutive of being. By claiming to be God, Adam rejected the Other as constitutive of his being and declared himself the ultimate explanation of his existence' (p. 43).[2]

## A Latinx Queering of Communion and Otherness

Theological explorations on diversity have been crucial for developing Latinx liberation theologies in the United States. Since their birth in the 1970s, theological explorations of mestizaje in the writings of Virgilio Elizondo and Orlando E. Costas and other Latinx theologians have opened the way to question erasure and oppression based on cultural differences. Responding to the socio-cultural marginalization of Latinx communities within the USA and the socio-economic consequence that follows from this marginalization, the writings of Latinx theologians often address the themes of otherness and human othering (Elizondo, 1988; 1993; Costas, 1979; 1982).

Rejecting the model of the USA as a 'melting pot' of peoples, these theologians propose an alternative perspective. They offer theological constructions that challenge the erasure of cultural differences and affirm the popular expressions of faith rooted in our cultural and racial histories. As Fernando Segovia (1992) writes, summarizing the vision for Latinx theology:

> The theology I envision is a theology that, because of its roots, cannot hide or disguise or reject mixture, for it finds that *mezcolanza* is life and gives life; a theology that given its very reality and experience, cannot bypass, assimilate, or annihilate the other, for again it finds itself that *otredad* also is life and gives life. (p. 28).

Exploring key political questions and implications related to the hybridity and othering of Latinx communities, Nanko-Fernández (2010) writes:

> At the same time, a critical appropriation of multiple belonging requires that attention be paid to the experience of multiple 'not fitting in.' Whether by choice or accident, as the result of others' cruelties or our own stances, this is also a reality that inclusion rhetoric glosses over. Explorations of our hybridity and multiple belonging must also include a sustained conversation regarding multiple not fitting in. Who gets left out in our constructions of identity and community? Who resides on our margins when we omit or ignore the stories of our intersections? Who is ostracized based on arbitrary criteria determining the norm? Who is privileged and who is excluded when a particular norm is assumed as common? Who is silenced? Who loses agency? Who are the gatekeepers controlling access. (pp. 19–20)

Nanko-Fernández's observations on power and socio-culturally constructed norms analogously apply to the hybridity that comprises LGBTIQ+ persons and, more specifically, queer Latinx communities who suffer from multiple forms of belonging and exclusion.

As I have discussed, Zizioulas offers a compelling Trinitarian construct that can be used to challenge the sinful socialization that excludes LGBTIQ+ persons. Queer bodies – in all their distinct differences – have been created, as any other body, in the image of God. Following Zizioulas, however, I would argue that as indispensable as our cultural, gender identities and sexual orientations are, these distinct expressions become theologically orientated when understood in relationship to the triune mystery of God. As Zizioulas would say, only by being *my* qualities do they become personal, but as indicated above, the ingredient 'me' is a claim to absolute uniqueness. In other words, my 'I' as a queer man does not ultimately emerge from my specific gender and sexual qualities but from God, who calls each one of us to participate in the triune mystery of communion and otherness. Let me be clear: it is not a question of undermining or rejecting these human qualities that mark our identities. In fact the social constructions and cis-heteronormative narratives that oppress and erase our distinct ways of being human must be rejected. That said, what this Trinitarian perspective offers is the possibility of grounding our queer ways of being human in the divine life of communion and otherness.

We know all too well the history of othering and the otrocide of queer bodies caused by what might be termed the reductionistic seduction that cis-heteronormative ideologies perpetuate. Judith Butler (1990) comes to mind when I think of challenging essentialist and social constructions obstructing inclusive realizations of human *ek-stasis*. Building upon the central arguments of Michel Foucault, Butler argues that what we understand by 'gender' is a social construct. Butler rejects essentialist understandings of gender identity, underscoring that gender is 'the repeated stylization of the body, a set of repeated acts within a highly rigid regulatory frame that congeals over time to produce the appearance of substance, of a natural sort of being' (p. 45). Rejecting essentialist perspectives, Butler writes:

> Hence, within the inherited discourse of the metaphysics of substance, gender proves to be performative – that is, constituting the identity it is purported to be. In this sense, gender is always a doing, though not a doing by a subject who might be said to preexist the deed. (p. 34)

Butler reminds us of Friedrich Wilhelm Nietzsche's claim that 'there is no "being" behind doing, effecting, becoming: the doer is merely a fiction added to the deed – the deed is everything' (p. 34). As Butler argues, gender is performed, and a person becomes intelligible 'through becoming gendered in conformity with recognizable standards of gender intelligibility' (p. 22). Butler challenges this reasoned intelligibility concerning gender that reduces certain persons to biological qualities, erases their human differences and boxes them into predetermined scripts. Like gender, 'sex' also functions as a 'regulatory idea', or as Butler (1993) states, 'an ideal construct which is forcibly materialized through time' (p. xii). The 'regulatory norms of "sex" work in a performative fashion to constitute the materiality of bodies and, more specifically, to materialize the body's sex, to materialize sexual difference in the service of the consolidation of the heterosexual imperative' (Butler, 1993, p. xii).

Butler's perspective is indispensable for gaining insight into various forms of gender and sexual othering. However, despite its theoretical and material value for queer critical denunciations of cis-heteronormativity, Butler's perspective is insufficient if we wish to theologically source – from a Christian perspective – human otherness and reject the otrocide that threatens queer bodies. Given the distinct trinitarian approach to otherness and communion I have just discussed, how might we take some initial steps to reconcile Zizioulas's theocentric theology with Butler's gender theory? Both are highly critical of an essentialist approach to human persons that reduces persons to biological determinants, qualities and attributes of persons. Both turn away from oppressive essentialism that turns persons into 'what' questions.

Given her interest as a gender theorist, Butler rightly places greater emphasis on the social constructions of our human condition. Zizioulas's theological interests lead him to underscore the construction of human persons within salvation history, within the unfolding story of a God who, in the otherness of Christ and the Spirit, offers a life-saving script for human persons. Both agree that embodiment really matters, especially when misguided fear of others and the human constructions we create that reject differences turn into oppressive divisions. Whereas Butler's response to otrocide is to denaturalize the body with respect to gender and sexuality to liberate us from sexist and cis-heterosexist constructs, Zizioulas not only wants to denaturalize bodies – regarding our focus on qualities and attributes – but he also seeks to theologize bodies. As a Christian theologian, however, Zizioulas cannot avoid the fundamental Christian teaching that our bodies have been divinized and scripted unto divine life: *El Verbo se hizo carne* [The Word has become flesh] (John 1.14). For a Christian, this divine deed is everything.

Gender-based and theological analysis of oppressive constructions of human existence need not be seen as irreconcilable. What if we made Christian theological discourse about the mystery of God as producing – following Butler – the effects that it ultimately names, namely deified persons who receive and respond to God's life through – and not despite – gender and sexual embodiments? What if we understood the intelligibility of persons not only through socially constructed scripts and norms that oppress us but also through liberating religious scripts that affirm traditional differences as reflections and refractions of the mystery of God?

In this theologically constructed vision, a queer God can come out of cis-heteronormative constructions to declare *their* preferential communion with those who have been othered. This is a God who interrupts and disrupts history to liberate LGBTIQ+ persons from all threatening social constructions and otrocides. In this revised and religiously constructed narrative, the divine deeds change everything. Thus it is not enough to highlight human deeds and social deconstructions in the struggle against sexism and cis-heterosexism. Following an integral approach to history – common to liberation theologies – that incorporates divine acting as salvific acting *in and through* historical actions, we might argue that it is through ordinary human acts on behalf of queer bodies, acts that include the dismantling of cis-heteronormativity – through critical gender theories and liberating praxis – that God destroys otrocide, grafts our queer otherness into divinity and realizes the call of LGBTIQ+ persons to exist in communion with all creation.

The theological notion of a queer God, a God who perpetually exits as communion in otherness, a God who – when brought out of cis-heteronormative closets – enables queer persons to embrace their distinct gender and sexual otherness as reflections and refractions of divine life, is not new in queer thinking (D'Costa, 2000; Althaus-Reid, 2003; Díaz, 2023). As Susannah Cornwall (2010) writes:

> Queering hegemony necessitates a willingness to travel off the path, to form alliances beyond those sanctioned by the colonizers; to seek God in unfamiliar places, in order not to take on all the assumptions and forced agreements of theological imperialism. Part of this entails acknowledging the 'shadow-side' of God, whose 'back' is 'made of difference'. Unless God is allowed to 'come out' of the closets of human construction, God's otherness will always be negated. (p. 97)

For Althaus-Reid, encountering God's otherness entails welcoming the divine presence in sites and persons and experiences outside cis-heteronormative constructions. This 'coming-out' of God is liberating for both divine and human lives: 'There is a need', she writes, 'to understand the possibility of the kenotic act coming from Godself as theologically liberative, even for divinity' (Althaus-Reid, 2003, p. 37).

This liberation of the otherness of God and human persons includes, among other things, not only challenging existing epistemologies and ethical stances but also developing new ones in accordance with LGBTIQ+ experiences. The otherness of our disruptive and fluid sexual lives can and must be brought into communion with the disruptive and queer otherness of God. As Althaus-Reid (2003) observes:

> This encounter in filial transgressions does not imply fixity, as in the case of a static God, fixed paradoxically in an idealist heterosexual transcendental position which implies God's encounter with a similarly strict subject. The Queer subject is nomadic, unsettled and does

> not have a sedentary vocation. Her boundaries of affiliations are constantly on the move, thus destabilizing the settling ideals of Christian ethics. (p. 44)

Drawing from the experience of Christian mystics, we can expand upon this nomadic nature of divine and human life. As ecstatic beings, divine and human beings encounter one another in openness to, giving to and receiving from distinct others. In embodied and ordinary hospitality acts, humans make room for others and their distinct otherness. As sexual beings, queer persons participate and reflect divine life by welcoming queer nomads into their relational lives. From a Christian and queer liberation perspective, this queer praxis denounces cis-heteronormative expectations that stand in the way of their God-given capacity to relate, love and embrace otherness in accordance with their way of being human. Through grace-filled sexual relationships, LGBTIQ+ persons make room and commune with those who have been othered. These relationships enable communal solidarity with other marginalized bodies and participation in the liberating mystery of God (Córdova Quero et al., 2024). As I (2023) argue in my book *Queer God de Amor* concerning the practice of effecting communion *in* otherness: 'Queering ecstasis means making room for those who have been rendered invisible, recognizing that the divine preferential option incarnated in Jesus's love for marginalized bodies includes "sexiled bodies and their cultures"' (pp. 112–13).

## Conclusion: A Queer *Nos-otrxs*

If someone questioned our identity as Latinx and Latin American queer persons, we might respond not with an 'I' pronoun but with a communal 'we'. We are a queer body, *Nosotrxs somos un cuerpo queer*. The Spanish word 'nos-otros' culturally, anthropologically and theologically captures the central argument of my Trinitarian reflections (Goizueta, 1992; Díaz 2011, pp. 265–8). Unlike in other modern languages (e.g. the English 'we', the German *wir*, the French *nous* or the Italian *noi*), this frequently used Spanish pronoun invites us to conceive of communal unity in terms of diversity. The pronoun 'literally means "we others," a community of *otros*, or others' (Goizueta, 1992, p. 57). This chapter has highlighted this intrinsic relationship between comm-union and otherness by discussing the Judaeo-Christian Creation narratives and the doctrine of the Trinity.

I pointed to the Creation narratives as biblical building blocks that can be useful in constructing theological anthropologies that challenge othering, embrace the diversity of creation and recount divinely willed and life-sustaining communion with others. I turned to Zizioulas's metaphysics and his Trinitarian theology as an example of how a prominent and contemporary theological voice has retrieved the ancient theme of communion and otherness in the Trinity. I also offered some reflections on Butler as a queer theoretical alternative to Zizioulas's theocentric perspective on questions that relate to human differences, othering and otrocide. Butler's groundbreaking arguments on performativity and her critique of rigid regulatory frames and narratives that congeal and yield a metaphysics of substance offer an indispensable resource for understanding the social basis of human othering.

Notwithstanding the value of her gender-anthropological critique of cis-heteronormativity, I believe that a queer-theological reading that affirms the diversity, non-essentialized and nomadic nature of LGBTIQ+ persons can benefit from considering the ways we too have been 'grafted' to reflect and refract divine life. In this sense I initially discussed the all-important building blocks of communion and otherness in Trinitarian theologies. This theological perspective allows us to reconceive the words of Ignacio Ellacuría and affirm that queer humanity can be read as a grafting *ad extra* of Trinitarian life. By humanity I do not understand an abstract human nature but rather a historical experience, always and everywhere embodied in diverse and nomadic ways of being human.

## *Notes*

1 On life-giving – soteriological – ways to relate God, historical persons and concrete human experiences, see Ignacio Ellacuría (1993, p. 277).

2 On the role of Christ and the Spirit in deification, see Zizioulas (2006, pp. 237–45).

## References

Althaus-Reid, Marcella (2003), *The Queer God*, New York: Routledge.

Butler, Judith (1990), *Gender Trouble: Feminism and the Subversion of Identity*, New York: Routledge.

Butler, Judith (1993), *Bodies that Matter: On the Discursive Limits of 'Sex'*, New York: Routledge.

Cornwall, Susannah (2010), 'Stranger in Our Midst: The Becoming of the Queer God in the Theology of Marcella Althaus-Reid', in *Dancing Theology in Fetish Boots: Essays in Honour of Marcella Althaus-Reid*, edited by Lisa Isherwood and Mark D. Jordan, London: SCM Press, pp. 95–112.

Córdova Quero, Hugo, Miguel H. Díaz, Anderson Fabián Santos Meza and Cristian Mor, eds (2024), *Mysterium Liberationis Queer: Ensayos sobre teologías queer de la liberación en las Américas*, St. Louis, MO: Institute Sophia Press.

Costas, Orlando E. (1979), *Christ Outside the Gate: Mission Beyond Christendom*, Grand Rapids, MI: William B. Eerdmans.

Costas, Orlando E. (1982), *The Integrity of Mission: The Inner Life and Outreach of the Church*, San Francisco, CA: Harper & Row.

D'Costa, Galvin (2000), *Sexing the Trinity: Gender, Culture, and the Divine*, London: SCM Press.

Díaz, Miguel H. (2006), 'Human Beings at the Crossroads of Divine Self-Disclosure: Otherness in Black Catholic and Latino/a Catholic Theologies and the Otherness of God', presidential acceptance speech delivered at the Annual Meeting of the Academy of Catholic Hispanic Theologians of the United States (ACHTUS), San Antonio, Texas, 6 June.

Díaz, Miguel H. (2011), 'The Life-Giving Reality of God from Black, Latin American, and US Hispanic Perspectives', in *The Cambridge Companion to the Trinity*, edited by Peter Pham, New York: Cambridge University Press, pp. 259–73.

Díaz, Miguel H. (2023), *Queer God de Amor*, New York: Fordham University Press.

Elizondo, Virgilio (1988), *The Future is Mestizo: Life Where Cultures Meet*, Denver, CO: University Press of Colorado.

Elizondo, Virgilio (1993), *The Mexican-American Promise*, Maryknoll, NY: Orbis Books.

Ellacuría, Ignacio (1993), 'The Historicity of Human Salvation', in *Mysterium Liberationis: Fundamental Concepts of Liberation Theology*, edited by Ignacio Ellacuría and Jon Sobrino, Maryknoll, NY: Orbis Books, pp. 137–68.

Ellacuría, Ignacio and Jon Sobrino, eds (1993), *Mysterium Liberationis: Fundamental Concepts of Liberation Theology*, Maryknoll, NY: Orbis Books.

Fox, Patricia A. (2001), *God as Communion: John Zizioulas, Elizabeth Johnson, and the Retrieval of the Symbol of the Triune God*, Collegeville, MN: Liturgical Press.

Goizueta, Roberto S. (1992), 'Nosotros: Toward a U.S. Hispanic Anthropology', *Listening: Journal of Religion and Culture* 27, no. 1, pp. 55–69.

LaCugna, Catherine Mowry (1991), *God for Us: The Trinity and Christian Life*, New York: HarperCollins.

Nanko-Fernández, Carmen (2010), *Theologizing en Espanglish: Context, Community, and Ministry*, Maryknoll, NY: Orbis Books.

Segovia, Fernando (1992), 'Two Places and No Place on Which to Stand: Mixture and Otherness in Hispanic American Theology', *Listening: Journal of Religion and Culture* 27, no. 1, pp. 26–40.

Trible, Phyllis (1978), *God and the Rhetoric of Sexuality*, Philadelphia, PA: Fortress Press.

Zizioulas, John D. (1985), *Being as Communion: Studies in Personhood and the Church*, Crestwood, NY: St. Vladimir's Seminary Press.

Zizioulas, John D. (2006), *Communion and Otherness: Further Studies in Personhood and the Church*, edited by Paul McPartland, New York: T&T Clark.

# 15

# In Search of Queer *O/utopia*: A Haunting (Impossibility of) Queer Archive

MAYUKO YASUDA

## Queer Theology in Japan: Where to Start?

I feel I am lost, or rather, I am not supposed to find a way as long as every trodden road appears to be haunted by the ghosts of imperialism, fascism, queer-phobia and all sorts of violence, leading to where I do not wish to go. Assuming my role here in this book of global queer theologies is to present a Japanese queer theology, I fear – or dare – to fail. As a Japanese anti-cis-heteronormative biblical scholar, it is hard for me to find a ground to start thinking about myself, theology and god, gender and sexuality, and how they relate with one another. I do not have 'my people' in Japan to collectively form a counter-discourse against the West-centric, cis-heteronormative theology since my sense of belonging to either queer community or Christian community in Japan is unsecured. One of the main factors behind it is the small Christian population in Japan – less than 1 per cent of the total population (Shūkyō Kenkyūjo, 2023) – making non-cis-hetero Christians doubly marginalized. Here are some other significant factors I see.

First, my unlearning of cis-heteronormativity did not start in Japan but in Chicago, when I was doing my PhD. I learned vocabularies and concepts to articulate my sexuality beyond cis-heteronormative language when I was introduced to queer studies, theories and theologies. It was quite a journey to tear down the patriarchal theology and to explore how and with whom I wanted to build close relationships, but I had friends and colleagues in Chicago to think it through together. They were my queer Christian community. After five and a half years in Chicago I returned to Japan to teach Bible-related courses at higher education institutions. Japan is a highly patriarchal society and it has been a new challenge to deal with cis-heteronormative – or even homophobic – churches without the close support of a queer Christian community.

Second, forming a Japanese counter-discourse against Western academia is extremely difficult. While some marginalized scholars celebrate and strategically use their identity categories and social locations, be they for example blackness, indigenousness, global South, it seems impossible for me, a Japanese, to do so. Japan was – and technically still is – an empire that colonized the neighbouring Asian countries from the end of the nineteenth century to the mid-twentieth century. During the Second World War, inculturation and contextualization of Christianity in Japan ended up supporting the Emperor and his colonial violence as part of the Christian God's plan to build God's Kingdom on earth. Given such a history there seems to be a thin line between celebrating Japanese culture, history and tradition and promoting nationalism, a slippery slope to imperialism, colonialism and fascism. When I was in Chicago, however, the labels of 'people of colour' and 'Asian' were assigned to me. These categories neglect the history of Japanese colonization and eradicate the differences among various Asian people. Sometimes the labels also function to position 'Asians', regardless of their ethnicity, against whiteness altogether. In a sense, being categorized as 'other' in the USA made me see how Japan is othered, just like other Asian countries, in the West-centric global context. Japan is even culturally colonized and partially occupied by US military bases. Sensing the tension of being the (former) colonizer and the culturally colonized, I cannot use the flag with the red sun as a banner against colonial occupation; I refuse to sing the national anthem, the ode to the Emperor; I do not find 'pride' in being a Japanese. Thus, I stumble to find a ground to do *Japanese* queer theology, whatever that means.

Third, the archives of the marginalized, the subaltern history, in Japan are hard to access. When I lived in Chicago there were stories – highly accessible even to a foreigner like me – of those who fought for freedom and justice, such as Martin Luther King Jr and Rosa Parks. The archive of justice seekers was everywhere in the seminary classes, church activities and casual conversations with my friends and colleagues. Then, I wondered what kind of archives we had in Japan. I did not know many. For my excuse, it was not only my lack of interest but also other factors that made me ignorant. Namely, the Japanese education system, the influence of the defective – mass and social – media, and the work–life imbalance that deprives people of time and energy for engaging with sociopolitical matters. The masses also have low political literacy due to the circumstances described. People – especially the oppressed and exploited – are too busy and tired even to care about their needs and wants. It is what the ruling people wish the masses to be. Because people do not/cannot care much, stories of social change are limited. The less the narratives of success are circulated, the less people are empowered. The sense of helplessness and fatigue grows, and so does the negative cycle. While people are archiving the struggles for justice and liberation in Japan, they are not easy to access. When one cannot find a story they connect to, the language and discourse to shape their life is insufficient.

In the journey towards justice – a utopian vision – for the marginalized, it is crucial to acknowledge and archive the under-represented struggles, contributions and achievements. For the ways we remember history and (re)tell narratives (in)form the world and us within the world. At the same time, history-making has often been cis-heteronormative work; chaotic, messy and tangled events are put into a 'straight' sequence that is universally legible and makes sense to the majority, often by forgetting moments of queer eu/dysphoria. When history-making/archiving is such a cis-hetero project, queerness would agitate for rejection of the project and staying in and with the chaos, the nonsense that is made illegible by/in the cis-heteronormative society. Below, I analyse and respond to how Japanese theologians use and create archives of queer theologies. It is an attempt (destined to be failed) to build an archive of queer theology in Japan. I might wish this chapter can succeed in doing so but I am afraid it will not. Instead, this is a first-person representation of my queer desires, torn between the painful longing to be recognized, accepted and affirmed even in cis-heteronormative spaces like church and academia and the twisted pleasure of refusing to be understood (Halberstam, 2011). It is a manifestation of queer negativity against meaning-making in and through the cis-hetero normative social order (Edelman, 2004), a desire to be in illegible chaos, nonsense against hegemonic and constructive storytelling, against mastery (Singh, 2018).

## Archiving Queer Theology in Japan

Queer theologies and queer readings of the Bible are not trendy, let alone mainstream, in Japan. The number of those who engage with queer issues in the realm of theology is limited. Nevertheless, the last two decades have seen increasing publications on the related matter, raising awareness to a certain extent.[1] In terms of translations, *Radical Love* (Cheng, 2011), the chapter on John in the *Queer Bible Commentary* (Shore-Goss, 2022) and *Queer Theologies: The Basics* (Greenough, 2020) are now available in Japanese (Cheng, 2014; Greenough, 2024; Maekawa, 2023).

Here, I take up three scholars who have been writing on queer theology: Yuri Horie, Tomoki Asaka and Marie Kudo. While I recognize that scholars with PhDs do not have a monopoly on queer theology, I focus on these scholars and their ways to use and create their archive of queer theology. Their works have fissures that queerly challenge and destabilize the academic discipline even when they prove themselves to be meeting the academic standard that restrains queer creativity and defiance. Besides, these theologians continually refer to one another as credible sources in citations and bibliographies. In a sense, I select them as the focal scholars by following their steps of listing their works in the archive of queer theology in Japan.[2]

The first theologian is Yuri Horie, an openly lesbian sociologist, theologian and pastor of the United Church of Christ in Japan (UCCJ). She was involved in a resistance movement against a gay discrimination case in UCCJ and has been questioning and resisting sexism and cis-heterosexism in Christianity through both activism and academic works. Horie's works are rooted in her activism, the site of her constant battle, and seek potential in queer theology to fight against homophobia in the church. Her commitment and sense of responsibility not only to fight but also to record the history of the fight is remarkable. I – like many other feminist and/or queer scholars – am empowered by her writings. Horie is regarded as a pioneer of queer theology in Japan.

The second theologian is Tomoki Asaka, who made significant contributions by introducing queer theology developed in Western academia with sharp analysis and critical questions. Published in 2011, his paper is the first article known to summarize and examine the prior research on queer theology. He interrogates what queer theology is/does by inspecting the frictions in binarism, including the boundary between the insider and the outsider (Asaka, 2021) and the tension between essentialism-based lesbian and gay theology and constructionism-based queer theology (Asaka, 2011). Especially his careful approach to the definition and the origin of queer theology (Asaka, 2018) demonstrates that such binaries are not as precise or stable as we would think.

The third theologian is Marie Kudo (2022), who published a book based on her PhD dissertation on (feminist) queer theology, focusing on Carter Heyward, Elizabeth Stuart and Marcella Althaus-Reid. It highlights connections and gaps between feminist and queer theologies, clarifying the challenges and possibilities of diverse queer theologies. It was the first thorough study on the topic written in Japanese and would play the role of a navigator to walk through the journey of queering theology 'without a map' (Kudo, 2022, p. 217; Althaus-Reid, 2008, p. 108). Its chapter on the prior research is helpful for this chapter because it is not only an extensive archive of queer theology but also displays different views on how queer theology has developed over time.

In the following sections I look into how these three theologians use and make an archive of queer theology, highlighting and responding to some key points – history and contexts, citations and origins, and developments of an academic field.

## Story and Context

When we tell a (hi)story, we want to tell it right, in a way it deserves, preferably from the beginning, locating events in a correct order (Luke 1.1–3), hoping not to leave out anything while knowing no story can tell *everything* (John 21.25). No, it is not even the point of any story to include *every* this and that. A storyteller selects the events and moments for the plot so the story makes sense. This is why (hi)story-telling is world-making: 'In making history, an author, wittingly or unwittingly, excludes and even effaces some histories, which then become hidden. In this respect, making history is an exercise of power' (Choi, 2015, p. 78). Thus, queer (hi)stories are too often left out or on the margin due to the exercise of hegemonic cis-heteronormative power.

It is violence – Horie argues – to eliminate the (hi)stories and memories of the marginalized from history. In order to resist such violence, she keeps writing and recording what she witnesses and experiences (Horie, 2006, p. 210; 2008, p. 69). Her sense of responsibility for writing her version of history is rooted in the UCCJ gay discrimination case in 1998: when an openly gay seminarian was supposed to take an exam to become a UCCJ pastor, discriminatory comments regarding the ordination of gay people – oral and written – were shared at the UCCJ Executive Council meeting and the General Assembly. The participants in the meeting and the Assembly – including Horie – acted promptly to raise their voices of protest. However, their voices were mostly ignored. Their struggle for justice did not make it to the minutes of the Assembly, which means it was erased from official history. The subaltern *cannot* speak when there is no listening ear, but that does not mean they cannot write their version of history. Thus, Horie actively writes.

Horie's sense of responsibility is not only about telling the subaltern (hi)stories but also about paying attention and showing respect to the texts and contexts of others. When she writes about queer theology, Horie usually starts by explaining what the term 'queer' meant initially and how queer activism emerged (Horie, 2024, pp. 176–8). She also refers to feminist movements and feminist theology that prepared the ground for queer theology to develop (Horie, 2008, p. 93). For her, to disregard the context is to be oblivious to the social structure and power dynamics around the matter. Considering decontextualization as depoliticization, Horie is careful about using the imported term 'queer' – transcribed as *kuia* in Japanese – out of its original context. Horie observes that the term *kuia* is so decontextualized that it merely indicates celebrating diversity without considering power dynamics or questioning the social structure among and around the sexual- and gender-minoritized groups (Horie, 2006, p. 158; 2024, pp. 178–9; Kudo, 2022, pp. 25–6). Horie points out that such a use contradicts the original derogatory tone of the term and the original emphasis on differences among gays and lesbians made by Teresa de Lauretis when she introduced queer theory (Horie, 2006, p. 156). In her first monograph, *Rezubian to iu Ikikata* ['Lesbian' Way of Life: Questioning Heterosexism in Christianity] (2006), therefore, Horie expresses her preference for 'lesbian' over 'queer'. According to Horie, 'lesbian' – as a term and a way of life – represents and resists the systemic discriminations caused by sexism (against women) and cis-heterosexism (against non-hetero people) better than the term *kuia*/ queer in the Japanese context (Horie, 2006, pp. 158–9). Nevertheless, Kudo highly values this book as a pioneer of Japanese queer theology, and Horie did not stop exploring the potential of queer theology.

Both Asaka and Kudo also pay attention to the specific context of queer theologies and theologians they refer to. Kudo takes this matter seriously, as the first chapter of her monograph is on the history of queer theology, starting with the original meaning of the term 'queer' and the context of the USA where queer activism emerged. Mapping the research history, Kudo (2022) poses a question of 'what counts as the history of queer theology in the first place' (p. 27) since she is not satisfied with counting only the theological works that emerged after the rise of queer activism and theories. Instead she emphasizes the 'prehistories' of the long struggle fought by gays, lesbians, feminists and so on for liberation: '[T]he history of "queer theology" must include *all* of the gay, lesbian, bisexual and transgender theologies that started actively addressing issues of homosexuality and Christianity in the 1980s and 1990s, as well as the various attempts of feminist theologies' (Kudo, 2022, pp. 27–8; translation and emphasis mine). What is at stake here seems not the 'all' but the connection between feminisms and queer, given the fact that Kudo repeatedly highlights the contributions of lesbian feminist theologians in her book. Nevertheless, my attention keeps being pulled back to the 'all' and the impossibility of accounting for *all* the history. There is no way we can consider the prehistories of *all* the struggles for justice, leading up to the theological struggle.

## The Impossibility of Archiving *All*

There are things forgotten, erased or meant to be off the record between all and nothing. These events and people eradicated from (hi)stories, while we have no access to them, haunt us through between the lines of written texts. Such spectrality, the weight of absence manifesting through the presence of others (Derrida, 1994), disrupts the idea of context concerning a text or the whole concerning its part, as described by the hermeneutical circle.

Contexts matter. As a scholar of the Christian Bible – or, formerly, the New Testament – I have no opposition to that. A reader makes sense of a biblical text by referring to the whole chapter, a letter or a book. Contexts can also refer to what lies outside the text, the sociopolitical location of the text, the identity categories assigned to the author and so on. As such, interpretation is a circular movement of expanding understandings of an individual part in relation to the whole. However, the question of what counts as the 'whole' remains. Especially when it comes to a closeted queer writer, disguising as a cis-hetero person would be part of who they are, and there is little a reader can know through the layers of interwoven 'lies', 'truths' and the silence in between.

While Horie reveals who she is – including her sexuality – in her academic writings, it is not common for theologians in Japan to *be* and to come out as a sexual minority. There is always room to speculate if an author of a queer theology book/article is queer unless they clearly state that they are cis-hetero, just like Kudo (2022, p. 294) does in the Afterword. We cannot know who the closeted queer theologians are or *all* those who have shaped queer theologies today, as context crucially matters. This haunting impossibility is one of the fatal limitations of academic endeavour, which depends on what is present in the written, verified texts.

Needless to say, queer theology does not exist only in academically verified texts but also in our lived experiences and vernacular talks. A queer theologian can refer to blog posts, church newsletters or even a personal diary (with the consent of the author, of course). However, ethical problems reside there, according to Kudo (2024). Working in academia, scholars agree that their works are open to severe critiques, so the arguments get deepened and developed. Non-academics, on the other hand, do not consent to such a process, and it is violent to put non-academic works under the scrutiny of scholarship. Kudo is concerned that there is even a risk of appropriating activists/activism when academic works draw on them for the sake of scholarship. Thus, Kudo focuses on academic writings when she does queer theology.

Since scholarship forms hegemonic discourse, as Edward Said indicated (1978), it is relevant, I believe, to offer a critical reflection on queer theology as an academic study. The following section closely examines what makes academic works academic: verifying and identifying the sources, especially the origin.

## Where did it Come from? Who Said it First?

We use citations and bibliographies in academic works so that readers can trace back the arguments prior to the one they are reading. This traceability of chronicles of accumulated knowledge is what maintains academic rigour. Citations indicate that the author has studied the past works back to the source or the person who coined the term of significant importance and critically engaged with them, often with a new angle to develop the argument further. By referring to the verified sources, an academic work connects itself to the authorized history of the field and registers itself at the end of the archive.

Knowing the pain of alienation, marginalized scholars would be cautious not to omit the underprivileged people from histories of scholarship and physical space like conference rooms. Giving credit correctly (particularly to those in the shadows), telling the subaltern history, recognizing power dynamics around the author – these practices of citations and bibliographies are sometimes not only about maintaining academic rigour but also a political and affectional gesture, a way to honour those who have come before you. That seems to be what Horie, Asaka and Kudo do when they pay close attention to the context, history and the origin of queer theology. They show a serious commitment to telling the scholarship history of the marginalized properly. It mainly draws my attention that Horie repeatedly refers to the first theologians who wrote about queer theology, namely Robert E. Shore-Goss in the USA and Asaka in Japan. Where there are pages to spare, Horie unfolds the circumstances of Shore-Goss, an openly gay, former Roman Catholic priest who had been involved with AIDS activism in the 1990s (Horie, 2019, pp. 167–70). She also clarifies her respect for Asaka being the very first scholar to introduce queer theology to an audience in Japan (Horie, 2014, p. 101). This practice of paying homage to the original works aligns with her sense of responsibility to accurately tell the – subaltern – history.

While *Jesus Acted Up* (hereinafter cited as *JAU*) by Shore-Goss (1993) appears to be the first academic writing to use the term 'queer theology', it is debated if his theology is rather gay than queer (Córdova Quero,

2019). Horie (2014, p. 94) briefly mentions that Stuart does not see *JAU* as queer theology. Asaka takes a closer look at the critiques by Stuart and Patrick S. Cheng towards Shore-Goss, asking what counts as queer theology (Asaka, 2018). Asaka's argument is summarized as follows: according to Shore-Goss, *JAU* recognizes the difference between lesbians and gays, considers the experience of solidarity among lesbians/feminist women and gays during AIDS activism, enables inclusion by using Foucauldian analysis. Concurrently, it illustrates Jesus deviating from the social norm – such as his 'protest' at the temple in Matthew 21.12–16 – as the model for the Stop the Church movement in the 1990s. To investigate why this book is not regarded as queer theology, Asaka turns to Cheng's *Radical Love* (2011). Cheng offers three definitions of the term 'queer' that steer different approaches to queer theologies: 1) an inclusive term for identity categories of LGBTQI+; 2) an attempt/act to transgress the social norm; and 3) an attempt/act to erase and deconstruct the boundaries. Asaka (2018) considers *JAU* – rooted in activism that challenges social norms – to align with Cheng's second definition. However, Cheng (2011) critiques it as 'not queer *enough*' since it 'was still grounded in a liberationist conception of lesbian and gay identity' (pp. 37, 52; emphasis mine).

What is at stake here are the queer theories around identity and social construction. When a person regards the term 'queer' as equal to non-normative gender or sexuality, any theology done by, about and for lesbians or gays can count as queer theology. This is probably why Kudo mentions that queer theology can be traced back even to the 1950s (Kudo, 2014, p. 35). On the other hand, when a person highlights queer theories, especially their destabilization of the naturalized notions of gender, sexuality and identity, queer theology is queer as long as it is based on queer theories. Still, Asaka's reading of Shore-Goss and Cheng indicates that the line between the two sides is unclear. Each theologian's queer theology is nuanced from one another, and it is hard to define queer theology and identify its origin. It would not be too much of a stretch to say that Asaka's inspection destabilizes the origin and definition, intentionally or not.

## Gatekeeping and Queer Expansion

Who can decide who/what is queer and who/what is not? While queer people and scholars can theorize and analyse the criteria of what it means to be queer, whether it is a simple equation to being gay or a radical disobedience against the cis-heteronormativity, gatekeeping and policing do not appear queer. 'Am I queer enough?' is a silly but exhausting question; 'Is s/he queer enough?' can be a harmful one. Nobody is entirely queer. Of course, there is a difference between asking whether a person is queer and asking whether something is unquestionably queer. When queer action or narrative is meant to fight the system, it is crucial to investigate if it genuinely dismantles the system and how. Too often the cis-hetero-based patriarchal system takes queer things in, absorbs them and makes them work for the system, and thus the scrutiny is required. For instance, Jack Halberstam (2011, pp. 55–9) analyses male stupidity, a supposed failure to perform proper masculinity, and argues that it is accepted on many occasions as an alternative – even attractive – masculinity.

In the theological field it is crucial to articulate how queer theology challenges and deconstructs the cis-heteronormative 'T-theology' (Althaus-Reid, 2003, p. 172) or how it fails to do so. Nevertheless, I sense a sort of anxiety if it is *queer enough* – *queer* as in resisting, destabilizing and deconstructing the norm – to pursue and reinforce academic mastery, hearing the invitation by Julietta Singh (2018) to post/anti/decolonial non-masterful modes of knowledge and being. Articulating the link between colonial mastery and seemingly harmless mastery, she articulates:

> as a pursuit, mastery invariably and relentlessly reaches toward the indiscriminate control over something – whether human or inhuman, animate or inanimate. It aims for the full submission of an object – or something *objectified* – whether it be external or internal to oneself. In so doing, mastery requires a rupturing of the object being mastered, because to be mastered means to be weakened to a point of fracture. Mastery is in this sense a splitting of the object that is mastered from itself, a way of estranging the mastered object from its previous state of being. (Singh, 2018, p. 10; emphasis original)

When a scholar of queer theology aims for academic mastery by rigorously scrutinizing the sources, clarifying the definitions, identifying the origin and delivering their idea with a convincing argument, what is put into complete submission? It might lie in the messy, tangled and self-contradictory lived experiences and emotions of queer people. It could also encompass their understanding of who they are – an essential identity, even though it is socially constructed. Or it could be our admiration for those who have fought the battle, paved the way and woven the words that allow us to live. In pursuit of mastery we scholars learn to package our respect and affection for our queer predecessors in a rigid box with flawless format. It is sad, to be honest, *and* remarkable to see a queer scholar learning to do so and even being creative to exploit any given opportunity to squeeze their personal feelings into academic writing. An author's queer affect, hidden between the lines, haunts those who are willing to be haunted.

## Developing (Hi)story

A story needs a plot, it is believed. A beginning and an end and a narrative arch to connect the two. It cannot include everything, only the important and necessary things. We assume that we cannot throw in random episodes and memories non-sequentially. Nor can a writer leave all the pages of a storybook blank. (Or can we? Just like *4'33"* by John Cage (1952)?) Academic archives also seem to require a (hi)story, a plot on how the subject, the concept, the methodology have developed over time. As argued above, the origin stories and the contexts from which a theory, concept, perspective or term is developed are significant in academic studies. To tell a compelling (hi)story, events need to be put in a legible order by straightening out their tangled correlations and contexts. There is no room for argument that a neatly arranged narrative is more accessible to the audience than a chaotic mumbling. Nevertheless, I feel some friction with such a legible, linear (hi)story-telling. I will explore my desire for illegibility later, but for now let me turn to Kudo's summary of how theologians tell the history of queer theology.

Keeping the connection between queer theology and its prehistory – liberation movements, activisms, feminisms and theologies inspired by those – intact, Kudo summarizes different views of queer theology's history offered by Mary E. Hunt, Stuart and Cheng. Hunt and Stuart draw a clear developing line from the (male) homosexuality-centred theology to more liberational and queer theology. Hunt divides the development into three stages whose focus shifts from 1) homosexuality; 2) lesbians, gays and bisexuals; to 3) queer. Meanwhile Stuart sees four stages of 1) gay liberal theology; 2) gay liberational theology; 3) erotic theology; and 4) queer theology. Either way, both of them present the narrative of linear and step-by-step progress of queer theology. Cheng, on the other hand, suggests four *intertwined* stages of apologetic, liberational, relational and queer theologies. Cheng's difference from the former two theologians lies in the looseness of the periodization and non-linear understanding of the history of queer theology. Multiple stages and perspectives rely on one another and co-exist in one theologian simultaneously. Kudo evaluates Cheng's analysis as more queer than that of Hunt and Stuart, referring to queer resistance against a linear and progressing view of history, encapsulated by Lee Edelman (2004) as 'reproductive-futurism'.

Based on the prior argument, Kudo summarizes three key developments of queer theology as follows: first, the attitude shifted from apologetic to prophetic, from seeking acceptance by the church to raising a prophetic voice against homophobia in the Christian church. Second, it gradually moved from an essentialist approach to a social constructionist approach regarding identity. Third, it developed a sharper awareness of differences as more lesbian, bisexual and transgender theologians started raising their voices in the white-male-centric field. These developments are, of course, not irreversible nor strictly linear.

For the record, Kudo is aware that the history of queer theology she reviewed in her book consists mainly of English-written works in the USA and the UK. Thus, Kudo tries to pay attention to scholarship outside of the West. It is another way to disrupt the idea of singular and linear development. One heavily footnoted paragraph is dedicated to diverse works from the Americas and Asia. The Japanese context is paid more attention, as might be expected, and Kudo starts with Horie and Asaka.

## Re-membering/Forgetting a Subaltern (Hi)story

Given the fact that trans women of colour played a significant role at the beginning of queer activism in the USA – such as Marsha P. Johnson at the Stonewall riot – I am concerned about the diversification of the field, as highlighted by Kudo in the key developments. It implies that theology, church and academia were – and probably still are – more occupied by white elite men than the fields of activism and social struggle for justice. It is only natural, of course, that activism starts with the marginalized, and it takes time to reach the top of the ivory tower. As white elite men have long occupied theology, there must have been the lost archives of non-white-elite men. On countless occasions, non-cisgender men, women, transgender, nonbinary and so on, and scholars of colour, have been silenced in seminaries, theological conferences, church meetings and elsewhere. There would be several queer women who have given up pursuing higher theological education. Queer students of colour are again and again 'encouraged', read 'forced', to stay in the 'comfort' zone – comfortable for the white or hetero advisors or reviewers rather than for themselves – when choosing the study topic since they are already 'too much'. Then where is their archive?

Queer theology or a queer reading of the Bible has often been an attempt to recover, or 'take back' (Shore-Goss and West, 2000), what had been lost from and to queer and trans people – their presence, voice, perspective, experience, subjectivity and so on in the theological sphere; a safer way for the queer to read the Bible, ponder about God and simultaneously express their faith and sexuality; and above all, access to power for knowledge production. While remembering what is lost is crucial – and today's scholars owe much to those who undertook the labour of remembering – forgetting is a vital part of (hi)stories and memories too. As articulated by Halberstam (2011), in the act of remembering, we distort what is incapable of being understood into something we can handle. On the other hand, forgetting something we cannot comprehend is not a denial of what/who happened. Still, it opens a 'new way of remembering' to recognize and live with the 'traces' of the haunting loss (Halberstam, 2011, p. 82). Furthermore, Halberstam (2011) affirms, 'forgetting becomes a way of resisting the heroic and grand logics of recall and unleashes new forms of memory that relate more to spectrality than to hard evidence, to lost genealogies than to inheritance, to erasure than to inscription' (p. 15).

When academic mastery requires queer theology to make a queer perspective convincing and reasonable even to the cis-heteronormative eyes, a queer theologian would have to omit or distort their too radical and queer – or too inconvenient and shameful – thoughts, experience and relationality, be it with the divine, other living beings or objects, to remember them. Or they can forget what is so queer that feels not ready to be shared with the rest of the world, leaving it beautifully and chaotically deviant as it is.

## Epilogue: The Desire to be Lost in the Haunting Abyss

When storytelling is history-making, and history-making is world-making, the more we recover from history, the better the world becomes for the marginalized. Not a few biblical scholars have attempted to reconstruct the queerness of biblical figures, and it made a significant impact on queer people in and around Christianity. While admitting its importance, I also find it necessary to question the desire to improve the world: '[D]esire never belongs to an individual subject but is constantly produced in the matrices of relations in which the subject finds herself. How can one then be free if one's desires are not one's own?' (Braun, 2024, p. 3). If my desires are not my own but produced out of connections with others, it would not be my desire to free myself but to get caught or tangled with the lost spectres, or at least haunted by them. Instead, it might be their desires – to be remembered or be left forgotten – that nudge me towards the spectrality's realm. The haunting calls, and I look into the chasm found in the margins of a book, (hi)stories or my memories, with the longing for queer utopia, which is nowhere – *ou-topia* – to be found.

You remember. The moment you feel shattered inside – whether by queer pleasure or queer pain – the world around you trembles and nothing feels the same. You lose the body's outline in the overwhelming waves of euphoria, letting go of the illusion of the self and falling into the haunting abyss where forgotten beings and actions dance. You want to be lost, forgotten, in a dim room enclosed by four walls that have witnessed all your guilty pleasures, unhinged rants, sacred tears and laughter, secret lovers, blasphemous acts and more. It feels safe here. You want to hide and protect these secrets so fiercely, even to the point of wanting to forget these precious moments of queer intimacy, whether with yourself or others, so the world would never discover them. Therefore, you will not be destroyed by the weight of carrying these memories. Yet in the next moment you remember being remembered – not lost, not yet. You remember that you have shared words with others and left a trace. When you review something once written not for yourself but for a broader audience, the dry and stiff words appear like a dress too tight to cover what you hide from public view. It could explode at any moment – it is evident to your eyes, but you wonder if anyone who knows you only through your words can see the tension. It may just appear formal and neutral, as it was intended to be.

We are so much more than our words, more than what we *can* say in the presence of others. We are elusive; tomorrow we might no longer believe in what we had yesterday. This cannot be more true for queer people. Some are closeted and in disguise of being cis-hetero. For some, the binary language around gender and sexuality restrains how they think of themselves or constantly fails to represent how they live. There is only so much queerness we can capture in writing like this chapter. However, when (the) word is valued in theology as the primary means for academic communication *and* as the presence of the divine through scripture, sermon and Jesus in the flesh, we are to believe that (the) word is fundamental to form our subjectivity. The word creates the world; the word forms us.

I am not sure how – or whether I even want – to inscribe the moments of queer eu/dysphoria into theology – the God-talk/the Word-wording. Notwithstanding, the fact that (the) word cannot exist without flesh invites me to believe in the possibility of queer theology. Just as Judith

Butler (1997) sheds light on the hand that writes a text questioning the existence of the body of the self, a word cannot come into existence without a mouth to utter it. It cannot remain in the world without a hand to write and the physical labour to produce inks and papers. The words written by bodies with queer experiences carry more than what they signify, ever-expanding the meanings as the selves/bodies push their porous boundaries, hiding and leaking what is contained inside. As we search for alternative approaches of queering theology that are more forgetful, messy and boldly failing, may the absence haunt those who dance with the lost and the forgotten.

## *Notes*

1 According to the CiNii, a Japanese 'database service which can be searched with academic information of articles, books, journals, and dissertations', the number of articles related to queer theologies increased from the 2000s to the 2020s: while there is one article from 2008, there are three between 2010 and 2014, rising to ten between 2015 and 2020, and reaching 14 in the period from 2021 to 2022.

2 Of course, more people raise their voices to do the queering of theology and Christianity inside and outside academia in Japan – Sawako Fujiwara, a feminist theologian; Yuki Nagao, a feminist and queer theologian/pastor; Reina Ueno, an openly lesbian pastor, Kazumi Usui, an openly pansexual former pastor and chaplain, to name a few.

## References

Althaus-Reid, Marcella (2003), *The Queer God*, London: Routledge.

Althaus-Reid, Marcella (2008), 'The Bi/Girl Writings: From Feminist Theology to Queer Theologies', in *Post-Christian Feminisms*, edited by Lisa Isherwood and Kathleen McPhillips, London: Routledge, pp. 105–16.

Asaka, Tomoki (2011), 'Kuia Shingaku no Kanōsei' [The Development of Queer Theology: Problems and Prospects], *Nihon no Shingaku* [Theological Study in Japan] 50, pp. 55–73.

Asaka, Tomoki (2018), 'Kuia Shingaku no Teigi wo Meguru Shomondai' [Problems around the Definition of Queer Theology], *Fukuin to Sekai* [Gospel and World] 73, no. 7, pp. 12–17.

Asaka, Tomoki (2021), 'Kuia Shingaku to Jissen' [Queer Theology and Praxis]. *Fukuin to Sekai* [Gospel and World] 76, no. 12, pp. 12–17.

Braun, Adam F (2024), 'The Bible without a Cure (As Emancipatory Praxis)', *The Bible and Critical Theory* 20, no. 1, pp. 3–4.

Butler, Judith (1997), 'How Can I Deny That These Hands and This Body Are Mine?' *Qui Parle* 11, no. 1, pp. 1–20.

Cage, John (1952), *4'33"*, New York: C.F. Peters.

Cheng, Patrick S. (2011), *Radical Love: Introduction to Queer Theology*, New York: Seabury Books.

Cheng, Patrick S. (2014), *Radikaru Rabu: Kuia Shingaku Nyūmon* [Radical Love: Introduction to Queer Theology], translated by Marie Kudo, Tokyo: Shinkyōshuppansha.

Choi, Jin Young (2015), *Postcolonial Discipleship of Embodiment: An Asian American Feminist Reading of the Gospel of Mark*, New York: Palgrave Macmillan.

Córdova Quero, Hugo (2019), 'Straddling the Global South: Bridging Queer Theologies in Asia, Latin America, and Africa', in *Siapakah sesamaku?: Pergumulan teologi dengan isu-isu keadilan gender* [Who is my neighbour? Theology's challenges with gender justice issues], edited by Stephen Suleeman and Amadeo D. Udampoh, Jakarta: Sekolah Tinggi Filsafat Teologi, pp. 157–84.

Derrida, Jacques (1994), *Specters of Marx: The State of The Debt, the Work of Mourning, and the New International*, translated by Peggy Kamuf, New York: Routledge.

Edelman, Lee (2004), *No Future: Queer Theory and the Death Drive*, Durham, NC: Duke University Press.

Greenough, Chris (2020), *Queer Theologies: The Basics*, London: Routledge.

Greenough, Chris (2024), *Kuia Shingaku Nyūmon: Sono Fukusū no Koe wo Kiku* [Queer Theologies: The Basics], translated by Yoshiko Usui, Tokyo: Shinkyōshuppansha.

Halberstam, Jack (2011), *The Queer Art of Failure*, Durham, NC: Duke University Press.

Horie, Yuri (2006), *Rezubian to iu Ikikata: Kirisutokyō no Iseiaishugi wo Tou* ['Lesbian' Way of Life: Questioning Heterosexism in Christianity], Tokyo: Shinkyōshuppansha.

Horie, Yuri (2008), 'Shūkyō ni okeru <Datsu-Iseiaishugi> no Jissen' [A Praxis of De-Heterosexualism in Religions], *Jinken Kyōiku Kenkyū* [Journal of Human Rights Education and Research] 16, pp. 77–102.

Horie, Yuri (2014), '<Tomurai> wo Meguru Oboegaki: Kuia Shingaku kara no Ichi Kōsatsu' [A Note on 'Funeral': An Analysis from the Perspective of Queer Theology], *Josei, Sensō, Jinken* [Women, War, Human Rights] 13, pp. 86–103.

Horie, Yuri (2019), 'Kirisutokyō ni okeru "Kazokushugi": Kuia Shingaku kara no Hihanteki Kōsatsu' [A Critical Analysis of 'Familiism' from the Perspective of Queer Theology], *Shūkyō Kenkyū* [Journal of Religious Studies] 93, no. 2, pp. 163–89.

Horie, Yuri (2024), 'Kuia Shingaku no Kanōsei' [Possibilities of Queer Theology], in *Todoki Hajimeta SOS* [SOS Starting to Reach], edited by Hanazono Daigaku Jinken Kyōiku Sentā [Hanazono University Human Rights Centre], Tokyo: Hihyōsha.

Kudo, Marie (2014), 'Kuia Shingaku he no Izanai' [An Invitation to Queer Theology], *Fukuin to Sekai* [Gospel and World] 69, no. 11, pp. 30–5.

Kudo, Marie (2022), *Kuia Shingaku no Chōsen* [The Challenge of Queer Theology], Tokyo: Shinkyōshuppansha.

Kudo, Marie (2024). The interview was conducted in Tokyo on 4 October.

Maekawa, Yutaka (2023), '<Hon-yaku> Robāto·E·Shoa=Gosu Cho "Yohane ni yoru Fukuinsho" Kuia Sēsho Chūkai (Dai 2 Han)' [Translation of Robert E. Shore-Goss, 'John', in *The Queer Bible Commentary* (2nd edn)], *Kwansei Gakuin Daigaku Ripojitori* [Kwansei Gakuin University Repository] 24, pp. 43–87.

Said, Edward W. (1978), *Orientalism*, New York: Pantheon Books.

Shore-Goss, Robert E. (1993), *Jesus Acted Up: A Gay and Lesbian Manifesto*, San Francisco, CA: Harper San Francisco.

Shore-Goss, Robert E. (2022), 'John', in *The Queer Bible Commentary*, edited by Robert E. Shore-Goss and Mona West, 2nd edn, London: SCM Press.

Shore-Goss, Robert E. and Mona West (2000), *Take Back the Word: A Queer Reading of the Bible*, Cleveland, OH: Pilgrim Press.

Shūkyō Kenkyūjo [Institute for Religious Studies] (2023), *Shūkyō nenkan: Reiwa 5 nen-ban* [Religious Yearbook], Tokyo: Shūkyō Kenkyūjo.

Singh, Julietta (2018), *Unthinking Mastery: Dehumanism and Decolonial Entanglements*, Durham, NC: Duke University Press.

PART 6

# Mariology and Hagiography

# 16

# Manifesting the Mediatrix: Queering Ecclesiology through Spiritual Activism

MOLLY GREENING

## Introduction

This chapter is a reflection on the spaces where systems of belonging break down and overflow, where hierarchies of value constrain but ultimately cannot determine a final definition. It attempts to name the power dynamics of borders that claim neat separations, whether separations of religious traditions, gender binaries, sexualities or nationalities. It is a personal account of spiritual activism with my chosen family of queer and trans-Roman Catholics. We sometimes refer to ourselves as *Qatholics* with a Q, a term we coined when speaking with those who doubt that one can be queer, trans and Roman Catholic with a C. It is an experiment in creating a path for queer and trans-Roman Catholics beyond the binary of exclusion and assimilation and relating this process to protesting unjust structures of immigration in the United States.[1]

It is a narration of where the mechanisms of exclusion mark my body – sometimes in ways that benefit me and sometimes in ways that do not. I reflect on the inextricable interconnections of race, gender, sexuality, nation and religion, where the open wounds of these structures demand attention, care and the possibility of coalitional resistance, regardless of one's social position. Relying on insights from Gloria Anzaldúa's (2015) concept of spiritual activism, it is also an attempt to counter the constructed nature of these separations. I question the usefulness of the term 'ecclesiology' to describe this queering of Christian community building, asking if the term can be repurposed when ecclesiology has often determined the boundaries of sexual and religious queerness that break eligibility for Christian church belonging. I look to other images as more fruitful for standing amid legitimacy scripts, whether the Christian church or the state maintains those.

Through intentionally telling stories of interconnection, blurring, meeting and mutual influence that coalesce in artistic retrievals of Mary the Mother of God, I look to the Mediatrix or the holy one who stands in between as a necessary cry against that which would desecrate those who find themselves in between systems of power. I end with a reflection on Anzaldúa's model for coalition building with *el árbol de la vida*, suggesting that this metaphor of the tree of life can affirm connections of the chosen family without falling into the trap of adhering uncritically to a belief in the church as a 'chosen people'. Knowing our ancestral roots and connecting through the open wounds of our past and present demonstrates how spiritual activists can work together to creatively challenge structural oppression through multireligious, queer, politically activated liturgies.

Taking the legacies of border crossing and border defining seriously within theology and the US immigration system, this is a story of two queer and trans Roman Catholics with citizenship in the United States questioning strategies of confinement. With inspiration from Chicana experiences of reclaiming the sexual and the sacred amid borders of exclusion that must be skilfully navigated, my Irish-Hungarian-German roots and my adopted queer daughter's roots in Kerala, India, grafted together, forming bonds of family across religious, racial and sexed/gendered borders.

## Manifesting the Mediatrix

Headmistress Geethanjali Mar Ulysios (2024) – or Geetha as we lovingly call her – raised a handmade clay chalice in the air. Right before we attended a protest for immigrant children who were under the custody of the US government, Geetha insisted on an impromptu liturgy in the living room. On reflection, she says, 'Our queer liturgies take into account the discarded and disregarded members of the world and put them at the forefront of our endeavors' (Ulysios, 2024).

I sang prayers and circled the dining room table as we both blessed our eucharist found in haste in Geetha's studio apartment. The eucharist was made from what we had on hand at this spontaneous moment – vodka and Cheetos. We made our daily surroundings sacred by pouring cheap vodka into this vessel Geetha made with her hands, a cup she shaped with a hole in one side. We sprinkled Cheetos on a plate, which also cracked. We repurposed clothes for priests and bishops that Geetha had from trips back home. We prayed with Jesus, Mary, Shiva and Kali, with our sexualities, our fears, with the broken things in our lives, and the things that others say are broken but, in reality, are not. She says: 'The karmic cycle of life allows us to transcend and be in communion with each other as we break bread, share the cup, and laugh from the depths of our liver' (Ulysios, 2024). She refers to the Jewish understanding of our life force being located in the liver, a call for a depth of joy that comes from the most essential core of our being. Remembering bodies that are broken, dismembered, forgotten and thrown out, we made a liturgy connecting transgressions of national, sexual and religious borders.

Geetha took a shawl I was wearing that covered the shape of my body and placed it on my head to mimic the images of Mary. With clothes designed to enforce modesty and vestments that create hierarchies between clergy and lay people, we broke the rules and became bigger. It was not just the Mediatrix, but we who became, who have always been, the body, the blood, the sacramental site of the sacred. In Geetha's interpretation, Mary, not Jesus, said it first: 'This is my body, this is my blood.' Then *we* said it too: 'This is my body, this is my blood.' We became the Mediatrix in this space of in-betweenness, building a church from our bones with Christmas lights and the incense Geetha bought in India.

It was Halloween night in Rogers Park, a neighbourhood on the north side of Chicago. According to Celtic mythology, this was a night when the world of the living and the world of the dead intermingle, a time when the veil, or the borders that separate this life and the otherworldly realm of spirits, is said to be especially thin (Hutton, 1996). People dressed up in Halloween costumes passed each other on the sidewalks: skeletons, vampires, Disney princesses, even someone in a full mesh bodysuit with perfectly placed fig leaves – Eve, the mother of all herself – came out to roam the streets of one of Chicago's most diverse parts of the city, a place where over 100 languages are spoken, and many immigrants from all over the world call home. In every direction in Rogers Park one encounters a vibrant array of temples, synagogues, masjids, gurdwaras and churches, where communities actively preserve traditions from around the globe. However, Chicago is also one of the most segregated cities, with its policies offering the rest of the United States a blueprint for racially segregating neighbourhoods (Moser, 2017).

By 2019 the Trump administration had officially ended its 'zero tolerance' policy that criminalized all immigrants coming to the United States, including people seeking asylum (Chishti and Bolter, 2018). This law separated thousands of families, with the majority from Guatemala, Honduras and El Salvador. However, after the official termination of this deterrence policy, many children were still not reunited with their families (Diaz, 2021; Santana, 2024). Combining the impacts of civil wars in Central America financed by the United States and immigration laws from 1996, the policies of my country created the conditions for violent groups like Mara Salvatrucha that many people were fleeing. It was often undocumented Salvadoran youth trying to escape violence within highly segregated US neighbourhoods that formed the original gangs that were then deported, spreading the seeds for international networks of organized crime (Taddonio, 2018). Families and young people escaping such conditions were called criminals for breaking immigration law, even if they were exercising their human rights to apply for asylum.

People under the age of 18 were supposed to have even more legal protections than adults, especially after legal settlements ruling that minors should not be detained, like the Flores Settlement of 1997 (National Center for Youth Law, 2019). In place of detention there are 'shelters' where young people wait in conditions that are not the same as in buildings that are prisons (Office of Refugee Resettlement, 2024). Nevertheless they are not able to leave; they are highly monitored and exist in a liminal space between legality, countries and complex processes that sometimes take years to sort through, especially since in 2024 the Flores Settlement was overturned by a federal judge in Los Angeles (Wiessner, 2024).

The United States bears painful legacies that have led state officials to justify separating indigenous people (Adams, 1995), black people (Dettlaff, 2023) and Latinx immigrants (Hillstrom, 2020) from those most vital to their survival. The history of boarding schools for indigenous children that churches ran demonstrates the lie of the separation of the church and the state in the United States. Many of these shelters are run by Roman Catholic, Lutheran and other Christian organizations (McKellips, 1992). Many young people inside of these shelters run by the Office of Refugee Resettlement are indigenous too. Multiple shelters are in the neighbourhood where my university was located, where young people from Central America, but also India, China, Syria, Nepal and Bangladesh, were waiting for a date in court, reunification and the following steps of their journey, all without physical contact with people not authorized by the facilities.

We took to the streets with a local group of activists and a cacophonous full-on marching band, exclaiming that there are detention centres in this neighbourhood, that the children inside were not forgotten or alone, that we need other solutions that do not involve cages, weapons, militarized borders. With signs on recycled cardboard we protested the cis-heterosexual ideas that determine what counts as a family and the old racist ideologies with a long history in the United States. We stood at the locked gate separating the inside of the facility from the outside. Undoubtedly the young people inside could hear our music and chanting outside. Locked arm in arm with our queer chosen family, we protested the mechanisms of family separation legalized through US immigration policy.

## Refusing Compartmentalization: Queer Liturgies

Geetha gave me the confidence to prepare an ecstatic liturgy in the living room where we broke the rules and claimed space for ourselves as queer and trans Roman Catholics, where we screamed when the church hierarchy asked us to remain silent, to disappear. However, I also gave Geetha the political analysis of this liturgy, the invisible but sacred threads that connect everyone with everyone. Together we demonstrated what Marcella Althaus-Reid (2004) called a 'theological cry' that comes from queer liturgies, as well as a form of what Anzaldúa (2015) called 'spiritual activism'.

Althaus-Reid (2004) wrote about the importance of queer people making 'camp chapels' in response to their deep theological yearning for a wholeness that refuses the separation of their sexualities from their spiritualities. As she says, we are 'sexual dissenters ... who make camp chapels of their living rooms simply because there is a cry in their lives, and a theological cry, which refuses to fit life into different compartments' (p. 2). Refusing this compartmentalization and listening to one's theological cry is especially important when queer and trans Roman Catholics have often been asked to choose between assimilation or exclusion.

Spontaneous living-room liturgies can tend to the wounds of being thrown out of liturgical spaces for refusing to assimilate into cis-heterosexual norms. Still, it can also tend to the wounds of feeling pressure to abandon one's spiritual life completely. Due to the commonly held belief by both religious and non-religious people that being queer and/or trans and being religious are antithetical, spontaneous liturgy reclaims a space of in-betweenness. It challenges the mechanisms that enforce opposition and neat distinctions, which often fail to reflect the lived experiences of queer and trans people. In Geetha's perspective:

> Liturgies are coined as work of the people. As queer people who live and breathe rituals of love, we are called to remember those who have gone before us, those currently fighting for their life, and those who will come after us. (Ulysios, 2024)

## Spiritual Activism in the Borderlands

Anzaldúa's (2012) theory of the borderlands was mainly received as a geopolitical concept about national borders. In her later work Anzaldúa refused compartmentalization even further, claiming that while the borderlands were geographical and physical they were also emotional, sexual, psychological and spiritual.

> The US/Mexico border was 'una herida abierta' where the Third World grates against the first and bleeds. Before a scab forms it hemorrhages again, the lifeblood of two worlds merging to form a third country – a border culture. (Anzaldúa, 2012, p. 25)

The borderlands were created from this collision, a 'vague and undetermined place created by the emotional residue of an unnatural boundary' (p. 25). It is a space between us and others, a slash that separates us from them. However, these spaces are not solely within geopolitical borders; there are also spaces between oversimplified understandings of binary gender that trans and non-binary people inhabit or between binaries of monosexuality that bisexual and pansexual people defy. There are many borders, and varied people crossing these borders in different ways. Early in *Borderlands/La Frontera*, she defined the inhabitants of this space broadly as those who were 'prohibited and forbidden', such as 'the squint-eyed, the perverse, the queer, the troublesome, the mongrel, the mulato, the half-breed, the half-dead; in short, those who cross over, pass over or go through the confines of the "normal"' (Anzaldúa, 2012, p. 109). In between life and death, racial categories, sexual acceptability – anyone challenging the limits of what dominant culture considers typical – were inhabitants of this space in between. As the description shows, these categories often bled into each other. In her later work Anzaldúa (2015) named the conditions of the twenty-first century as ones where all humans, all living species and even the planet itself were 'caught between cultures and bleed-throughs among different worlds – each with its own version of reality' (p. 118); this is experienced as 'a personal, global, identity crisis in a disintegrating social order that possesses little heart and ... justif[ies] a sliding scale of human worth used to keep humankind divided' (p. 118). The borderlands could be found within one city, within one body, anywhere where two opposites pressed together and met. These value categories reinforced hierarchies even as the social order was collapsing. From this space in between, Anzaldúa calls for reimagining more just worlds through art, activism and coalition building.

I argued in previous work that Anzaldúa brought together her theories of the borderlands and spiritual mestizaje through the concept of spiritual activism (Greening, 2023, pp. 175–81). For Anzaldúa, the multiplicities of the borderlands were a vital stepping stone for building action-orientated coalitions that could fight the violence of the borders that arbitrarily separate and obscure our interconnectedness. The borderlands could be sites of resistance, personal and political spaces of challenging dominant norms, a space of the 'queer' that questioned the normalcy of any borders, geographical, racial, religious, sexual or religious.

Our sexuality was not broken but the wounds of these messages of exclusion, of otherness, were still present, needing to be attended to. Unfortunately the immigration system we were protesting was not broken either – it worked the way it was supposed to through displacement, criminalization, racial hierarchies of citizenship and state-sanctioned exploitation of migrant labour, as Harsha Walia claims in *Undoing Border Imperialism* (2013, p. 5). This immigration system also contained messages of gender and sexuality and showed its racist contradictions. Separating the ideal of the cis-heterosexual family – the parent and the child – showed how these xenophobic contortions racialize cis-heteropatriarchy, further compartmentalizing the ideals of normalcy that often accompany court hearings for asylum or citizenship.

## *La Virgen* in Between

Anzaldúa interpreted *La Virgen* with Nahua goddesses, concluding that Guadalupe was the name Coatlalopeuh, meaning in Nahuatl 'she who is one with the beasts' (Anzaldúa, 2015, p. 67). One day she saw a branch cut from her favourite tree, and in the severed branch she saw the shape of the Virgin, inviting her to connect with trees, rocks, ocean and all creation. For Anzaldúa, *La Virgen* was a mediator between cultures of humans, humans and animals, nature, systems of religion and planes of reality. Mediation requires comfort with ambiguity as Chicanas navigate structures such as colonialism, racism and sexism that fix their bodies in hierarchies of value. With this potent symbol of Chicanos/Mexicans, she found a figure between various worlds.

There is a vibrant history of Chicanas in the United States, which manifests representations of the Virgin of Guadalupe with creativity for survival. They have reinvented the story of Juan Diego on the Tepeyac hill and the image of a humble Virgin. Yolanda López created art with her own body, with shoes and t-shirts, and in the image of her mother and grandmother, showing the effects of changed borders, work, homeland and gender (Miranda, 2022). Like Yolanda, Alma López also has feminist representations, reimagining how images dictate gender roles. With a rose bikini and a mantilla constructed from Coyolxauhqui, the Nahua goddess of the moon, López gives a picture of *Our Lady* that is powerful and fearless, with an implicit queer femme sexuality, symbolized by the Viceroy butterfly that looks like a monarch but is not (Lopez, 1999). In her earlier writings Sandra Cisneros (1997) claimed Guadalupe was a sex goddess, and later in her life, with the influence of Buddhism, designed a tattoo for her bicep she calls *Buddhalupe*, a mixture of Guan Yin and *La Virgen* on her arm (Paljor, 2022).

I take inspiration from these feminist theorists for conceptualizing the Mediatrix, which manifested through a spontaneous living room liturgy. Christians have used the title 'Mediatrix' for centuries, and in 1896 there was a proposal to create a dogma that states that the mother of Jesus would be the mediatrix of all graces. However, Vatican II did not formalize this request because there were concerns that people placed too much emphasis on Mary. Nonetheless, many people who feel excluded turn to Mary in search of healing. Therefore the Mediatrix is more powerful than the tools of church control. Sometimes, when these symbols are too powerful, official church legitimization is a way of trying to control an outpouring larger than doctrinal statements. I imagine the Mediatrix as one who embodies the influences of the past that are here in the present. She also holds possibilities for a future filled with more ambiguity and connection through denaturalizing lines of separation. This type of mediation is manifested in a spirit of art and activism that challenges cis-heterosexual and patriarchal institutions.

These connections in ambiguous spaces destabilize the separation of different identities, inviting people to change through intimate encounters. The continued change and impermanence of being in between always create spaces where systems of belonging break down and spill over. The Mediatrix always resists a final definition. Therefore she is the Mediatrix of all graces by inviting honesty about our co-construction, the ways that we are all shaped in national institutions and religious hierarchies that are always gendered and sexed.

## Concerns of Queering Ecclesiology

What are the possibilities and limits of a model of the Christian church centred on multireligious, political and spiritual engagement that challenges fixed identities and borders between religious traditions, genders, sexualities and nationalities? There are many concerns with using terms that denote classical church structures that need to be attended to, lest queer theologies repeat the wounds of dominant forms of Christian theology. Queer ecclesiology would need to give attention to the dynamics of power that accompany belonging in interconnected structures. Althaus-Reid (2004, pp. 2–3) invites us to consider that 'queering' means honestly questioning cis-heterosexuality and how cis-heteronormativity informs the basic conditions of our particular human contexts. In ecclesiological terms this would mean queering the structures of belonging, and Anzaldúa's contributions help imagine models of connection that are rooted in political and multireligious experiences without reinforcing assimilation within or exclusion from communities that take the interconnections of religion, nation, gender, race and sexuality seriously.

What does it mean to get bigger when asked to be small? When does belonging become something claimed in the marrow of your bones rather than granted from a structure that has 'turned you out'? Specifically, I wish to explore in-between spaces as possible sites of resistance concerning institutional legitimacy, whether ecclesial or state. I believe that the Mediatrix holds this space better than a concept of queer ecclesiologies and connects with Anzaldúa's theory of spiritual activism, offering a reconnection with endless opportunities for realizing our fundamental inseparability.

## *El Árbol de la Vida*

Critics of Anzaldúa questioned how her dependence on the concept of mestizaje might erase indigenous and Afro-Latinx identity. María Lugones wondered whether it was so true that all *atravesados* – or people who crossed these limits of normalcy – could build a coalition together, given their different social positions. Anzaldúa's concept of *el árbol de la vida* – or the tree of life – responds well to both critiques. *El árbol de la vida* is also a visual model for the necessary steps of building diverse coalitions through spiritual activism. First, one can know *sus raíces* – or their roots – that ground them within the historical legacies of their own cultures and lineages. Then, they can share stories with others and find places of connection where connections can be formed, like a process of grafting a branch to another tree's rootstock that tends to the wounds of unjust material conditions. With this connection the branches can flourish and expand towards the sky, holding multiple religious and spiritual practices to build a more just world that honours our interconnectivity (Anzaldúa, 2015, pp. 67–8). The language of grafting can give another method of looking at colonial violence, a matrix of power that interconnects us all into a single tree.

I supplement this theory of spiritual activism, particularly the first step of understanding one's roots, with contributions from indigenous feminists and queer theorists. The native feminists Arvin, Tuck and Morrill (2013) echo Patrick Wolfe (1999) in reinforcing that colonialism is a *structure* and not an event. It is not a moment in history that passed; it manifests in the present and impacts all aspects of our lives. Indigenous and non-indigenous people need to understand how this structure permeates and interrelates with dominant notions of nation, gender and sexuality in colonial societies (Driskill et al., 2011, pp. 145–7). The forces of exclusion and assimilation require that this history of oppression be forgotten. Recovering our roots requires retelling the stories that connect us to these systems that try to separate us but continue to influence us. Amid the forces of exclusion and assimilation, memory can be perilous. We must also investigate how our counter-narratives to these histories often manifest as political narratives of desire (Morgensen, 2011, p. 141). When we tell a story there are always motivations. Still, in this case the hope is that this theory offers a way to heal the wounds caused by the unnatural separation that accompanies the immigration policies that interlock nation, gender and sexuality. A queer theological analysis shows the ways that religion is inextricably connected to these categories as well.

## Grafting Through Stories

At this point in my life I was a graduate student at Loyola University Chicago. I came to the academy looking for language for my experiences but I struggled to name the different influences that informed my theological cry. I had been a teenager in a wealthy suburb with an immense love for the mystical and a correct suspicion of the Roman Catholic Church, its hierarchies, patriarchy, sex abuse and monetary exploitation; a 20-year-old from the United States living in India, looking for a 'good kind of religion' that you could juxtapose with the ills of the Roman Catholic Church, lulled by an illusion that could only exist for so long, a sort of positive orientalism that exculpated religions of 'the East' from hierarchies, patriarchy, sex abuse, monetary exploitation. Then, a mid-twenties idealist living in a Roman Catholic anarchist community in small-town Minnesota tried to live a life of integrity while grappling with the structural inequalities that seemed so distant yet interconnected on local and global scales. Now I was a late-twenties queer and non-binary ethicist-in-training feeling my connection with my own body for the first time without the mediation of religious guilt, finding my way through the contradictions of my life outside of religious communities that once called me sister, mother, sinner.

I needed to meet Geetha, someone boldly practising liturgy on her terms. As a first-generation immigrant, Geetha was the only child of her parents, and the liturgy and Roman Catholic faith had captivated her since she was little. She grew up in a South Indian Roman Catholic rite. As a child she dreamed of being at least a bishop, if not the Pope herself. However, when she realized that queer and genderfluid folks were not allowed to be out and in the Roman Catholic Church's ranks, it broke some of her life's aspirations.

Geetha and I met searching for a place where our spiritualities, gender expression and sexualities could exist. Headmistress Geethanjali Mar Ulysios started the School of Whores or SoW. Giving herself the name of the bishop used in South India, 'Mar', and taking a name from India for women that means a gift of songs, she rejected the binary of sacred and profane and decided to see God and love all around through her queer ministry. I saw Headmistress Geethanjali bless shots of tequila, dildos, cats and any person who is suffering or celebrating a life transition. Geetha adopted me as her mother and so, naturally, Geetha became my daughter – or my son, depending on the occasion. I am also a proud board member of SoW and the self-designated minister of sexual education.

Our social positions differed significantly but Geetha and I shared many things. We have family stories with addiction, sexual abuse and struggles where we were too queer for Catholics and also too Catholic for queers. Also, like all people in the United States who are not indigenous, our ancestors share the history of immigration to this country. With this we share navigations of the confluence of national identity, racism, religion and cis-heteropatriarchy that influence all laws, including ones that determine immigration and citizenship.

## Knowing Our Roots

Geetha and I can explore our roots through this lens, particularly narrating how immigration policy overlaps amid the categories of nation, gender, sexuality and religion. I am a Roman Catholic granddaughter on the Irish side of my family. My great-great-grandparents came to the United States in 1841 and had a farm in the 'ceded' land of the people of the Potawatomi, Odawa, Ojibwe and Wyandot nations with the

Cession 66 treaty of 1807 (Dunbar-Ortiz, 2014). In 1790 the Naturalization Act ruled that 'free and white people' could be citizens (Painter, 2011). Indigenous people would not be given citizenship in the United States until 1924 (Hoxie, 2012). It was unclear whether the Irish were white, and the price of exclusion was high (Haney López, 1996). Therefore they took the name of their colonizers (Ignatiev, 1995). For my family, for instance, the name Greenan – meaning 'green hill' – was Anglicized to its English version, Greening. The Roman Catholic branch of Christianity was the only apparent connection that they maintained with their roots. My other ancestors – who were Hungarian – forgot even more to assimilate into this national project. They arrived much later in Canada, where my great-grandmother survived in a town where Romani people traded horses. She crossed the border and returned as a single mother, hoping to forget the past for a stable future through marriage. She remarried and had nine children, letting go of her past and forging a new life.

With the benefit of European supremacist policies my ancestors – like many other immigrants – gained access to the racial category of being 'white' (Jacobson, 1999). By participating in the Second World War, all my grandparents on both sides of my family met. With policies like the GI Bill that benefitted white soldiers and excluded black soldiers, my grandfathers had the money for education, homes in the suburbs and the opportunity to actualize the 'American dream' within the cis-heteropatriarchal family structure built on stolen private property. I wrote the lyrics of a song that said, 'Swallow the lie for a piece of that white bread'. Swallowing this lie costs a lot: giving up one's roots, overwork and addiction. My US passport allowed me many opportunities for travel, education and intercultural and interreligious exchanges that woke me up from forgetting assimilation or – as Hugo Córdova Quero (2021, p. 48) labelled it – 'ethnic amnesia'.

The Hart-Cellar Act, the immigration and nationality law of 1965, changed the restrictions that privileged Europeans to migrate to the United States (Gjelten, 2015). An extension of the civil rights movement, the law abolished racist quotas, meaning that people from Latin America, Asia and Africa had more opportunities to obtain visas through work visas or family connections. This greatly influences the demographics of the United States, particularly religious diversity. However, many new immigrants were still Christians but with practices from many parts of the world. Geetha's father's sister was a nurse and citizen, and she left Kerala, the most southern state in India, in 1988 for the United States. Through the legitimacy of marriage her mother came to the United States shortly afterwards, also working as a nurse. Neither of us is disconnected from these legacies as we protest the mechanisms of citizenship expressed as a militarized border, a backlogged court system or a freezing prison cell.

Negotiations of racism shape our own families, the privileging of cis-heterosexual marriage, movement dictated by labour, and pursuing the 'American dream' from different contexts. These histories tell a much more nuanced story of what it means to know one's history and link arms with one's queer chosen family, especially when protesting the mechanisms of family separation legalized through US immigration policy.

I imagine our manifestations of the Mediatrix as an incarnated and incarnating, a destabilized and destabilizing symbol of the histories etched in our skin and the churches we have carved from our bones. It is an invitation to embrace the complexities and ambiguities that challenge naturalized borders. The Mediatrix traffics in the histories that the institutional church wants us to forget, as well as the spiritual and material connections that the church cannot control and the state cannot separate with decrees of legitimacy.

## Chosen Family in Place of Chosen People

I believe that the images of the Mediatrix and *el árbol de la vida* are both helpful in reflecting on another issue with defining a 'queer' form of ecclesiology. Grafting also has biblical imagery, with Romans 11.17–21 heralding the goodness of Gentiles being grafted into the community of believers, making essential statements about models of belonging connected to God's promise to his chosen people. Unlike Romans 11, this grafting does not depend on a correct and singular belief. In Anzaldúa's inspiration for this metaphor, her *tío*'s [uncle's] dying orange tree was sick, but with different branches grafted to it, it became healthy again. It is not necessary to maintain a monotony of beliefs but to know the differences and find places of connection that oppression can obscure. Another queer theologian (Worsfeld, 2010) offers a problematic metaphor when he says that grafting is 'unnatural', the same word that is used to describe homosexual sex. Worsfeld argues that God created the first 'unnatural' act with the grafting of Gentiles on to a Jewish tree, and thus homosexuality is not the first unnatural act. With Anzaldúa, *the separation of the border is the unnatural thing*. However, a healing and strengthening connection is possible through the openings that result from an unnatural boundary. Sometimes, with this cutting of a branch, the face of the Mediatrix can appear to be where the severed limb has been removed. I feel this is important for queer ecclesiology, where we can emphasize the *chosen family* rather than a chosen people.

## Conclusion

I have narrated a specific example with a member of my chosen family, my queer adopted daughter, from where we manifest the Mediatrix through our bodies, liturgies and activism against unjust immigration policy. I believe that this is a localized example of Anzaldúa's theory of spiritual activism, from where we know the roots of our ancestors, we connect through the open wounds of our past and present through the process of grafting, and we take creative actions that are spiritual, political and multi-religious. Anzaldúa was walking one day when she saw the figure of *La Virgen* in a severed branch from her favourite tree. Sometimes a cut into the tree of life shows the Mediatrix.

If there were to be a queer ecclesiology, it would have to address the wounds where there is an unnatural rupture of separation that disrupts the sacredness of our infinite interconnections. Perhaps imageries of in-betweenness and interconnectedness can create a better path for queer and trans Roman Catholics beyond the binary of exclusion and assimilation and inspire taking action against harmful structures that shape so many forms of belonging. When we, as J. Robin Kimball's (2016) poem suggests, build churches from our bones, particularly when we find ourselves in intermediary spaces concerning institutional legitimacy, whether that be with the Christian church or the state, we can become more prominent, become furious and become art as we resist from the spaces in between legacies of legitimacy.

If they were to exist, queer ecclesiologies would require the qualities of the Mediatrix. They must manifest outside of the control of the institutional church through spontaneous liturgies in the living room, in the cut branches of a tree and the bones of those refusing compartmentalization through their theological cries. The power of the Mediatrix's flexibility is also the rejection of purity, singularity or settledness in a sole culture. The appearance of the Mediatrix is usually hyperpersonal and often appears in moments of wounding between countries, cultures, religions and sexualities. Examples include the Black Madonna of Czestochowa with a rainbow halo, *Our Lady of Ferguson* by Mark Doox (2015) for victims of gun violence, and *La Ofrenda* by Ester Hernandez (1988), with an image showing her giving flowers to the tattoo on the back of her lesbian lover. They are a fraction of creative expressions that tie into this spirit of spaces in between. The Mediatrix also protects from reification and comfortable categorizations of us versus them. Queer ecclesiologies would need to pay attention to the wounding often caused by mainstream ecclesiology itself, tending to a rupture caused by the unnatural separations against our infinite interconnections.

## *Notes*

1 Special thanks to Carmen Gonzalez, André Musskopf and Headmistress Geethanjali Mar Ulysios for their invaluable feedback and thoughtful reviews during the development of this chapter.

## References


Adams, David Wallace (1995), *Education for Extinction: American Indians and the Boarding School Experience, 1875–1928*, Lawrence, KS: University Press of Kansas.

Althaus-Reid, Marcella (2004), *The Queer God*, London: Routledge.

Anzaldúa, Gloria (2012), *Borderlands/La Frontera: The New Mestiza*, San Francisco, CA: Aunt Lute.

Anzaldúa, Gloria (2015), *Light in the Dark/Luz En Lo Oscuro: Rewriting Identity, Spirituality, Reality*, edited by Ana Louise Keating, Durham, NC: Duke University Press.

Arvin, Maile, Eve Tuck and Angie Morrill (2013), 'Decolonizing Feminism: Challenging Connections between Settler Colonialism and Heteropatriarchy', *Feminist Formations* 25, no. 1 (Spring), pp. 8–34.

Chishti, Muzaffar and Jessica Bolter (2018), 'Family Separation and "Zero-Tolerance" Policies rolled out to Stem Unwanted Migrants, but may face Challenges', *Migration Information Source*, 24 May, at https://www.migrationpolicy.org/article/family-separation-and-zero-tolerance-policies-rolled-out-stem-unwanted-migrants-may-face?utm_source=chatgpt.com, accessed 01.12.2024.

Cisneros, Sandra (1997), 'Guadalupe the Sex Goddess', in *Goddess of the Americas: Writings on the Virgen of Guadalupe*, edited by Ana Castillo, New York: Riverhead Books.

Córdova Quero, Hugo (2021), 'Whatever happened to the lemon vendors?: West African im/migrants and the (re)ethnization/(re)sexualization of erotoscapes in the streets of Buenos Aires', in *The Indecent Theologies of Marcella Althaus-Reid: Voices from Asia and Latin America*, edited by Lisa Isherwood and Hugo Córdova Quero, London: Routledge, pp. 46–69.

Dettlaff, Alan J. (2023), *Confronting the Racist Legacy of the American Child Welfare System: The Case for Abolition*, Oxford: Oxford University Press.

Diaz, Jaclyn (2021), 'Justice Department Rescinds Trump's "Zero Tolerance" Immigration Policy', *NPR*, 27 January, at https://www.npr.org/2021/01/27/961048895/justice-department-rescinds-trumps-zero-tolerance-immigration-policy?utm_source=chatgpt.com, accessed 01.12.2024.

Doox, Mark (2015), *Our Lady of Ferguson* (acrylic collage icon), Cathedral of Saint John the Divine.

Driskill, Qwo-Li, Chris Finley, Brian Joseph Gilley and Scott Lauria Morgensen (2011), *Queer Indigenous Studies: Critical Interventions in Theory, Politics, and Literature*, Tucson, AZ: University of Arizona Press.

Dunbar-Ortiz, Roxanne (2014), *An Indigenous Peoples' History of the United States*, Boston, MA: Beacon Press.

Gjelten, Tom (2015), *A Nation of Nations: A Great American Immigration Story*, New York: Simon & Schuster.

Greening, Molly (2023), 'Belonging in the Borderlands: Questioning Catholic Ethics', doctoral dissertation, Loyola University Chicago, at https://ecommons.luc.edu/luc_diss/4024, accessed 01.12.2024.

Haney López, Ian F. (1996), *White By Law: The Legal Construction of Race*, New York: New York University Press.

Hernandez, Ester (1988), *La Ofrenda* (screenprint on paper), Smithsonian American Art Museum, Gift of the Wight Art Gallery, University of California, Los Angeles, at https://americanart.si.edu/artwork/la-ofrenda-national-chicano-screenprint-taller-1988-1989-32720, accessed 01.12.2024.

Hillstrom, Laurie Collier (2020), *Family Separation and the U.S.–Mexico Border Crisis*, Santa Barbara, CA: ABC-CLIO.

Hoxie, Frederick E. (2012), *This Indian Country: American Indian Activists and the Place They Made*, New York: Penguin Books.

Hutton, Ronald (1996), *The Stations of the Sun: A History of the Ritual Year in Britain*, Oxford: Oxford University Press.

Ignatiev, Noel (1995), *How the Irish Became White*, London: Routledge.

Jacobson, Matthew Frye (1999), *Whiteness of a Different Color: European Immigrants and the Alchemy of Race*, Cambridge, MA: Harvard University Press.

Kimball, J. Robin (2016), 'The Bigger We Get' (letterpress), printed by Maggie Campbell, Brooklyn, NY: Campbell Raw Press.

Lopez, Alma (1999), *Our Lady* (digital print), at http://almalopez.com/ourlady.html, accessed 01.12.2024.

McKellips, Karen K. (1992), 'Educational Practices in Two Nineteenth Century American Indian Mission Schools', *Journal of American Indian Education* 32, no. 1 (October), pp. 12–20.

Miranda, Carolina (2022), 'How painter Yolanda López gave the Virgen of Guadalupe a Feminist Tweak', *Los Angeles Times*, 2 April, at https://www.latimes.com/entertainment-arts/newsletter/2022-04-02/essential-arts-yolanda-lopez-portrait-of-the-artist-mcasd-essential-arts, accessed 01.12.2024.

Morgensen, Scott Lauria (2011), *Spaces Between Us: Queer Settler Colonialism and Indigenous Decolonization*, Minneapolis, MN: University of Minnesota Press.

Moser, Whet (2017), 'Chicago isn't Just Segregated, it Basically Invented Modern Segregation', *Chicago Magazine*, 31 March, at https://www.chicagomag.com/city-life/march-2017/why-is-chicago-so-segregated/, accessed 01.12.2024.

National Center for Youth Law (2019), 'The Flores Settlement Agreement & Unaccompanied Children in Federal Custody' (briefing document), February, Oakland, CA: National Center for Youth Law.

Office of Refugee Resettlement (2024), 'Unaccompanied Children', Administration for Children and Families, U.S. Department of Health & Human Services, 22 January, at https://www.acf.hhs.gov/orr/programs/uc?utm_source=chatgpt.com, accessed 01.12.2024.

Painter, Nell Irvin (2011), *The History of White People*, New York: W. W. Norton & Company.
Paljor, Angelica (2022), 'The Sacred Work of Sandra Cisneros', *Lion's Roar*, 3 August, at https://www.lionsroar.com/the-sacred-work-of-sandra-cisneros/, accessed 01.12.2024].
Santana, Rebecca (2024), 'Migrant Families separated under Trump still feel the Fallout and they fear his Return to Office', Associated Press, 26 October, at https://apnews.com/article/election-family-separation-trump-immigration-zero-tolerance-ef77a181712149bb5edbd8dae4df4604, accessed 01.12.2024.
Taddonio, Patrice (2018), 'How the U.S. Fueled the Rise of MS-13', *Frontline*, 13 February, at https://www.pbs.org/wgbh/frontline/article/how-the-u-s-fueled-the-rise-of-ms-13/, accessed 01.12.2024.
Ulysios, Geethanjali Mar (2024), The author conducted the interview in Skokie, Illinois, on 13 November.
Walia, Harsha (2013), *Undoing Border Imperialism*, Chico, CA: AK Press.
Wiessner, Daniel (2024), 'Biden Administration wins Partial Nix of Court Pact on Child Migrant Detention', Reuters, 1 July, at https://www.reuters.com/legal/biden-administration-wins-partial-nix-court-pact-child-migrant-detention-2024-07-01/?utm_source=chatgpt.com, accessed 01.12.2024.
Wolfe, Patrick (1999), *Settler Colonialism and the Transformation of Anthropology: The Politics and Poetics of an Ethnographic Event*, London: Cassell.
Worsfeld, Matthew (2010), 'A Queer Ecclesiology', *Religion at the Margins*, 22 September, at http://religionatthemargins.com/2010/09/a-queer-ecclesiology/, accessed 01.12.2024.

# 17

# Queer Mary: A Reflection on Gender, Sexuality, Violence and Resistance in the Symbol of the Virgin in Latin America

GIOVANNA SARTO

## Introduction

A study of the Marian symbols[1] and their relations with Latin America is fundamental for those who wish to understand the memory of violence and actions of resistance in the formulation of religion, gender and sexuality forged in a territory ruled by coloniality. Researchers and theologians have drawn attention to and reflected on the intentionality of the arrangement of general and specific elements in these symbols in Latin American territory and the power effects of these arrangements. Many have insisted on the centrality of the statement that Marian symbols are not fixed and immutable but quite the opposite: they are a territory of dispute and are constantly being transformed. Recognizing this implies the possibility of also denouncing the fact that the interpretations attributed to them often contribute to reinforcing restrictive discourses that shape – and conform to – restrictive meanings of gender and sexuality, which are experienced in people's bodies and affect all spheres of social life. They teach, for example, that the 'good behaviour' or 'ideal behaviour' expected of women is that of submission, passivity and unrestricted servitude, which creates, reinforces and maintains inequalities inside and outside the religious space (Althaus-Reid, 2000; 2004; 2019; Azcuy, 2001; Gebara and Bingemer, 1989; Vuola, 1993).

However, interpretations that undermine spontaneity and the possibilities of (re)signifying gender and sexuality are not the only ones possible within the dispute over Marian symbols. The most spontaneous experiences can reveal stories about the diversity of sexual and theological behaviours, including transgressive ones. Recovering these stories is fundamental for a Queer Mariology committed to a radical liberation project.

In this sense this chapter can be used by scholars, Christians and/or the LGBTIQ+ community as a tool that can be helpful to reveal the unstable aspects of human relationships, articulating gender and sexuality as forms of power that are articulated in and through the Marian symbol, while at the same time establishing theoretical foundations for an in-depth evaluation of the sexual foundations that underpin religious symbols in general. My proposal will be on the following pages. My starting point is a story about the case of the symbol of Our Lady of Aparecida, recovering the disputes and tensions in Latin America to reflect on the Marian symbol from pragmatically less restrictive and potentially more liberating theological approaches, articulating gender and sexuality in an understanding that shifts the axis of Mary's symbolic meaning in the mystery of redemption.

## Counterpoint: A Black Virgin in a Samba Circle

Samba circle. Wednesday night. City of Aparecida do Norte. I was passing through as part of my research activities. It was the eve of 12 October, when we celebrate Brazil's patron saint – *Nossa Senhora de Aparecida* [Our Lady of Aparecida].

Our Lady of the Conception Aparecida – its official name – is one of more than two thousand names by which Mary is claimed. The term *Aparecida* – 'the one who appeared' – refers to the story of her apparition in 1717 and emphasizes devotion. Marcelo Pedro de Arruda (2005) points out that in the popular and official narrative, Aparecida is a black Mary who appears to black and impoverished fishermen in Brazil, deeply marked by the memory of enslavement, 'shackled for almost four hundred years to a brutal system of production and labor relations, discriminated because of their status as slaves and the color of their skin' (p. 26). From a symbol that initially gained strength among the poorest people in the inland region of São Paulo – in south-eastern Brazil – it gradually came to be celebrated and devoted to different parts of the country and Latin America. It is currently one of the most popular Marian symbols in the territory.

On that October evening the city was congested with pilgrims from all over the country, and all the restaurants and bars were crowded and festive. It was an area on the margins of the immense complex that today is home to the National Shrine of Aparecida. A group of seven women and five men gathered in the small bar, sharing music, beer and good laughs. In the centre a black lady was playing a tambourine. Next to her a black man complemented the rhythm by drumming on the bar's wooden table. It was an improvised samba circle. The lyrics were authored and spoke of devotion and love for 'Aparecida, holy woman, who guides the road and enchants me.' A woman took out of her pocket a small holy card of Our Lady of Aparecida and kissed it. In their way those people were experiencing a rich and engaging expression of devotion.

This situation may be unusual for a researcher or theologian unfamiliar with Marian devotion's presuppositions in Latin America. But for someone born and raised in a territory where samba was and is such a meaningful expression, particular experiences such as a samba dedicated to Aparecida fit into a broader framework of collective memory with deeper meanings. Historically, samba circles have been more than a cultural element; they have been spaces of collectivity and creativity, where the experiences of marginalized bodies are strengthened in a community that creates new possibilities for signifying the world together. For example, during Brazil's civil–military dictatorship (1964–85), samba circles were fundamental to express cultural resistance. They served as a mechanism for denouncing the order imposed by the violent regime (Almeida, 2024). It was through samba circles that marginalized populations, black people and sexual and gender dissidents transgressed the brutality of the dictators while remembering that life consistently breaks free of the rigidity of norms. Thus it was precisely for this reason that the military censored many of these spaces. They were spaces that called into question authoritarian and supposedly standard sexual, theological, social, political and economic systems because of the spontaneous and sincere communion of bodies and affections, shifting Marcella Althaus-Reid's (2019) reflection to my topic of interest, 'mixed the rights to pleasure' (p. 189). In this sense a samba to Aparecida is perhaps a good starting point for examining and drawing up reflections on the sexual assumptions of a more traditional reading of Marian symbols in Latin America, seeking to observe ambiguous elements that can be brought to the light of queer studies.

For context, it's important to situate my starting point and presuppositions. From a very early age, like hundreds of my Latin American sisters and brothers, my *existence* was shaped by Marian devotion. I choose the word *existence* – rather than religious experience – because in Latin America, devotion to Mary is not just an expression of faith and certainly not restricted to the Roman Catholic tradition. It is part of the most profound identity elements of women and men who grew up in a territory marked by a type of Christianity that was not only part of the colonial process but was also responsible for maintaining it. Devotion to Mary has been one of those ambiguous and complex keys that many people found to see between the cracks in the wardrobe of the colonial system other possibilities for understanding and giving significance to more spontaneous experiences that escape the rigour of officialdom. Through this devotion many women and men have also articulated their understandings of the body, affection and identity.

Notwithstanding, in my case, like that of many other Brazilian women, the devotion that ran through me was not for any representation of Mary. The Mary in question had a locality and a location: Aparecida – the black saint of the poor – was proclaimed queen and patron saint of Brazil, Our Lady of Aparecida. It is noteworthy that in the first chapter of *Deus Cuir* [The Queer God], Althaus-Reid (2019) makes a distinction between 'locality' and 'localization'. While 'locality' refers to the ideological/institutional/habitatal place of occupation and affiliation, the sexual geography that the theologian/he occupies, the second term, 'localization', is broader and refers to the system that organizes the location. In the words of the author:

> The locality is the event of bending the knee (in confessional act) and its special configuration; it is also the model of affectivity (or lack of) present in the church. And location is theology as a type of knowledge that orders these spaces of determination for the theologian and her love life. (Althaus-Reid, 2019, p. 30)

I was born into a Roman Catholic family in São Paulo. From my grandmother (the daughter of an enslaved black person) and my mother (a white immigrant woman from rural southern Minas Gerais) I inherited a cultural and religious habit that was quite common among the Roman Catholic women in my neighbourhood at the time: for several years in a row we would inevitably go on *excursões*[2] to the city of Aparecida to visit the *house of the Virgin*, as we called it, and to express devotion in front of the original statue that is on display at the end of the main corridor in the Aparecida National Sanctuary.

In the past, and even nowadays, there is always a characteristic mass of people taking over the main streets of the riverside city, which today is the municipality of Aparecida do Norte but which in the past used to be a small fishing village linked to the Province of Guaratinguetá. The mixture of smells, colours, sounds and people is remarkable: the smell of sweat, the river, fish, perfumes, candles, urine, fresh roses, hot coffee, blood, tears ... all mixed. From the city's edge you can experience samba circles dedicated to Our Lady of Aparecida. At the same time, from a distance you can see, on the highest hill, the immense beige and gold structure that houses the National Sanctuary.

During my childhood I did not realize the implications that devotion to Our Lady of Aparecida would have on me. I did not know about the Marian dogmas. Let us remember that in the context of the Christian faith, dogmas are irrevocable truths. Specifically for the Roman Catholic Church, dogmas have a normative and definitive character. According to the *Catechism of the Catholic Church* (Roman Catholic Church, 1994), dogmas are above even the authority of the Pope because they are understood as explicit, immutable and permanent doctrines revealed by God through the Bible, tradition or the clergy. That is an essential topic for those who venerate Our Lady of Aparecida. Rádio Aparecida (2020) instructs:

> The [Roman] Catholic Church proclaims the existence of many dogmas, with 43 being considered the most important. These are divided into eight different categories: dogmas about God, dogmas about Jesus Christ, dogmas about the creation of the world, dogmas about humanity, Marian dogmas, dogmas about the pope and the Church, dogmas about the sacraments, and dogmas about the last things.

At the time I did not even understand what hermeneutics was. Or pedagogy. I had not read the works of Ivone Gebara or Althaus-Reid. I did not understand the theoretical debates on class, race and gender. I was not familiar with queer studies, religious studies or theology. I had not read ethnography manuals that would have alerted me to the necessary precautions to avoid reproducing relations of domination to which social groups are subjected. However, I did know one thing: I had always been located much more at the bottom of the hill, among the people outside the institutional hierarchy, than at the top.

From a very early age I knew that the implications of my instabilities, such as my gender, my (bi)sexuality and my patched-up body, marked by the scars of the multiple surgeries I went through due to a congenital disability, would always be a problem for that structure at the top. That is because it was a structure that seemed to want to guarantee itself stability, cis-heteronormativity and perfection that I could never achieve. Which none of the women I knew could achieve. A place without a smell, I thought. Not down there. Down there was a place where people and samba could move freely. And in the freedom of each person's imperfection it was possible to create alternative readings of faith and devotion.

All these insights were taken to the next level when André Musskopf and Ana Ester Pádua Freire offered a course on Queer God in the Post-graduate Programme in Religious Studies at the Federal University of Juiz de Fora. It was in the second half of 2021 when I was still an MA student. That experience pushed me to revisit the reading of the symbol of the Virgin through the lens of Althaus-Reid's 'indecent theology'.

I first encountered a sincere, radical, critical and profound study of the Virgin's symbolic complexity in Latin America – particularly the tensions, disputes and effects of gender and sexuality – through Althaus-Reid's works like *Indecent Theology* (2000), 'When God is a Rich White Woman who does not Walk: The Hermeneutical Circle of Mariology in Latin America' (2004, pp. 30–43), *Deus Queer* (2019) and what she called 'indecency'. The author's use of the term 'virgin' was intended to denounce the construction of an idealistic sexual system that functioned as a violent model of behaviour and conduct, arbitrarily imposed on the women of the territory. This is a phenomenon that has occurred and is occurring in the maintenance of cis-heterosexual ideology, which consists of the suppression of authentic sexuality in the name of idolatrous sexuality. This idolatrous sexuality was constructed under a theological pretext based on the privileged experience of a primarily white, male and cis-heterosexual elite trained in colonial schools of thought, who see spontaneity as a threat because it destabilizes any pretence of stability.

Althaus-Reid hypothesized that the institutional power of the Christian church invested in transforming the symbol of Mary into a portrait of what colonialism wanted from enslaved peoples. This implied rejecting sexuality while at the same time hypervaluing virginity, associating it with an essentialist perspective of what it meant to be a 'true woman' in a context where women and children were and still are systematically raped, subjugated and exploited in the most violent ways. Placing virginity as a central theme and linked to a sign of sexual purity represented an attack on the vertical power of the divine mystery over human nature, which distorted the meaning that Mary had for the Christian faith in its origins and reduced the different interpretations to a single one, which came to mean a body separated from the flesh, a body without sex, a dismembered body (Córdova Quero, 2023).

Moreover Marian devotion is significant in the region, where the name conjures notions of chastity, elegance and nurturing motherhood. Mario Ribas (2006) makes the contention that this veneration has evolved into an instrument of female subjugation, perpetuating traditional roles and limiting women's agency. For Althaus-Reid (2000), the Marian symbol twisted by hegemonic theology has stigmatized the real experiences of all those who are dissidents, sweeping under the carpet the violence, damage and suffering that colonialism has caused and elaborating unrealistic sexual and gender assumptions. This system has been guaranteed, and continues to be guaranteed, due to a cis-heterosexual ideology built into a wardrobe that hides, or seeks to hide, all its perversions and indecencies while claiming a supposed consensus that is far from being consensual.

In the particular case involving the symbol of Our Lady of Aparecida, the issue observed by Althaus-Reid is further linked to Brazil's social and political context in the 1700s and 1800s. According to authors such as João Corrêa Machado (1976), José Oscar Beozzo (1984), Arruda (2005) and Pedro Carlos Cipolini (2010), devotion to the symbol of Our Lady of Aparecida gained ground in 1717, initially among poor fishing families, predominantly Roman Catholic laywomen. These people were responsible for naming the two-part broken statue of a dark bronze-coloured woman, which was found on the margins of the River Paraíba do Sul in the region of São Paulo. At the time, they chose the name *Aparecida*. It was, however, a time when the monarchical regime in Brazil was falling apart, and the local mercantile elites were beginning to have republican aspirations.

In the early years of devotion to Aparecida the image was passed from hand to hand within the community. Notably the symbol's dark colour was significant, evoking a unique sense of identity. This was especially meaningful in a predominantly black and impoverished community, still profoundly marked by the recent memory of slavery, where fishing served as the primary source of sustenance and trade. It did not take long for narratives that attributed supposed miracles to the symbol to begin to grow: from abundant fishing to cures for illnesses, protection, strength and care, Our Lady of Aparecida became a powerful symbol of the Roman Catholic tradition in the region (Corrêa Machado, 1976). Beozzo (1984) also points out that between 1717 and 1904 there was no consensus on the celebration dates of the symbol of Our Lady of Aparecida. Furthermore the title of queen and patron saint was also not part of the popular vocabulary of devotees, and the festivities were more spontaneous (Arruda, 2005; Cipolini, 2010).

Despite this the clerical hierarchy strongly invested in the symbol throughout this period. Before, the symbol's seal was in the hands of lay women and poor fishing families, but the authority – and discourse – over Our Lady of Aparecida was gradually shifted to the limits of institutionality. A specific place was set for the celebration, and the image no longer circulated from hand to hand but now remained within the confines of the Roman Catholic Church. The date of 12 October was established as the official day of the patron saint. The black statue was given a dark blue cloak with the flags of Brazil and the Vatican side by side. The image also received a golden crown representing the Portuguese crown.

Arruda's (2005) central thesis is that this transformation meant, especially in the transition from the Brazil Empire to the Brazil Republic, when Our Lady of Aparecida was proclaimed queen and patron saint of Brazil, the Roman Catholic triumph over the secular world at a time when the political and economic elites were rearranging themselves. I would even dare to say that this triumph only happened because the symbol of the Virgin in Latin America was already, as we have seen, a symbol that captured notions of gender and sexuality that were functional to coloniality and had been incorporated into common sense by then. In this regard the capture and conformation of the symbol of Our Lady of Aparecida was not strange.

## A Maria Who Sambas Among Us

Nevertheless, even when presumed stability exists, something invariably seems to elude the control and rigidity of an authoritarian theological narrative. Despite extensive efforts to regulate what, where and how the Marian symbol is discussed and celebrated, it remains profoundly influential among laypeople – in bars, in samba circles and both within and beyond the boundaries of traditional theology.

André Musskopf (2005) reflected on the existence of a gap in the wardrobe. For him, using Althaus-Reid's reflection in depth, the valorization of sexual histories and dissident experiences can bring to light discomforts and areas of tension. Althaus-Reid believed that these areas of tension could destabilize the economy and racial structures of suppression of subjectivities around official constructions in theology, including elaborations such as the symbol of the Virgin (Althaus-Reid, 2000, p. 65). In this sense, just like a samba circle dedicated to the symbol of a black Mary by impoverished black people on the margins of the National Sanctuary dedicated to her, for example, some popular expressions of devotion seem to have the potential to fit into a broader phenomenon of popular spirituality that can be useful for recovering aspects of indecency in the symbol of the Virgin. 'Popular spiritualities are not just sexual dissidence but are sometimes an elaborate and complex symbology designed to help people deal with the aberrations of heterosexual systems' (Althaus-Reid, 2019, p. 21).

However, unlike the reference to the white, wealthy, passive virgin who does not walk, the case I have taken here is a counterpart: Our Lady of Aparecida does not seem to be just a symbol that expresses a faith designed to help people deal with the 'aberrations of heterosexual systems' but, beyond that, it can be articulated as a complex that sometimes escapes the onslaughts and attempts to capture it by hegemonic power. In popular devotion, individual and collective experiences are integrated. Together, it teaches, always in an ambiguous and sometimes contradictory way, among other things, notions of rebellion, social justice, economy, community, race, body, gender and sexuality that can be positive when brought to the light of queer studies under the commitment of a radical liberation project.

As Althaus-Reid (2004) herself pointed out: 'The everyday lives of people always provide us with a starting point for a process of doing a contextual theology without exclusions, in this case without the exclusion of sexuality struggling in the midst of misery' (p. 4).

Especially in a Brazil that is still strongly marked by poverty, inequality and the maintenance of the ideology of the racial and cultural inferiority of black, indigenous and mestizo populations, a legacy of the colonial and slave-owning processes, a saint like Aparecida can represent an interpretative turn of a Marian symbol that is no longer that of the rich, passive, white European woman who doesn't walk, but that of a black Brazilian woman who frequents samba circles and who, on the margins of officialdom, helps people to elaborate meanings of resistance and rebellion. This Maria can denounce – announce – that the most spontaneous theological meanings are forged mainly from the experiences of the devotees' and/or theologians' bodies: bodies that become queer by admitting their presuppositions and opening up their ambiguities; bodies that overlap, intersect and therefore claim equally intersectional hermeneutics: queer hermeneutics.

By queer hermeneutics in studies of Marian symbols I mean one that is necessarily diasporic because so is the body of the theologian and/or researcher. According to Althaus-Reid (2019, p. 25), a diasporic hermeneutic is continually getting to know, deconstructing, constructing and exploring issues related to gender, sexuality, class and race at the 'crossroads of Christianity'. The challenge here is that shifting the axis and our starting point takes courage. We need to rebel against boundaries and upset the order of our theological, sexual, economic and social systems.

Putting the sexual presuppositions of these more traditional readings of Marian symbols under suspicion means touching on a range of silences not generally dealt with and observing who has benefited from them. It means going to the roots of the more traditional readings, valuing above all elements of freedom, strangeness and nonconformity, even if this means renouncing the wardrobes they have created. It means opening up the possibility of seeing beyond them.

However, it is not enough to go beyond. Tina Beattie (2007) states that for those dissidents who:

> have played no part in the history of Mariology but who find themselves bodily inscribed within its war-like discourse, the task of liberating theological symbols is complex and multi-dimensional. It requires going beyond the systematized domain of Mariology itself, in order to construct an alternative theological narrative which draws on different aspects of the Marian tradition. (p. 295)

In this task of deconstruction and reconstruction, one possible path is to use the tool of indecency to question theology and hegemonic power drawing on the potential of lived experience. It means sambaing with Mary and, in body-to-body friction, allowing other possibilities of devotion, theology, gender, sex and life to emerge. Because in the end, a queer hermeneutic comes about like this: despite the attempted capture of officialdom, between theological-sexual experiences that experience God (and Mary) as 'queer'; that is, 'as a disturbing presence with the potential to disrupt the order of our systems' (Beattie, 2007, p. 294).

## Some Final Considerations

To investigate a Marian symbol, whatever it may be, from a dissident, queer perspective is to enter into a complex and tangled sexual system that has been articulated and interpreted for centuries by white, cis-heterosexual men, generally linked to the priestly hierarchy of the Roman Catholic Church. This priestly hierarchy has operated – or at least tried to operate – the symbol of the Virgin in an idealistic, decent way, from a cis-heterosexual ideology capable of creating truths conditioned by cultural, political, social and moral factors in different times, cultures and societies, whose meaning can and has been used to defend and sustain a binary and restrictive sex-gender system. A supposedly sexless, odourless, colourless Virgin. A perfect and uniform model for a wholly imperfect and heterogeneous reality. By establishing this model as an ideal, systematic violence has been reinforced, especially against those who dissent from the hegemonic model. In Latin America, Althaus-Reid reminds us of the damaging effects that an authoritarian and colonizing construction of the Virgin had and how it functioned as a simulacrum to guarantee and keep under control a system of exploitation that even today has left a legacy of daily rape, deprivation of liberty, abandonment, exploitation and misery.

But where hegemonic power strikes, there is also resistance. Such resistance happens between the lines of life despite the officialdom, in the most spontaneous and intimate experiences. For this reason, thinking about the relationship between the Marian symbol and humanity, rather than the Marian symbol and theology, can be a valuable invitation to shift the axis of our analyses towards a radical examination of the sexual presuppositions behind the interpretations of religious symbols.

For queer hermeneutics radically committed to an actual project of liberation it is essential to recover sexual-theological histories that may have gone unnoticed; it is crucial to assume creativity and mutability as fundamental keys to theological exercise. It is a hermeneutics that is born in the ground, that sprouts like a seed, that is always under construction and deconstruction because it is, in the end, a hermeneutics made in our body and by our body, with all its imperfections and ambiguities, with all the memories and stories that are ours but which are also those of others, and which we tell and retell every day because that is how we have learned to survive: in the cracks.

As the many Marias appear, many Black women in Brazil preserve the memory of their pain and reveal the strength of a transgressive narrative – or *indecent*, if we adopt Althaus-Reid's term. A dissident virgin who has sex, who smells and who is coloured. She inhabits samba circles and communicates, together with her companions, other possibilities for experiencing the body, sex, religion, economics and politics.

Finally, it's important to emphasize that Aparecida is just one possible example, and perhaps a pedagogical one, to help us understand that the Marian symbol's indecency – or queerness – can be found in the recognition that any symbolic language is an unstable complex that operates in different ways, from different intentions and understandings. For this very reason it is subject to subversion and tension.

For a Queer Mariology it is crucial to recognize that the most sincere and transgressive hermeneutics take place simultaneously with, and are complementary to, a larger structure, penetrating the cracks in the priestly hierarchy and denouncing the limits of the more authoritarian dynamics that impose themselves on life and relationships. In this sense it opens up the possibility of using queer as a tool that nourishes and inspires sexual and gender dissidents to dare to find in the cracks of dominant positions other strategies for elaborating religious symbols, whether they are Marian symbols or not. Ultimately it is a radical, sincere and courageous call for redemption, which lays bare the 'decent' assumptions of patriarchal ecclesiastical power while recovering many vital elements that escape the control of officialdom.

## *Notes*

1 I have chosen to use the term 'Marian symbols' to refer to the plurality of communications and representations of Mary mentioned in the works of feminist theologians without going into the model of the Virgin criticized by many of them, which I will refer to later (Vuola, 1993; Azcuy, 2001; Althaus-Reid, 2000; 2004; 2019).

2 In the Brazilian context, *excursão* is the word used, in popular terms, to refer to long walks or family recreational outings, which may or may not be led by a guide. Excursions are typical on religious holidays, especially among poor and/or middle-class families.

## References

Almeida, Cleiton França de (2024), '(Re)Invenções do Corpo na Irredutível Liminaridade do Samba: A teoria Cuíca', *Revista Brasileira de Estudos da Presença* 14, no. 1, e131996.

Althaus-Reid, Marcella (2000), *Indecent Theology: Theological Perversions in Sex, Gender and Politics*, London: Routledge.

Althaus-Reid, Marcella (2004), *From Feminist Theology to Indecent Theology*, London: SCM Press.

Althaus-Reid, Marcella (2019), *Deus Queer*, translated by Flavio Conrado, Río de Janeiro, RJ/Brasília, DF: Metanoia/Novos Diálogos.

Arruda, Marcelo Pedro de (2005), 'Triunfo Católico no Calendário Republicano: N.S. Aparecida no Calendário Secular (1930–1980)', doctoral dissertation, Universidade de São Paulo.

Azcuy, Virginia Raquel (2001), 'El lugar teológico de las mujeres', *Proyecto* 13, no. 39 (May-August), pp. 11–34.

Beozzo, José Oscar (1984), 'A Igreja entre a Revolução de 1930, o Estado Novo e a Redemocratização (1945)', in *História Geral da Civilização Brasileira, Tomo III: O Brasil Republicano, Volumen 11: Economia e Cultura (1930–1964)*, edited by Fausto Boris, São Paulo, SP: DIFEL, pp. 337–422.

Beattie, Tina (2007), 'Queen of Heaven', in *Queer Theology: Rethinking the Western Body*, edited by Gerard Loughlin, Malden, MA: Blackwell Publishing, pp. 293–304.

Cipolini, Pedro Carlos (2010), 'A devoção mariana no Brasil', *Teocomunicação* 40, no. 1 (January-April), pp. 36–43.

Córdova Quero, Hugo (2023), *Teologías Queer Globales*, St. Louis, MO: Institute Sophia Press.

Corrêa Machado, João (1976), *Aparecida na história e na literatura*, 2 volumes, Campinas, SP: Gráfica Editora.

Gebara, Ivone and Maria Clara Bingemer (1989), *Mary, Mother of God, Mother of the Poor*, Maryknoll, NY: Orbis Books.

Musskopf, André Sidnei (2005), *Uma brecha no armário: Propostas para uma teologia gay* [A Gap in the Closet: Proposals for a Gay Theology], São Paulo, SP: CEBI.

Rádio Aparecida (2020), 'O que é e quantos são os dogmas de fé?', A12 Rádio

Aparecida, 14 December, at https://www.a12.com/radio/noticias/o-que-e-e-quantos-sao-os-dogmas-de-fe , accessed 01.12.2024.

Ribas, Mario (2006), 'Liberating Mary, Liberating the Poor', in *Liberation Theology and Sexuality*, edited by Marcella Althaus-Reid, Aldershot: Ashgate, pp. 123–35.

Roman Catholic Church (1994), *Catechism of the Catholic Church*, London: Geoffrey Chapman.

Vuola, Elina (1993), 'La Virgen María como ideal femenino, su crítica feminista y nuevas interpretaciones', *Revista Pasos* 45 (January-February), pp. 11–20.

# 18

# Into Queer Silence: Resisting the Theological Voice

ZACCARY HANEY

Theological disciplines in higher education – at least in the United States – seem to be facing a crisis. Even colleges and universities with religious affiliation have cut or folded into other departments their programmes of theology and religion. My alma mater – a Roman Catholic liberal arts college in the US Midwest – has not filled positions as senior faculty members retire, has rejected tenure to younger theology faculty, and is maintaining only the faculty necessary to meet its theology requirements. Theology becomes a window dressing, a marketing tactic, a conveyor belt of academic obligation that seems to contribute little to educational curricula and students' professional goals. In response to this crisis, some recent analyses have reasserted theology's connection to the Western European history of the university, stating that a university education lacking theology seems almost unimaginable (Faggioli, 2024). However, the tenuous relationship between theology and the university is not new. 'Distorted formation', the US black theologian Willie James Jennings (2020) reminds us, 'has been with Western education for centuries' (p. 5). Recognizing this, some have encouraged theologians 'to make a leap to new institutional forms' with reference to Christianity's eschatological vision (Smith, 2023, p. 15). Others have suggested that we take up theology's university setting as the subject of theological analysis, particularly regarding how the university and its forces impact what we do and how we do it (Tonstad, 2020). All seem to agree that something needs to be done about how theology is done.

Professionalized theologians[1] often lament the existence of 'distorted' or 'bad' theologies and their impact on the world, arguing that we must figure out how to do theology 'better'. The US queer theologian Hanna Reichel (2023, p. 5) argues that theologians typically ignore other vital questions that arise in light of this argument. What is a bad theology, and how do we know? If theology is – at least according to its name

– discourse on or speech about God, how can one conclude what is good or bad speech about God? Theologians often agree that theology is more than words we say or write since 'theology is not a noun, but a verb'. Theology is something we *do*, not something that *is*. It is not, therefore, simply good or bad; theology can be done poorly or well, so we can do it better. How, then, do we *do* theology better? What does it look like to do a good or bad theology? What does theology hope to do? What does it mean to do theology at all? If we do need to do theology better, then for whom? And how?

Liberation theologians have defined theology as a praxis that helps build a more just, equitable, free and loving world, modelled on the example of Jesus' activity and ministry in the world with specific reference to a preferential option for the poor. The twentieth-century Spanish Jesuit and liberation theologian Jon Sobrino (1996) has written that 'in terms of primacy of the poor, the need for a praxis in [*sic*] behalf of the Reign [of God] is evident ... It is in practice that we learn what generates hope in the poor' (p. 64). Suppose theology is understood first and foremost as a praxis of liberation. In that case it must seek out those persons, communities, even regions and nations that have long suffered under various, unique and intersecting forms of oppression, discrimination and marginalization. The goal has been to create a more just, equitable, free and loving world through the addition of a more significant number of voices from oppressed and marginalized communities, which proposes to help resolve, correct or at least counterbalance the dominance of a white, Western European, cis-heterosexual and male voice within theology. Kwok Pui-lan (2021), a postcolonial feminist theologian from Hong Kong, questions the formation of theological speech itself and how theology students are formed within structures that continue to favour some experiences and perspectives over others even when those departments claim to be liberative in the way that Sobrino describes. She writes that although much has changed in how theology is taught since her graduate studies in the 1970s, she is not confident that white theological institutions have developed the ability to teach outside their Western European structures. Even if those whose access had previously been restricted receive invitations to professionalized academic theology, she argues that it is still the case that 'students need to acquire the white tongue of theology and learn the intricacy of its grammar before they can speak *theologically*' (p. 1008; emphasis in the original). While there is something wrong with how we do theology, this is bound up with how we form students to speak. Therefore the structure of theological speech and what it proposes to do are the concerns of this chapter. I understand theological speech and discourse as primarily a performative utterance, a form of speech that hopes to do or to accomplish something. The voices may all sound different but the goal of a speech about God often remains the same. We rely on authoritative speech, with a touch of social magic, to compel the divine to arrive among us in a way that lines up according to our desires, a God who is the God we already know to be true. In other words, theology has an impulse to the familiar that risks reinforcing the structures that liberative theologies – especially queer and postcolonial theologies – at their best critique.

The question is not whether we can improve the theology we are already doing. It is not whether we can speak of God 'better' if we mean in a more liberative, more freeing or more loving way. If 'to do theology' is to make prescriptive and normative determinations of who God is and who God is not, then doing this better reproduces only what has already been said and established as obviously true. I suggest we consider Christian mystical and monastic traditions, especially where there has been resistance to normative and prescriptive discourse. Although I recognize that reliance on these traditions does little to dislodge the dominance of certain voices and may cause us to think that the Christian tradition itself will 'save us', this is not my intent. Mysticism and monasticism contain an impulse of silence regarding normativized structures and epistemologies. We look for texts and persons who, in their way, reflect this resistance not as perfect fixes but as guidance through distorted theological formation. If theology will continue to have a place in the university, then it may not be through a reproductive style of teaching that asserts to students who God is and who God is not. Suppose it will offer a critical presence that appears to be so desperately needed today in religious, cultural, political and social discourse. In that case the discipline needs not more professionalized talk about God but a pedagogical silence.

Theologians, our work and those whom we address may be better off when we listen, becoming more chroniclers of the divine than we are its arbiters. In the end I turn to the twelfth-century English Cistercian abbot, Aelred of Rievaulx (1110–67),[2] who has been noted for his uniqueness within the Cistercian tradition and in the larger Benedictine tradition for his discussions of human friendship as a metaphor for our relationship with the divine (Henn, 1979). He places a unique value on creative dialogue with his students and monks. Unlike the *Rule of St Benedict* (written in the sixth century), which states that the 'student' ought to incline their ear to the 'teacher' (Benedict of Nursia, 1980), Aelred flips this pedagogical model and writes that the teacher must open their attentive ear to the words, insights and questions of the student.

Aelred has particular ideas of friendship and God, but these become less important than his dialogue partner's concepts, images and arguments – theologies. Together, but beginning with the student's experiences, they determine who God is and how God is experienced. Likewise the theologian can allow the 'student', those for whom we think we need to do better theology, to speak, to open their ears to the student and encounter the God who already exists within the lives of those desperately seeking liberation. However, it is this God that arrives.

## Should the Theologian Speak?

The dominance of certain theological texts and the voices they carry has suggested a strange universality: because of their 'classic' status (Tracy, 1987, p. 102) they are deemed closer to 'truth' than texts and perspectives considered more contextually grounded. A 'classic' text or voice appears to be a trans-cultural text. Elevated to heightened status are those writings, ways of knowing, images and narratives of the divine that reproduce precisely what has come before. Anything else can be ancillary at best if not dismissed and ignored altogether. The US queer minister and writer Cassidy Hall (2024) has recently written that this kind of silencing is 'toxic' insofar as it 'causes harm, shame, minimization, and damage to our world' (p. 42). Liberation theologies, however, raise voices from marginalized positions historically peripheral to theological discourse. These voices contain a kernel of liberation that theology desperately needs, and in adding their experiences to theological discourse, these groups and communities likewise contribute to their liberation. Suppose Kwok (2021) is correct in her diagnosis that theology and theological education remain entrenched in whiteness, patriarchy and cis-heteronormativity. In that case it is the 'theological formation' itself that must be critically examined. Can liberation theologians – especially subaltern theologians – speak theologically from the experiences of those most needing liberation?

Recall, for instance, the US feminist theologian Elizabeth Johnson's (1992) primary argument that 'the symbol of God functions'. How we talk about God matters for how we structure our societies, politics, communities, churches and academic spaces, and even how we understand ourselves concerning them. Far from wanting to suppress the male voice of theological disciplines, Johnson uses the argument of negation that expresses the absolute mystery of the divine to assert that theological discourse ought to have an expansion of metaphors for God. It is not in silencing voices but in an increase in the variety of divine names that liberation is possible: 'Language is informed by the particularity of women's experience carried in the symbol. Women thereby become a new specific channel for speaking about God ... so that the community of disciples may move toward a more liberating life' (Johnson, 1992, p. 47). The male voice of theology must be diminished but it is also retained, persisting alongside and balanced out by the growth of other less dominant images and metaphors. Adding voices to established discourse, the suggestion goes, leads inevitably to the liberation of these communities.

This is an understandable response to decades and centuries of suppression of the experiences and voices of various groups that has led to the exaggerated importance of some experiences over others, especially those voices that align most closely with what is imagined to be the white, Western European, cis-heterosexual, male voice of theology. Subjectivity and freedom of the subaltern and marginalized are often bound up with the ability to speak for and about oneself, especially among queer persons whose experience of 'coming out' is an announcement of the self to the world, and thus, according to the US queer and crip theorist J. Logan Smilges (2022, pp. 35–6), crucial for one's liberation. However, does adding a significant number of marginalized voices to discourse already taking place produce the kind of liberation it claims to produce? And if so, what kind of freedom is this? Is it possible that one may be opened up to new forms of oppression and marginalization in announcing oneself and using one's voice? Smilges (p. 213) likewise observes in their recent work on queer silence that keeping quiet and not 'coming out' may sometimes prevent oppression, which may be favourable where there is an even greater threat.

Speaking from one's position can help establish subjectivity and authority in social and political spaces. It can provide the coherence of identity and even help uncover how one has been embedded within oppressive and marginalizing structures, both as the 'victim' of marginalization and, at times, as a complicit agent. Hall (2024) thus writes that 'Voicing queerness has allowed me to recognize my silent acceptance of patriarchy more quickly, the subliminal disguise of heteronormativity, hidden Eurocentricity, and internalized capitalistic views that move me away from interdependence' (p. 43). Giving voice to our own experiences of ourselves, the world and the divine, conditioned as these are within the settings of power and dominance, can indeed be a move towards the liberation of ourselves from them, from our complicity with them. They will provide a platform to build new epistemologies, ways of understanding the world, and even social, political and ecclesial structures uniquely inflected by our experiences.

Pamela Lightsey (2015) – a US queer womanist theologian and pastor – urges young black lesbians and other queer persons of colour to study theology, noting that even church communities change for the better when these persons contribute to spaces already noisy with white, straight cis-men. The church, she adds, needs to learn from the experiences of the marginalized. As Lightsey writes: 'Exploring the lives of any culture is good and necessary work. We need to learn from the experience of lesbian, bisexual, transgender, and queer Black women how the church has been helpful and hurtful' (p. 2). Institutional conversion begins when those previously prevented from accessing authoritative positions are in this discourse. She continues:

> We also need to discover how we as scholars can help train a new generation of clergy and faculty to affirm LGBTQ [*sic*] persons as people whom God loves as they live out their lives as same gender loving persons. (Lightsey, 2015, pp. 2–3)

The immediate benefit of this is obvious, though we should not limit our work to affirmation and validation within an already established system.

All of these efforts, we hope, will result in greater inclusion for LGBTIQ+ persons, among other groups to whom access has historically been restricted, within ecclesial and academic spaces. Where this is done, according to Hall, Christian institutions are often forced to confront their often horrific histories of colonization, their failure and 'refusal to honor and elevate the leadership and dignity of women, people of color, refugees, people with disabilities, and people from other marginalized communities' (2024, p. 43). And yes, speaking from a positionality of marginalization can and ought to be a liberating action for the marginalized. It should even be liberating for those institutions themselves, whether academic or ecclesial, to release themselves from their colonial, cis-heterosexist and patriarchal structures and the perpetuation of these histories. Lightsey, however, also writes that we must be attentive to the kind of language and labels we use from within queer communities: 'Language is a powerful resource, and we must always consider how it influences and is influenced by our social locations' (2015, p. 13). Giving language and words to our experiences can be liberating, but Lightsey continues: 'We may debate the viability of LGBTQ [*sic*] lexicons internal to community expressions' (p. 13). Are there expressions that may be improper – that is, unviable – for the purpose of queer liberation within theological discourse? Are there restrictions on the kinds of words, vocabularies and grammars that can be used within theological disciplines? Do these place restrictions on the divine itself?

Kwok (2021) notes that historically there have been limits to the kind of reflection made possible within a theological education. If we aim to train more marginalized persons to speak theologically and within the established discourse, are these limits ever indeed lifted? How are theologians 'trained' to speak about God? What sources and texts are deemed acceptable within this training, or at least elevated to the kind of significance required for 'doing' theology? And even where scholars are trained within 'contextual' forms of theology (already a peripheral field, as it fails to measure up to the so-called universality of other fields), does this automatically promise these scholars, especially those from marginalized positions, access to any of the discourses, including classrooms, outside of their immediate positionality as 'marginalized'? These persons are often seen as 'diversity hires', intended to fill identitarian gaps within theology or religion departments. They get relegated to only teaching courses that align most closely with that marginalized identity. As Kwok (2021) argues:

> Once a person's career is boxed in such a way, it can be limiting because she or he is supposed to work in a particular archive of knowledge and always speak from a certain designated 'perspective.' And there is hypervigilance to check if the person is black enough, Asian enough, or queer enough. (p. 1008)

The invitation to marginalized persons to, finally, *speak* for themselves about experiences of God may in some ways be liberating, but liberation is not a linear progression that is always granted to those speaking; they may yet run into other limitations.

The title of Kwok's article, 'Can the Native Speak Theologically?', indicates these limitations with its echoing of Gayatri Chakravorty Spivak's (1988) foundational article in postcolonial thought, 'Can the Subaltern Speak?' The answer for Spivak was that the subaltern cannot speak without relinquishing what it means to be the subaltern. If they were to try speaking from their position, then they could not be understood within the dominant structure. To insert oneself within the dominant discourses of theology one must learn to approximate (to the greatest extent possible) the 'white tongue' of theology, the 'straight tongue', the 'cis tongue', the 'male tongue' that has characterized theological work for the last several centuries. To begin addressing this the theologian must take an approach similar to the US queer theologian Linn Marie Tonstad's (2020, p. 505): to examine the very structures within which our discipline is situated, for we do not remain untouched by these governmental, educational and economic pressures. Beyond the university structures in which theological discourse finds itself, although this analysis is also necessary, we must analyse the structures of speech and discourse that allow theologians to obtain any authority. What does it mean to *speak theologically* from a professionalized stance? What does it mean to *do* professionalized theology?

There is no real difference between speaking and doing regarding professionalized theological discourse. The emphasis that liberation theologians have placed on speaking – as an inevitably liberating act – tends to ignore that speech, like anything else that human beings do, is an act that we do to someone or something; that is, speech has an object. Theology is a performative utterance, which is to say that it is an attempt at making, doing or accomplishing something as opposed to simply describing it (Austin, 2018, pp. 6–7). Although theology may often hide how its discourse is prescriptive, suggesting instead that its task is only to describe how the divine comes into the world, it is more often the case that theologians speak prescriptively about who God is and who God can be. For instance, liberation theologies intend to create conditions for a more just, equitable, free and loving world. We do this by critiquing the structures in which we already do our work and by demonstrating the oppression and marginalization within political and social spaces, with particular regard for race, ethnicity, gender, sexuality, disability and socio-economic status and by proposing more liberative images of an all-loving God. We hope that theological utterances themselves will – perhaps magically – *do* the work of liberating.

Underlying every speech act is the hope that such an act will do what it proposes – shaping objects – through the authorization of social magic that allows the efficacy of some speech acts over others insofar as the speech act has met particular specifications that would enable it to be successful (Austin, 2018, pp. 12–15). These specifications can take the form of proper use of grammar following a prescribed ritual text. Speech acts become successful when uttered by someone who has attained social, political and, in our case, theological authority. For theologians, this today means acquiring specific kinds of theological training and sometimes the conferral of ecclesiastical authority (Bourdieu, 1991, p. 223). Through various ways of speaking, especially reproductive and ritualistic repetition, the professionalized theologian proposes to do what they say they do. Theological speech tries to be efficacious and generative of the divine as something material that has a real effect within and on the world. To speak *about* God, especially from a position of authority, is to speak *like* God (Butler, 2021, pp. 50–1). The promise of liberation, more often celebrated than questioned, may be crueller than we would like to admit. Although a speech act requires some object that can be moulded and shaped, God is not an object (Tonstad, 2020, p. 495).

Trained theologians claim a magical social authority that allows us to call upon God – as a strange object – to arrive in a specific manner that is 'familiar' to us; that is, we claim to bring into existence the very thing that we name in our discourse. We dictate who this God is or who God can be, hoping that this is the God we will encounter. We desperately desire that God arrives according to what feels most comfortable and affirming for us, and we assert that this is the God that we have – loving, queer, on the side of the oppressed. God could be nothing else. The impulse of speech to shape its object according to what is familiar allows us to treat God as 'obvious', lacking the potential to arrive otherwise. Familiarizing discourses force certain things – objects – to take the shape of something so familiar or evident that they escape our attention, including critical attention by scholars, limiting their disruptive potential. The queer and feminist theorist Sara Ahmed (2006) has examined this trend with particular regard to race and ethnicity, noting that some racialized persons disrupt spaces that historically have been orientated towards specific kinds of bodies. While the bodies – for whom these spaces are orientated – are 'familiar' within the space, those that fall outside of this familiarity drag across it; they feel the weight of their body, as do the rest of us (p. 121). Having become an object, God 'fits in', no longer gets noticed. The hope for a liberative voice is the problem that ought to be addressed since it is this hope that conditions the desire of the theologian, and through the speech act of theology, this theologian compels the 'arrival' of the divine (p. 127).

My central concern is this desire for familiarity, and our words work to ensure it. The oftentimes uncritical stance of adding more voices to theological discourse, in our eagerness to achieve this kind of linguistic liberation that is promised, may inadvertently cover up forms of theological discourse that continue to be oppressive. God becomes some 'thing' that no longer needs to be examined. God functions in the background of life, as an everyday object, and as commonly as the desk and chair I use to write this chapter. God is called upon to 'arrive' as an object. However, God is certainly not one, within a space that is always orientated towards a particular idea of who or what God is – God *is* love, God *is* liberator, God *is* queer – and anything otherwise is either ignored, rejected, 'compelled' into a familiar orientation to not cause a disruption. The God of the oppressor hides under the skirts of the theologian's pleasant and desirable utterances, turning God into an object that can be compelled in one direction or another, who can become familiarized and who loses all disruptive power. The familiar

God may not be the one who looks like the white, cis-hetero, male God that liberation, postcolonial and queer theologies critique, but instead may be the one who has been compelled through our discourse always to be the all-loving, queer God, covering up and ignoring how God arrives to the contrary.

## Listening for Divine Arrival

Aelred of Rievaulx provides one possible approach to this invisible problem of theological utterance through his dialogical method. My proposal is not that Aelred's pedagogical style of listening and dialogue will inevitably allow us to do theology 'better'. However, I do argue that it gives us guidance for doing theology differently, with particular attention to how some have described Aelred's dialogue as empathetic. His affective method in pedagogy has often been noted for its uniqueness even among his twelfth-century Cistercian peers to explain how God relates to us as human persons. This is to say that the experience of God, as the Cistercian scholar Elizabeth Freeman (2002) has written, 'is sought through the experiences *of* others and through experiences *with* others' (p. 14; emphasis in the original). Thus Aelred prays: 'you and I are here and we hope that the Christ will be between us' (2010, 1.1). God arrives between us, anywhere that relations between persons take place. To be attentive to these kinds of arrivals, however, means that the professionalized theological utterance must decrease in volume.

After a prologue in which Aelred describes his commitments to friendship, he turns to a dialogue that begins with a short anecdote from a visit that he made to Wardon Abbey, a neighbouring daughter house of Rievaulx:

> Not long ago while I was relaxing among a crowd of brothers, on every side everyone was adding to the din. One was questioning and another debating. One was raising questions about Scripture, another about ethics, a third about the vices, and a fourth about the virtues. You alone were silent. Suddenly raising your head in the group, as you were about to add some remark, your voice seemed to stick in your throat. Then lowering your head, you fell silent. (1.2)

Aelred takes notice of the monk Ivo, who has grown quiet amid the noise of the rest of the brothers but is unable to speak even when he desires to do so. J. Stephen Russell (2012) argues that this scene sets an empathetic tone for Book One of the treatise, which would also resound through the second two books. Aelred initiates a 'duet' in which he and Ivo articulate relational and theological truths together (Russell, 2012, p. 51). He invites Ivo into this dialogue, not condescendingly but out of an interest in the monk's insights and questions. Ivo has a distaste for large crowds and prefers a one-on-one, intimate meeting. Aelred thus writes: 'Yes, most beloved, open your heart now and pour whatever you please into the ears of a friend' (2010, 1.1). A few lines later the abbot of Rievaulx restates his purpose and invitation, recognizing his monk's capacity for knowing, teaching and indeed for learning: 'Share with a friend all your thoughts and cares, that you may have something either to learn or to teach, to give and to receive, to pour out and drink in' (1.4).

At the opening of their dialogue, Aelred has to convince Ivo of the worth of his idea and the value of his thoughts and questions. The tone that he takes demonstrates a slight departure from what is typically expected of the abbot according to the *Rule of St Benedict*, or at least an openness to how one might interpret the *Rule* (La Corte, 2017, p. 69). While in the *Rule* the abbot takes the place of the authoritative teacher, here the abbot is a learner alongside his monks, nurturing their thoughts and opinions instead of authoritatively compelling them towards his own. Aelred's model of authority can remind us that the persons we want so desperately to liberate through the right words and better ways of doing theology already have their understandings of who God is that may not – or indeed may – line up with what we desire to be true. Theology, therefore, may look different if we, like Aelred, adopt a stance of listening empathetically to how the divine already arrives in the lives of those around us. The professionalized theologian, resisting the temptation of authoritative speech, crafts descriptions of the divine presence in the lives of the marginalized and oppressed that are then used to respond to the conditions of oppression of which God is often – though not always – a part.

According to Grace Jantzen (2001), theologians need to listen to and feel out the contours of the divine, the contours that are queer, that follow the very curves and shapes of the human body and of all of creation. These contours, for Jantzen, constantly affirm diversity and difference; they value the marginalized and oppressed, and they always resist the structures of dominance – white supremacy, cis-heterosexism and colonialism. Of course, we ought not to ignore how accurate and true these contours are. However, the contours of the divine cannot all look the same, especially in the lives of those for whom we seek liberation. It is the responsibility of the theologian who seeks liberation for any group to attend to how we *do* our craft and perpetuate the underlying structures that allow for racialized, gendered, sexualized and socio-economic forms of oppression. Taking up this responsibility, inspired by the silent empathy of the listening ear, we theologians are confronted by how our very speech and attempts to orientate the divine in specific ways cover up how and when God does not arrive on the side of the marginalized, reminding us that God may arrive on the side of the oppressor (Williams, 2013, p. 20).

Theologians cannot encounter this God until we have taken a step back, have reduced our speech to – at most – a whisper and have developed a sense for listening and feeling attentively to how the divine moves through the contours of human life in both the good and the bad, as the oppressed and as the oppressor. The theologian who accepts silence as a methodology in what we *do* and how we teach does not, however, sit idly by waiting for others to dominate the conversation. A chronicler of the divine arrival does more than simply uncritically argue the value of whatever arrives. Allowing marginalized individuals – non-professionals – to speak, even in unviable ways, about their experiences of God will help us recognize how God, even as an *oppressor*, is intimately woven into the materiality of life – a God to whom theologians must respond, rather than reject or ignore. Listening and chronicling offer an opportunity for the theologian to craft a response to the God who is there, already felt materially on the side of the oppressed or even on the side of the oppressor. When we listen, touch, feel and taste, taking pleasure in wandering and stumbling around through a dark room (Boquet, 2017, p. 186), directed only by the thoughts and words of the one next to us who alone knows the path through their own experiences, we begin to liberatively sense the who, the what, the where, the when and the how of the divine arrival. To become silent means we wait attentively, listening to our students' experiences, knowledge and desires, for the arrivals of the divine. To do theology 'better' and renew our place in the university may require precisely this.

## Notes

1 There are no 'professional' theologians but only those who have approximated 'professionalized' status through training regimens and the adoption of various norms within the discipline.

2 Aelred was the second abbot of Rievaulx Abbey (1147–67), often noted in scholarship for his uniqueness. His most significant writings include his *Mirror of Charity* (1990) and *Spiritual Friendship* (2010), among other spiritual and critical historical works.

## References

Aelred of Rievaulx (1990), *The Mirror of Charity*, translated by Elizabeth Connor, Kalamazoo, MI: Cistercian Publications.

Aelred of Rievaulx (2010), *Spiritual Friendship*, translated by Lawrence C. Braceland, edited by Marsha L. Dutton, Collegeville, MN: Cistercian Publications.

Ahmed, Sara (2006), *Queer Phenomenology: Orientations, Objects, Others*, Durham, NC: Duke University Press.

Austin, John L. (2018 [1962]), *How to Do Things with Words*, edited by J. O. Urmson and Marina Sbisà, Eastford, CT: Martino Fine Books.

Benedict of Nursia (1980), *The Rule of St. Benedict, in Latin and English with Notes*, edited by Timothy Fry, Collegeville, MN: The Liturgical Press.

Boquet, Damien (2017), 'Affectivity in the Spiritual Writings of Aelred of Rievaulx', in *A Companion to Aelred of Rievaulx (1110–1167)*, edited by Marsha L. Dutton, Boston: Brill, pp. 167–96.

Bourdieu, Pierre (1991), *Language and Symbolic Power*, translated by Gino Raymond and Matthew Adamson, edited by John B. Thompson, Cambridge, MA: Harvard University Press.

Butler, Judith (2021), *Excitable Speech: A Politics of the Performative*, New York: Routledge.

Freeman, Elizabeth (2002), *Narratives of a New Order: Cistercian Historical Writing in England, 1150–1220* (Medieval Church Studies Series #2), Turnhout: Brepols.

Faggioli, Massimo (2024), 'Theology between the University and the Church as a "Field Hospital"', in *Theology and the University*, edited by Fáinche Ryan, Dirk Ansorge and Josef Quitterer, New York: Routledge, pp. 39–54.

Hall, Cassidy (2024), *Queering Contemplation: Finding Queerness in the Roots and Future of Contemplative Spirituality*, Minneapolis, MN: Broadleaf Books.

Henn, Katherine (1979), 'Friendship: The Mysticism of Aelred of Rievaulx', *Journal of Dharma* 4, no. 2, pp. 113–25.

Jantzen, Grace (2001), 'Contours of a Queer Theology', *Literature and Theology* 15, no. 3, pp. 276–85.

Jennings, Willie James (2020), *After Whiteness: An Education in Belonging*, Grand Rapids, MI: William B. Eerdmans.

Johnson, Elizabeth (1992), *She Who Is: The Mystery of God in Feminist Theological Discourse*, New York: Crossroad.

Kwok Pui-lan (2021), 'Can the Native Speak Theologically?', *Modern Theology* 37, no. 4, pp. 1006–15.

La Corte, Daniel (2017), 'Aelred on Abbatial Responsibilities', in *A Companion to Aelred of Rievaulx (1110–1167)*, edited by Marsha L. Dutton, Leiden: Brill, pp. 48–72.

Lightsey, Pamela (2015), *Our Lives Matter: A Womanist Queer Theology*, Eugene, OR: Pickwick Publications.

Reichel, Hanna (2023), *After Method: Queer Grace, Conceptual Design, and the Possibility of Theology*, Louisville, KY: Westminster John Knox Press.

Russell, J. Stephen (2012), 'The Dialogic of Ælred's *Spiritual Friendship*', *Cistercian Studies Quarterly* 47, no. 1, pp. 47–69.

Smilges, J. Logan (2022), *Queer Silence: On Disability and Rhetorical Absence*, Minneapolis, MN: University of Minnesota Press.

Smith, Ted A. (2023), *The End of Theological Education*, Grand Rapids, MI: William B. Eerdmans.

Sobrino, Jon (1996), 'Central Position of the Reign of God in Liberation Theology', in *Systematic Theology: Perspectives from Liberation Theology*, edited by Jon Sobrino and Ignacio Ellacurría, Maryknoll, NY: Orbis Books, pp. 38–74.

Spivak, Gayatri Chakravorty (1988), 'Can the Subaltern Speak?', in *Marxism and the Interpretation of Culture*, edited by Cary Nelson and Lawrence Grossberg, London: Macmillan, pp. 66–111.

Tonstad, Linn Marie (2020), '(Un)wise Theologians: Systematic Theology in the University', *International Journal of Systematic Theology* 22, no. 4, pp. 494–511.

Tracy, David (1987), *The Analogical Imagination: Christian Theology and the Culture of Pluralism*, New York: Crossroad.

Williams, Delores S. (2013), *Sisters in the Wilderness: The Challenge of Womanist God-Talk*, Maryknoll, NY: Orbis Books.

# PART 7

# Apologetics and Prophetic Witness

# 19

# Visions of Hope from a Transgender Perspective

ANDRÉS HERRERA GRÉ

## Introduction

In this chapter we will journey together through different visions of hope mainly found in the Judaeo-Christian tradition. This text aims to identify and show different concepts of hope, ways of understanding them and how they play a role in people's daily lives. The turning point that I want to present, which differs from what previous authors have proposed about hope, is to connect the theology of hope with my own experiences as a transgender man and with the experiences of other queer and trans people who have shared their spiritual journeys with me.

Before we begin, sharing the social and geopolitical location from where I am writing is meaningful and transparent. I am not an academic, but I am a theologian who believes hope can be transformational if used correctly, which is not to say there is only one unique way to 'use' hope. Even talking about hope as something that can be 'used' feels inaccurate, but as you will see in this chapter, hope can be a tricky concept to define and pinpoint. Also, there has been a lot of bad publicity about hope, relating it to optimism, wishful thinking and positive psychology, which have nothing to do with hope and only misconstrue what hope is and has the potential to be, which ideally will become clear as you read this chapter.

My thoughts and ideas have been shaped by my unique experiences of growing up and coming out as a transgender man in Latin America, serving as a hospital chaplain in the United States and working within the Episcopal Church. Since 2020 I have been involved with St. Stephen's Episcopal Church in Houston, Texas, where part of my work has included producing a podcast that highlights the stories of LGBTIQ+ people of faith. Alongside this, since 2021 I have been part of Otros Cruces, an organization dedicated to promoting religious freedom and human rights. This non-profit works to ensure that diverse religious and spiritual perspectives are represented in public spaces, creating platforms for dialogue on topics such as religion, politics, gender, diversity and environmental justice. Currently I reside in Santiago, Chile, my birthplace. My spiritual and gender transition, which began in 2005, is not a new chapter but rather a continuous journey of self-discovery and growth.

Throughout this chapter I will reference, at one end, what could be considered more classical theologians, others from the pastoral/spiritual care world and, last but definitely not least, black feminists and black liberation theology, as well as non-Christian authors who have researched the topic. My influences are as diverse as my own identity, and I will mix and match the ideas of these authors with my own because theology and life are beautifully messy and cannot be contained in rigid categories.

## Why Do I Want to Write About Hope?

As I finished the last touches on this text, Donald Trump won the 2024 presidential election in the United States. The fear that my trans siblings feel is real as they prepare for a period when a lot of their rights are at risk of being taken away completely. In the short time since the election results we have already seen an increase in hateful messages to LGBTIQ+ individuals on social media platforms.

The topic of hope is profoundly important to me, especially in the context of the narratives surrounding trans lives. Too often the media perpetuate a hegemonic story that frames trans people's lives as inevitably marked by suffering, violence and death. This narrative erases our full humanity and reduces us to victims of circumstance, ignoring the resilience, joy and transformative power that we embody. By focusing on hope we can reclaim our stories and shift the conversation towards the possibilities of thriving, healing and creating a future that celebrates our identities and experiences.

We also have devoted a lot of time and energy to creating materials to defend ourselves from fundamentalist religious groups and leaders who continue to interpret the Bible in literal ways and pick and choose passages to discriminate against and attack trans folks. This work has been vital and, at the same time, takes a different approach because it uses the Bible to demonstrate that trans people are sacred and divine. That is not up for debate in this chapter. Thus my focus involves dedicating our time and energy to life-giving practices for our community. For me, life-giving practices are intrinsically connected to hope and our ability to hope when the world wants to erase us constantly. In this case hope seems counterintuitive and serves as an act of resistance. Cis people will not dictate our lives and our bodies, and they won't be allowed to use God and their religious beliefs to do that because hope can serve as a tool for our response. Instead of defending ourselves or trying to respond with biblical verses or theological arguments, living fully with hope can be a strong witness for them and the whole world.

First, we cannot talk about hope without referencing the work of Jürgen Moltmann (1967). He proposes several ideas that can be connected to how queer and trans people use hope as a tool for survival. For Moltmann, there is only one authentic issue in Christian theology: the future and how hope is an 'inseparable accompaniment' of faith. He explains that without hope, faith dies. Furthermore, for him the Christian faith is fundamentally eschatological, meaning it has to be orientated towards the future, and that future cannot be passive. Christian eschatology has to present itself in connection with hope, and this hope has the role of contradicting the human experience of suffering, pain, evil and death.

Moltmann (1967) invites us to explore the concept of hope concerning Jesus' death and resurrection, emphasizing that by connecting the present with the resurrection, we open ourselves to the possibility of a new world. This vision enables us to imagine a future filled with hope, moving beyond the perpetual pain and suffering of the crucifixion. Jesus' resurrection becomes a powerful symbol that despair is not eternal and that transformation is not only possible but tangible. While this interpretation may appear simplistic in light of the deep and intricate theology Moltmann offers, I have come to realize that the essential truths are often simple and easily overlooked amid complex theological questions. As we progress through this chapter we will continue to engage with Moltmann's work, as his insights remain foundational to our understanding of hope and transformation.

Writing about hope is not something I chose at random. The way that hope has played a role in my life has been different through the years. For example, hope initially appeared to me as a possibility when I discovered for the first time that other people felt the same way that I did. At that time in my life I did not have the language to define myself; I did not know trans men existed, nor had I ever met in real life someone who was trans. So when the internet showed me the possibility of transitioning and living a fulfilling, happy life as my true self, I was invaded with hope.

Even before this reality presented itself, hope lived within me as an undercover current. What I mean is, for those of us who live with the weight of oppression, even if it is self-imposed, for those of us who live in and with fear, there is a considerable desperation flowing through our veins. Because of that intense desperation there is also a fierce hope, even if we cannot recognize it or name it as such at the lowest and darkest moments. This might seem contradictory and that is OK. What I mean is that living authentically as a transgender person is both an act of liberation and an act of confronting fear. In this way, existing as a transgender person in this world becomes an act of hope, whether we consciously name it as such or not.

As you can see, this hope is not necessarily connected to Christian belief or theology, although it can be. We do not need to be Christians to have hope, and hope should not be expected to be the same for everyone, regardless of whether they have a religious or spiritual belief or no belief at all.

## What is Hope?

Andrew D. Lester (1995) shares what the theologian David Woodyard describes as the attitude and potential of hope:

> What is most authentic about [human beings] is the disposition to hope, to live from the future rather than in terms of the past and present. In hoping, [humanity] reaches beyond every apparent limit with anticipation, inquiry, and vision ... Hope is not the calculation of a new future based on extrapolations from present data; it is a confidence that the unpredictable will happen. The most fundamental consciousness [...] is a passionate longing for what is 'not yet'. When [human beings are] truly in possession of [their] existence, [they] experience the process of hoping as a militant aspiration for something new in the future. (p. 62; Lester's substitutions)

Donald Capps (1995) brings into the conversation the view of psychology from a psychoanalytic perspective and its relation to hope. He references Paul W. Pruyser, who also bases his work on the paper written by W. Clifford M. Scott about depression. Scott proposes that hope is part of a dynamic sequence divided into four stages: waiting, anticipation, pining and hoping. Taking Scott's theory, Pruyser connects hope to the relationship between a mother and her infant child, where the mother needs to give what she can to her child. He explains it this way:

> Thus, hope involves the belief that our desire is reciprocated by the one whose presence is desired. Even as we know we want the other to come, we believe the other wants to come and therefore will come. Our desire and that of the other are reciprocal. It is not that infant and mother necessarily desire the same thing, but that their desires are interrelated. What the infant desires, the mother desires to provide. (Capps, 1995, p. 35)

Another relevant element of what Pruyser proposes refers to the difference between hoping and wishing and some of the characteristics of the images of hope. The first point has to do with the feeling of relatedness. In hope, the other – let us say the infant – has internalized the mother, and when she is absent the infant still feels related to her. This means that the images of hope originate in the capacity to be alone. From this idea Pruyser parallelizes the relationship between God and self, meaning that the images of hope in God are based on our internalization of God. An example of this is that God is 'within us' and thus always present and with us.

Another relevant concept that Capps proposes is the idea of hope as projection. This means that as human beings we can project on to others our desires, fantasies, aggressions and so on, which could be one way to view how we engage in hope or the process of hoping. On the other hand, Capps suggests that hope can be a projection in a photographic sense more than a physiological sense. Photographic projection is the process of causing an image to appear on a screen. The photographic projection's main characteristic is that this way of seeing is the work of a creative mind. In both cases the projection is an illusion but the photographic one allows us to imagine a different reality from the one we live in. It shows us other possible worlds.

Both Moltmann and Capps offer another way of understanding hope, which is also a way of understanding God. For example, Moltmann sees God as dynamic and – in future terms – 'I will be what I will be' instead of a God with a set of qualities that never change. This means that our images of God, whether conscious or unconscious, will reflect our views about hope.

Byung-Chul Han (2024) offers a more contemporary look that does not come from a Christian perspective. This author notes an essential factor affecting how we function in the twenty-first century and how we view hope as a society. This factor is fear. We live in a society dominated by fear, and fear opposes freedom. More importantly, for Han fear does not allow us to embrace diversity and the differences between human beings. Thus fear wants us to be the same and imposes a logic of sameness. Such an idea is highly relevant when we consider how mainstream media in the USA portray transgender people, often spreading inaccurate information. This portrayal is frequently manipulated to provoke fear, creating an image of trans people as enemies, as highlighted in a report published by the Pew Research Center (Parker, Horowitz and Brown, 2022).

Finally, I also wanted to include the view of Mariame Kaba, who discusses hope as a discipline. In an interview, Kaba shares that hope is not optimism for her and does not preclude feelings like sadness, anger or frustration (Decoloniza, 2022). She understands it as a discipline based on a nun's view years ago: hope must be connected to ensuring we are of-the-world and in-the-world. Instead of thinking about living in the afterlife in the present, the invitation of this nun is to practise hope where we currently are. That is why Kaba describes it as a discipline that must be practised daily. Kaba adds that this has required her to choose how she sees the world and people. For example, she decides to believe and act differently by trusting that people are trustworthy until they prove untrustworthy.

The dread doula, Ominira Mars, proposes a contrary position to Kaba's. She explains:

> Hope as a discipline becomes restrictive, monotonous, exhausting. We must be able to occupy a multifaceted consciousness and way of reasoning with what could be that makes room for both the pragmatic and the impossible. We must practice a regenerative and expansive hope, or else hope becomes contained only by what we assume and/ or are told is not possible. (James, 2022, p. 19)

Mars adds that to practise hope as a discipline, we have to lower our expectations of liberation. She quotes Nicholas Brady, who explains that the most hopeful people are those who have no hope in the system. That statement resonates with me and with many trans people I have met, who remain hopeful because we have not placed our hope in systems, leaders or institutions, but we have placed our hope in our community. To end this section, I also wanted to include what Rebecca Solnit (2016) shares about hope:

> Hope locates itself in the premises that we don't know what will happen and that in the spaciousness of uncertainty is room to act. When you recognize uncertainty, you recognize that you may be able to influence the outcomes – you alone or you in concert with a few dozen or several million others. Hope is an embrace of the unknown and the unknow-

> able, an alternative to the certainty of both optimists and pessimists. Optimists think it will all be fine without our involvement; pessimists take the opposite position; both excuse themselves from acting. It's the belief that what we do matters even though how and when it may matter, who and what it may impact, are not things we can know beforehand. We may not, in fact, know them afterward either, but they matter all the same, and history is full of people whose influence was most powerful after they were gone. (p. xiv)

Solnit also adds something similar to what Han mentioned about the frequency with which hope gets confused with something it is not, such as optimism and positive thinking. Solnit says that hope is not the belief that everything will be all right since we have evidence all around us – now and in the past – and are surrounded by pain and suffering.

For all the authors mentioned so far, hope emerges as the singular, unwavering response to the overwhelming tide of fear, hate, anxiety, despair and distress that consumes and dominates our world today. Hope is a radical act of resistance, offering a vision of transformation, healing and resilience in the face of such adversity and illuminating pathways forward.

As I reviewed these opinions and ideas about hope, you might think my goal will be to critique them, especially the work of more classical or 'older' theologians. Instead my purpose is to invite you to sit with these ideas and explore which resonate with you and which do not make sense to you. You can also pick and choose what works for you from these concepts. One of my struggles throughout the process of writing this chapter has been to find other trans theologians/thinkers/writers who are working on the topic of hope. Two theologians and authors who have inspired me and motivated me without knowing it have been Roberto Che Espinoza and Alex Clare-Young, who also contribute to this collection.

Espinoza is a transqueer Latinx scholar and activist who engages deeply with themes of hope, justice and liberation in their work. Espinoza is known for their theological and philosophical reflections, particularly on how marginalized identities intersect with spirituality and the pursuit of social transformation. Their writings emphasize hope as an active, communal practice grounded in justice and resistance rather than a passive or abstract ideal. One notable work by Espinoza (2019) explores the intersection of theology, activism and identity. In this book Espinoza challenges readers to move beyond individualistic understandings of faith and embrace collective action rooted in love and hope. They frame hope as a radical act of imagining and creating a world where marginalized communities can thrive. Espinoza's perspective is particularly compelling because it ties hope to accountability and action, insisting that genuine hope cannot exist without a commitment to justice.

Clare-Young is a pioneering non-binary trans theologian whose work focuses on inclusion, justice and hope within Christian theology. Clare-Young integrates their lived experience with their theological insights, offering a unique perspective on how faith communities can embody radical hospitality and hope for marginalized individuals, particularly transgender and non-binary people. Clare-Young (2020) explores their personal journey and theological reflections. They discuss how hope emerges through embracing one's authentic self while navigating the complexities of faith, identity and community. In Clare-Young's work, hope is not detached optimism but a grounded trust in the transformative power of God's love, even amid struggles and marginalization. Their work emphasizes the need for churches to be spaces of genuine belonging and restorative justice, grounded in the belief that every person reflects divine diversity. Hope becomes an active process fostered through inclusive relationships, advocacy and deep engagement with faith traditions.

## Images of God, Images of Hope

As I shared at the beginning of this chapter, the way we perceive God – the images, metaphors and projections we hold of the Divine – significantly shapes how we engage with hope and, by extension, how we interact with the world. Our understanding of the Divine often influences whether we approach life in a hopeful or non-hopeful manner. Within the context of hospital chaplaincy I had the unique opportunity to explore the various images that can represent the chaplain's work. Two of these images stand out to me, as they deeply resonate with the concept of hope. These images not only inform the chaplain's role but also invite us to consider how we embody hope in the midst of suffering and uncertainty.

### *The Intimate Stranger*

The first one is the image of the Intimate Stranger (Dykstra, 2005), which proposes that the chaplain, the family, the patient and even God themselves can be strangers and strange. This does not mean God is distant and disconnected. Instead it means that 'in the *very strangeness of the situation itself* we may find sanctuary' (p. 135; emphasis original). God reveals Godself in the mysterious, and so does hope. We can find and form hope in and within the uncertainty. Such a transformative practice involves embracing the unknown as a space for growth, possibility and connection. That practice also involves seeing waiting as sacred and trusting that what we need will be revealed in time.

In many of my conversations with other trans folk, inside and outside of Christian spaces, we have found ourselves embracing uncertainty and seeing it as something that is not as threatening for us compared to how non-trans individuals see and experience uncertainty. This could be because a lot of uncertainty surrounds our lives. For instance, deciding to come out as trans or disclose our trans history or experiences is an ongoing process, one filled with uncertainty and vulnerability. We never truly know how people will respond. In my life, people I thought would be supportive have turned out to be judgemental, while others whom I did not expect to understand have been more compassionate. Another example relates to physical transitions. We do not have control over how our bodies will change, which brings many unknowns. We must learn to embrace or welcome these changes in our lives, navigating them the best we can with the tools and understanding we have.

## *The Hospital Chaplain*

Another image I have found useful and helpful in my journey as a hospital chaplain and now as a future licensed therapist is that of the wounded healer. This concept resonates deeply, as it speaks to the healing potential that comes from our experiences of suffering and struggle.

A simple Google search will reveal the latest statistics, news reports and academic research regarding the trans community worldwide, showing that our community continues to endure significant hardship. From high rates of violence, discrimination and mental health challenges to the stigma faced by trans people in various cultural contexts, these wounds are widespread. For example, trans communities in countries like Brazil (Lobato et al., 2019), Russia (Buyantueva, 2018), Uganda (Rodríguez, 2018) or Pakistan (Kasmani, 2023), among others, experience alarming rates of violence and discrimination. Concurrently, trans people in more conservative regions, such as parts of the Middle East, face severe persecution and legal challenges (Noralla, 2022). Despite these challenges, trans individuals worldwide are finding strength in their communities, embracing their identities and offering support to one another in the face of adversity.

### *The Wounded Healer*

The image of the wounded healer, introduced by Henri Nouwen (1972), illustrates that a wounded healer has personally faced pain, suffering and challenges and uses that experience to guide, support and heal others. This idea speaks to the power of vulnerability – by acknowledging our wounds we can connect with others struggling similarly. I find this image particularly powerful because it speaks to the transformative nature of suffering: if we, who have borne much pain, can still find hope, then indeed others too can find pathways to healing and joy.

However, I want to be clear that this is not about competing over who has endured the most suffering. Instead the essence of this approach is the deep understanding that comes from sharing in pain and suffering. It is about being there for one another with empathy and compassion, even if we have not experienced the same struggles. We can embrace a more profound sense of compassion and acceptance when we open ourselves to understanding our wounds.

Moreover recognizing our wounds reminds us that there is more to us and humanity than pain. There is a side of us capable of responding with tenderness, care and hope, and this side can be a source of light for others. In this way our pain does not have to define us – it can fuel the possibility of growth, healing and a more compassionate world.

## Transforming Hope

A concept that captured my attention as I was doing research for this chapter is the one that the Vietnamese American writer Viet Thanh Nguyen (2023) shares about *nothingness*:

> Rather than despising the refugees who come with nothing and are nothing, we could identify with them and their nothingness, a blankness from which we can imagine a world free from the forces that negate all of us – exploitation and violence, fear and terror, greed and selfishness. (p. 279)

This idea suggests that the future we envision is not simply a continuation of the present or a repetition of what already exists; instead it is an entirely new creation that emerges from nothingness. This blank canvas provides a powerful opportunity to imagine something different, free from the limitations of the current state. It is worth noting that trans people, at times, are treated as if they are 'nothing' – invisible, disregarded or erased from society. While this often serves as a form of profound oppression it can also be reframed as a source of strength. By acknowledging this invisibility we can break free from societal norms and create a new reality filled with hope, fulfilment and self-authorship.

## What Can We Offer the World?

When exploring the themes of liberation and self-discovery we encounter powerful concepts that challenge the status quo. Transness, in particular, becomes a symbol of transformative freedom – an act of living authentically that transcends societal norms. It opens the door to a more inclusive world where self-expression and truth are celebrated.

Central to this journey is the pursuit of self-knowledge and self-truth, which empower individuals to break free from external expectations. Understanding and embracing our inner selves creates the foundation for genuine liberation, allowing us to live fully and authentically. These ideas reflect the profound connection between inner freedom and the broader quest for societal change.

### *Transness as Liberation*

One of the greatest gifts we can offer the world is the freedom to live authentically, regardless of societal expectations or judgements. As trans people our existence and journey embody the power of transformation and the courage to embrace change. By simply being who we are we challenge the limitations imposed by rigid norms and inspire others to envision lives beyond the boundaries of convention.

Our authenticity becomes a beacon, showing that it is possible to create a different, more inclusive world where everyone's truth is celebrated. This perspective resonates deeply with queer theologies, particularly in the works of Marcella Althaus-Reid and Hugo Córdova Quero, who explore liberation and inclusivity through diverse and subversive lenses. In her groundbreaking book *Indecent Theology*, Althaus-Reid (2000) challenges traditional norms by inviting theology to embrace the margins. She argues that the truths of marginalized identities, including trans and queer lives, reveal the liberating power of the divine in ways that dismantle oppressive systems. Similarly, Córdova Quero (2008) highlights the fluidity of identities and spiritualities across transgender issues. He frames queerness as a sacred journey that challenges fixed binaries and opens pathways to new, transformative understandings of self and community.

By embodying authenticity, trans people live out the liberative ethos present in these queer theologies. We challenge the status quo, illustrating that no identity or reality is confined to societal expectations. Instead, as Althaus-Reid and Córdova Quero suggest, we create possibilities for reimagined lives where liberation is personal and collective. In this way our existence inspires hope and transformation for ourselves and the broader world.

## *Self-knowledge and Self-truth*

These concepts – self-knowledge and self-truth – are deeply connected to pursuing freedom, as true liberation begins within. We must first understand ourselves and embrace our complexities, desires and unique identities to be free. Self-knowledge involves the courage to look inward, recognizing our strengths and vulnerabilities without judgement.

On the other hand, self-truth demands that we live authentically and be honest with ourselves and others. These principles guide us towards a life of integrity, where our actions align with our inner realities. Only by knowing and honouring our true selves can we break free from the expectations and limitations imposed by the world, paving the way for genuine liberation.

For instance, André Sidnei Musskopf (2015) emphasizes the importance of self-knowledge and self-truth in transforming religious and theological spaces for LGBTIQ+ individuals. Musskopf critiques traditional Christian teachings that often marginalize queer identities, advocating for a theology of inclusion that encourages individuals to embrace their true selves. For Musskopf, self-knowledge involves understanding one's identity beyond societal norms and religious dogma. On the other hand, self-truth demands living authentically and unapologetically expressing one's identity within faith communities. By creating a 'gap in the closet', Musskopf envisions a space where LGBTIQ+ individuals can explore and affirm their identities without fear of rejection. This self-knowledge and self-truth process is liberating and transformative, fostering both spiritual growth and social change. Musskopf's vision calls for faith communities to celebrate diversity, challenge oppressive structures and affirm the dignity and worth of all people, allowing them to live fully and authentically in their truth.

## *Spiritual Flexibility*

When I think about spiritual flexibility I mean the capacity to embrace multiple beliefs or religious traditions. Another way to describe it would be multi-faith. Throughout the many conversations that I have had with different groups of trans folks, many of them grew up in a specific religious tradition. Then they embraced other spiritualities or beliefs without giving up the spiritual tradition in which they were raised. In other cases these trans folk have moved on from the religious beliefs in which they grew up and have integrated new religious beliefs and practices from multiple faith traditions. This might sound difficult for many people but it is a common practice among trans people, at least in my experience. This is common because we have learned not to be confined by spaces and people that limit us and want to impose their truth. Spirituality should be freeing, life-giving, caring and nurturing, among many other things. Therefore it makes sense to move within traditions and beliefs and find what resonates.

For example, Anderson Fabián Santos Meza (2024) delves into the concept of spiritual flexibility as a central element of queer liberation theology. He critiques the rigid and exclusionary theological frameworks that have historically marginalized LGBTIQ+ individuals, advocating for a more dynamic and inclusive understanding of faith. Spiritual flexibility, according to Santos Meza, allows for the creation of a theology that can adapt to the evolving realities of queer lives and experiences. By embracing this fluid approach, individuals can reimagine their spiritual identities without being bound by oppressive norms. Such a perspective challenges traditional religious teachings and encourages the formation of faith communities that honour diversity and promote liberation. Santos Meza's work calls for a transformative spirituality that supports queer individuals in navigating both their faith and identity in empowering and flexible ways.

## Thinking About the Future

According to Capps (1995), how a person thinks and feels about the future – the not-yet – is crucial to physical, emotional and spiritual health. A source of inspiration as I thought about how we can foster hope and overall well-being was Natasha Marin (2020). She explains that imagination can be a transformative force that enables black people to envision futures free from oppression. Her book *Black Imagination* frames this act of envisioning as both rebellious and necessary in a world shaped by systemic racism and marginalization. Marin invited a diverse group of black folks to participate in the project by reflecting on these questions:

- What is your origin story?
- How do you heal yourself?
- Describe/Imagine a world where you are safe, loved and valued.

In our case this can be an invitation to think about how imagination can be a crucial tool for our liberation, spiritual healing and growth. Hope can be constructed by telling our stories and continuing to make trans spirituality visible and known. I believe that if we continue to show up in ways that are safe and authentic to us, the narratives about trans people will begin to shift from despair, suffering, abuse and violence to love, care, compassion and hope. Of course, we cannot do this alone. It takes our whole community to work collectively in this movement of hope. If our hope is not a catalyst for action it is not serving us for liberation.

These actions, though seemingly small or subtle, carry immense power. They do not require grand gestures or dramatic displays; they often go unnoticed by those who may not be attuned to their significance. However, these quiet acts – moments of compassion, resistance or solidarity – are the building blocks for more significant, more visible transformations. They plant the seeds of change, creating momentum that gradually ripples through communities. Over time these seemingly insignificant actions accumulate, fostering a collective energy that challenges the status quo and paves the way for more significant societal shifts. In this way even the most understated efforts contribute to a broader movement, proving that actual change often begins in the smallest moments. Let us dream and hope together!

## References

Althaus-Reid, Marcella (2000), *Indecent Theology: Theological Perversions in Sex, Gender and Politics*, London: Routledge.

Buyantueva, Radzhana (2018), 'LGBT Rights Activism and Homophobia in Russia', *Journal of Homosexuality* 65, no. 4, pp. 456–83.

Capps, Donald (1995), *Agents of Hope: A Pastoral Psychology*, Minneapolis, MN: Fortress Press.

Clare-Young, Alex (2020), *Transgender. Christian. Human*, Glasgow: Wild Goose Publications.

Córdova Quero, Hugo (2008), 'This Body Trans/Forming Me: Indecencies in Transgender/Intersex Bodies, Body Fascism and the Doctrine of the Incarnation', in *Controversies in Body Theology*, edited by Marcella Althaus-Reid and Lisa Isherwood, London: SCM Press, pp. 80–128.

Decoloniza (2022), 'Dear Mariame Kaba, Hope is Not a Discipline', *Grassroots Thinking*, 11 October, at https://grassrootsthinking.com/2022/10/11/title-dear-mariame-kaba-hope-is-not-a-discipline/, accessed 01.12.2024.

Dykstra, Robert C. (2005), *Images of Pastoral Care: Classic Readings*, St. Louis, MO: Chalice Press.

Espinoza, Roberto Che (2019), *Activist Theology*, Minneapolis, MN: Fortress Press.

Han, Byung-Chul (2024), *The Spirit of Hope*, Barcelona: Herder Editorial.

James, Joy (2022), *In Pursuit of Revolutionary Love: Precarity, Power, Communities*, Brussels: Divided Publishing.

Kasmani, Omar (2023), *Pakistan Desires: Queer Futures Elsewhere*, Durham, NC: Duke University Press.

Lester, Andrew D. (1995), *Hope in Pastoral Care and Counseling*, Louisville, KY: Presbyterian Publishing Corporation.

Lobato, Maria I., Bianca M. Soll, Angelo Brandelli Costa, Alexandre Saadeh, Daniel A. M. Gagliotti, Ana Fresán, Geoffrey Reed and Rebeca Robles (2019), 'Psychological Distress Among Transgender People in Brazil: Frequency, Intensity and Social Causation – An ICD-11 Field Study', *Brazilian Journal of Psychiatry* 41, no. 4 (July), pp. 310–15.

Marin, Natasha, ed. (2020), *Black Imagination: Black Voices on Black Futures*, San Francisco, CA: McSweeney's Publishing.

Moltmann, Jürgen (1967), *Theology of Hope: On the Ground and the Implications of a Christian Eschatology*, translated by James W. Leitch, New York: Harper & Row.

Musskopf, André Sidnei (2015), *Uma brecha no armário: Propostas para uma teologia gay* [A Gap in the Closet: Proposals for a Gay Theology], São Leopoldo, RS: Centro de Estudos Bíblicos/Fonte Editorial.

Noralla, Nora (2022), 'Confused Judiciary & Transgender Rights: Inside the MENA Region's Case Law on Legal Gender Recognition', *Manara Magazine*, 17 March, at https://manaramagazine.org/2022/03/confused-judiciary-transgender-rights-inside-the-mena-regions-case-law-on-legal-gender-recognition/?utm_source=chatgpt.com, accessed 01.12.2024.

Nouwen, Henri J. M. (1972), *The Wounded Healer: Ministry in Contemporary Society*, Garden City, NY: Doubleday.

Nguyen, Viet Thanh (2023), *A Man of Two Faces: A Memoir, a History, a Memorial*, New York: Grove Press.

Parker, Kim, Juliana Menasce Horowitz and Anna Brown (2022), 'Americans' Complex Views on Gender Identity and Transgender Issues', *Pew Research Center*, 28 June, at https://www.pewresearch.org/social-trends/2022/06/28/americans-complex-views-on-gender-identity-and-transgender-issues/, accessed 01.12.2024.

Rodriguez, S. M. (2018), *The Economies of Queer Inclusion: Transnational Organizing for LGBTI Rights in Uganda*, Lanham, MD: Lexington Books.

Santos Meza, Anderson Fabián (2024), 'Desviaciones teológicas para retornar al Edén. Aproximaciones, preguntas e indagaciones desde las teologías queer/cuir' [Theological Deviations to Return to Eden], in *Mysterium Liberationis Queer: Ensayos sobre teologías queer de la liberación en las Américas*, edited by Hugo Córdova Quero, Miguel H. Díaz, Anderson Fabián Santos Meza and Cristian Mor, St. Louis, MO: Institute Sophia Press, pp. 369–422.

Solnit, Rebecca (2016), *Hope in the Dark: Untold Histories, Wild Possibilities*, Chicago, IL: Haymarket Books.

# 20

# Caledonian Antisyzygy: Defiantly Dissonant Theology for a Quantum Generation

JUDITH TATTON-SCHIFF

## Introduction

The term 'Caledonian Antisyzygy' [*anti-si-zi-gee*] describes the ways in which opposites, contradictions, dissonance and even impossibilities coexist within Scotland. It draws our attention to the binaries of Scotland: Britishness and Scottishness, Highlands and Lowlands, Protestantism and Roman Catholicism, nationalism and unionism, sovereignty and subservience, feudal lairds and housing schemes, progressive politics and xenophobia (Abrams and Brown, 2010, p. 184). It is noteworthy that in parts of Glasgow, life expectancy – even today – goes only slightly beyond forty.

Whether born in Scotland, adopted by Scotland or living elsewhere, Scottish hearts remain bound to our Caledonian home. Perspectives, vernacular and a shared sense of 'something', reaching deeply back into the mists of time, have all been shaped by the multifaceted – often contested – tendrils of history, tradition and mystery. For the generation of today, those who are of an age to exert the most significant influence on the ongoing direction of Scotland, the prevalence of justice and identity in their lives, set within increasingly normalized deconstructed and quantum frameworks, the Caledonian Antisyzygy is a particularly relevant construct.

The term 'Caledonian Antisyzygy' was first coined by the Scottish literary critic George Gregory Smith (1865–1932) and made popular by the poet Hugh MacDiarmid (1892–1978), referring to traits present within Scottish literature and the Scots themselves:

> We find at closer scanning that the cohesion at least in formal expression and in choice of material is only apparent, that the literature is

> remarkably varied, and that it becomes, under the stress of foreign influence, almost a zigzag of contradictions. The antithesis need not, however, disconcert us. Perhaps in the very combination of opposites ... we have a reflection of the contrasts which the Scot shows at every turn ... we need not be surprised to find that in his literature the Scot presents two aspects which appear contradictory. Oxymoron was ever the bravest figure, and we must not forget that disorderly order is order after all. (Smith, 1919, p. 5)

Well-known literary works such as Robert Louis Stevenson's *The Strange Case of Dr. Jekyll and Mr. Hyde* (2014) and Muriel Spark's *The Prime of Miss Jean Brodie* (1961) have all wrestled with the dissonant themes of identity, both national and personal. The Antisyzygy embodies the many polarities and coexisting contradictions of the Scottish zeitgeist. However, it also represents a defiant deconstruction: transgressively imaginative, irreverent subversive and, necessarily, multidimensional (Carruthers, 2009). It is playful, contextual and intersectional, queering (Althaus-Reid, 2003, p. 175) its binaries, as it uncloaks their absurdities; at once both mocking and earnest. Such a preposterous mouthful as 'Caledonian Antisyzygy' could not be less 'Scottish' in its pretentiousness, yet all that the Caledonian Antisyzygy represents is nevertheless true. It reflects a profound existential reality, a long-established history of subaltern, anti-establishment and subversive ethics rooted within the Scottish experience of marginalization within the United Kingdom, and a long history of struggle for equality and justice within that union.

## Dissent

I love Scotland passionately. I have personally known her darker, more brutal and dangerous realities. Yet these experiences have never driven me to disconnect from Scotland, which is proud, justice-loving, joyful, inclusive, 'left-leaning' and intellectually rich. As a queer, Scottish, Christian individual, the Scottish zeitgeist has continued to reflect me, just as my own life has itself borne out its narrative. I have lived through – and survived – the myriad contradictions of what Scotland is 'about', what life can be in Scotland and what it is to be Scottish, along with the many contradictions and dissonances manifest within both Christianity and the queer community. Further, I have also embodied the contradictions of these identities, along with many unique only to me, within myself. The Caledonian Antisyzygy is me, and it is us: Scottish, queer and Christian alike.

Scots have long exemplified an innate contempt for any airs or graces, perpetually holding up two fingers to the world – especially 'the man' or 'the system' – with sleeves rolled up for the fight. A shared cultural adherence to the biblical words of Acts 10.34 underscores this attitude. To be 'no respecter of persons' in terms of rank, position, birth or any such other supposed vestige of authority is a resolutely Scottish attitude, as urged by John Knox – one of the most significant characters of the Protestant Reformation within Scotland – resisting, by any means necessary, 'persecution and tyranny' from 'princes or emperors'.[1]

In all its many forms Scottish Presbyterianism has always occupied a dissenting position, acknowledging only the sovereignty of God above any human authority (Storrar, 1990, p. 26; Gay, 2013, p. 182). However, this dissenting tendency is applicable across denominations within Scotland. The Roman Catholic Church in Scotland has a long history of solidarity with those who are being oppressed and of speaking truth to power, right back to the Highland Clearances in the sixteenth and seventeenth centuries. In more recent history, women of 'The Kirk' (as the Church of Scotland is known) were trailblazers in their work with HIV/AIDS and sex workers in the 1980s, well before the need for this work had come to be recognized within the mainstream (Church of Scotland Guild, 2021). The United Reformed Church in Scotland, the Scottish Episcopal Church and the Congregational Federation in Scotland all supported same-sex marriage early in the life of its legislation in the UK. The first British same-sex marriage in a church was performed in a Scottish church – Port Glasgow URC – in 2016. The Methodist Church updated its legislation around marriage in 2021. However, The Church of England appears – as of 2024 – still a long way from making such a move.

## Deconstructive Queering

As Scotland makes sense of its place within the world – and within 'the Union' – suspicious of and resisting all earthly authorities, she exists within a continual state of deconstruction. It is very much 'the Scottish way' to queer any reading of who and what we are as Scots, and through this ongoing process there continue to be revealed profound seams of insight from deep within the Scottish ground: transgressive and provocative ways of seeing things, innovative survival skills and a distinctive, celebratory joy. It is therefore possible to queer any reading of Scotland – past, present and future – and therein find hidden jewels of great theological beauty without glossing over the problematic, the dark or the dissonant. Myriad coexisting 'truths', intersections and con-traditions are all integral aspects of what it is to be Scottish, what it is to be queer and, in a synergetic, dynamic relationship, also what it is to be a Christian, alongside these other identities.

Caledonian antisyzygical literature highlights the contradictions and impossibilities that coexist within the Scottish whole. It provides what can only be considered to be a queer(ed) view because it goes on, inevitably, to continue its deconstruction, revealing the true multidimensionality of the Antisyzygy. It is a naturally and necessarily quantum process, as it accommodates the contradictions, dissonances and impossibilities of the whole; Scottish-quantum-deconstructive-queering is naturally transgressive, subversive and irreverent, rooted within Scotland's complex and multifaceted identity and her long-held passion for justice. As it squares for the fight, it displays a mischievous smirk on its face. It begins with binaries but does not stop there, continuing until the resulting matrix is, inevitably, fluid, dynamic and multidimensional.

The ideas central to 'queer' and 'queering' speak deeply to the Scottish situation: resistance to patriarchy, establishment and injustice; solidarity with those considered to occupy the margins of sexuality and gender identity and beyond; and deconstruction of the texts of culture, politics and identity. Indeed, the queer struggle within the UK over recent decades seems inseparable from the struggle against Margaret Thatcher[2] through the 1980s and 1990s; the miners' strike, anti-'poll tax', Section 28/Stop the Clause movements and even that of the Scottish independence movement (McGhee, 2024). Through these movements there intensified a shared sense of 'we the marginalized', whether that be as Scots within a union whose leadership did not reflect the votes of Scotland, or as queers within a country whose legislation designated them as illegal, perverse or – in the case of lesbians – invisible.

## Woke

Scotland has come to be far more progressive, politically, than other parts of the UK, manifesting, as the Scottish theologian and Church of Scotland minister Doug Gay (2013) has observed, a 'strongly egalitarian, "liberal" and anti-discriminatory stance on issues of racism and immigration' (pp. 119–20), including the campaign 'One Scotland, Many Cultures' (2002), the Hate Crime and Public Order Bill (2021) and the Gender Recognition Bill (2022) (Seanan, 2002; Scottish Parliament, 2021; Scottish Government, 2022). At times this stance has led to Scotland being accused – from the outside – of being a 'woke nation' and the Scottish Government of having a 'woke agenda'. Writing in

*The Telegraph*, Jenny Hjul (2023) analysed 'how Scotland became the wokest country in the world'. She cited the high-profile case of a trans-identified (mtf) violent rapist who was – temporarily – remanded in a women's prison, alongside proposed legislation that would have enabled individuals to change gender without any formal medical diagnosis legally, and lowered the permitted age for this change to 16. The UK government blocked the bill (*The Observer*, 2022).

However, viewing 'woke' from an altogether different vantage point, Michael Russell (2023) – a Scottish National Party (SNP) Member of the Scottish Parliament (MSP) – argued that the so-called 'war on woke' is in truth actually an attack on good and ordinary people who are challenging institutional racism and systemic inequalities in society. He reminds us:

> The African American word 'woke' simply means being alert to racial prejudice and discrimination. That is something we should all be – awake to the injustices and cruelties that still abound, horrified by their past expression and focused on eliminating them for the future.
>
> Yet the word has increasingly become a term of right-wing and tabloid abuse which has almost replaced that old mantra about 'political correctness gone mad' which was regularly and offensively trotted out as an excuse for what used to be called, euphemistically, saloon-bar prejudice.
>
> We need, [in the words of] Amanda Gorman [American poet and activist] '... to lift our gazes not to what stands between us, but what stands before us.'
>
> We must continue to be awake to the problems that exist all around us and be ever more motivated to resolve them – problems such as racism, sexism, misogyny and discrimination. (Russell, 2023)

Furthermore, Russell urges: 'That is how you build a new country, by acknowledging what is wrong and collectively working to set it right. In other words, by being woke.' Such a 'woke' attitude is, as Kirsty Borthwick (2022, pp. 64, 71) argued (by inference), an identity deeply rooted in the values of Jesus Christ, as laid out in Matthew 25: to be concerned whenever anyone is hungry or thirsty; to welcome the stranger; to clothe those who are naked; to take care of those who are sick; to visit those in prison. All these imperatives are explicitly Christian values, given directly through the mouth of Jesus. However, by the standards upheld by tabloid media today they are inherently 'woke'.

Ultimately the increasingly woke-leaning nature of Scottish politics backfired on Nicola Sturgeon. These policies – manifested in Scotland's political direction of travel – became a significant catalyst for her resignation as First Minister (Keate, 2024). Although the 'Trans Bill' in particular had been crafted and approved across parties within the Scottish Parliament, some – including *The Telegraph* journalist Hjul (2023) – considered it to have gone 'too far'.

## Subaltern Ethics

> With recourse to such diverse historical-political, ideological and aesthetic avenues as nationalism, postcolonialism, and modernism (which have in both fields become somewhat inextricably interlinked), and more currently, postmodernism and post-nationalism, the general response strangely resembles the advice a desperate emperor is given in one of Alasdair Gray's short stories: 'You [have been] dreaming the disease. Now you must dream the cure' ... In Gray's 'The Start of the Axletree', the cure deemed capable of preventing the vanishing out of history of this doomed empire is the perpetuation of its existence in the form of a national monument, and it seems ironic that some of the various forms of 'national enjoyment' not only show the same desire but, in turn, reaffirm the anachronism of their nation's historical trajectory. (Lehner, 2008, p. 38)

The 'postcolonial approach' is, as Stephanie Lehner detailed further, 'a specific inclination to perceiving, registering and negotiating forms of marginalisation, oppression and disempowerment, related to aspects of class and gender' (2011, p. 3).

Lehner (2011, p. 30) notes the extent to which perceptions of both Scotland and Ireland have come to be 'refracted and distorted' by the 'quasi-colonial lens' of England/the English. Yet any Scottish self-identity that is based upon the idea of noble resistance within an oppressive situation must also be set against another strand of the Antisyzygy: Scotland's historical involvement in the empire, colonization and the slave trade through the tobacco industry and beyond cannot be ignored. A postcolonial Scotland must be understood holistically, embracing its often fragmented multi-dimensions, including all dissonances – even those embarrassing or shameful. That understanding should also prioritize individuals, issues and perspectives existing at its margins. Despite this need for inclusivity, Scotland continues to grapple with alarmingly high rates of deprivation – far exceeding those of England – and struggles with poverty, violence, drugs and alcoholism. Furthermore, the scourge of racism continues to be the most prevalent form of hate crime that exists within Scotland. Those who come from black and minoritized ethnic backgrounds continue to experience the poorest health outcomes, face persistent discrimination and under-representation in educational and vocational opportunities and endure the highest levels of poverty (Williams, 2022; CRER, 2024).

The Scottish alt-rock band Idlewild sing in their song 'Scottish Fiction':

> It isn't in the mirror
> It isn't on the page
> It's a red hearted vibration
> Pushing through the walls of dark imagination
> Finding no equation
> There's a red road rage
> But it's not road rage
> It's asylum seekers engulfed by a grudge
> Scottish friction, Scottish fiction.[3]

Scottishness – as understood by the band – is something that is in the blood, beyond the analogous yet also utterly rooted in the imagination. It is not only about identity, nor is it only a literary thing. It is not just romantic vistas. It may rage and not rage all at once. It may deal with the questions of asylum seekers and refugees coming to its doors while also – simultaneously – grappling with its complicity in the creation of the very situations that now generate asylum seekers and refugees. It is disease, addiction, nuclear submarine bases and knife crime. Yet perhaps some of its greatest beauty – and truth – exists in this very dissonance, alongside the narratives that emerge to cocoon it.

The basis for the subaltern ethics argued by Lehner (2011) is wrought from the multidimensional margins of a complex, antisyzygical whole. Therefore it must be, as she argues:

> based on a sensibility and responsiveness to the ethos of the other, namely the specific position and place that a subaltern other occupies in a given society … A subaltern ethics thereby demands of the critic a careful scrutiny and negotiation of power relations, a deliberate taking of side, decisions and risks. (p. 22)

The term 'subaltern' refers to colonized people who are marginalized or oppressed within the hierarchy of an oppressive state, excluded from participation in the power structures of the empire they inhabit. The Scot can only be heard in the UK through political protest and action. Similarly, within Scotland the queer individual finds a voice only through political protest and action. For Christians, it is only by embracing the promises of Isaiah – directed to the marginalized and the outsider – and engaging with narratives like Matthew 25 that they can embody these inherently woke subaltern ethics.

## A Deconstructive Logic of Undecidability

As long ago as the eighteenth century the Scottish philosopher David Hume (1739) observed that it is 'possible for the same thing both to be and not to be' (p. 66). Indeed, Scotland's truth embodies myriad conflicting truths, a deconstructive logic of undecidability where, as Jacques Derrida (1999) challenged 200 years later, 'an event or an action can be both/and, neither/nor, or in ethical terms both good and evil, neither good nor evil' (p. 65). Lehner (2011, p. 34) highlights – in the 'modern self-fashioning' of Scotland – whether through necessity or towards some particular goal, there is an ongoing development of a Scottish narrative which is, just as pointed to by both Hume and Derrida, simultaneously both 'true' and invented.

Such an acknowledgement of the existence of potentially infinite coexisting truths is crucial when it comes to an understanding of the Caledonian Antisyzygy. It is a quantum view; binary, polarized and static limitations are shown to be a premature view. Within the broadened quantum perspective, things may occupy more than one location or state simultaneously or, somehow, exist in a manner that is neither in a single location nor state, or neither as particles nor waves (George, 2017, p. 138). Individuals, situations and issues are likely to be fluid, and multiple interpretations may coexist and be interconnected as each possibility or dimension maintains its particularity yet continues to move through each other fluidly, with intersections, synergies and dissonances.

Accordingly, Scotland is a complex, quantum whole comprising myriad crucial dimensions that orbit – often erratically – around one another, intersecting, combining and repelling. Whether these dimensions are ethnic, religious, historical, geographical or pertain to sexual or gender identity, politics or football, they function as vectors, each carrying direction, velocity and time inherent to their nature. Points of intersection may be intricate or clumsy, transitory or lasting, seemingly ordered or chaotic. There may be consonance or dissonance, synergy or even destruction.

## A Quantum View

Albert Einstein, through his theories of General and Special Relativity, argued in the 1920s that 'time' is non-linear, as it embodies both movement and direction; space and time come to be part of a 'four-dimensional phenomenon' (Leath, 2023). As the North American theological ethicist and professor of black religion Jennifer Susanne Leath (2023) observes:

> In a sense, quantum physics offers a curving correction to the linearity of Newtonian physics that builds on Euclidean geometry ... this correction is not necessary when mathematics (and physics) begin with a 'curvilinear' approach. (p. 33)

This author refers to the ways in which space, time and matter manifest, ways that cannot be made sense of within the confines of contemporary (Western) cultural frameworks. Based primarily on the understandings of the Enlightenment and modernity, she argues: 'These complexities have a great deal to do with the uncertainties and infinite possibilities to which quantum mechanics points' (p. 33).

Hence it is also with the multi-identity, multi-contextual model of Scotland herein proposed. Each particle, identity or context is part of a universe-wide interconnectedness that transcends the limits of 'old thinking' (Al-Khalili, 2003, p. 16; O'Murchu, 2004, p. 29; George, 2017, p. 151). This phenomenon is known as 'entanglement'. Within a queer(ed) view of Scotland, even though each of the myriad identities and dimensions that exist within her may appear at times to be far removed from one another, they still can also be seen to be utterly connected, 'in relationship' and even interdependent with one another (George, 2017, pp. xiii, 9). Within quantum thinking, 'nonlocality' and 'decoherence' are additional concepts related to entanglement. Any change to the quantum state of one may change the state of the other, no matter how far apart they may be (George, 2017, pp. 28, 47).

The quantum view shows that alongside all visible particularities lie infinite further possibilities, all equally 'true' or valid. This utterly interconnected, multidimensional reality-matrix therefore inevitably queers a concept such as identity because any individual can only be viewed in terms of their being a particularity – also encompassing its own set of potentially infinite possibilities – that further exists *among* myriad coexisting particularities and possibilities (Al-Khalili, 2003, p. 119). 'Who I am' is therefore inevitably and necessarily contextual and fluid, ripe with imaginative potential.

Particular dimensions of Scotland's whole cease to exist in isolation as they become entangled both with one another and with the complexities of their environment (Al-Khalili, 2003, p. 114). All things must be considered relative to one another in myriad, multidimensional ways. Within this multidimensional whole, as Leath (2023) argues, such a mass of entangled yet self-differentiated particularities leaves no space for any notion that binaries could be 'all that there is' (p. 133). Roberto Che Henderson-Espinoza (2018, pp. 129, 130) has also argued that there can be no 'outside' in the 'matted knot' revealed by entanglement. Differentiation is replaced by interconnectedness.

Thus the Caledonian Antisyzygy initiates an ongoing journey of deconstruction, deep into the Scottish subconscious, to reveal multiple elastic and dynamic layers and dimensions of contradictions, dissonance and impossibilities. The 'matted knot' described by Henderson-Espinoza is integrally intersectional yet apparently chaotic, resistant to any attempts to detangle or unravel it. Within the fluid intersections of this dynamic, quantum (en)tangled knot, a historically and culturally embedded consciousness is also revealed. Every intersection has multiple 'horizons': personal, cultural, linguistic and spiritual; 'fusions', where new quantum worlds open up (Gadamer, 2007, p. 217). It is as though it were 'a stream in which we move and participate, in every act of understanding' (p. 117).

Quantum thinking considers the interrelatedness of all things within the universe, all matter or particles, to be 'in a relationship'. Quarks are considered to be that from which all things are built, yet are only observable through their innately relational qualities. Just as C. S. Lewis (1943, pp. 1, 20, 21, 49) proposed with his concept of the 'Tao', quarks can be seen in a closely analogous way: as a connecting and interflowing energy grounded in justice and humanity, representing a foundational, shared morality or conscience from which human beings derive all value judgments. The Tao encapsulates a core, entangled truth rooted in relationship.

Walter Rauschenbusch (1861–1918) – a North American theologian and pastor – argued that the essence of Christian ethics emanates from the intersection between identity and justice. Writing in 1907 he urged Christians to express Christlike love through service and solidarity with all, a Christ-identity manifesting through social justice action. He identified an instinctive, innate 'sympathy' within all human beings for those who are marginalized and impoverished (Rauschenbusch, 2007, p. 11). Such an innate state – or perhaps Tao – is undoubtedly an integral dynamic of the Scottish zeitgeist; a shared preoccupation with identity – however diversely interpreted – and passion for justice.

Clearly, for the majority of Scots this identity/justice Tao is not consciously connected to Christ Jesus. Nevertheless it remains clear that the identity/justice Tao *is* a core attribute of the Scottish zeitgeist. It can be readily observed in dissent, politics, literature, sport and ingrained, shared attitudes throughout Scottish history. Further, there exists within Scotland a profound interconnectedness, often across seemingly impossible divides. Scotland can therefore only be treated holistically. It is multidimensional, fluid and quantum, both synergetic and volatile in its intersectionality. Consequently any model that properly accommodates the Scottish whole must also accommodate the movement, growth, change, connections and repelling energy that occurs between each particularity, person, issue and identity. The quantum Scottish whole encompasses myriad multidimensional intersections involving geographical location, age, gender, class, ethnicity, ability/disability, sexuality, faith, football teams, political perspectives, subculture adherence and myriad other particularities and dimensions. Each of these may also be further deconstructed and subcategorized. Each one overlaps, intersects and synergizes.

As old ideas of binaries inevitably give way to relativistic and pluralistic understandings (Tomlinson, 2008, p. 78), within a fluid, elastic landscape, everything, including gender and sexuality, comes to be naturally deconstructed. This perspective recognizes not only spectra but also complex, fluid and dynamic matrices contained within further matrices and so on (Marsh, 2016). Each identity or dimension, whether that be 'Scottish', 'Gael', 'black', 'disabled', 'lesbian' or 'trans', contains potentially infinite further – intersecting – dimensions of nuance, contextuality and possibility, merging past experiences, cultural influences, contexts and more, none of which could be linear or binary.

Within the whole of Scotland, it can only be the instinctive process of deconstructive queering that enables the great Caledonian melting pot of celebration and strife to – almost inexplicably – 'work'. The Scottish nation continues to be forged through every synergetic moment of connection between diverse strands, identities and dimensions and in every point of dissonance and reaction. In Scotland, people are inseparable from the land, from our 'idea of Scotland' or even from one another. Multiple identities and contexts coexist and intersect within Scotland. These intersections can blur, so that those who are today part of a generation preoccupied with matters of identity and justice may come to feel connected to social justice movements not directly their own. Examples of such movements include Black Lives Matter, #MeToo and Pride. More specifically, in Scotland this would also include the marked uptake of adult Gaelic language learning and Gaelic medium schooling by those who do not have any particular connection to the Western Isles of Scotland, where the language has traditionally been found in recent history.

This is what 'wholeness' means for Scotland: a progressive political and cultural movement that is integrally relative, subjective, intersectional and contrary, quantum, reactionary and synergetic. This understanding of wholeness is very much echoed in the writings of North American womanist theologians, who embrace the challenge to 'celebrate life in its totality' (Cannon, Townes and Sims, 2011, p. xvi). 'Who we are determines ... our worldview' (p. xv).

## Womanism

Rooted in the experiences of black women, particularly within North America, womanism is integrally holistic, as it considers, in particular, the intersectional dimensions of sexism, racism and classism (Cannon, Townes and Sims, 2011, p. xv) alongside social and political identity (Weems, 2011, p. 51). It acknowledges and appreciates a breadth of traditions and dimensions of potential influence, which 'challenge us to continue to recover and discover resources and sources that point to a reality beyond ourselves' (Cannon, Townes and Sims, 2011, p. xv). The African American context of womanism, while entirely particular in its own right, may fruitfully be presented in parallel with Celtic, subaltern and queer(ed) ethics, wrought from the margins, in reaction and resistance to patriarchal, imperialistic hegemony. Although there are, of course, many clear differences in context and detail, the Scottish situation shares with that of African Americans a sense of marginalization and of being 'less than' within one's own country.

This justice and identity-centred, holistic approach of womanism offers a tangible way – within the quantum framework – to draw together the myriad polarities of the Caledonian Antisyzygy. That includes age, national identity, ability/disability, peer groups past and present, church backgrounds and the particularities of individual political preferences and subculture adherence (Borthwick, 2022, pp. 64, 71). It accommodates far more than simply sets of spectra. Dissonance and celebration, in the flux of the movement of this boundless, apparently chaotic matrix, reveal each individual, context, situation and issue to be a dynamic vector, directional and progressive, through time and space. There can no longer only be binaries; now, instead, multiple, nuanced orbits manifest constantly moving vectors.

## To Conclude

Accordingly, Scotland is a multidimensional, quantum whole comprising myriad crucial dimensions that – often erratically – orbit around one another, intersecting, combining and repelling. Whether these dimensions are ethnic, religious, historical or geographical, or relate to sexual identity, gender identity, politics or football, they are vectors, travelling with direction, velocity and time intrinsic to their nature. Points of intersection may be intricate, transitory or chaotic. Within each intersection that occurs there may be consonance or dissonance, synergy or even destruction. Only a fluid, intersectional and synergetic model can accommodate the complexities of the Caledonian Antisyzygy, a quantum, entangled whole made sense of through the holistic, justice- and identity-focused, integrally holistic lens of womanism.

The multidimensional, multidirectional and matrix-like nature of the whole of Scotland is innately playful, transgressive and subversive, dreaming of 'cure and disease' simultaneously. The myriad antisyzygies of Scotland pulse, orbit and intersect with one another, constituting a unique whole. As we unpick the knot, we deconstruct, queering our reading, a natural and integral thing to do for those blessed to be Scottish, whether by birth, adoption, personal choice or other route. Today's generation is intrinsically queer(ed) and quantum, to an extent never seen so naturally, explicitly or comfortably before.

As Smith (1919) urged: 'Oxymoron was ever the bravest figure, and we must not forget that disorderly order is order after all' (p. 5).

## *Notes*

1 The term comes from: 'Ye lawfully may, yea, and thereto are bound, to defend your brethren from persecution and tyranny, be it against princes or emperors, to the uttermost of your power' (Knox, 1745, p. 209).

2 Margaret Thatcher was the leader of the Conservative (Tory) party and British Prime Minister for three periods between 1979 and 1990.

3 Idlewild, 2002, 'Scottish Fiction', on *The Remote Part*, Parlophone Records.

## References

Abrams, Lynn and Callum G. Brown (2010), *A History of Everyday Life in Twentieth-Century Scotland*, Edinburgh: Edinburgh University Press.

Al-Khalili, Jim (2003), *Quantum: A Guide for the Perplexed*, London: Weidenfeld & Nicolson.

Althaus Reid, Marcella (2003), *The Queer God*, London: Routledge.

Borthwick, Kirsty (2022), 'Comfortable Feminism is not Enough: Following Christ's Call for Abundant Life', in *Young, Woke and Christian: Voices of the Missing Generation*, edited by Victoria Turner, London: SCM Press, pp. 62–73.

Cannon, Katie Geneva, Emilie M. Townes and Angela D. Sims (2011), 'Preface', in *Womanist Theological Ethics: A Reader*, edited by Katie Geneva Cannon, Emilie M. Townes and Angela D. Sims, Louisville, KY: Westminster John Knox Press, pp. xv-xvii.

Carruthers, Gerard (2009), *Scottish Literature*, Edinburgh: Edinburgh University Press.

Church of Scotland Guild (2021), 'Projects Though the Years', *Church of Scotland*, 14 June, at https://www.churchofscotland.org.uk/__data/assets/pdf_file/0005/19049/Past_guild_projects.pdf, accessed 01.12.2024.

Coalition for Racial Equality and Rights (CRER) (2024), 'Ten Things We Need to Say about Racism', at https://www.crer.org.uk/ten-things-we-need-to-say-about-racism, accessed 01.12.2024.

Derrida, Jacques (1999), 'Hospitality, Justice and Responsibility: A Dialogue with Jacques Derrida', in *Questioning Ethics: Contemporary Debates in Philosophy*, edited by Richard Kearney and Mark Dooley, London: Routledge, pp. 65–83.

Gadamer, Hans-Georg (2007), *The Gadamer Reader: A Bouquet of the Later Writings*, edited by Richard E. Palmer, Evanston, IL: Northwestern University Press.

Gay, Doug (2013), *Honey from the Lion: Christianity and the Ethics of Nationalism*, London: SCM Press.

George, Alison (2017), *The Quantum World: The Disturbing Theory at the Heart of Reality*, London: John Murray Learning and *New Scientist*.

Henderson-Espinoza, Roberto Che (2018), 'Queering Desire', in *Contemporary Theological Approaches to Sexuality*, edited by Lisa Isherwood and Dirk von der Horst, London: Routledge, pp. 124–31.

Hjul, Jenny (2023), 'How Scotland Became the Wokest Country in the World', *The Telegraph* (London), 28 January, at https://www.telegraph.co.uk/news/2023/01/28/how-scotland-became-wokest-country-world/, accessed 01.12.2024.

Hume, David (1739), *A Treatise of Human Nature, Book 1: Of the Understanding, Part 1: Of Ideas, their Origen, Composition, Abstraction etc., Section 7: Of Abstract Ideas*, London: Penguin.

Idlewild (2007), 'In Remote Part / Scottish Fiction' [song], in *Scottish Fiction: Best of 1997–2007* (3:50), London: Parlophone.

Keate, Noah (2024), 'Nicola Sturgeon says Trans Rights Abuse Pushed her to Quit as Scottish Leader', *Politico*, 20 May, at https://www.politico.eu/article/scotland-nicola-sturgeon-trans-rights-abuse-pushe-quit-leader-snp/, accessed 01.12.2024.

Knox, John (1745), *Select Practical Writings: Issued by the General Assembly of the Free Church of Scotland, for the Publication of the Works of Scottish Reformers and Divines*, Glasgow: William Collins.

Leath, Jennifer Susanne (2023), *Black, Quare, and Then to Where*, Durham, NC: Duke University Press.

Lehner, Stefanie (2008), 'Subaltern Aesth*ethics*: Tracing Counter Histories in Contemporary Scottish, Irish and Northern Irish Literature', doctoral dissertation, University of Edinburgh, at https://era.ed.ac.uk/bitstream/handle/1842/3305/Lehner2009.pdf?sequence=1&isAllowed=y, accessed 01.12.2024.

Lehner, Stefanie (2011), *Subaltern Ethics in Contemporary Scottish and Irish Literature: Tracing Counter-Histories*, London: Palgrave Macmillan.

Lewis, C. S. (1943), *The Abolition of Man*, Grand Rapids, MI: Zondervan.

Marsh, Sarah (2016), 'The Gender-Fluid Generation: Young People on Being Male, Female or Non-Binary', *The Guardian*, 23 March, at https://www.theguardian.com/commentisfree/2016/mar/23/gender-fluid-generation-young-people-male-female-trans, accessed 01.12.2024.

McGhee, Kelly Ann Cecillia (2024), 'The Destruction Caused by Clause 28', *LGBTQ Collections Online, Glasgow Women's Library*, at https://womenslibrary.org.uk/explore-our-collections/lgbtq-collections-online-resource/the-destruction-caused-by-clause-28/, accessed 01.12.2024.

*The Observer* (2022), 'The Observer View on Scotland's Controversial Proposed Gender Reforms', *The Guardian*, 18 December, at https://www.theguardian.com/commentisfree/2022/dec/18/scotland-controversial-proposed-gender-reforms, accessed 01.12.2024.

O'Murchu, Diarmuid (2004), *Quantum Theology: Spiritual Implications of the New Physics*, New York: Crossroad.

Rauschenbusch, Walter (2007), *Christianity and the Social Crisis in the 21st Century: The Classic that Woke up the Church*, edited by Paul Rauschenbusch, New York: HarperOne.

Russell, Michael (2023), '"Woke" will be the Foundation of an Independent Scotland', *The National*, 27 May, at https://www.thenational.scot/politics/23551407.woke-will-foundation-independent-scotland/, accessed 01.12.2024.

Scottish Government (2022), 'Gender Recognition', at https://www.gov.scot/policies/lgbti/gender-recognition/, accessed 01.12.2024.

Scottish Parliament (2021), 'Hate Crime and Public Order (Scotland) Bill', at https://www.parliament.scot/bills-and-laws/bills/s5/hate-crime-and-public-order-scotland-bill, accessed 01.12.2024.

Seanan, Gerard (2002), 'Push to Promote Scots Tolerance after Survey finds One in Four is Racist', *The Guardian*, 25 September, at https://www.theguardian.com/uk/2002/sep/25/race.scotland, accessed 01.12.2024.

Smith, George Gregory (1919), *Scottish Literature, Character and Influence*, London: Macmillan.

Spark, Muriel (1961), *The Prime of Miss Jean Brodie*, London: Macmillan.

Stevenson, Robert Louis (2014), *The Strange Case of Dr. Jekyll and Mr. Hyde*, London: Vintage Books.

Storrar, William (1990), *Scottish Identity: A Christian Vision*, Edinburgh: Hansel Press.

Tomlinson, Dave (2008), *Re-Enchanting Christianity: Faith in an Emerging Culture*, Norwich: Canterbury Press.

Weems, Renita J. (2011), 'Re-Reading for Liberation: African American Women and the Bible', in *Womanist Theological Ethics: A Reader*, edited by Katie Geneva Cannon, Emilie M. Townes and Angela D. Sims, Louisville, KY: Westminster John Knox Press, pp. 51–63.

Williams, Sarah (2022), 'Are you Guilty of "Transwashing"?' *The HR Grapevine*, November, at https://www.hrgrapevine.com/content/article/2022-11-25-are-you-guilty-of-transwashing, accessed 01.12.2024.

# 21

# Folding, (Un)Folding and (Re)Folding the World: An Approach to the Intellectual Itinerary of Darío García Garzón

ANDERSON FABIÁN SANTOS MEZA

## Introduction

Folding the world is an operation that not only (de)organizes chaos but also reveals its internal tensions. Each fold hides within itself a memory, a wound or a power of the yet unsaid. When we speak of folding the 'queer world', for example, the metaphor is amplified and complexified, for it implies not only recognizing the queer archive but also opening the fissures it contains. Queer – in its genealogy – is often presented as a globalizing category, exported from the centres of academic power to the peripheries and diasporas. (Un)folding its folds and (re)folding them when necessary is a critical action: letting out what has been compressed and what has not been seen. In this process of (de)folding, the '*marica* [sissy or pansy] world' appears as that which does not seem to fit, nor does it want to fit into the framework of the Anglo-Saxon queer. The folds are not only folds. They are also cracking and jumping. There we find the fractures that break with the colonial logic that pretends to order bodies and subjectivities. When it breaks, the queer fragments into a thousand pieces that cannot be reabsorbed into the totality. These fragments are the traces of the dissidence that insists, the insistence of the bodies-territory that do not allow themselves to be domesticated.

The work of the Colombian theologian and philosopher Hemberg Darío García Garzón is inscribed precisely in this Deleuzian logic of *folding*, *unfolding* and *refolding*. His intention was not to import foreign theories to impose them in his context but to break them from within, to submit them to the test of the territory. His walk through the Colombian streets, his dialogue with academic spaces and his listening to subaltern voices allowed him to fold the world of imported theories and unfold them again on his terms. It was not a simple 'adapting' but a 'folding'; that is, returning the theory to its initial folds, but with the marks of lived experience: (un)folds and (re)folds.

Folding, (un)folding and (re)folding the world, then, is not only an exercise in understanding but a way of doing epistemic (theo)politics. It is to recognize that there is no homogeneous and linear world but a set of worlds in tension, each with its folds, which are sometimes (un)folding and (re)folding (Conley, 2011). Therefore to fold, (un)fold and re(fold) is not to order, nor to define, but to allow the emergence of what was silenced, subway, clandestine and camouflaged ... as happens with that which is folded. It is – ultimately – a way of writing, (un)writing and (re)writing the collective memory from the perspective of those who have always been closer, next door, although they have always been called 'rare', 'others' and 'strangers'. Thus the fold becomes a horizon of understanding and a crack where resistance germinates.

Aligned with this horizon, this chapter provides a bibliographical synthesis of the work of García Garzón, recognized as the first queer theologian in Colombia. It begins with an overview of key elements of his biographical profile. Next it delves into an exploration of his academic output from 2004 to 2012, followed by an analysis of his proposal for creole, mestizo and bastard hermeneutics as a lens to understand Colombia's sex-gender dynamics. The chapter concludes with a reflection on the challenges a *marica* theology faces.

## About Hemberg Darío García Garzón

Hemberg Darío García Garzón – he preferred to be called Darío – was born on 5 August 1969. He studied Philosophy at the Major Seminary of Bogotá. He graduated in Philosophy and Religious Sciences at the Saint Thomas University. He received a degree in Theology from the Pontifical Xavierian University (PUJ). He has two master's degrees from the National University of Colombia: one in Sociology and the other in Gender Studies. He was a doctoral candidate in Theology at PUJ.

He was a professor-researcher assigned to the Virtual Bachelor's Degree in Religious Sciences academic unit. He was a member of the Theology and Gender research group at the Department of Theology, PUJ. He was also a member of the Seminar of Analogical Hermeneutics of the Instituto de Investigaciones Filológicas of the National Autonomous University of Mexico (UNAM). On the back covers of *Viaje de emperador a loco* [Journey from Emperor to Madman] (2009b), *Camino del ángel* [Path of the Angel] (2010) and *Mundo de las princesas* [World of Princesses] (2011a), the author presents himself as 'philosopher and theologian, pro-feminist, Colombian, and professor-researcher'. As a queer theologian, he affirms his theoretical positioning in this way:

> I place myself in queer theory because since I was initiated in feminism and gender studies, I have assumed a critical stance towards the logics of production and consumption of the gay market, which imposes a dominant identity and generates structures of alienation based on the hegemony of virile capital contained in beauty, youth and genital hyper-anatomy. (García Garzón, 2010, pp. 77–8)

Some of the theoretical references most consulted by this Colombian thinker were Mauricio Beuchot, Jacques Derrida, Gilles Deleuze and Félix Guattari, Martin Heidegger, Michel Foucault, Pierre Bourdieu, Oscar Guasch, Rosa María Rodríguez Magda, Julia Kristeva, Judith Butler and Clodovis Boff, among others.

## Behind the Heartbeat of Darío's *Senti-Pensar*:[1] His Works, His Thoughts and His Research

It was 2022, and my desire to trace my predecessors in Colombian queer theology was growing. I was walking through the same corridors where more than ten years ago the first person to talk about queer theologies in the country had walked. I had hunches, which were simultaneously profound certainties. I knew that nothing is ever done from scratch – that there are always others walking disruptive paths, resisting toxic and unhealthy logic, leaving testimonial traces and causing indecent, unforgettable scandals. Without even knowing his name, his face or his works, I paid attention to the reactions of many people who discovered in me a young *marica* theologian who spoke of transvestites and dissidents.

One day, after a presentation I made, someone said: 'It has been a long time since I heard someone talk about theology as Darío did.' After that statement there was an uncomfortable silence. I did not understand what that meant because I did not know that person. They tell me that he used to dress in black, wear cowboy boots and long leather coats and sometimes let his hair grow long and make a bun. Also, I am told that he used to offer himself as a 'symbol', dressing symbolically and trying to communicate with his body many things that become complex when theoretical language and its limitations enter the scene. Without knowing who that theologian was, I already knew that he walked these paths that I walk in my daily life. This filled me with mixed feelings, questions, suspicions and desires to know everything these cold walls can know. In Colombia – and throughout Latin America – they say with a tone of mischief, complicity and satire: 'Si las paredes hablaran ...' (If the walls could talk ...). What would these walls have to tell me? As a young theologian trying to discover the legacy of his predecessor in queer/*maricas* theologies in Colombia, this interested me.

I asked many people about García Garzón. Immediately silences and gestures of discomfort appeared, and explicit desires to evade the question and not answer. I noticed a systematic erasure of his history, work, relationships and faith experience. Someone told me: 'In the library, there are some texts that can tell you who he is' because 'people around here usually do not talk about him and his things.' This is how I found García Garzón's intellectual production, written between 2004 and 2012.

I found a small book (García Garzón, 2004a), which is part of the 'Nuevas Cartografías' Series of Instituto Pensar,[2] a text inspired by Darío's master's thesis in Sociology. It is a sociological study of the stylistic offerings of men's bathing houses in Bogotá.[3] In the work I found a striking sex-cultural ethnography nourished by methodological itineraries experienced by the author himself. Above all, inquiries into fundamental questions about homosexual relations in Colombia, about the *habitus* of the occupants of the saunas and clandestine steam rooms, and all the *symbolic capital* of masculinity and virility that is managed there.

I also found the 2004 book edited by him, together with Olga Consuelo Vélez and María del Socorro Vivas Albán, entitled *Reflexiones en torno al feminismo y al género* [Reflections on Feminism and Gender]. This collective volume compiles several research papers from the academic work of the Theology and Gender research group at PUJ, to which the authors belonged. García Garzón contributed two chapters (García Garzón, 2004b; 2004c). Some of the most relevant ideas developed therein are related to the critique of phallocracy, male domination and the cis-heterosexual division of labour, with the resistance of sex-gender dissidence to the modes of configuration of corporealities presented from the sex-gender binaries.

In this exercise of 'going back to the archive', to shake it all and sift through the dust of the shelves that are not usually visited, I found an article published in a student journal (García Garzón, 2008a) in which García Garzón unveils one of the epistemo(theo)logical problems of theology in the change of era: the *habitus* of the one who theologizes. It is an exercise of sociological reading of theological work to unmask the symbolic capital of theological knowledge. His methodology is based on 'relational thinking'; that is, on associative thinking from a sort of network logic. In his research, García Garzón makes explicit three issues of concern: (i) the 'stylistic offer' of theological epistemology, (ii) the socio-symbolic spaces in which theology is theologized, (iii) the theological capital; that is, the symbolic possession and possession of the knowledge of revelation. In response to this he asserts that it is essential to return to a perspective of uncertainty. To achieve this one must recognize that the theologian stands at the crossroads of the aporia created by multiple epistemological styles, alongside the risks of absolutizing these methods, no matter how eclectic or disruptive they may be. This uncertainty is overcome by embarking on 'a nomadic journey through the unsuspected desert of chaos' (García Garzón, 2008a, p. 64).

I learned that in 2008 he participated in the first Congress of Latin American and German Women Theologians on 'Biographies, Institutions and Citizenship. Theology and Society from a Women's Perspective', held from 25 to 27 March at the Schools of Philosophy and Theology of San Miguel, Province of Buenos Aires, Argentina. The book *Sentires teológicos en perspectiva liberadora* [Theological Sentiments in Liberating Perspective] compiled the papers presented by the participants of the Theology and Gender research group. The paper presented by García Garzón to the group (García Garzón, 2008b) is a reflection on the traditional logic of theological thinking and its practices of *epistemological transvestism*. For the author, it is urgent to recognize the trans becoming of theology – which is metaphorical, symbolic and literal – because there occurs a particular dynamic phenomenology of theological work about power and domination:

> Sometimes, to become masculine, that is, to become 'strong' again epistemologically speaking, theology resorts to transvestite itself with the theoretical accessories of the prevailing machismo of the knowledge that comes from the dominant philosophies of empiricism-positivism, or indeed it transsexualizes itself with the reassignment of methods that insist on the objectivity of data and suspect the subjective experience of the occurrence of divine revelation in the human. (García Garzón, 2008b, pp. 57–8)

With this, García Garzón encourages suspicion of the discourses that validate and legitimize specific epistemological and theological bets of rigid character while rejecting and silencing other perspectives. Likewise he points out the dangers of structuralist determinisms and theoretical and theological dogmatisms. Thus he invites us to pursue the paths of nomadic, relational, complex and rhizomatic thinking.

Simultaneously I found a conference paper (García Garzón, 2009a) in which it was proposed to suspect the issue of sexual and gender identity, constitutive of difference and sexual diversity. To this end García Garzón addressed the bipolarity perceived in (i) the phenomenon of 'demasculinization', understood as the transition that a male can make from masculinity to femininity, and (ii) the process of 'hypermasculinization', understood as the transfer of the male towards the more masculine. This text is understood as a synthetic preview of the postulates that the author will develop in his book *Camino del ángel* (García Garzón, 2010).

However, another book that came into my hands (García Garzón, 2009b) can be presented as a journey of metaphors accompanied by the Beuchotian pharmacist towards the hermeneutic threshold, an itinerary through which the imbrication between the question of gender and analogical hermeneutics is progressively approached, suggesting a sort of 'transcendental analogical feminism' that makes it possible to speak of trans masculinities. Borrowing Beuchot's words, it is sensible to say that:

> it is the hermeneutics of the threshold because it stops the chiaroscuro of the confluence between light and shadow, between metonymy and metaphor. Its characteristic of borderline, between the threshold, makes such interpretation suffer from certain indecision or ambiguity, but not so much that it cannot be held with certain clarity and definition ... Thus, the threshold has the peculiarity of being something partly given and partly built, precisely where the given and the built come together. (Beuchot, 2003, pp. 77–9)

Undoubtedly this is a text that criticizes androcentrism, cis-heterosexism and rigid sex/gender norms, recognizing that philosophies – and theologies – that are constructed on such logics are inherently destructive.

Together with Luis Mario Sendoya, Ángela María Sierra, Olga Consuelo Vélez and María del Socorro Vivas, García Garzón published an article (García Garzón et al., 2009) that was a systematic examination of the contribution of the gender perspective to the theological work and the academic curricula of some subjects of the Theology programme. Recognizing that boldness and determination are needed to advance in the implementation of the gender approach in theological studies, the researchers affirmed that 'current theology must be open to these new theological approaches if it wants to maintain its validity and relevance in today's society' (p. 126).

Pursuing his research interest he published a book chapter (2009c) in which he approached trans and sex-gender transits as 'steps of tension' that enable the emergence of fundamental questions in academic disciplines. According to the author, contemporary times evidence the need to seek a way out of the impasse in which we find ourselves, particularly about the struggle of bodies feeling trapped in the binary sex-gender system of female/male identity; this would imply, subsequently, a theologization of the epistemological transits of theology itself (pp. 10–19).

Additionally I found three books that trapped me in the library for several days, afternoons and evenings: *Camino del ángel* (García Garzón, 2010); *El mundo de las princesas* (2011a); and *Uróboros* (2011b). To put it in a heartfelt way, reading García Garzón not only shook my way of inhabiting religion and theology but also motivated me to immerse myself in the existential and historical phenomenology of sex-gender dissidence in Colombia.

In *Camino del ángel* the reader encounters an exercise of thought that seeks to investigate the paradox of the trans – from the transgender and the androgynous – and the binary polarities of the sex-gender division. From the recourse to the hermeneutics of facticity and analogical hermeneutics, García Garzón offers a reflexive approach to understanding the issue of 'trans existentialism', assumed as 'angelic and androgynous existentialism'. The work has seven chapters, which mark the itinerary of the approach: paths, point of view, look at everyday life, questionability, significance, horizon of the gaze and crossroads. Using Heideggerian thought, this investigative journey seeks to bring to light, discover and reveal [*Zum Vorschein bringen*] the urgency of propitiating uncoverings [*Unverborgenheit*] that imply deconstructions and reconstructions (García Garzón, 2010, p. 16).

*Uróboros* attempts to raise a reflexive inquiry into *alquimia criollizada* [creolized alchemy] within the practice of analogist thinkers in Latin American theological hermeneutics (2011b). It is structured in two main sections: the epistemological suspicion based on Beuchot's concept of *pensamiento otro* [other thought] – which aligns with analogical hermeneutics – and the critique of the *Eurocentrism* inherent in Martin Heidegger's work.

In *Mundo de las princesas*, García Garzón concludes the 'triptych' of books framed in theological hermeneutics in which he presents relational, repetitive and recurrent writing.[4] In this work he continues with his purpose of marking the reflective itinerary with the metaphor, which is why he states that:

> the enunciated *world of the princesses* is a *metaphor* that allows us a *hermeneutic alloy* of the mentioned approach ... The particular framework of the *world of the princesses* is woven between the *brocade* of the *fold* in the *Leibnizian* style. (2011a, p. 15; emphasis original)

On this occasion he used the Deleuzian tern *folding/unfolding/folding*[5] to make his journey through the 'world of princesses' in three stages: (i) the consideration of folding and the action of folding; (ii) the analytic of (un)folding; and (iii) the exercise of (re)folding. In this book the author suggests that the way to approach hermeneutics and *queer* theology is to recognize that it is the 'doing of folding': one fold follows another fold to infinity. García Garzón's purpose is to invoke metaphors that make it possible to think about the prophetic (denunciation) and the soteriological (liberating) character of emancipatory theology.

> The triptych folding of the chapters, as we open this book, will allow us to invoke a formula: *hermeneutics and queer theology*, which could be a *poison* if it is apologetic of the gay; or a *remedy* if it is critical and deconstructive of the logics of production and consumption of the gay market. (p. 21; emphasis original)

However, one of García Garzón's last publications (2012a) appears in a book that gathers the papers presented at the First International Symposium on Queer Theology, held at the *Departamento Ecuménico de Investigaciones* [Ecumenical Research Department] (DEI) in San José, Costa Rica. His paper is a retrospective exercise that synthesizes his academic, spiritual and existential journey up to that point in life. The first section, 'Horizonte apología y defensa' [Horizon apology and defence], goes through the author's memories of theologizing (1992–98) and sociologizing (1999–2003). The second section, 'Horizonte sospecha y crítica' [Horizon suspicion and critique], presents some reminiscences of gender studies (2004–07). Finally, in the third section, 'Horizonte incertidumbres' [Horizon uncertainties], he alludes to his return to theology (2008), his exercises of theological inquiry from hermeneutics, metaphor and analogy (2009–10), and his itinerary along a new path beyond the sex/gender binary: queer theology (2011–12).

> Queer theology is part of the question about the existential. Still, at the same time, it marks the paths in the *criollismo* of the Colombian context, and particularly in Bogotá, in which I have thought and written my discourses. (2012a, p. 198)

Amazed by all these written testimonies of García Garzón's intellectual work, I was motivated to continue my research. I asked many people about his history and his academic path. Thus a person who asked to remain anonymous gave me access to a very special and confidential document: García Garzón's unfinished doctoral dissertation was tentatively titled 'De *analogia entis* a *analogia vitae*: Un giro hermenéutico de la comprensión de la analogía en teología fundamental' [From *analogia entis* to *analogia vitae:* A Hermeneutical Turn in Understanding Analogy in Fundamental Theology] (García Garzón, 2012b). This 124-page document explores the transition from *analogia entis* (analogy of being) to *analogia vitae* (analogy of life), presenting the idea that one of the most profound conclusions of the author's academic-existential pilgrimage is that the analogies guiding the paths of becoming must be sought within life itself.

No further publications by García Garzón have been documented since 2012. According to collected stories and interviews, this absence is attributed to a worsening of physical, mental and spiritual ailments that significantly impacted his life. These challenges ultimately led him to discontinue his professional work at the Department of Theology at PUJ.

## Towards a Creole, Mestizo and Bastard Hermeneutics: To Understand the Sex/Gender Folds of Colombia

The curious and attentive journey I made through García Garzón's works led me to the conclusion that his great intellectual project was the establishment of a Creole-mestizo-baroque phenomenological approach to the critique of sex-gender rationality from Latin America, especially from the territory he inhabited: Bogotá, Colombia (García Garzón, 2011a, p. 12). His broad theoretical and methodological framework was *folded* by the horizon of the world. He then narrowed his focus to the *(un)folding* of his reality, striving to consolidate a 'situated knowledge' of queer identity in his country: the *marica.*

The understanding of the Anglo-Saxon verb 'to queer', which has been translated into Spanish as *extrañar* [to miss, to surprise], *transgredir* [to transgress, to violate], *desviar* [to divert, to deflect], *extraviar* [to misplace, to lose], *dislocar* [to dislocate, to disrupt], alludes to a polysemic dance between meanings, signifiers and uses (Santos Meza, 2023; 2024). The word 'queer' raises acute issues of translation into Spanish because although in English it has a substantial charge of insult and insult, it encompasses many diverse sexualities and does not have a specific gender. In contrast, in Spanish it is presented as an obscure and confusing term. Faced with this, some researchers have argued that the use of the term 'queer' operates as a form of linguistic colonialism. In addition, it loses value in its 'subversive capital', since in some areas it has been translated as *torcido* [twisted or crooked] or *cuir* (Platero, Rosón and Ortega, 2017).

In this effort to translate the term, discussions arise about how we wish to be, and can be, named in Spanish. For example, in Spanish the expression *cuir* does not lead to adverse reactions provoked by the pejorative enunciation of the term as in Anglo-Saxon contexts. Instead it seems that the use of *cuir* manifests a kind of 'aura of respectability' that makes it seem 'better, more sophisticated and international in an academic context' (Mizielinsksa, 2006, p. 90) and even harmless in ultraconservative environments (Platero, Rosón and Ortega, 2017). Some authors point out that the conceptualization of 'Latin American queer', *cuir* or *kuir*, is a symptom that – from gender and Latin American studies – it is urgent to look at identities and bodies in a more transversal, creative and strategic way (Falconí Tráves, Castellanos and Viteri, 2013). Indeed, with the presentation of the range of alternate and dissident sex-gender identities – including non-identity – the term queer/*cuir*/*kuir* is placed out of place, showing 'talking bodies' that can be 'read' only from the marginalities of what they are expected to be according to our political geolocation (Lanuza and Carrasco, 2015).

Paul-Beatriz Preciado (2003) stated that '*queer* knowledge is in itself a theory of the necessity and inevitability of a constant retranslation' (pp. 196–7). The translation of the Anglo-Saxon 'queer' to the Latin American cannot consist merely in changing words, nor a transnational linguistic barter, because 'the Anglo-Saxon *queer* is not exactly the same as the Latin American *cuir*' (Santos Meza, 2023, p. 143). Amy Laminsky (2008, p. 879) proposes using *encuirar* as a possible translation of the verb 'to queer', given that this word insinuates a certain air of familiarity with *encuerar*, evokes the act of 'undressing' and allows 'un-covering' reality by removing the layer of cis-heteronormativity. These new words help a great deal; however, they may prove to be a blunder, at least in terms of the historical and social implications that burden the term 'queer'.

This issue will be more explicit when recognizing that the exercise of 'location' of concepts through 'dislocation' is evidenced in the practice of (de)folding carried out by García Garzón.

## Contextual (Un)Folding: The 'Colombian Queer' is Called *Marica*

It is true that in countries such as Colombia, people who are dissident from the sex-gender system are usually related to deviance, indecency, transgressions and dislocations. Still, when a person is labelled and catalogued in a derogatory way, they may be called *marica* [sissy or pansy], *maricón* [faggot], *mariquita* [sissy or queen], *mariposo* [fairy] and other words that preserve the 'family resemblance' – the *Familienähnlichkeit* of Ludwig Wittgenstein (Weiberg, 2022) – of *maricomprensión* [fusion of two words: *marica* and *comprensión* (understanding)], to use the expression of the Latin American writer Pedro Lemebel (2020). In Latin American countries this 'family resemblance' has been weaponized as a linguistic device to construct a stigmatized subject through humiliating interpellation (Butler, 2002, p. 318). However, it is very significant that such expressions have not been used to nominate theoretical, philosophical and theological reflections as in their Anglo-Saxon counterparts. On the contrary, foreign words continue to be imported for this purpose (Córdova Quero, 2018, p. 100), thus erasing the counter-cultural potential of those derogatory terms.

García Garzón realizes that speaking of 'queer' in Colombia is insufficient and counterproductive; moreover the literal and uncritical importation of this foreign term and its decontextualized use becomes a colonial and classist issue since the vast majority of Colombian *maricas* are not usually bilingual, nor do they have access to advanced professional formalization processes. In addition, the memory of their struggles for resistance to sex-gender control regimes does not seem to be explicitly related to this Anglo-Saxon concept. For instance, 'lo mataron por maricón' [they killed him for being *maricón*], 'aquí están las maricas resistiendo' [here are the *maricas* resisting], 'y no, y no, y no me da la gana de ser una *marica* mercantilizada' [and no, and no, and I don't feel like being a commodified *marica*], are some of the phrases most often heard in the streets of Colombia. It is urgent to 'infect' (Lemebel, 2020) the word 'queer' with this *mariquismo* [campiness] of the South. Such a Creole-mestizo-baroque 'infection' is the application of the hermeneutic-analogical apparatus that the Colombian thinker addresses in his works. The *maricas*, their personal experiences and the wisdom condensed in their *somatecas* – bodies understood as receptacles and places of knowledge – are unsurpassable. Therefore the exercise of perceiving the term 'queer' in the Colombian *marica* context consists of a much deeper *(un)folded understanding* of the life lived and suffered by the country's sex-gender dissidences.

> The *fold* applied in this case allows us to recognize that *queer* has many *folds* and can constitute a kind of *labyrinth* for the critical understanding of sexes and genders (…) we find ourselves inserted in the *world* as a *fold*. (García Garzón, 2011a, p. 18; emphasis original)

However, García Garzón never distances himself from the theories and approaches of the global North since there he finds essential knowledge of great value without necessarily uprooting himself from his context. Thus he manages to propose Latin American hermeneutics that recognizes itself as 'baroque'[6] or – as the feminist María Galindo (2022) puts it – 'bastard'. For him, it became urgent to recognize the need to develop a Latin American – and Colombian – hermeneutics based on hermeneutics in general; that is, on European and North American hermeneutics, but without being reduced to it (Arriarán, 2006, p. 26).

For the Colombian author, if his research is intended 'to be contextually *queer*' – that is, 'to be a *marica* investigation' – it had to have as a starting point of the (un)folding a strategic space that summons, year after year, multitudes of LGBTIQ+ people: the annual Pride March. Thus García Garzón describes his experience on the afternoon of Sunday, 27 June 2010, around three o'clock in the afternoon, when he arrived at Avenue 7 with 33 Street in Bogotá and joined the Pride March (García Garzón, 2011a, p. 25). He himself confesses that 'at the moment of walking among them, I felt perhaps *queerer than ever*, in terms of the *raro* [odd], before the *raro* [queer] happening through the existentialism of the walkers' (p. 29; emphasis original). Moreover he acknowledges that it was not enough to walk alongside other queer people but that he had to establish dialogic bridges: 'and I proceeded to dialogue briefly with some of them' (p. 30). In these conversations the author tried to discover what understandings of the term 'queer' his interlocutors have, noticing that 'in the proletariat, the *queer* concept is not yet internalized, not even to associate it with the popular idea of *loca* or *maricón*' (p. 39). Although for García Garzón the relationship between 'queer' and *marica* was evident because of his broad knowledge of the *status questionis* in the world, in the conversations he had with the people 'on the street', the people who *pone el cuerpo* [to put one's body on the line] and march, perceive that this terminological correspondence is dubious and confusing.

Similarly, García Garzón (2011a) observes a wide range of diverse experiences in this march. The Colombian researcher describes what his eyes – as a phenomenologist and sociologist – were witnessing in the flow of marchers. Among the expressions used by him are 'very masculine men', 'feminine men', 'masculine women', 'feminine women', 'transvestites who perform femininity', 'transvestites who perform masculinity', 'trans women' and 'androgynous people', among others. In another of his works he referred to this sex-gender multiplicity as follows: 'the presence of hybrid, eclectic, metamorphosing, revolutionized, changing, transgressive identities, in irruption, in transfer, in transit, in nomadism and in foreignness' (García Garzón, 2010, p. 72).

Hence García Garzón recognizes the (re)folds of the 'queer world' when he (un)folds the 'world of princesses' or the '*marica* world'. Thus in the case of the event of the march, he notices that 'the makeup, the tulle, the glove, and the sequin, accompanied their fictitious, delicate and courtly gestures, which linked them in an imaginary social class in the metaphorical world of the feminine' (García Garzón, 2011a, p. 32). During that walk – in which he affirmed feeling '*queerer than ever*' – he perceived a sort of 'Disney-fiction imaginary' (p. 16; emphasis original). That is, *princess* figures stand out and are performed by different marching artists:

> I intend to refer to the corporealized feminine metaphor with the term *princess* because, as I went deeper into the walk, I observed that most *transgender* people invoked the imaginary of the princess in their representation of their *bodies*, some representing her dressed and others naked, in the realm of *fairy tales*. Mainly, the dressed princess was repeatedly *observed* as a representation of Snow White. (García Garzón, 2011a, p. 30; emphasis original)

In this sense the metaphor of the 'world of princesses' used by García Garzón is a way of approaching the multiple realities of the diverse and the dissident, according to the existential he evidenced in Pride. In the 'world of princesses' he sees evidence that in the 'world of the march' there are 'other worlds' that coexist with his own or, perhaps, that he makes himself part of 'another world' very different from this one (Santos Meza, 2023). Along with this idea, several aspects are commonly described: feeling as if one were from 'another planet', sensing that one's feelings are incomprehensible 'on this earth', and suffering from the condition of indigence. It also involves the dismemberment of one's own body to force oneself to fit in, disguising oneself to pass the gender test, camouflaging one's gender identity and sexual orientation and pretending to be something one is not. Ultimately it is about knowing oneself to exist in a state of incessant clandestinity in order to cross borders and courageously dwell on the margins, the limits and the peripheries. The 'world of princesses' alludes to the notion of 'the abject' referred to by Patricia Soley-Beltrán (2009): 'The abject is precisely this *no man's land*, a space that defines the outer limits of what is acceptable, outside of which a person is not considered *someone* human' (p. 374).

## Among the (Un)Folds, the Presence of (Homo)Normativities

Already in *Camino del ángel* García Garzón had warned of the problems that are triggered when some queer people proclaim the 'utopia of sexual diversity' (p. 49). For him it was essential to recognize that in many cases:

> the ludic and hedonic activities of the world of the so-called sexual diversity, in rumba, carnivals, and orgy, lead us unbridledly to the reproduction of the sex/gender duality among males and continue perpetuating patriarchy and androcentrism in the *gay* version. (García Garzón, 2010, p. 50; emphasis original)

Indeed, several aspects should be considered, among which at least two stand out: (i) not everything related to sex-gender diversity should be considered as 'revolution' and 'liberation'; (ii) we should be suspicious of the spaces and practices that are usually presented as places and actions of sex-gender liberation, because they may be replicating the violent and oppressive logics of cis-heteronormativity.

In this order of ideas García Garzón proposes an essential difference between 'gay homosexuality' and 'homosexuality associated with queer':

> Homosexuality associated with *gay* is configured in a structuring strategy of the subjects in such logic determined by neoliberal and globalized capitalism, reproducing a type of hegemonic identity imposed on the same subjects. The strategy can configure an alienating game emphasizing another form of male domination. A possible emancipatory way out of the labyrinths of the logic of gay production and consumption as an alienating structure may be, at the same time, to leave enunciated now the approach of the becoming of the *antigay* as a condition to give way to the formulation of the *transgender* from the *queer* meaning. (García Garzón, 2010, p. 27; emphasis original)[7]

According to the author, cis-homonormativity (Duggan, 2002) is an expression of cis-heteropatriarchy and gay androcentrism, two structures that produce misogyny and homophobia. Misogyny because they repudiate the presence of women in the establishments but at the same time reserve the right of admission for 'effeminate men', and if they manage to enter they are seen as 'fake men' (García Garzón, 2010, pp. 45–6). García Garzón evidences this in many places of LGBTIQ+ socialization, but his research focuses on the phenomenology of relationships in men's bathhouses (García Garzón, 2004a). In such places it is evident that:

> the *illusio* or belief in phallic capital on the part of the occupants determines the *habitus* or behaviors internalized in their lives and disposes them to the taste of the phallus of other males, corresponding to the archetype of male domination, represented simply in a large penis, but which symbolically represents strength and virility. (García Garzón, 2010, p. 45)

Among the many people attending the 2010 Pride march there were also numerous hypermasculine bodies, bodies of 'real men', which represented a particular hegemony of gayness.

These 'real males' were not considered *maricas* in the derogatory sense in which the category is used. In the same way that García Garzón does, Lemebel affirms that history gives an account of the countless laughs that disorder the dominant sex-gender assumption, of the dislocated dances that rearrange the world, of the *maricas rites* in which bodies that do not classify in the imported category of 'gay man' are contemplated. Nowadays this category is increasingly exclusive since it has also witnessed a neoliberal and capitalist co-optation of identity, in which only a tiny group of hegemonic homosexual men have a place, with all that being hegemonic implies.

Undoubtedly cis-homonormativity has become one of the new segregation devices since we no longer only face the normative cis-heterosexual logics that are based on the petro-sexual-racial system. Still, within what is called 'sex-gender diversity' there are countless phobic, exclusionary and violent practices. The *maricas* of the South know we are doubly bastardized; we are not only wounded but *too* wounded (Lemebel, 2020, pp. 13–68). Paraphrasing the 'bastard feminist', as María Galindo (2022, p. 41) describes herself, we have numerous reliable testimonies. These testimonies emphasize that the goal is not for LGBTIQ+ people to occupy positions of power, such as leadership roles in churches, police departments, armies, universities, parliaments, mayor's offices, governments or sports organizations. These numerous wounds highlight that the real challenge lies in the ability to question the structures, logic and meanings underpinning each of these cis-hetero-patriarchal institutions. This requires acknowledging that 'the arena of interrelations between civil society and the state continues to be key to the processing of social contradictions' (Cadahia and Coronel, 2021, p. 60).This is what Pedro Lemebel (2020) recalls in his *Crónicas de sidario* [Chronicles of a 'poz']:

> Perhaps, affluent homosexuality was never a subversive problem that altered their neat morals. Perhaps there were too many right-wing nuts who supported the regime. Possibly their corpse-like stench was muffled by the French perfume of the barrio alto queers. But even so, the death stench of the dictatorship was a foretaste of AIDS, which made its debut in the early 1980s. (p. 22)

Due to the cis-normativities that emerge in the unfolding of gender diversity, we need to *maricomprendernos* (Lemebel, 2020, p. 163). Amid all that others say we are and all they claim we should be, we face an identity, socio-cultural, political and religious crisis. This crisis is triggered by several factors, among which two stand out:

1. Structural violence, which mobilizes forces of control and oppression over our dissident existences;
2. Endless clichés and neoliberal practices that fragment our existence and impose new asphyxiating binarisms, erasing any difference.

We need to *maricomprendernos* to transform the political, epistemic and symbolic coordinates, and to be able to dispute the common meanings established in the spaces of legitimization of knowledge and political-religious practices (Cadahia, 2024, p. 22). We should strive to *maricomprendernos* to contaminate the academy, the companies, the churches and the streets with our *marica* bastardism. We must go beyond the identitarian and the nominalist, beyond that sort of *naive voluntarism of nomination* (Cadahia, 2024, p. 28), because it is not the deliberate self-denomination that will allow us to find the way out of 'the prison of phallocentric language' (Braidotti, 2004, pp. 91–2). Enunciating ourselves as dissidents of the sex-gender system does not imply an automatic transformation of the material structures of power. To liberate our subjectivity we need more than mere acts of nomination; we must free ourselves from socio-historical constraints through tropes rooted in the popular collective imagination. These tropes should enable genuine socio-symbolic interventions. To achieve this, however, we need to *maricomprendernos*.

Assuming the *marica* life experience, Lemebel presented himself from an 'old reality with a new, incisive, challenging light, and from an extremely marginal condition. I am *maricón* and poor, my two noble titles ... [As well as] Indian and poorly dressed' (Checa-Montúfar, 2016, p. 164). According to Fernando Checa-Montúfar (2016), Lemebel made visible a collective that represents the dispute against the construction of a geocultural, political and racial subalternation, which:

> privileges and values logocentric metropolitan western knowledge and rejects knowledge that does not correspond to its epistemological parameters and that has ways of knowing and knowing with different logics and cultural dynamics structured in popular cultures configured by the crossing of the traditional and the modern, the historical and the new, the massive and the popular ... and prevents seeing those who produce that alternative knowledge as legitimate agents, 'only sees them as informal' of the cultural market. (p. 163)

That is why, in his literary narrative, we find *la maricada* [nonsense queer stuff], *el loquerío* [madness or craziness] and *el mariconaje* [queer marronage]. These expressions are accompanied by terminological mutations that share some syllables or simple euphony, as with *maricomprenderse* or *depre-sidas* [AIDSpair]. On the other hand, combinations appear that seek to resignify the available lexicon from the formulation of new substantive construction. Some examples are: *Lágrimas de maricocodrilo* [queer crocodile tears], *hermanas sidadas* [AIDS-stricken sisters], *loca sidada* [AIDS-stricken queen], *paranoia sidática* [AIDS-related paranoia], *complicidad maricueca* [sissy complicity], *bambolear homosexuado* [homoeffeminate swaying], *amancebado culeo* [cohabiting hookup], *el control ciudad-ano* [citizen-anus control] (Paredes, 2023). These 'linguistic infections' (Lemebel, 2020) were not simple nominative acts. Nevertheless, disruptive political actions were mobilized through them, such as those executed by *Las Yeguas del Apocalipsis* [The Mares of the Apocalypse], a collective founded by Lemebel that was active from 1987 to 1993. They engaged in a form of *maricomprensión*, aimed at dismantling unilateral truths, shattering social determinism and compelling the imagination to turn inward. All of this was achieved by resorting to the margins, folds and interstices that allowed for critical questioning through '*loca* homosexuality' as a vital hypothesis. Such a questioning functioned as:

> a brilliant way of perceiving and perceiving herself, of constantly reassembling her imaginary according to survival strategies. The *loca* is continuously zigzagging in her political becoming, she is always thinking about how to subsist, how to get by, perhaps without being

> noticed, or very much noticed. And it is a wandering way of thinking, it is not the fixed and solid form of the male. The *loca* is a hypothesis, a question about herself. (Risco, 1995, p. 16)

Undoubtedly when García Garzón speaks of the 'men of lies' he is not alluding to the gay, modern and whitewashed version of homosexual identity, that which benefits from bourgeois acquiescence for filling the quota of tolerance, inclusion and diversity. *Mariquismo* [campiness] does not fit in such quotas because it is part of the old popular homosexualities marginalized by this integration, and precisely for this reason the *marica* has a potential of 'deterritorializing subversion'. Its power lies in its constitution as becoming, as a process, as flow and – in this way – it claims its world, knowledge, corporealities and culture. Doing so gives them legitimacy and summons them to a more organic and widespread political practice, to a 'politicizing practice to *maricomprenderse*' (Sandoval Álvarez, 2018). Thus it fights against biopolitics and the coloniality of power (Checa-Montúfar, 2016).

From the descriptions I managed to gather about García Garzón, the most repeated is that he was not a *gay* man. Indeed, some people close to him recognize that he always positioned himself as *anti-gay* (García Garzón, 2010, p. 27). In his existential development, in the struggles he faced amid the *macho* and phallocentric Colombian society, he always tried to present himself as *loca* and *marica*; that is, as a person who 'se le moja la canoa' [plays for the other team] (García Garzón, 2010, pp. 36–40), taking the expression of a Vallenato popular song. This song describes *mariquismo* as the testimony that birds leave when they fly by the *pluma*. And the tracing of feathers implies, then, a recognition of the contextual (re)folds and of the infinite territorial ambiguities that make 'in our Latin American context, different from the Anglo-Saxon one, *queer* is even weirder and stranger' (García Garzón, 2011a, p. 63).[8]

## Towards a *Marica* Theology: (Re)Folding the Sex-Gender System in the '*Habitus* of Theologization'

The exploration of García Garzón's works has immersed me in numerous questions that cannot be postponed and demand an answer from anyone who seeks to theologize to *maricomprenderse*. As a *marica* I have become a theological question, a theological object, a theological subject, a subject who does theology and a theological space, a generator of theology. García Garzón's reflections act as stings, compelling me to confront the question of my own '*habitus* of theologization' (García Garzón, 2008a).

I continue my walk through the corridors of the School of Theology through which my fellow Colombian *marica* theologian once walked. My heart is anguished because I find the panorama of theology for those of us who declare ourselves as *maricas* in Colombia and all of Latin America to be hopeless. After researching in the archive the work done by this Colombian dissident theologian in the past and returning to the present, I feel a profound nausea. My body, my head, heart, legs, hands, blood and, in a word, everything I am, shudders with pain. I wish I had many answers and lights to illuminate the future. However, I do not see them. I long to embrace García Garzón wherever he may be – because no matter how much I searched, I could not confirm if he is still alive, has passed or is here or somewhere else. I yearn to hold him and his immunodeficiency close, to kiss his wounds and to comfort his vulnerability. I ache to weep with him and tell him that I am here, that I am another queer theologian like him. I want to assure him that I am striving to follow his path and confront the profound loneliness that accompanies the work of queer/*cuir* theologies in Colombia, a loneliness that deeply wounds me. If I feel all these emotions now, I cannot even fathom what García Garzón endured and suffered in his own time.

I am currently pursuing my doctoral studies in theology. Studying theology as a *marica* is complex, challenging and painful. Moreover trying it is already revolutionary, dissident and emancipating. Perhaps the failure of *maricas* in theology symbolizes the failure and death of theology itself, its liberation project and its utopias of justice. This may be so. However, I want to keep trying, even when strength feels lacking. The feeling of abandonment is constant and the necessary economic resources are scarce. Month after month I must grapple with how I will manage to continue. I am caught in 'epistemological limbos' and subjected to ongoing epistemic injustices. The incomprehension and violence I face make it all deeply difficult and painful. I try to coexist with the uncertainty that appears with every small act of resistance within the cis-heteropatriarchal academy and its theological conditioning. I do it because I resist stepping aside, and I hope to withstand even more the colonial efforts to silence the *mariquismo* and hide the *plumas* [feathers].

The research presented in this chapter has compelled me to decentre myself from the answers and return to García Garzón's questions, which remain highly relevant to the Colombian context. Still, I extend them to all of Latin America: What thresholds of secrecy must be crossed in theology? What is the *habitus* of theologization that predominates today? What theological sentiments do I perceive in myself and those around me? What advances and/or setbacks are evident in the theological hermeneutics that addresses the trans and queer/*maricas*? How is analogy applied in theology? Are we aware of everything that remains undeveloped? Where is the pen in Latin American theology? Where is *mariquismo* in Latin American theology?

If I want to follow in the '*maricas* footsteps' of García Garzón I must recognize that his queer/*marica* theology consists of 'a retracing of steps' (García Garzón, 2011a, p. 110). Thus in the existential questions that emerge repeatedly lies a prophetic force (denunciation) that can be transformed into a soteriological – liberation – flow – or not. Raising these questions incessantly requires the daring of the *loca*, the theological cry of the *marica* because 'daring in itself is an abject behavior that generates a transgression or an irruption' (García Garzón, 2010, p. 76). Among the tears that writing this research has caused me I want to conclude with this passage from García Garzón, where he makes explicit one of his greatest desires: 'to place this issue on the table of theologians in dialogue with activists, LGBTI scholars, and social scientists is of vital importance' (García Garzón, 2011a, p. 31). Only in this way will it be possible to 'say a word about faith through rare and incomprehensible statements' (p. 64).

Reflecting on García Garzón's life and work I am filled with awe and find myself compelled to affirm: 'Y miré la noche y ya no era oscura ... era de lentejuelas!' [And I looked at the night, and it was no longer dark ... it was sequined] (Trevi, 2006). This metaphor encapsulates the transformative power of García Garzón's contributions to *marica* theology, shedding light on the previously unspoken and turning darkness into a celebration of brilliance and resilience. His legacy inspires and challenges us to reimagine *marica* theology in all its complexity and beauty, urging us to find – even in the darkest alleys – the sequins that make it shine.

## *Notes*

1 The expression *senti-pensar* is used because it returns to the approach of the Colombian sociologist Orlando Fals-Borda (2009), for whom there is no other way to understand Latin American territories than by feeling and thinking simultaneously. For more information, see the research by Arturo Escobar (2014).

2 García Garzón's work was presented in the context of the Ciclo Rosa [Pink Series] of Bogotá from 26 June to 8 July 2004. The 2004 edition was entitled 'Para que todos luzcan' [So that everyone shines].

3 The ethnographic research fieldwork was conducted during 2001 and 2002 in Bogotá (García Garzón, 2010, p. 43).

4 This is what García Garzón (2011a, p. 12) states at the beginning of the section 'folding', making a brief synthesis of what was his Creole and mestizo phenomenological project around the critique of the rationality of sexes and genders from Latin America.

5 Gilles Deleuze (1989) says that 'we discover new ways of folding ... because it is always a matter of folding, unfolding and refolding' (p. 177).

6 In this sense, Deleuze (1989) stated that: 'The Baroque does not refer to an essence, but rather to an operative function, to a feature. It never ceases to make folds' (p. 11).

7 For more information, see Córdova Quero's (2023, pp. 222–3) synthetic approach to García Garzón's thought.

8 Deleuze (1989) points out about the Baroque that 'it is the fold that goes to infinity' (p. 11).

## References

Arriarán, Samuel (2006), 'La hermenéutica barroca', in *Ensayos sobre hermenéutica analógica-barroca*, edited by Samuel Arriarán and Elizabeth Hernández, Ciudad de México: Editorial Torres Asociados, pp. 25–35.

Beuchot, Mauricio (2003), *Hermenéutica analógica y del umbral*, Salamanca: Editorial San Esteban.

Braidotti, Rossi (2004), *Feminismo, diferencia sexual y subjetividad nómade*, Barcelona: Editorial Gedisa.

Butler, Judith (2002), *Cuerpos que importan: Sobre los límites materiales y discursivos del 'sexo'*, traducido por Alcira Bixio, Ciudad Autónoma de Buenos Aires: Editorial Paidós.

Cadahia, Luciana (2024), *República de los cuidados: Hacia una imaginación política del futuro*, Barcelona: Herder Editorial.

Cadahia, Luciana and Valeria Coronel (2021), 'Volver al archivo: De las fantasías decoloniales a la imaginación republicana', in *Teoría de la república y prácticas republianas*, edited by Macarena Marey, Barcelona: Herder Editorial, pp. 59–98.

Checa-Montúfar, Fernando (2016), 'Pedro Lemebel: Revelación y rebelión en sus crónicas desde el margen', *Palabra Clave* 19, no. 1, pp. 156–84.

Conley, Tom (2011), 'Folds and Folding', in *Gilles Deleuze: Key Concepts*, edited by Charles J. Stivale, London: Routledge, pp. 192–203.

Córdova Quero, Hugo (2018), *Sin tabú: Religiones y diversidad sexual en América Latina*, Bogotá/Santiago de Chile: REDLAD/GEMRIP Ediciones.

Córdova Quero, Hugo (2023), *Teologías queer globales*, St. Louis, MO: Institute Sophia Press.

Deleuze, Gilles (1989), *El pliegue*, translated by José Vésquez and Umbetina Larraceleta, Barcelona: Ediciones Paidós Ibérica.

Duggan, Lisa (2002), 'The New Homonormativity: The Sexual Politics of Neoliberalism', in *Materializing Democracy: Toward a Revitalized Cultural Politics*, edited by Russ Castronovo and Dana D. Nelson, Durham, NC: Duke University Press, pp. 175–94.

Escobar, Arturo (2014), *Sentipensar con la tierra: Nuevas lecturas sobre desarrollo, territorio y diferencia*, Medellín: Ediciones UNAULA.

Falconí Tráves, Diego, Santiago Castellanos and María Amelia Viteri, eds (2013), *Resentir lo queer en América Latina: Diálogos desde/con el Sur*, Barcelona: Editorial Egales.

Fals-Borda, Orlando (2009), *Una sociología sentipensante para América Latina*, Bogotá: Siglo del Hombre Editores.

Galindo, María (2022), *Feminismo bastardo*, Ciudad de México: Canal Press/ Mantis.

García Garzón, Hemberg Darío (2004a), *Cruzando los umbrales del secreto: Acercamiento a una sociología de la sexualidad* [Crossing the Thresholds of Secrecy: An Approach to a Sociology of Sexuality], Bogotá: Editorial Pontificia Universidad Javeriana.

García Garzón, Hemberg Darío (2004b), 'Escenarios, imaginarios y construcciones de los cuerpos' [Scenarios, Imaginaries and Constructions of Bodies], in *Reflexiones en torno al feminismo y al género*, edited by Hemberg Darío García Garzón, Olga Consuelo Vélez and María del Socorro Vivas Albán, Bogotá: Editorial Pontificia Universidad Javeriana, pp. 199–210.

García Garzón, Hemberg Darío (2004c), 'Misoginia, expresión antifeminista' [Misogyny, Anti-feminist Expression], in *Reflexiones en torno al feminismo y al género*, edited by Hemberg Darío García Garzón, Olga Consuelo Vélez and María del Socorro Vivas Albán, Bogotá: Editorial Pontificia Universidad Javeriana, pp. 33–40.

García Garzón, Hemberg Darío (2008a), '*Habitus* de teologización' [*Habitus* of Theologization], *Reflexiones Teológicas* 2, no. 1, pp. 55–65.

García Garzón, Hemberg Darío (2008b), 'Teología de la masculinidad. Crítica al androcentrismo y transgenerización de la epistemología teológica' [Theology of Masculinity. Critique of Androcentrism and Transgenderization of Theological Epistemology], in *Sentires teológicos en perspectiva liberadora*, edited by Amparo Novoa Palacios et al., Bogotá: Editorial Pontificia Universidad Javeriana, pp. 51–70.

García Garzón, Hemberg Darío (2009a), 'Exploraciones sobre la diferencia y la diversidad sexual. Hacia una teología transgénero: encrucijada en la teología' [Explorations on Difference and Sexual Diversity. Towards a Transgender Theology: Crossroads in Theology], in *Entremeses Teológicos 2008. Teología y hábitat juvenil. ¿Sabe Dios dónde andan nuestros jóvenes?*, edited by Hermann Rodríguez Osorio, Bogotá: Editorial Pontificia Universidad Javeriana, pp. 95–121.

García Garzón, Hemberg Darío (2009b), *Viaje de emperador a loco: Introducción a una hermenéutica analógica de la transmasculinidad* [Journey from Emperor to Madman: Introduction to analogical hermeneutics of transmasculinity], Coyoacán: Editorial Torres Asociados.

García Garzón, Hemberg Darío (2009c), 'Cruzando los umbrales del varón: Hacia una teología transgénero desde una ontología de la masculinidad' [Crossing the Thresholds of Male: Towards a Transgender Theology from an Ontology of Masculinity], in *Género y Religión. Pluralismos y disidencias religiosas*, edited by María Angélica Peñas Defagó and María Candelaria Sgró Ruata, Córdoba: Católicas por el Derecho a Decidir, pp. 11–19.

García Garzón, Hemberg Darío (2010), *Camino del ángel: Sendas hacia una hermenéutica de lo transgénero* [Path of the Angel: Pathways to a Hermeneutics of the Transgender], Coyoacán: Editorial Torres Asociados.

García Garzón, Hemberg Darío (2011a), *Mundo de las princesas: Hermenéutica y Teología queer* [World of Princesses: Hermeneutics and Queer Theology], Coyoacán: Editorial Torres Asociados.

García Garzón, Hemberg Darío (2011b), *Uróboros: Oficio del analogista en la hermenéutica teológica* [Ouroboros: The Office of the Analogist in Theological Hermeneutics], Coyoacán: Editorial Torres Asociados.

García Garzón, Hemberg Darío (2012a), 'Analogías en teología queer' [Analogies in Queer Theology], in *Teorías queer y teologías: estar… en otro lugar* [Queer Theories and Theologies: Being … Somewhere Else], edited by Genilma Boehler, Lars Bedurke and Silvia Regina de Lima Silva, San José de Costa Rica: Departamento Ecuménico de Investigaciones, pp. 191–8.

García Garzón, Hemberg Darío (2012b), 'De *analogia entis* a *analogia vitae:* Un giro hermenéutico de la comprensión de la analogía en teología fundamental', unpublished doctoral dissertation draft, Bogotá: Facultad de Teología, Pontificia Universidad Javeriana.

García Garzón, Hemberg Darío, Olga Consuelo Vélez and María del Socorro Vivas Albán (2004), *Reflexiones en torno al feminismo y al género*, Bogotá: Editorial Pontificia Universidad Javeriana.

García Garzón, Hemberg Darío, Luis Mario Sendoya, Ángela María Sierra, Olga Consuelo Vélez and María del Socorro Vivas (2009), 'El género en la disciplina teológica' [Gender in the Theological Discipline], *Theologica Xaveriana* 59, no. 167, pp. 101–28.

Laminsky, Amy (2008), 'Hacia un verbo queer', *Revista Iberoamericana* 74, no. 225, pp. 879–95.

Lanuza, Fernando and Raúl Carrasco (2015), *Queer & Cuir: Políticas de lo irreal*, Ciudad de México: Editorial Fontamara.

Lemebel, Pedro (2020), *Loco afán: Crónicas de sidario*, Bogotá: Editorial Planeta.

Mizielinska, Joanna (2006)', Queering Moominland: The Problems of Translating Queer Theory into a Non-American Context', *SQS: Journal of Queer Studies in Finland* 1, no. 1, pp. 87–104.

Paredes, Lautaro (2023), 'Transgredir la lengua: *El lugar sin límites* de José Donoso y *Loco afán. Crónicas de sidario* de Pedro Lemebel', *Revista de Estudios y Políticas de Género* 9, pp. 184–204.

Platero, R. Lucas, María Rosón and Esther Ortega (2017), *Barbarismos queer y otras esdrújulas*, Barcelona: Edicions Bellaterra.

Preciado, Paul-Beatriz (2003), 'Préface: Le Queer Savoir', in *Queer zones: Politiques des identités sexuelles, des représentations et des savoirs*, by Marie-Hélène Bourcier, París: Éditions Balland, pp. 195–212.

Risco, Ana María (1995), 'Escrito sobre ruinas', *La Nación* (Santiago de Chile), 18 June, pp. 16–17.

Sandoval Álvarez, Juliana (2018), 'Sospechas maricas de la cueca democrática: arte, memoria y futuro en "Las Yeguas del Apocalipsis" (1988–1993)', *Estudios de Filosofía* 58, pp. 9–39.

Santos Meza, Anderson Fabián (2023), 'Tránsitos, desvíos y dislocaciones. Hacia otro no-lugar con Paul-Beatriz Preciado y Marcella Althaus-Reid', in *El hilo de Ariadna Entretejiendo saberes en clave interdisciplinaria*, edited by Hugo Córdova Quero and Cristian Mor, St. Louis, MO: Institute Sophia Press, pp. 129–62.

Santos Meza, Anderson Fabián (2024), 'Desviaciones teológicas para retornar al Edén: Aproximaciones, preguntas e indagaciones desde las teologías queer/cuir', in *Mysterium Liberationis Queer: Ensayos sobre teologías queer de la liberación en las Américas*, edited by Hugo Córdova Quero, Miguel H. Díaz, Anderson Fabián Santos Meza and Cristián Mor, St. Louis, MO: Institute Sophia Press, pp. 369–422.

Soley-Beltrán, Patricia (2009), *Transexualidad y la matriz heterosexual: Un estudio crítico de Judith Butler*, Barcelona: Edicions Bellaterra.

Trevi, Gloria (2006), 'Todos me miran' [song], in *La Trayectoria* (CD), Santa Monica, CA: Universal Music.

Weiberg, Anja (2022), 'Familienähnlichkeit', in *Wittgenstein-Handbuch: Leben-Werk-Wirkung*, edited by Anja Weiberg and Stefan Majetschak, Stuttgart: Springer-Verlag, pp. 235–42.

# Glossary

**Abya Yala:** Indigenous name for the American continent, asserting pre-Columbian identity, sovereignty and cultural continuity, rejecting the colonial term 'Latin America'.

**AuDHD:** A dual diagnosis or self-labelling of autism and ADHD.

**Autoethnography:** The study of the self.

**Benedictines:** A Christian monastic order founded in the sixth century, following the life and teachings of Benedict of Nursia (AD 480–547) as conveyed in the *Rule of St Benedict*.

**Caledonian Antisyzygy:** The way Scots join opposites together.

**Capitalocene:** A monetary system that has led to the large-scale destruction of nature.

***Charis*:** Latin term that means 'grace'.

**Cis-heteronormativity:** Closely related to cis-heteropatriarchy, this term highlights societal preferences for specific sexual orientations and gender expressions. It also refers to the enforcement of a rigid male/female gender binary.

**Cis-heteropatriarchy:** Refers to the political, social, cultural, religious and epistemological systems that privilege male experiences, reinforce specific ideals of masculinity and marginalize those who do not conform to cisgender and heterosexual norms.

**Cis-homonormativity:** Refers to societal norms within LGBTIQ+ communities that privilege cisgender identities and traditionally masculine or feminine expressions, often marginalizing nonbinary, gender-non-conforming and intersectional queer experiences.

**Cistercians:** A late eleventh-century reform movement of Benedictine monasticism founded in Cîteaux, France. Often referred to as a 'school of charity', this movement follows the teachings of Robert of Molesme (1028–1111), Stephen Harding (1050–1134), Alberic of Cîteaux (d.1109) and Bernard of Clairvaux (1090–1153).

***Cuir*:** Spanish alternative word for 'queer'.

**Deconstruction:** The process of unpicking and examining theological concepts.

**Epistemology:** How we come to know the structures of human knowledge. It refers to the cultural, religious and even sexual dominance of specific experiences over others in shaping an understanding of the divine.

**Eschatology:** A theological concept that generally deals with the 'end times'. It is future-orientated and considers the end of humanity and the history of salvation.

**Essentialism:** Belief that specific sets of attributes are necessary for identity.

**Eurocentricity:** A term expressing overreliance on thought, ideas, texts and persons from Western European cultures – including the United States of (North) America – in shaping how we understand religion, culture and the divine.

**Indecent theology** shows the connections between politics, economics, sexuality and theology and enables a sexual reading of systematic theology.

**Intersectionality:** The overlapping or intertwining effect of multiple oppression (e.g. being black and female as in Kimberle Crenshaw's original usage).

***Izitabane*:** A term used in Southern Africa to refer to LGBTIQ+ people. Initially an indigenous word, it is often employed derogatorily to dehumanize and objectify sexually diverse individuals, framing them as the 'other'.

***Izitabane Zingabantu*:** South African phrase meaning 'queers are human'.

***Izitabane Zingabantu* Ubuntu theology:** A transformative framework reclaiming language and queer embodied experiences, challenging toxic theologies, restoring dignity and fostering inclusive African spirituality rooted in Ubuntu's communal and compassionate principles.

**Kairological:** A time when conditions are right for crucial action. It may also mean God intervening to enable those actions.

**Latin American liberation theology:** This school of theology was developed in the twentieth century, especially by the Peruvian theologian Gustavo Gutiérrez (1928–2024), whose work placed the experience of the socio-economic poor at the centre of theological reflection.

***Logos*:** A Greek term meaning 'word', 'verb', 'reason' or 'principle', central to Christian theology as the divine Word of God, embodied in Jesus, signifying ultimate truth and cosmic order.

**Mariology:** doctrines relating to the Virgin Mary, mother of Jesus.

**Neurodivergence:** Atypical cognitive, social and communication style. For example, a person who is autistic may use the term 'neurodivergent' to describe themselves.

**Nomadic subjectivity:** Philosophical concept that refers to the subject as constantly in flux, in a state of becoming.

**Non-binary:** A person who identifies outside of, between or variously as the binary gender identities of male and female.

**Performativity:** A linguistic term that refers to the ability of language and words to craft the worlds and persons they speak. Relatedly, to be 'performative' is to have no actual original referent.

**Postcolonial theology:** A critique of theological systems and reflection from the perspective of historically colonized populations, including those still directly experiencing the effects of Western European colonization. This is an attempt to rebuild epistemology from these often dismissed perspectives.

**Posthuman:** A philosophical movement that challenges the idea that humans are the centre of the world.

**Praxis:** The combining of theory and practice.

**Queer hermeneutics:** A way of studying biblical texts through queer eyes.

***Ruâh*:** The Hebrew word for Spirit.

**Sophianic:** A theology of divine wisdom – Sophia.

**Stabanize:** A verb derived from *Izitabane*, a term used to describe individuals who defy the econo-heteropatriarchal ideal. To Stabanize is to embody, affirm and centre the experiences and realities of *Izitabane*, much as 'queering' relates to 'queer'. The word seeks to highlight and celebrate the unique perspectives of those who challenge normative frameworks.

**Standpoint theory:** The feminist theory of deep subjectivity critiques claims of objectivity because there is no view from nowhere.

**Trans/Transgender:** A person who has transitioned away from their sex assigned at birth.

***Trans-Struere*:** A term coined to describe the process of transing deconstruction.

**Trans-apologetics:** The defence of trans identities.

# Acknowledgements

The editors and publisher acknowledge with thanks permission to use the following material under copyright:

Seth Pinnock, (2024), 'Night Watch', *Inclusive Evangelicals*, 29 July, at https://www.inclusiveevangelicals.com/post/watch-night-a-poem-by-seth-pinnock, accessed 01.12.2024, p. 143.

Carlos Márquez Peralta (2024), 'Tiempo de Mujer', p. 161.

Idlewild (2002), 'Scottish Fiction', on *The Remote Part*, Parlophone Records, p. 322.

# Index


Abya Yala (Latin America) 5, 7–9, 355
academic writing 242–3
Adam and Eve 221–3
Aelred of Rievaulx 287–8, 294–5
aesthetics 159–69
Africa
  European evangelization 64–71
  understanding of sexuality 57–70, 122–34, 185–98
African Americans 320, 327
African women's theology 23–4
Agamben, Giorgio 9
Ahmed, Sara 293
AIDS 243–4, 318, 346–7
Aihiokhai, SimonMary Asese 144, 145
Alison, James 123, 125
*alquimia criollizada* [creolized alchemy] 337
Althaus-Reid, Marcella 16, 19, 112, 126–8, 157, 206, 259, 279–80, 311
analogy, in theology 339
antisyzygy 316–28, 353
Anzaldúa, Gloria 255, 260–1, 263, 267–8
Aparecida, national shrine 273–80
apologetics 91–3
*Árbol de la vida* [Tree of Life] 263–4
Armour, Ellen T. 93
Arruda, Marcelo Pedro de 279
Asaka, Tomoki 239, 244
Asian countries
  and Japanese colonization 237
  LGBTIQ+ theologies in 109–11
Athanasius of Alexandria 224
atonement 205–6
autoethnography 355
Aztec belief system 42

Benedictines 287–8, 355
Beuchot, Mauricio 336, 337
biblical hermeneutics 23–32
binary thought 4, 20, 27, 74, 89, 98–9, 204
  in theology 337
Black Lives Matter 326
blessing 78–87
bodies 6–7
  freedom of 19
  in Mexico 163–5
  purity and pollution 208, 210–11
  sanitized language about 208
  as sites of salvation 212–13
  as technique of liberation 13–19
  and theology 16–17, 21
  violence on 163–4, 172–83
borderlands theory 260–1
'born again' 14–15
Boswell, John 127
Brazil, patron saint of 272–82
Brazilian 279
Butler, Judith 164, 230–1, 234

Caledonian antisyzygyny 316–28
Capitalocene 355
Cappadocian Fathers 224
Capps, Donald 304–5, 313
Castro-Gómez, Santiago 3–4, 11–13
Celtic beliefs 99, 257, 327
charis 355
Cheng, Patrick S. 124, 176–7, 244, 246
Chicana feminisms 261–2
chosen family 267–8
Christian Left 71
Christian missions 69
Christian mysticism 233, 287
Christianization 58, 59

Church of England 318
cis-heteronormativity 28, 123–4, 130, 355
cis-heteropatriarchy 27, 189–91, 261, 355
cis-heterosexuality 174
cis-homonormativity 355
Cistercians 355
citizenship 261, 265–7
'civilization' 65–6
Clare-Young, Alex 308
colonial ideology 59, 132
colonialism, as a structure 264
coloniality 3–6, 60, 70
Columbia 331–50
communion, and Trinitarian theology 219–34
Cone, James 126–7, 131, 215
Congregational Federation in Scotland 318
Contextual Bible Study 187, 191–6
Córdova Quero, Hugo 19, 311
Cornwall, Suzannah 93
Costas, Orlando E. 228
creation narratives 174, 220–3, 233–4
creativity 20
cruising 37, 39, 41–2, 48, 50
*cuir* theology 19, 82–7, 153–69, 340, 355
Cumes, Aura Estela 4, 5

Dalit theology 172–83
DARE forum xvii
De Lauretis, Teresa 241
decoloniality 60
decolonization 58, 58–9
of sexuality 71–4, 163
deconstruction 89, 356
deprivation 321–2
Derrida, Jacques 7, 323
diasporic hermeneutic 280
dispossession 4–5
dissent 317–18
diversity 128–9, 136
Latinx liberation theologies 228–33
domination 17
of bodies 20, 174
techniques of 13
through biblical hermeneutics 10–11, 20

ecclesiology 255–69
Econo-heteropatriarchy 28–9, 32
ecumenism
blessing 78–9, 87
cooperation 55–6, 58, 71, 73, 83
Einstein, Albert 324
*ek-stasis* 227, 230
*Ekklesia* 17
Elizondo, Virgilio 228
Ellacuría, Ignacio 220
empires
European 65, 71, 74, 321–2
Japanese 237
Roman 173, 179–83
entanglement 324–5
epistemology 356
Epprecht, Marc 127–9
erotic tension 153–8
eschatology 356
Espinoza, Roberto Che 307–8, 325
essentialism 225–6, 230, 356
Ethiopia 68
Ethiopian eunuch 123, 130–1
eucharist 256–7
Eurocentricity 356
Eurocentrism 356

faggotting 36–47
failure, value of 32
familiarity 292, 340
families 145–6
fear 305–6
Female Genital Mutilation (FGM) 63
feminism 7, 10, 27–8, 159–61
aesthetics 165–7
and queer theology 239–41
*Fiducia Supplicans* 79–82
Flores Settlement 258
folding 331–50
Foucault, Michel 5–7
Francis (pope) 79–80
Freeman, Elizabeth 294
friendship 287
fundamentalism 87, 160

Gadamer, Hans-Georg 325
Gaelic language 326–7

García Garzón, Hemberg Darío
331–50
Gay, Doug 319
gay men 15–16
gender
as a social construct 230
and theology 336–7
gendered theologies 10
God, love of 86, 140–1
grace 153–69
grafting 267
group values 61
Guadalupe 261–2
guilt 155–6
Gutiérrez, Gustavo 215, 356

*habitus* 333–5, 348–9
Hall, Cassidy 288, 289
Halloween 257
Han, Byung-Chul 305–6
Hartley, Grant 139–40
hermeneutics
biblical 23–32
Foucault's reconstruction 5–7
Latin American 342
queer 9–13, 339–40
Hjul, Jenny 320–1
Holy Spirit 154
homophobia 68, 131, 172–3, 205, 239, 247, 344
homosexuality 38–40, 44–6, 49
in African cultures 67–9, 128–9
as sin 23, 25, 111, 132
hope 301–14
Horie, Yuri 239, 240–2
House of Rainbow 126–7
human rights 71, 128, 133
humanity 3–4, 11
Hume, David 323
Hunt, Mary E. 246

identity 177–80
African 71
and faith xvii–xviii
gender 19–20, 27–8, 45–6, 186
and justice 325–7
multifaceted xix
reconfiguration 5, 17
of Scotland 324–8
of trans people 89–91, 93
Idlewild (rock band) 322
immigration policy 257–9
inclusivity 128, 130–1, 198
indecent theology 19, 356
India
LGBTIQ+ people in Lushai Hills 211–12
Naga beliefs 203–16
theologies of liberation 172–83
indigenous worldviews 7
individualism 214
intersectionality xix, 326, 328
intimate stranger image 308–9
Islamic law 109
*Izitabane* 23–32, 185–98, 356

Jantzen, Grace 295
Japan 236–50
Jennings, Willie James 285
Jesus
challenges the empire 182–3
disciples 179
incarnation 12, 212–14
kingdom teaching 14–15
as liberator 215
and the marginalized 140, 173, 179–80, 205
prophetic mission 207, 215
resurrection 303
as saviour 205, 214
servanthood 140, 175, 320
teaching on love 125, 128, 134, 140
Johnson, Elizabeth 288–9
justice 126, 131
and identity 325–8
as utopian vision 238

Kaba, Mariame 306
Kahlo, Frida 36–46
Kairos 156–61, 168
Kingdom of God 15, 17, 179–80
Kirk, the (Church of Scotland) 318
Koch, Timothy 39
Kronos 156
Kudo, Marie 239, 242, 244, 246–7
*kuia* 240–1
Kwok Pui-lan 286, 291
*kyriarchy* 17

Latin America, and symbol of the Virgin 272–82
Latin American liberation theology 356
Latinx liberation theologies 228–33
Leath, Jennifer Susanne 324
Lehner, Stefanie 321–3
Lemebel, Pedro 341, 345–7
Lewis, C. S. 325
LGBTIQ+ people 24
 in Africa 122–34, 185–98
 and the Bible 29–32
 and divine otherness 220, 226–8
 and faith 122–34
 and guilt 137, 155–6
 and love 86
 and pastoral care 107–18, 136–49
 and Pope Francis 79–80
 in the Roman Catholic Church 255
 and salvation 206
 solidarity between 233
 suppression of 289–90
 theology 176–7, 214, 246–7, 285–96
 varieties in Pride march 342–3
 *see also Izitabane*
liberation 127
 of the body 19, 196
 Jesus' mission 207
 techniques 3–4, 13
 theology 134, 172–3, 193, 228–33, 286, 292, 356
Lightsey, Pamela 290
listening 73, 117, 137, 287–8, 295–6
*loca* 342, 347–8
*Logos* 12, 356
Lorina Muñoz, Lorina 214
Lugones, María 7, 263
Lushai ethnic group 212

Malaysia, LGBTIQ+ communities 108–18
marginalized people 95, 319, 322–3, 327
 cooperation 183
*marica* theology 36, 331–50
Marin, Natasha 313
Mariology 281, 357
Márquez Peralta, Carlos 161–2, 169
Mars, Ominira 306
Mary (Mother of God)
 as Mediatrix 256–7, 262–3
 symbols of 272–82
masculinity 334–6
'matted knot' 325
Mediatrix 256–7, 262–3, 268–9
Messiah 15
Methodist Church 318
#MeToo 326
Mexico
 the disappeared 163–4
 equal marriage law 78
Meza, Santos 313
ministry
 of Jesus 182–3, 286
 of reconciliation 127, 129, 134
 to marginalized people 90–1, 98, 111
Mizo ethnic group 212
Moltmann, Jürgen 303, 305
monasticism 287
money 355
monogamy 69
Mugabe, Robert 125
Muslims, views of homosexuality 132, 204
Musskopf, André Sidnei 312
mystery, of God 219–31, 277, 288
mysticism 287

Naga beliefs 203–16
names 155
Nancy, Jean-Luc 154, 164
nationalism 204, 237
neurodivergence 357
new birth 14–15, 17
Nguyen, Viet Thanh 310
Nicodemus 14–15, 18–19
Nietzsche, Friedrich Wilhelm 230
Nigeria 129
nomadic subjectivity 357
non-binary people 357
North America 55, 58, 70, 205, 327, 342
*Nos-otrxs* 233–4
nothingness 310–11

otherness 219–34
otricide 220
Otros Cruces 301–2

Our Lady of Aparecida 272–82

paganism 69, 99
pain, in Dalit theology 175–6
pastoral care 107–18, 136–49
pathos, in Dalit theology 175–6
patriarchy 3–4, 128–9
performativity 357
personal identity 5
Pharisees 18
Pinnock, Seth 142–3
pollution, and bodily purity 208, 210–11
polygamy 58, 69
postcolonial theology 357
power 6
  challenged by CBS 194–6
praxis 357
*praxis* 286
Preciado, Paul-Beatriz 6, 340
Pride march 342–3
Pride (organization) 326
*Prime of Miss Jean Brodie* 317
princess figures 327, 332, 338, 443
Pruyser, Paul W. 304–5
purity culture 205, 207–8, 212–13

quantum perspectives 323–7
quarks 325
queer activism 247
queer archive 236–50
queer Christian communities 237
queer God 50, 231–3, 275–6, 294
queer hermeneutics 9–13, 20, 282, 357
queer Mariology 272–82
queer people
  in Colombia 341
  definition 244–5
queer sex 172, 213
queer theologies xix–xx, 16, 19, 134, 338
  in India 172–83
  in Japan 236–50
queer theory 26, 176, 241, 333
queering 339–40
  as disrupting 219, 263, 281, 318–19

racism 146–7
  as sin 72
Rajkumar, Peniel 175
Rauschenbusch, Walter 325
reconciliation 126–7, 128
redemption 157, 159, 163, 208–13, 273, 282
Reichel, Hanna 285
relatedness 305
relational thinking 335
relational Trinity 219–34
relativity 324
Ribas, Mario 277
Roman Catholic Church
  pastoral work 136
  priestly hierarchy 281
  queer and trans members 255
Roman empire 179–83
Ruâh 12, 154, 357
Rule of St Benedict 287, 295
Russell, Michael 320

safe spaces 73
salvation
  and liberation 207, 214–15
  in Naga Baptist theology 203–16
same-sex marriage 318
same-sex relationships 69, 71, 78–82, 87
  condemned in Africa 187–8
same-sex unions 79–84, 87, 127
Schüssler Fiorenza, Elizabeth 17
Scotland 316–28
Scott, W. Clifford M. 304
Scottish Episcopal Church 318
Sebastian (Saint) 38, 44–5
Section 28 319
segregation 257–8, 345
self-knowledge 312
self-truth 312
*senti-pensar* 333
sex education, in African traditions 63–4
sex-gender binary 337–8
sex-talk 64, 70
sexual union 16–17, 57, 61–2
sexuality
  in African communities 57–8, 60–71
  and belief systems xvii–xviii
  celebration of 58, 65–6, 70, 74
  defined 56–64

denial of 141–2
and erotic tension 165–8
*see also* LGBTIQ+ people
Shore-Goss, Robert E. 243–4
silence 287, 289, 296
sin 86, 140
and atonement 205
systemic 215
as tool of control 155
Singh, Julietta 245
Smilges, J. Logan 289
Smith, George Gregory 316–17
Sobrino, Jon 286
Sodom and Gomorrah 136–40
sodomy laws 69–70
Solidarity Hub 89–91, 98–100
Solnit, Rebecca 206–7
*somatecas* 341
souls 6
South Africa 28, 185–98
Spark, Muriel 317
spiritual activism 255–69
spiritual flexibility 312–13
Spivak, Gayatri Chakravorty 291
Stabanized hermeneutics 23–32
standpoint theory 357
Stevenson, Robert Louis 317
Stonewall riot 247
stories 25, 193, 208–15, 240–1, 246–7, 264–5
*see also* creation narratives
*Strange Case of Dr. Jekyll and Mr. Hyde* 317
Strassfield, Max 92–3
Stuart, Elizabeth 244, 246–7
Sturgeon, Nicola 320–1
subaltern history 240, 243, 321–3
*see also* marginalized people
subalternity 237, 240, 243
suffering, in Dalit theology 175–6

Tao 325–6
theologies
in dialogue 288
gendered 10
trans 90–102
theology
and gender 336–7
in higher education 285–96
theopastoral competence 107–18
trans existentialism 337
trans(gender) people 89–96, 301–14, 357
tree of life 263–4
Trevisan, João Silvério 37–9
Trible, Phyllis 221
Trinity 86, 219–34

Ubuntu 194–8
Uganda, Anti-Homosexuality Act 55–6, 62, 146
Ugandan martyrs 62–3
Ujamaa Centre 24–5
Ulysios, Geethanjali Mar 256–9, 265
uncertainty 309
uncleanness 154, 164, 213
United Church of Christ in Japan 239
United Reformed Church 318
United States of America
citizenship 266
immigration policy 257–9
university education 285

Victorian sexuality 70–1
Virgen de Guadalupe, La 261–2
virility 334

white supremacism 59, 72
whiteness 6
wholeness
of creation 47, 215–16
of male and female 27
of Scotland 327
of sexual and spiritual 259
Wilcox, Melissa M. 196–7
'woke' 319–20
womanism 327
women
expected to be submissive 272
and patriarchy 4–5
World Council of Churches (WCC) 56–7
World Health Organization (WHO) 56
Worsfeld, Matthew 267
'wounded healer' image 309–10

Zizioulas, John 219–34
Zuma, Jacob 125

www.ingramcontent.com/pod-product-compliance
Lightning Source LLC
Chambersburg PA
CBHW022026290426
44109CB00014B/763

* 9 7 8 0 3 3 4 0 6 6 8 2 8 *